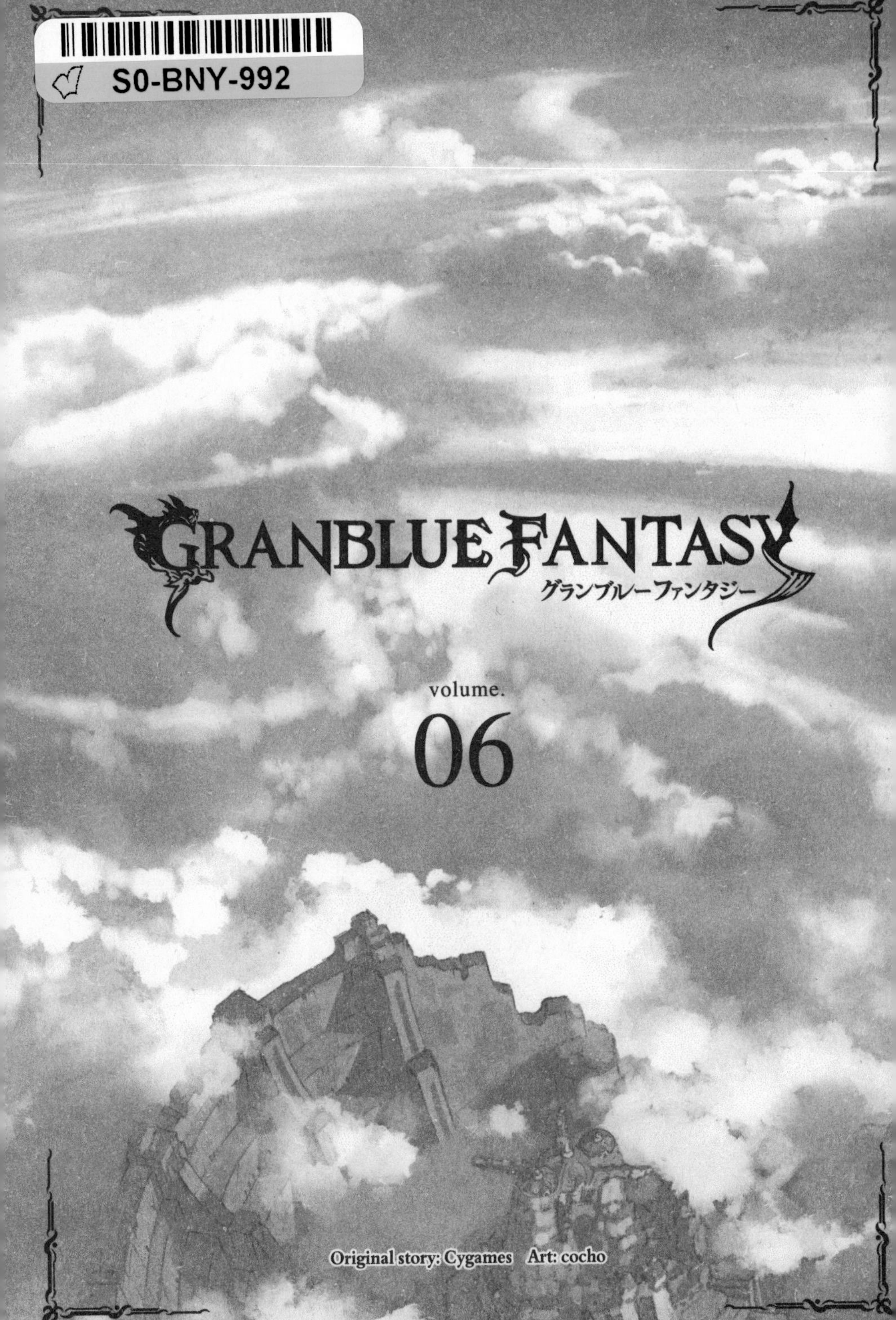
GRANBLUE FANTASY
グランブルーファンタジー
volume.
06
Original story: Cygames Art: cocho

CONTENTS

GRANBLUE FANTASY

volume.

06

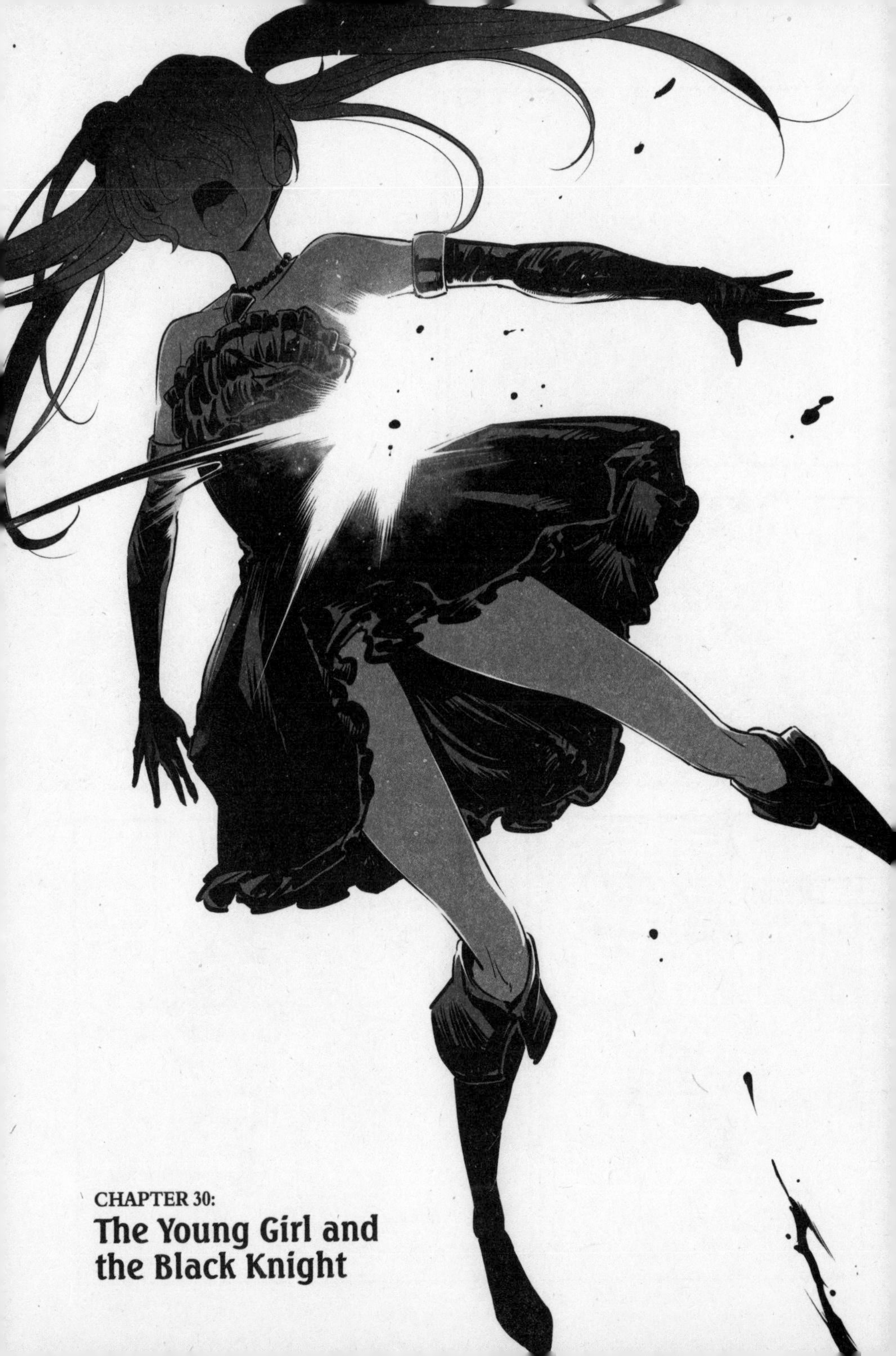

CHAPTER 30:
The Young Girl and the Black Knight

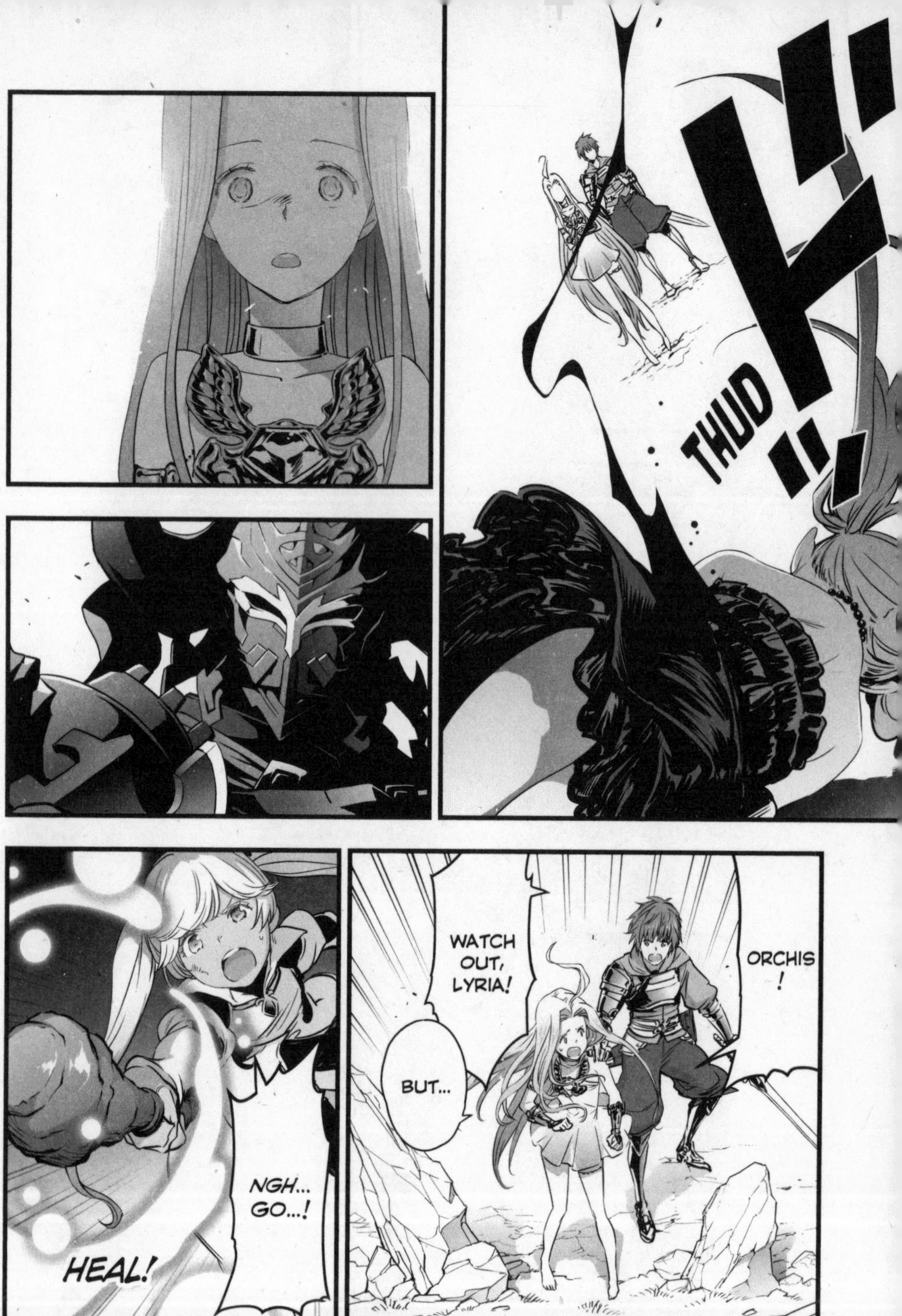
THUD
ORCHIS!
WATCH OUT, LYRIA!
BUT...
NGH... GO...!
HEAL!

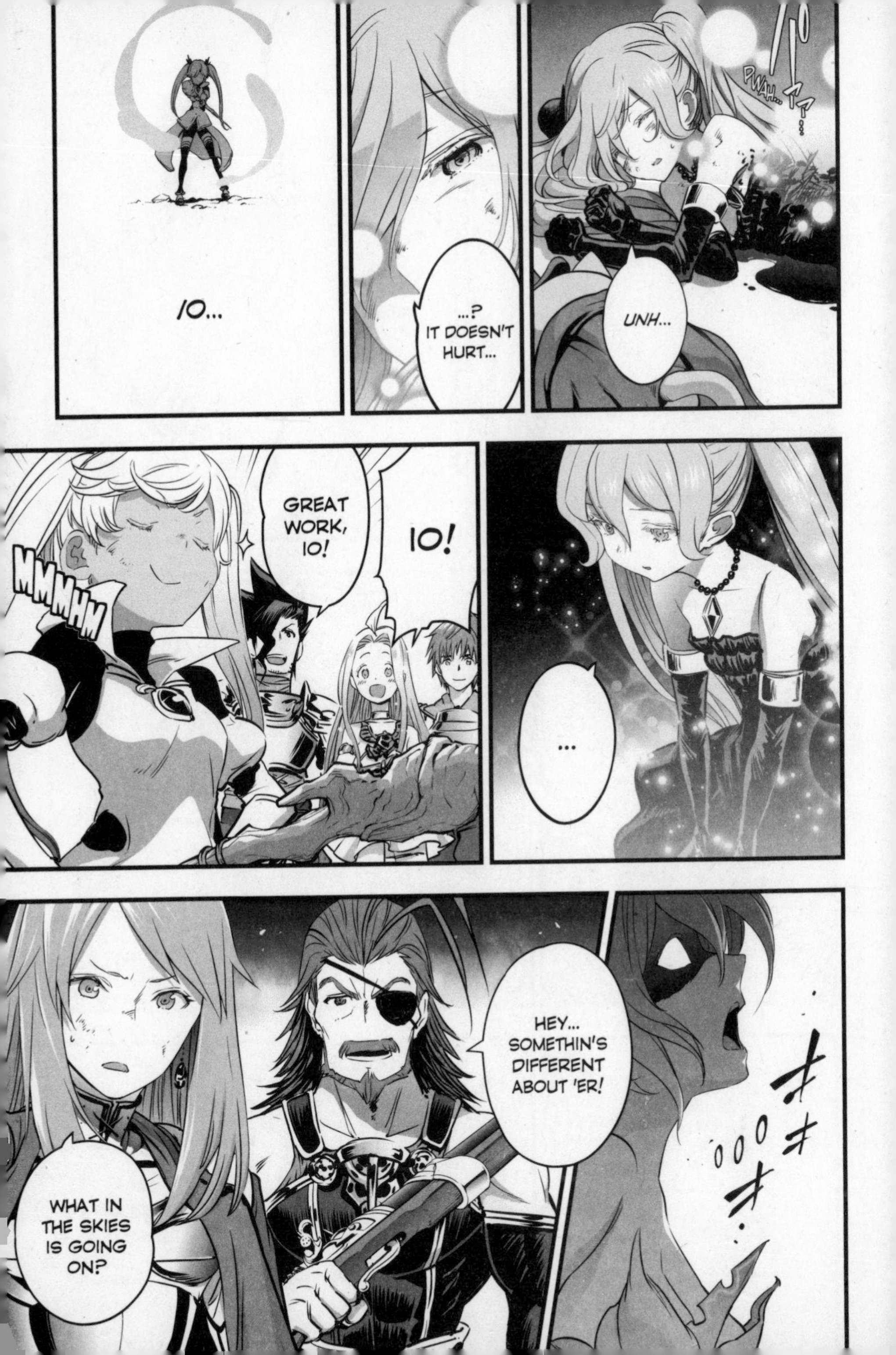

PWAH...
UNH...
...? IT DOESN'T HURT...
IO...
...
IO!
GREAT WORK, IO!
MMMHM
HEY... SOMETHIN'S DIFFERENT ABOUT 'ER!
WHAT IN THE SKIES IS GOING ON?

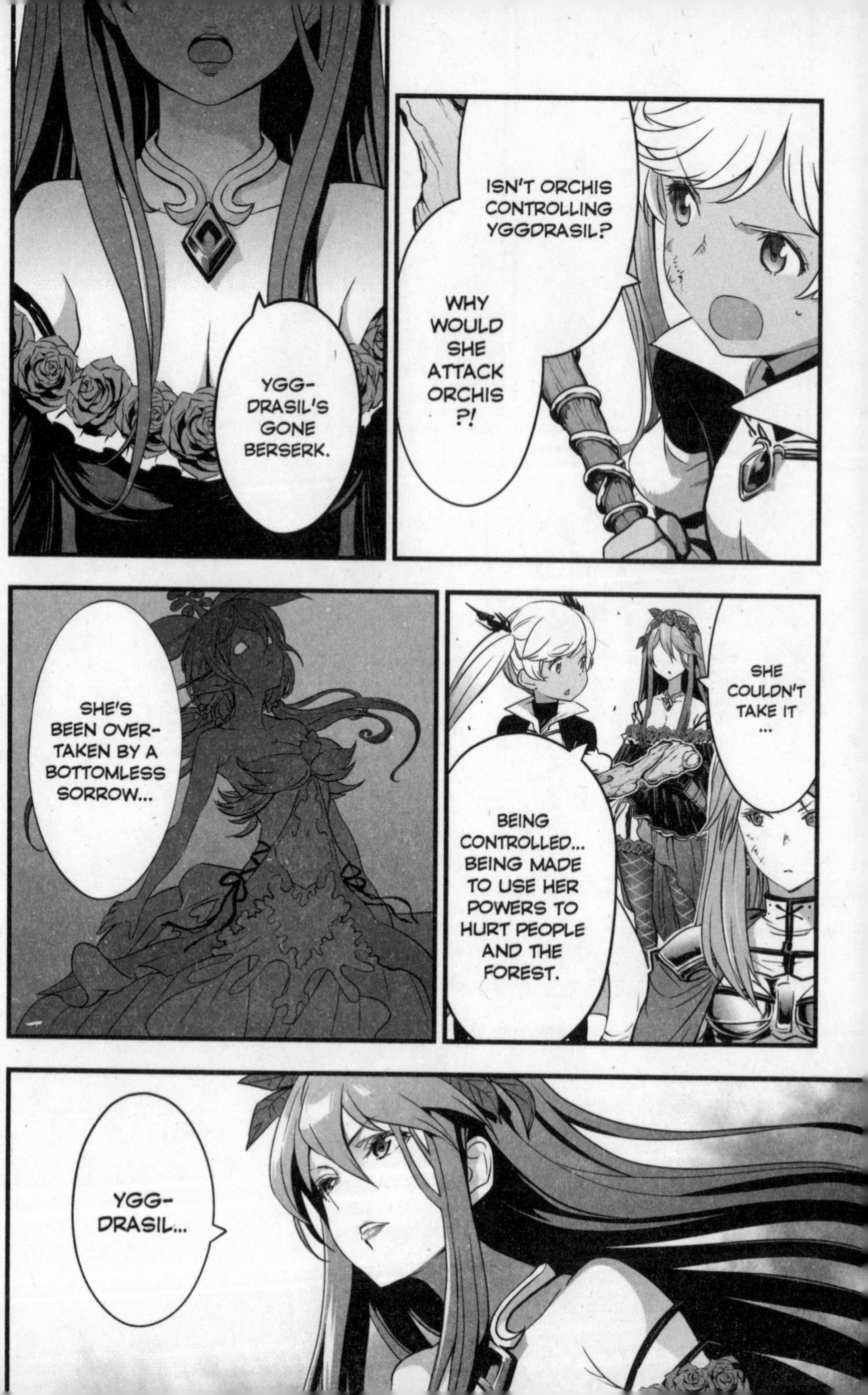
ISN'T ORCHIS CONTROLLING YGGDRASIL?
WHY WOULD SHE ATTACK ORCHIS ?!
YGG-DRASIL'S GONE BERSERK.
SHE COULDN'T TAKE IT ...
BEING CONTROLLED... BEING MADE TO USE HER POWERS TO HURT PEOPLE AND THE FOREST.
SHE'S BEEN OVER-TAKEN BY A BOTTOMLESS SORROW...
YGG-DRASIL...

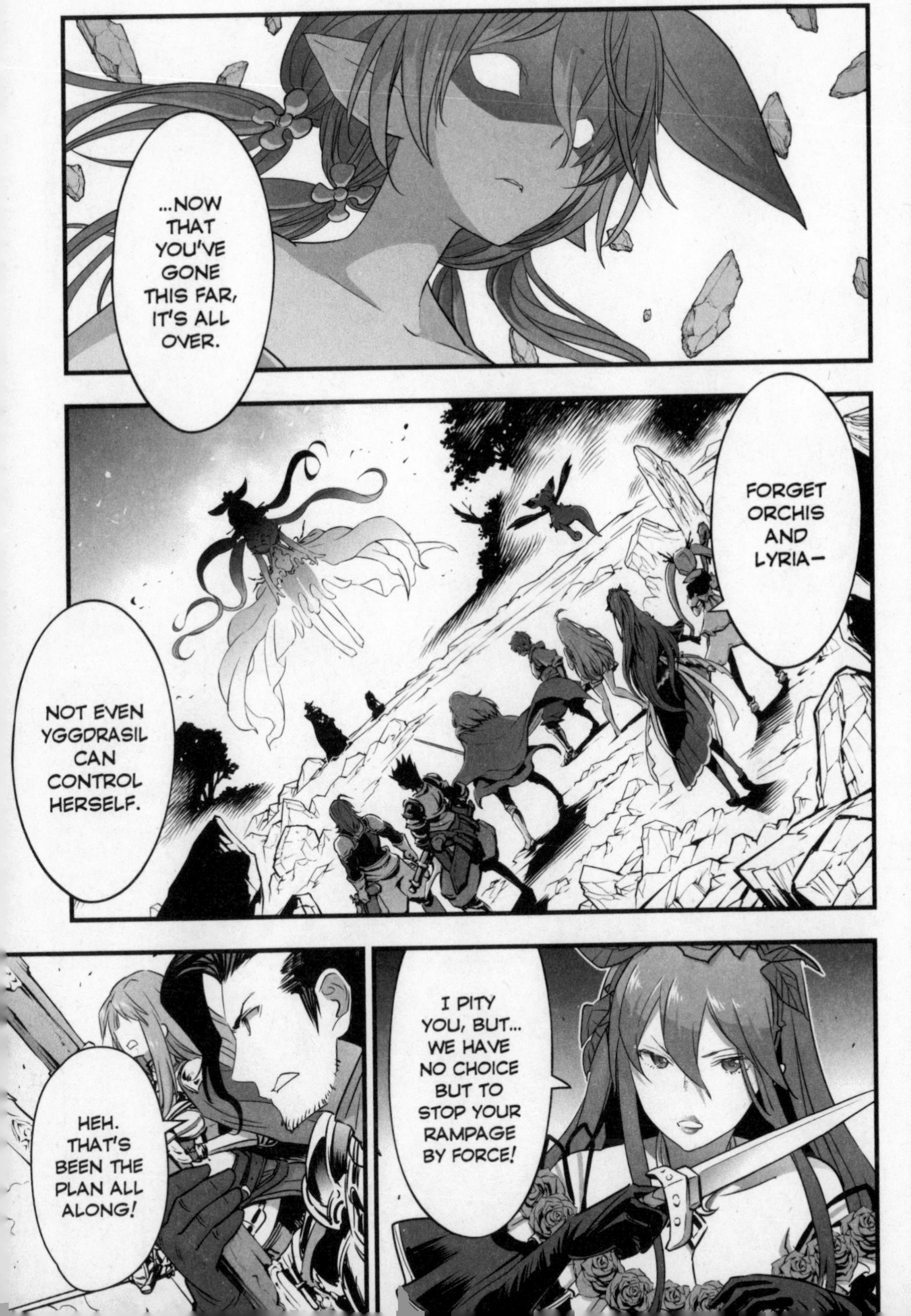
...NOW THAT YOU'VE GONE THIS FAR, IT'S ALL OVER.
FORGET ORCHIS AND LYRIA—
NOT EVEN YGGDRASIL CAN CONTROL HERSELF.
I PITY YOU, BUT... WE HAVE NO CHOICE BUT TO STOP YOUR RAMPAGE BY FORCE!
HEH. THAT'S BEEN THE PLAN ALL ALONG!

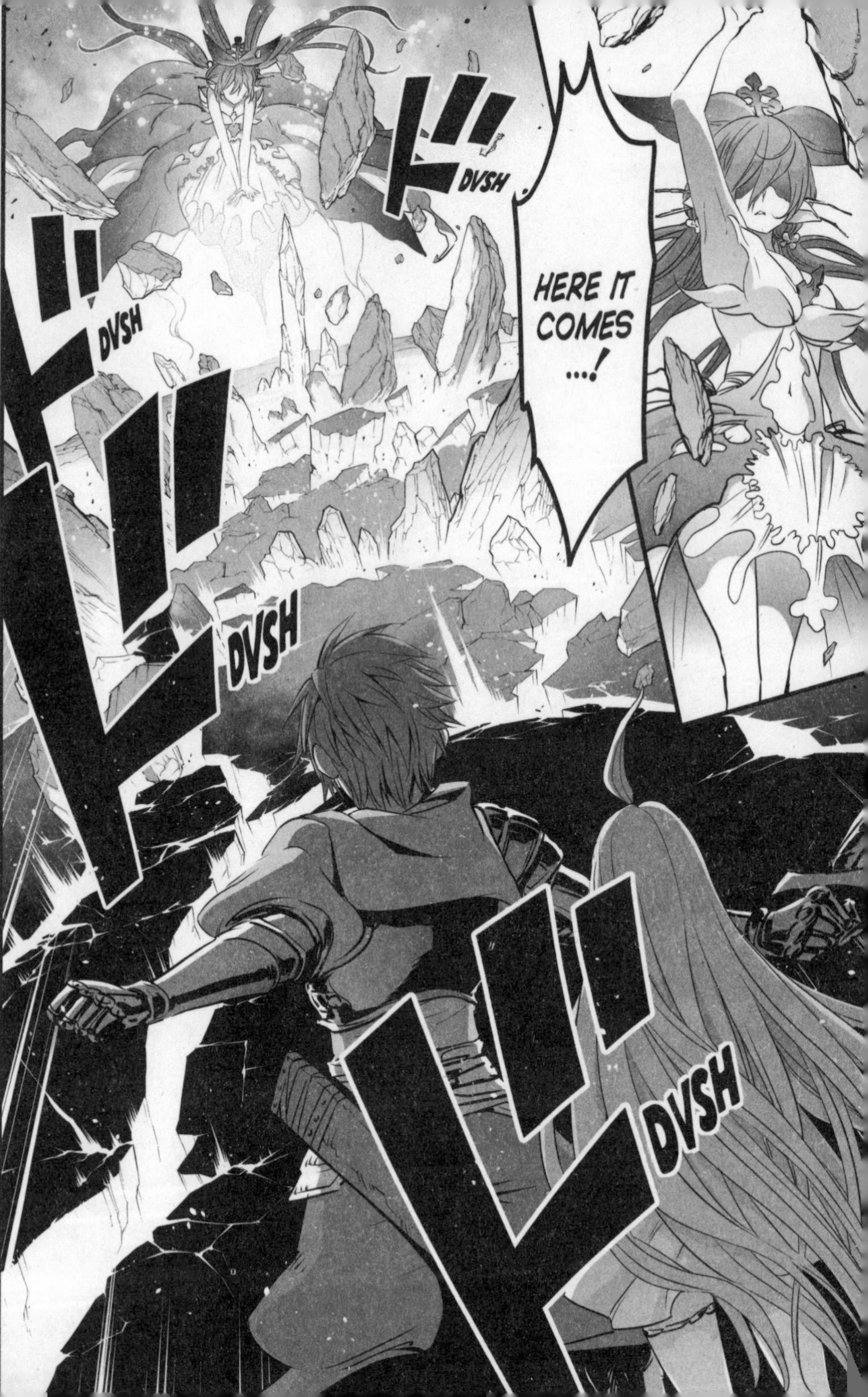
HERE IT COMES ...!
DVSH
DVSH
DVSH
DVSH

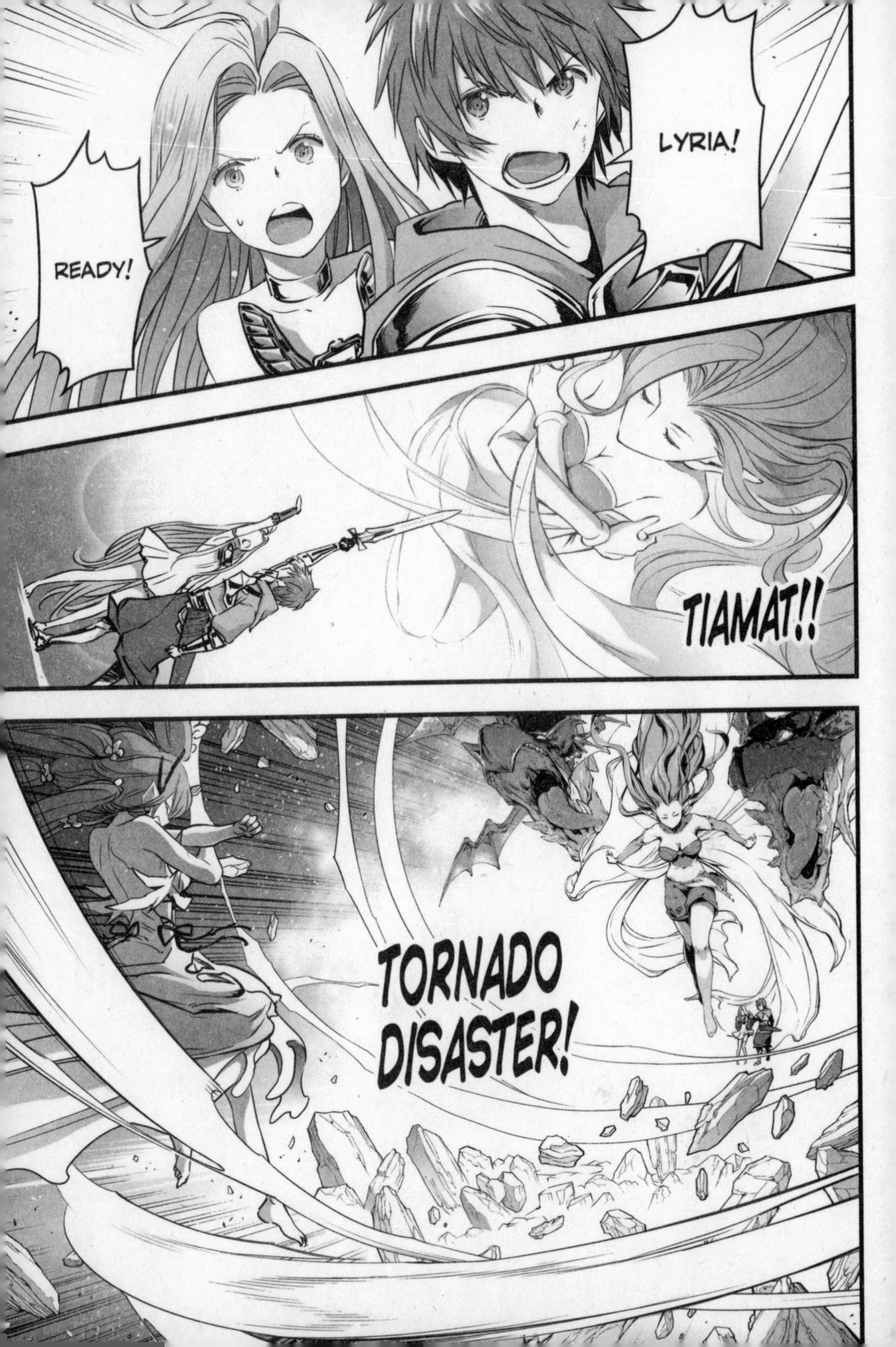
LYRIA!
READY!
TIAMAT!!
TORNADO DISASTER!

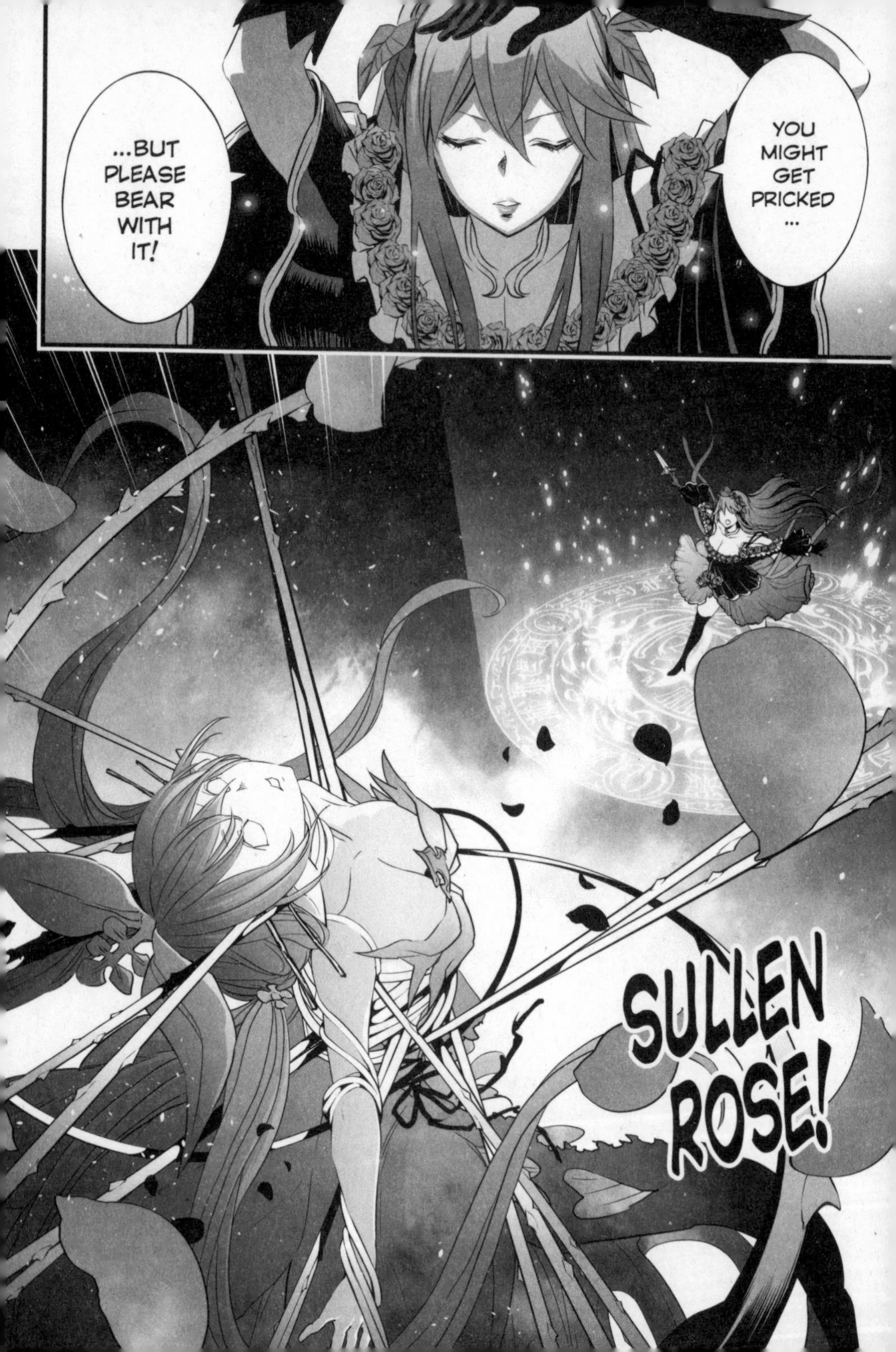
YOU MIGHT GET PRICKED ...
...BUT PLEASE BEAR WITH IT!
SULLEN ROSE!

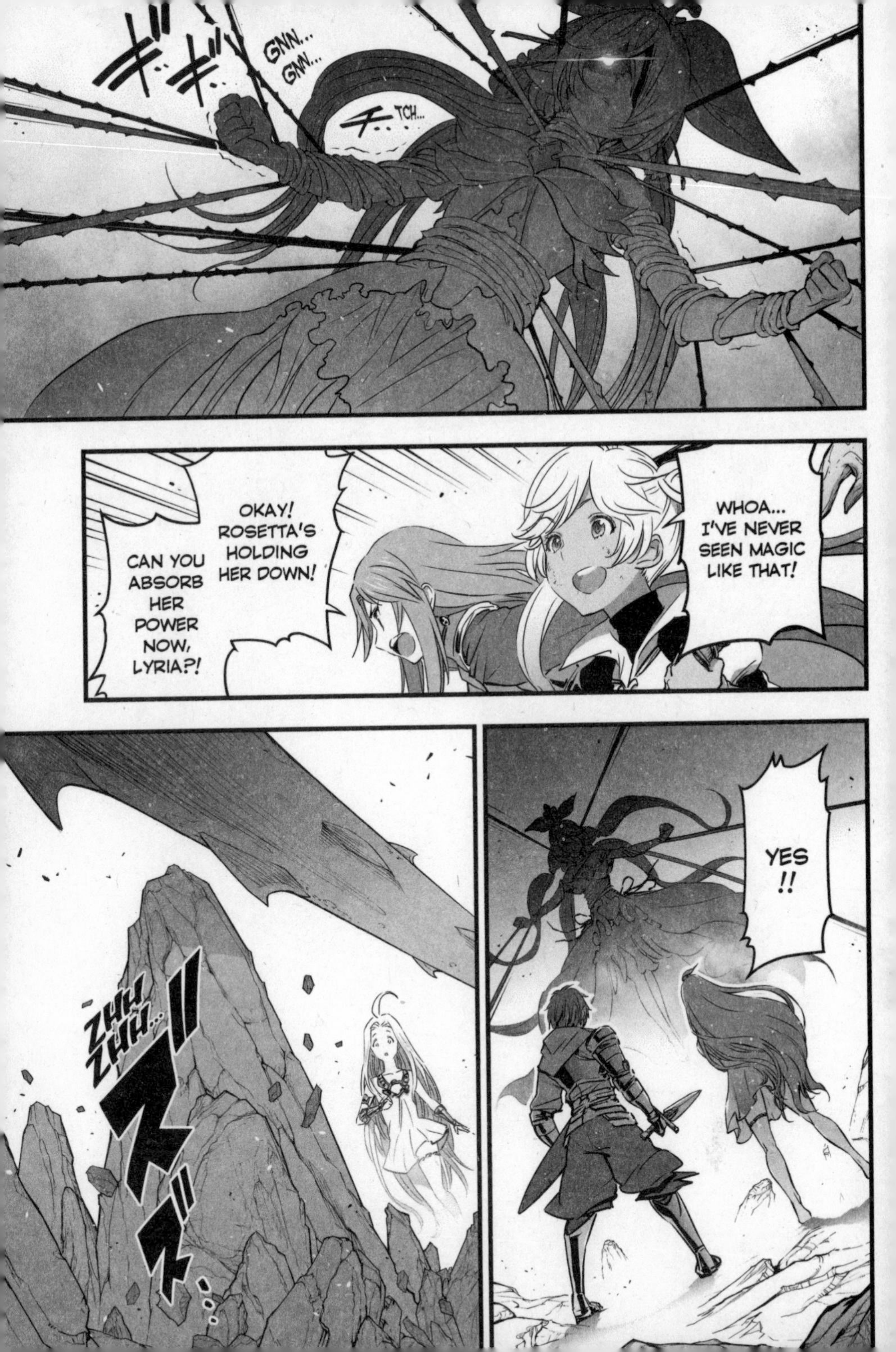
ギ.. ギ..
GNN... GNN...
チ..
TCH...
WHOA... I'VE NEVER SEEN MAGIC LIKE THAT!
OKAY! ROSETTA'S HOLDING HER DOWN!
CAN YOU ABSORB HER POWER NOW, LYRIA?!
YES !!
ZHU ZHU...
ズズ..

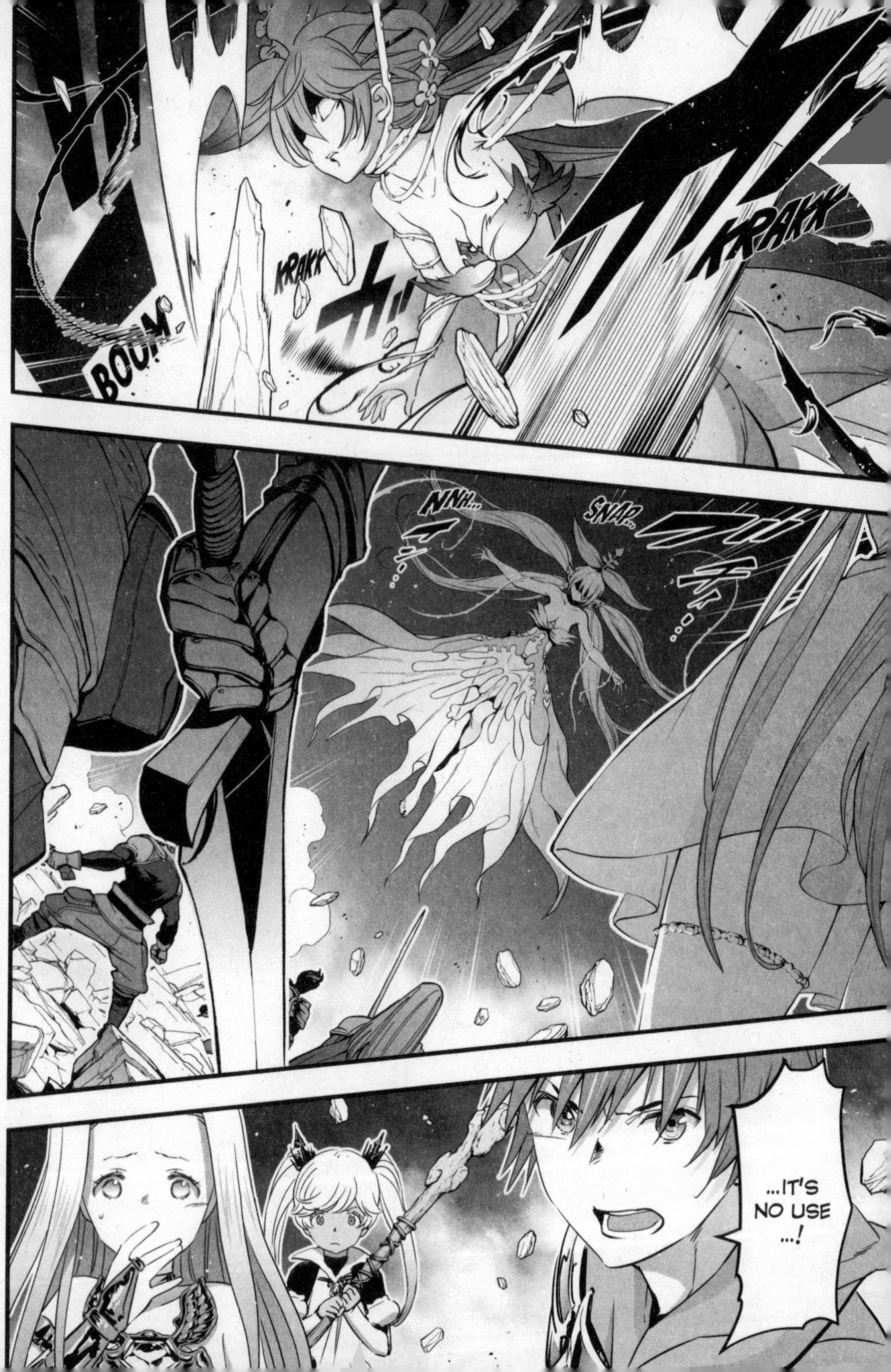
KRAKK
KRAKK
BOOM
SNAP...
NNH...
...IT'S NO USE ...!

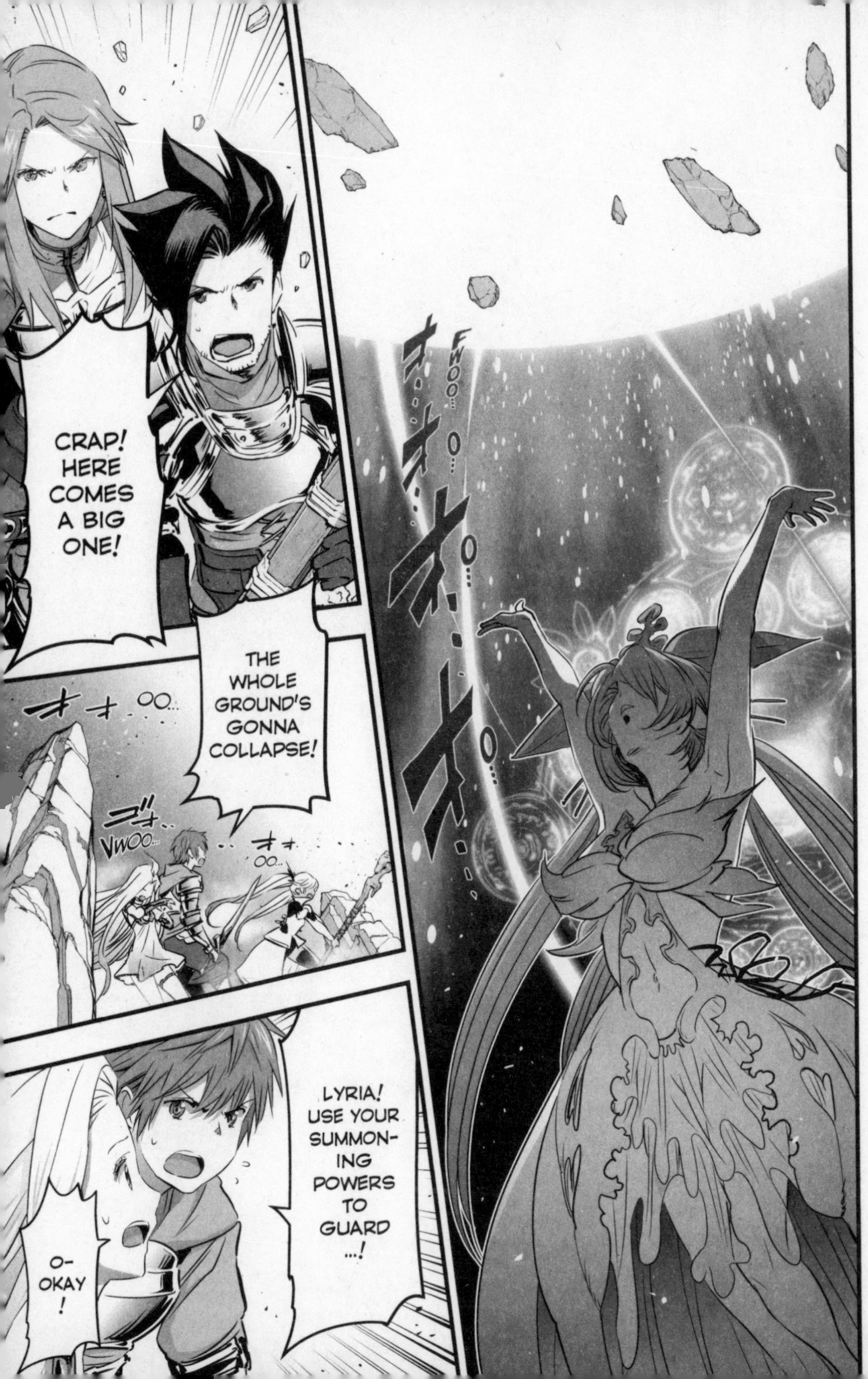

FWOO... O... O... O...
CRAP! HERE COMES A BIG ONE!
THE WHOLE GROUND'S GONNA COLLAPSE!
OO...
VWOO...
OO...
LYRIA! USE YOUR SUMMONING POWERS TO GUARD ...!
O-OKAY!

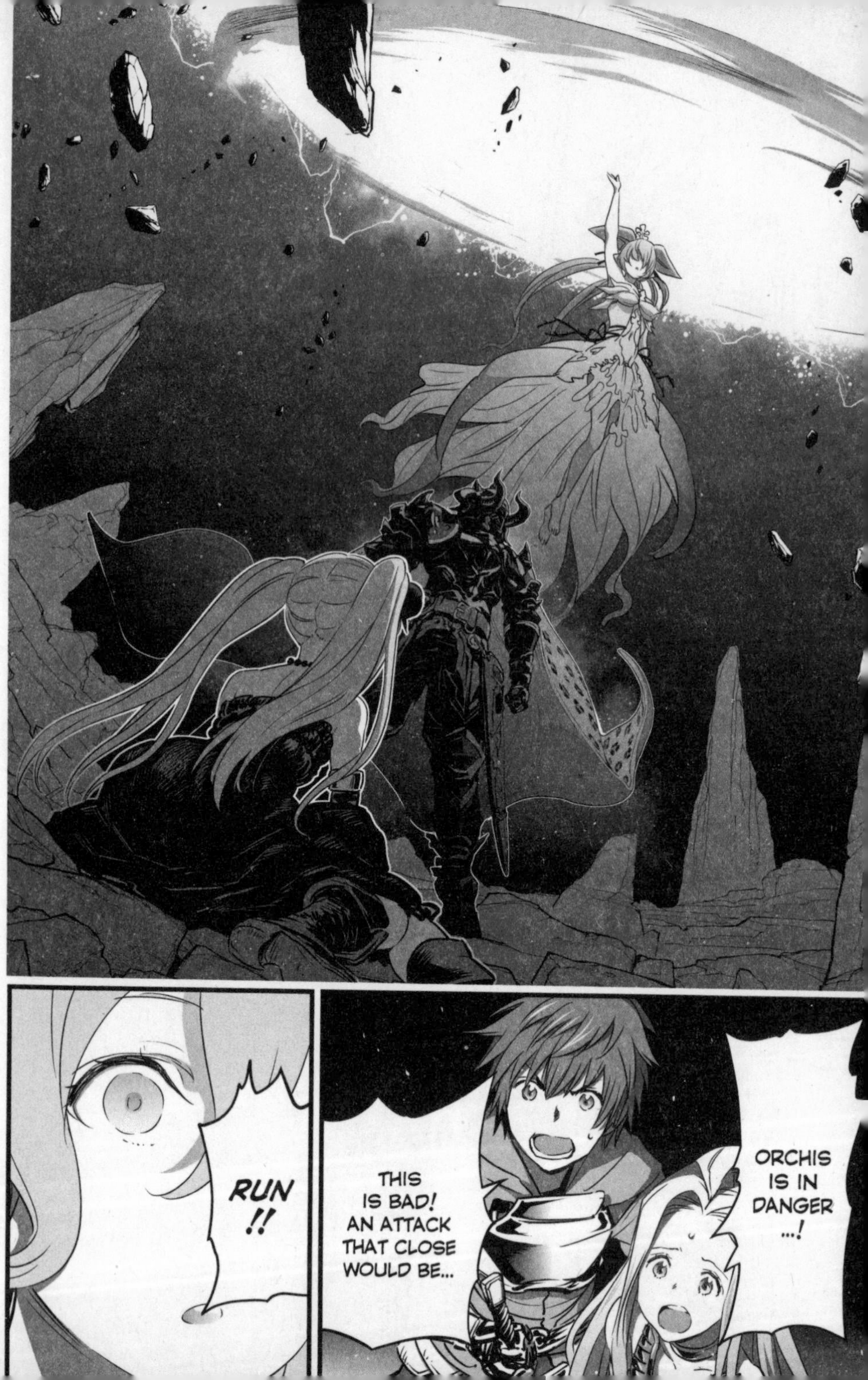
ORCHIS IS IN DANGER ...!
THIS IS BAD! AN ATTACK THAT CLOSE WOULD BE...
RUN !!

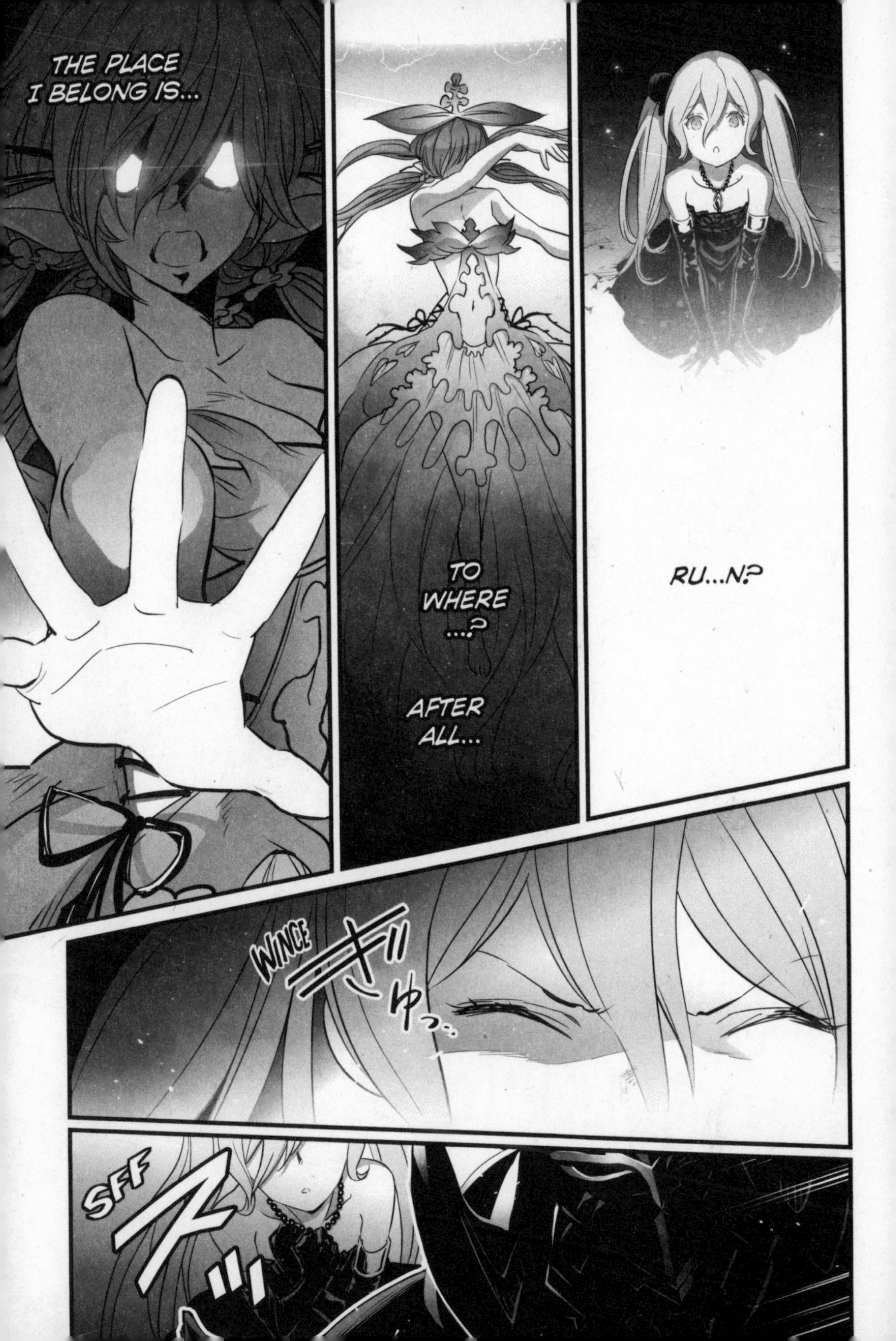
RU...N?
TO WHERE ...?
AFTER ALL...
THE PLACE I BELONG IS...
WINCE
SFF

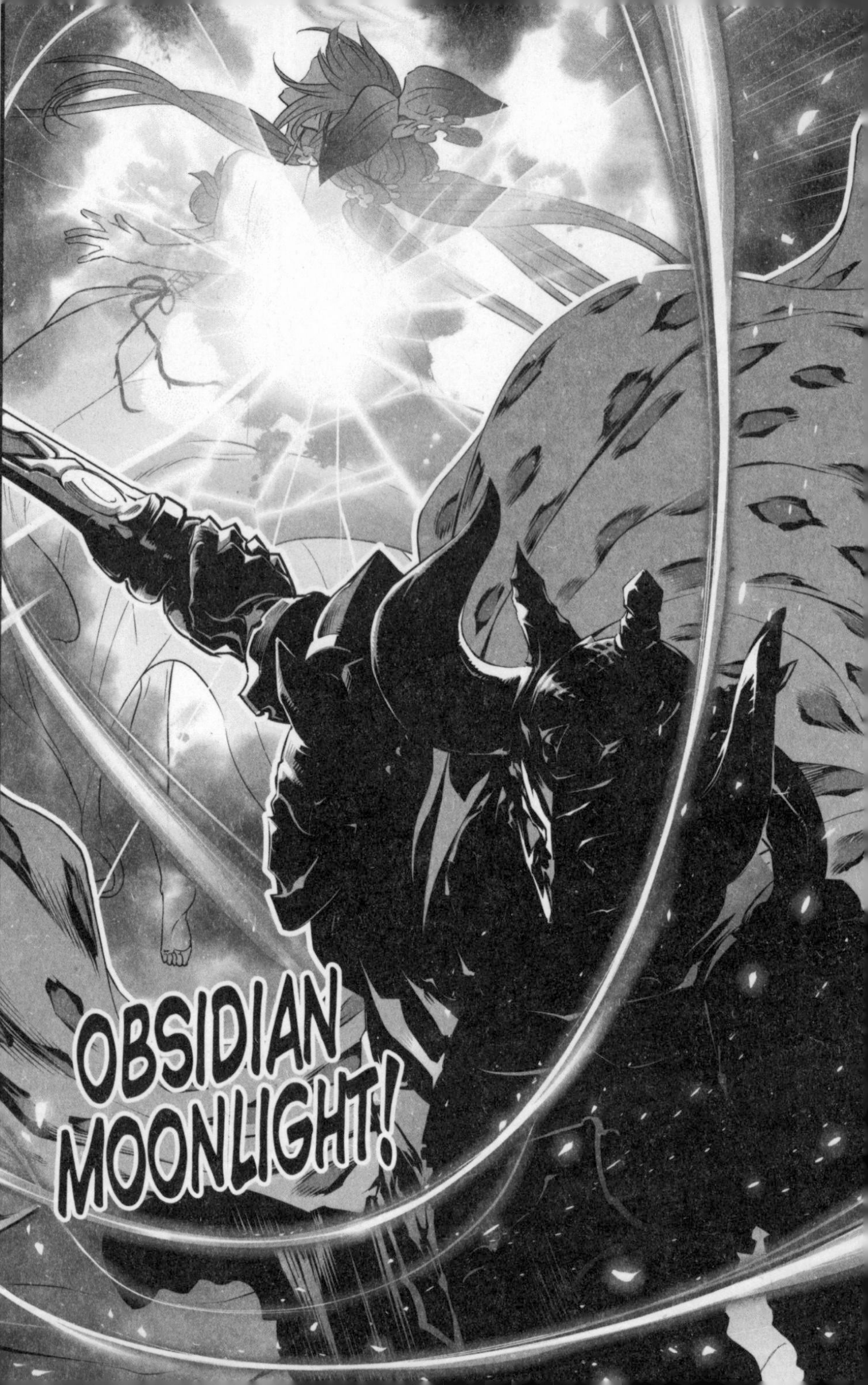
OBSIDIAN MOONLIGHT!

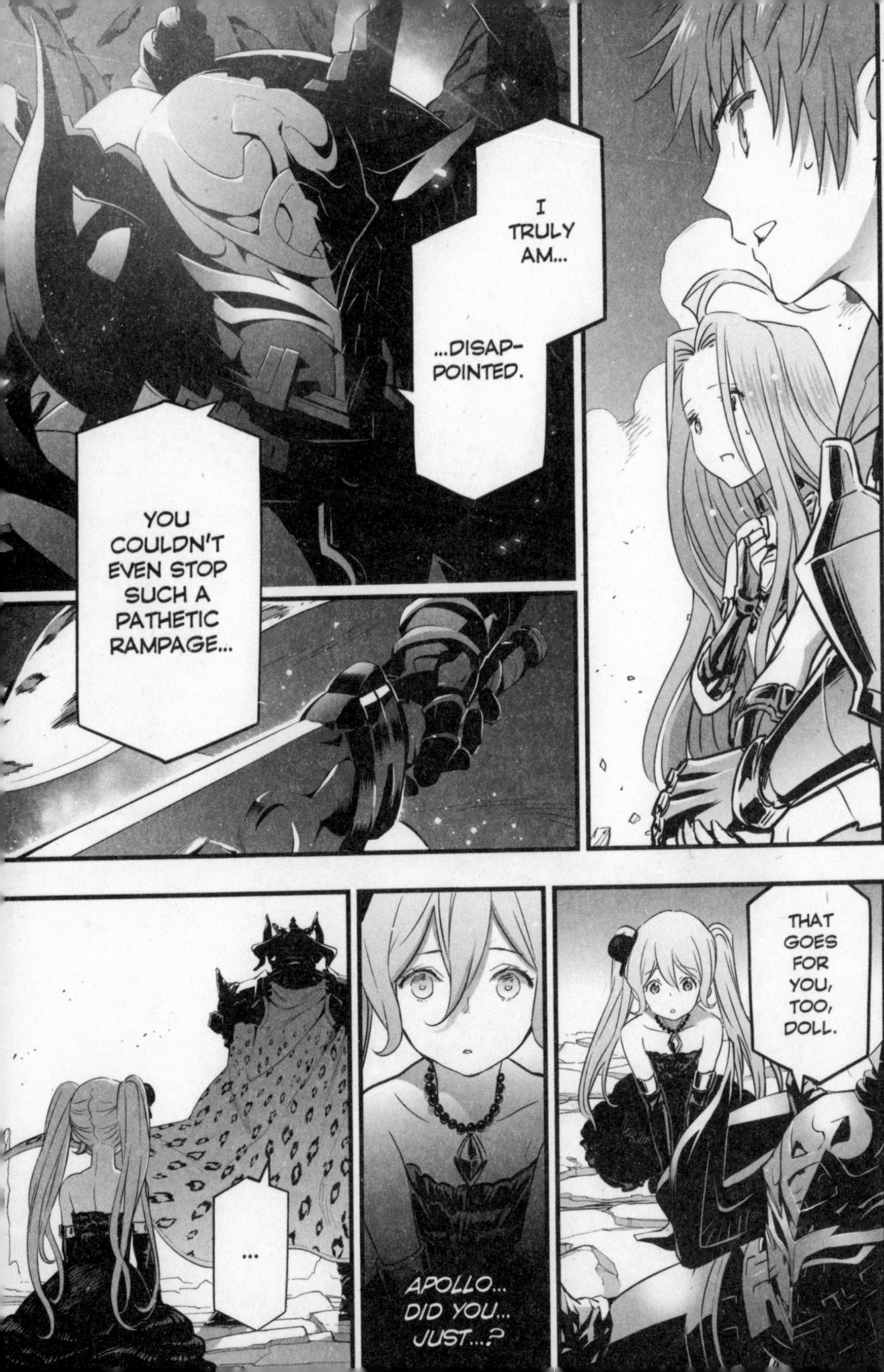
I TRULY AM...
...DISAP-POINTED.
YOU COULDN'T EVEN STOP SUCH A PATHETIC RAMPAGE...
THAT GOES FOR YOU, TOO, DOLL.
APOLLO... DID YOU... JUST...?
...

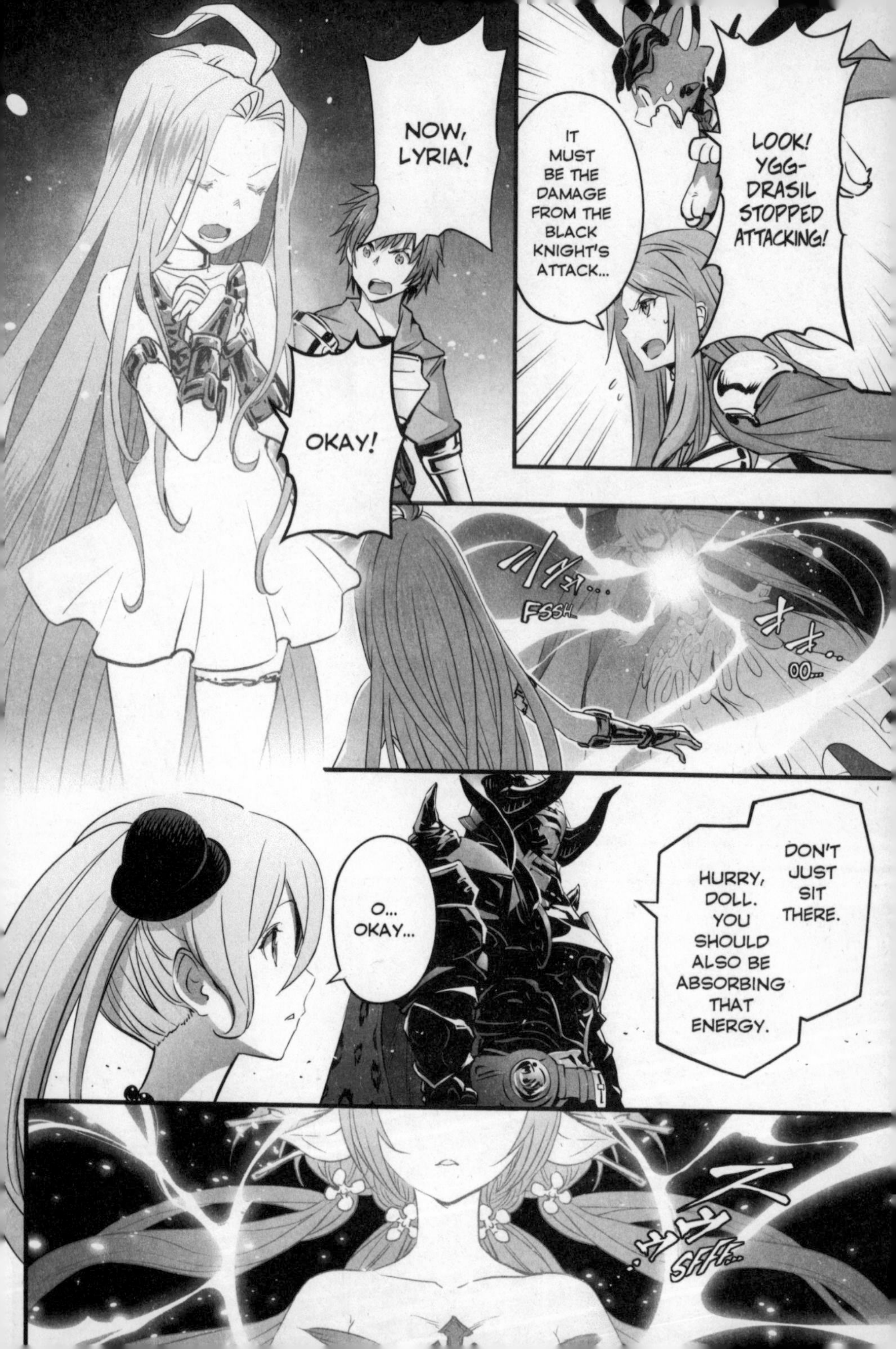
LOOK! YGG-DRASIL STOPPED ATTACKING!
IT MUST BE THE DAMAGE FROM THE BLACK KNIGHT'S ATTACK...
FSSH...
OO...
NOW, LYRIA!
OKAY!
DON'T JUST SIT THERE.
HURRY, DOLL. YOU SHOULD ALSO BE ABSORBING THAT ENERGY.
O... OKAY...
SFFT...

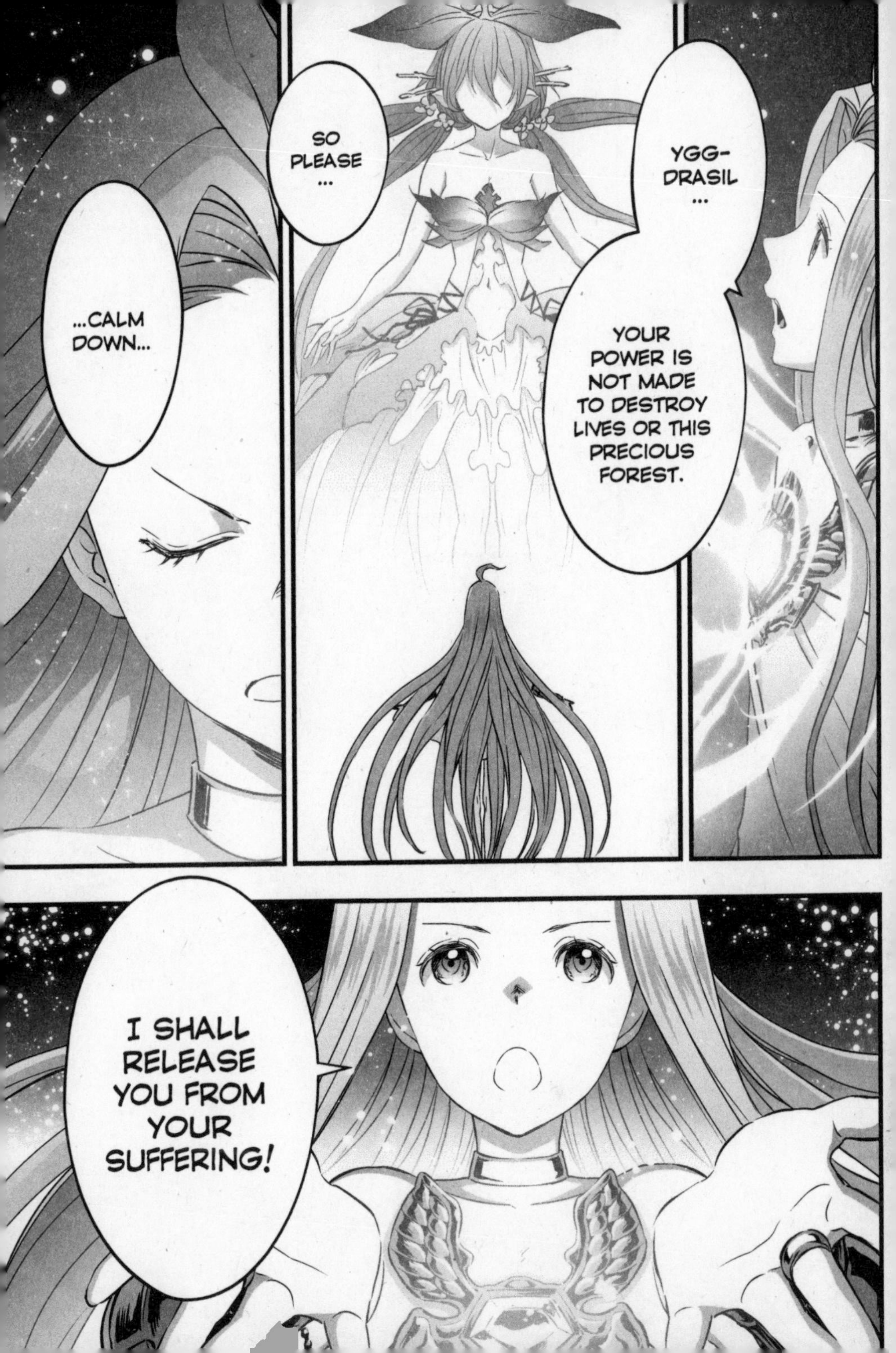
YGG-DRASIL ...
YOUR POWER IS NOT MADE TO DESTROY LIVES OR THIS PRECIOUS FOREST.
SO PLEASE ...
...CALM DOWN...
I SHALL RELEASE YOU FROM YOUR SUFFERING!

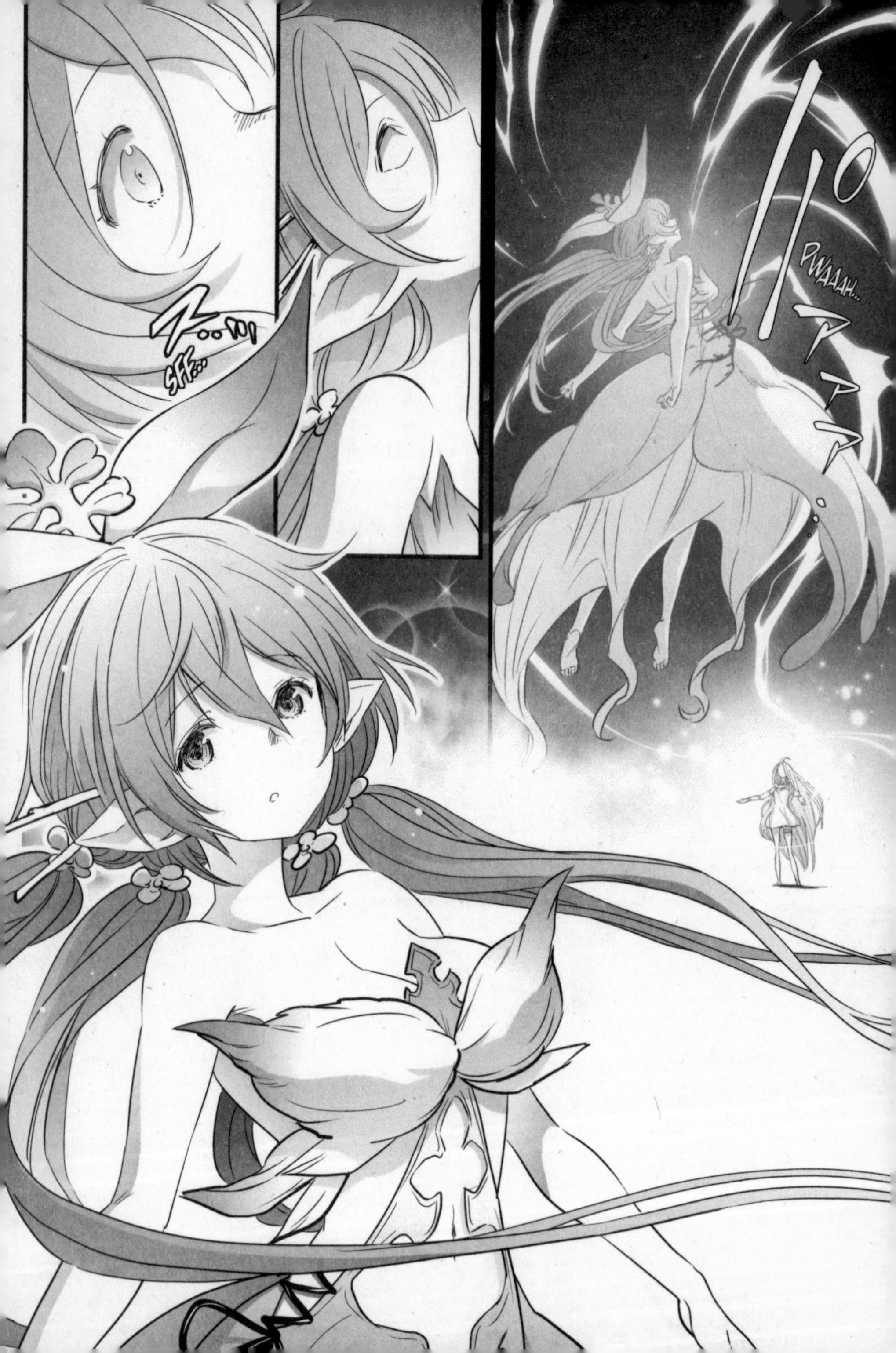
パァァァ…
PWAAAH...
ス…ッ!
SFF...

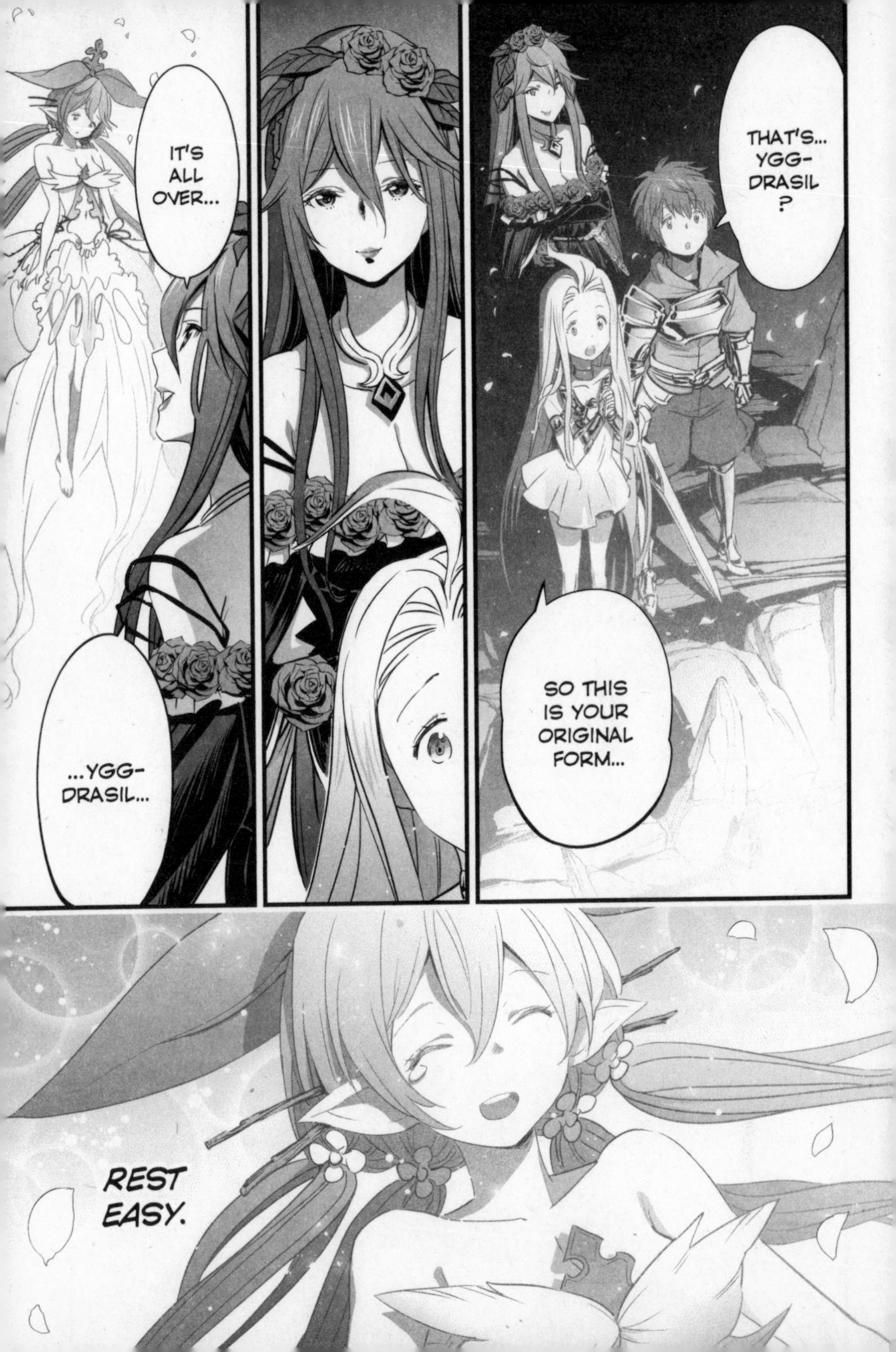
THAT'S... YGG-DRASIL?
SO THIS IS YOUR ORIGINAL FORM...
IT'S ALL OVER...
...YGG-DRASIL...
REST EASY.

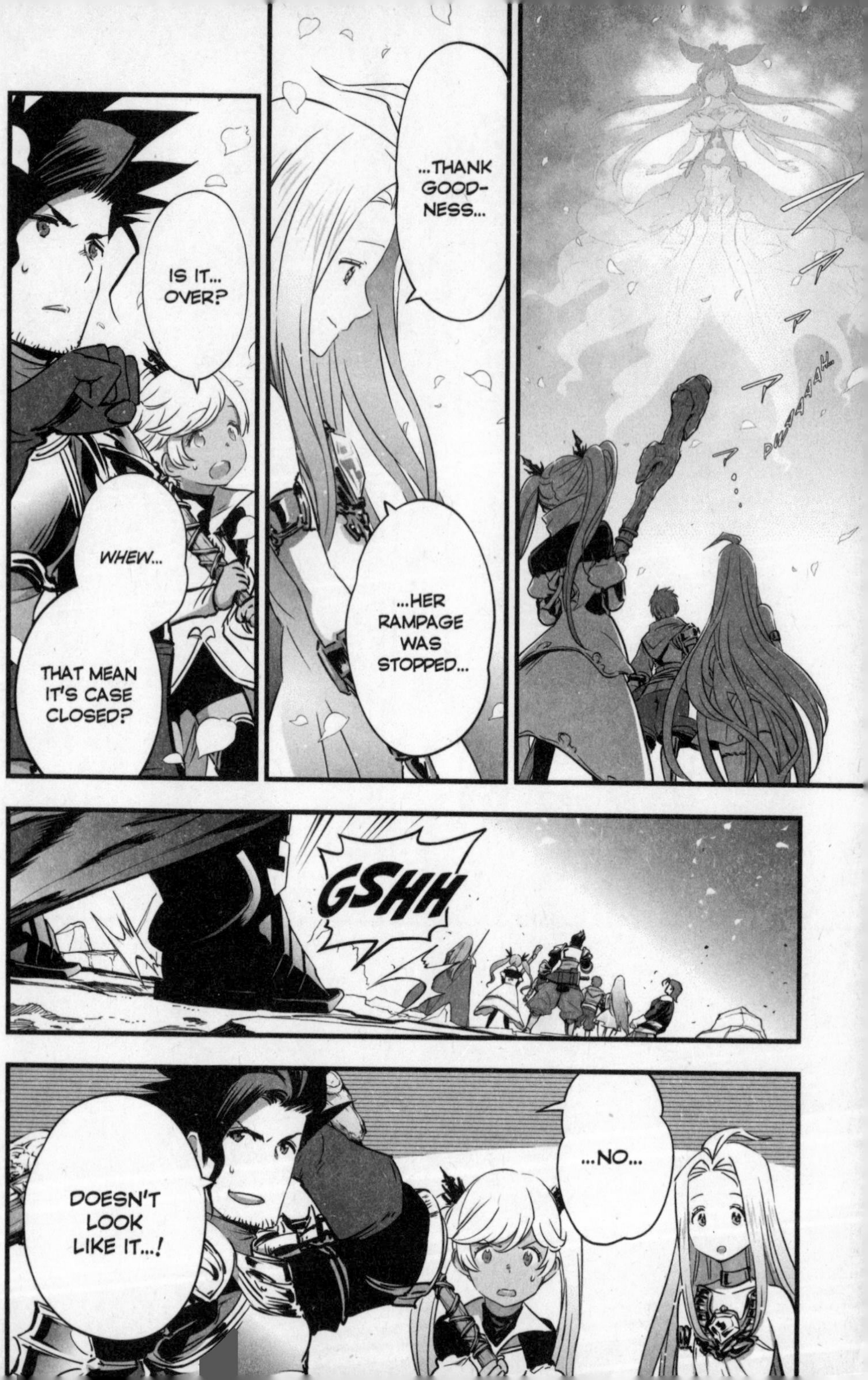
DWAAAAH...
...THANK GOODNESS...
...HER RAMPAGE WAS STOPPED...
IS IT... OVER?
WHEW...
THAT MEAN IT'S CASE CLOSED?
GSHH
...NO...
DOESN'T LOOK LIKE IT...!

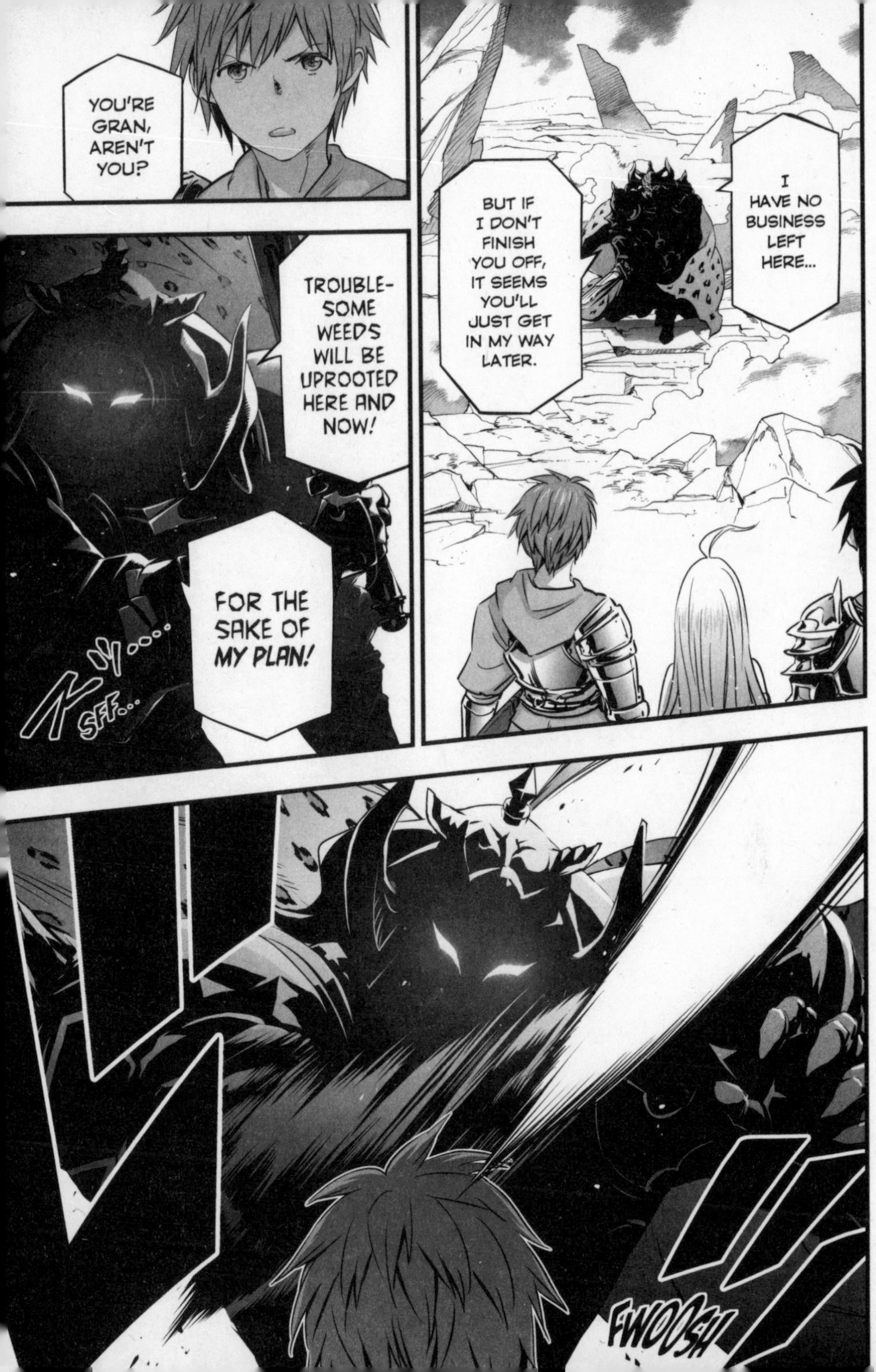
I HAVE NO BUSINESS LEFT HERE...
BUT IF I DON'T FINISH YOU OFF, IT SEEMS YOU'LL JUST GET IN MY WAY LATER.
YOU'RE GRAN, AREN'T YOU?
TROUBLE-SOME WEEDS WILL BE UPROOTED HERE AND NOW!
FOR THE SAKE OF MY PLAN!
SFF...
FWOOSH

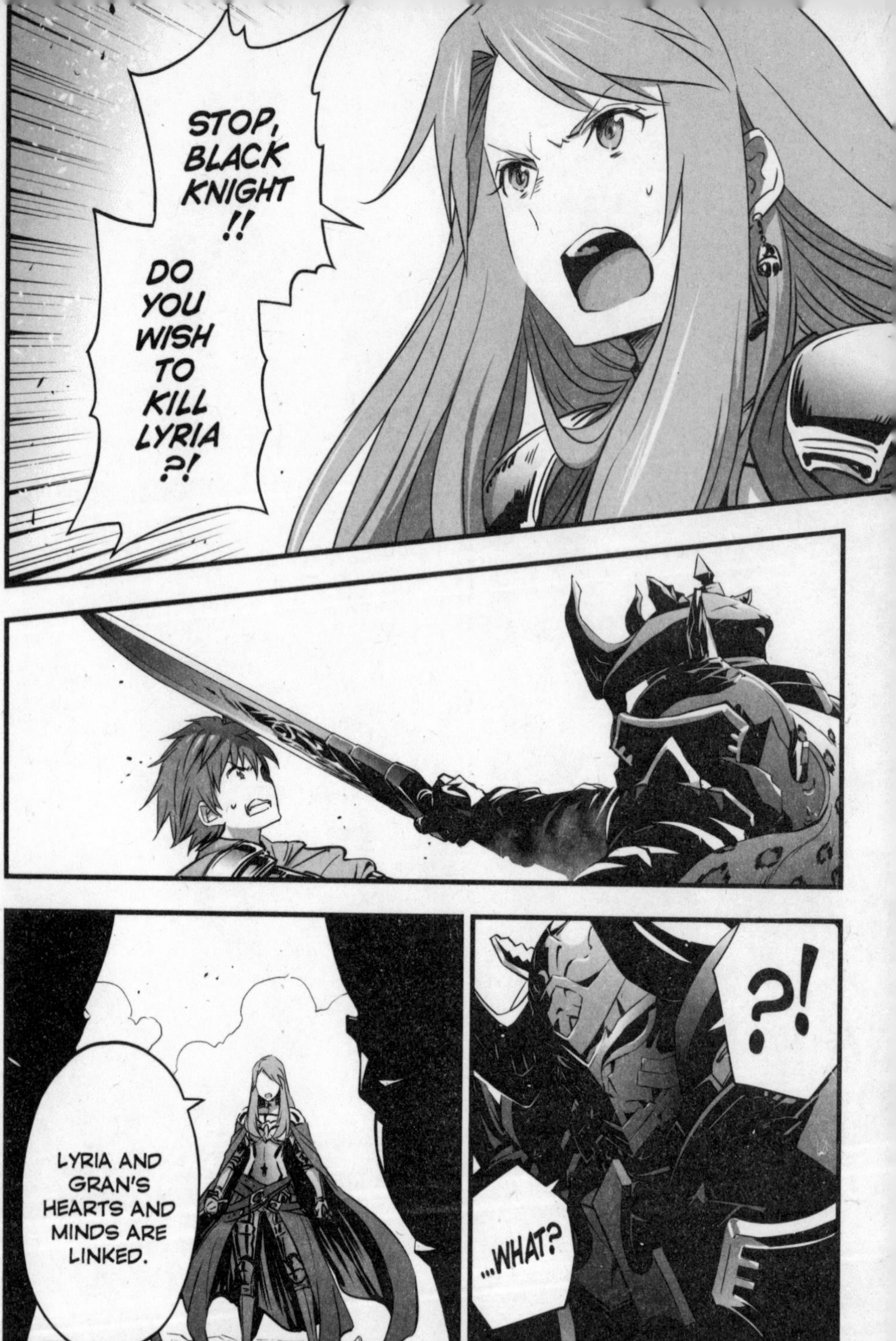
STOP, BLACK KNIGHT!!
DO YOU WISH TO KILL LYRIA?!
?!
...WHAT?
LYRIA AND GRAN'S HEARTS AND MINDS ARE LINKED.

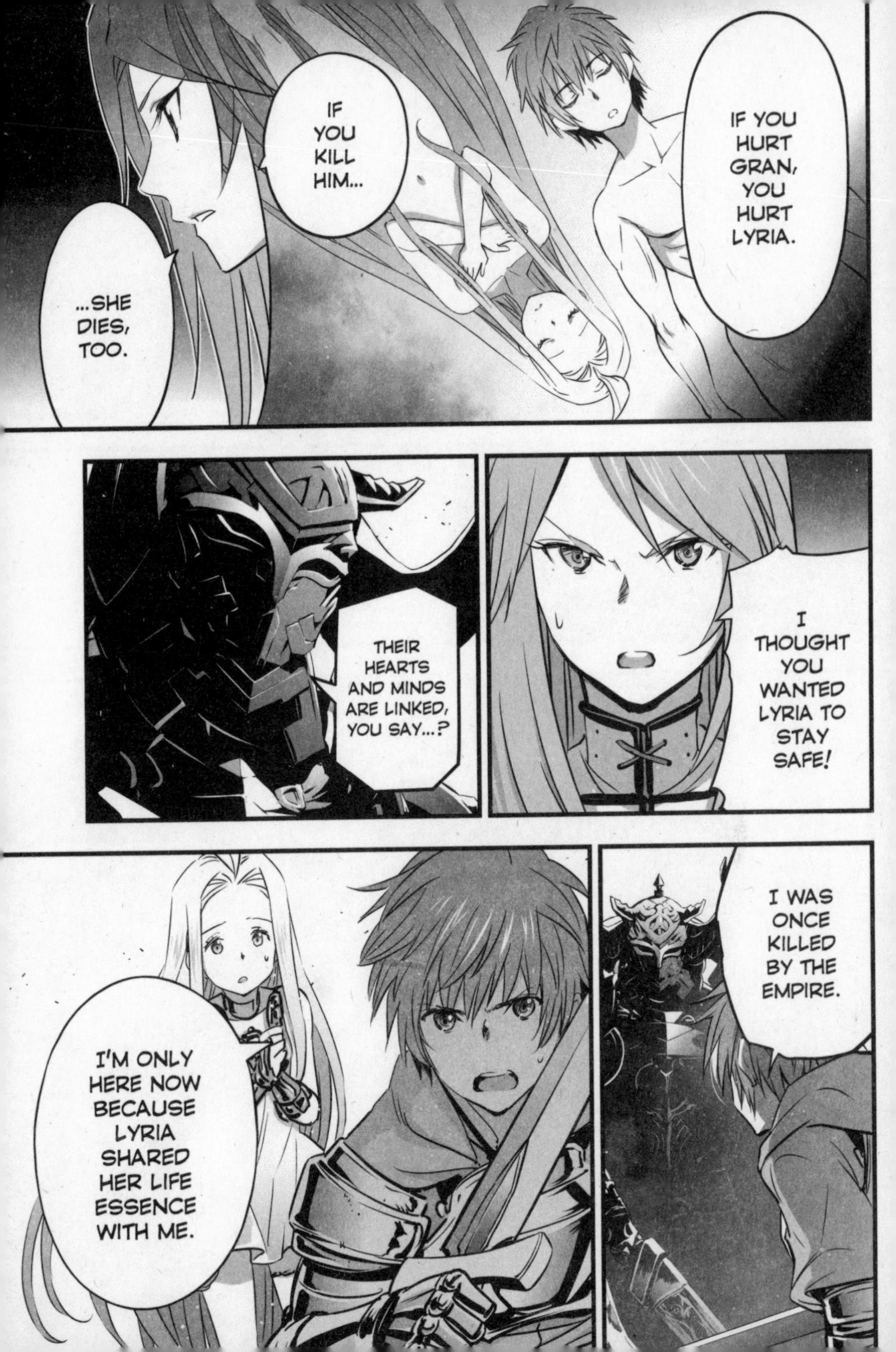
IF YOU HURT GRAN, YOU HURT LYRIA.
IF YOU KILL HIM...
...SHE DIES, TOO.
I THOUGHT YOU WANTED LYRIA TO STAY SAFE!
THEIR HEARTS AND MINDS ARE LINKED, YOU SAY...?
I WAS ONCE KILLED BY THE EMPIRE.
I'M ONLY HERE NOW BECAUSE LYRIA SHARED HER LIFE ESSENCE WITH ME.

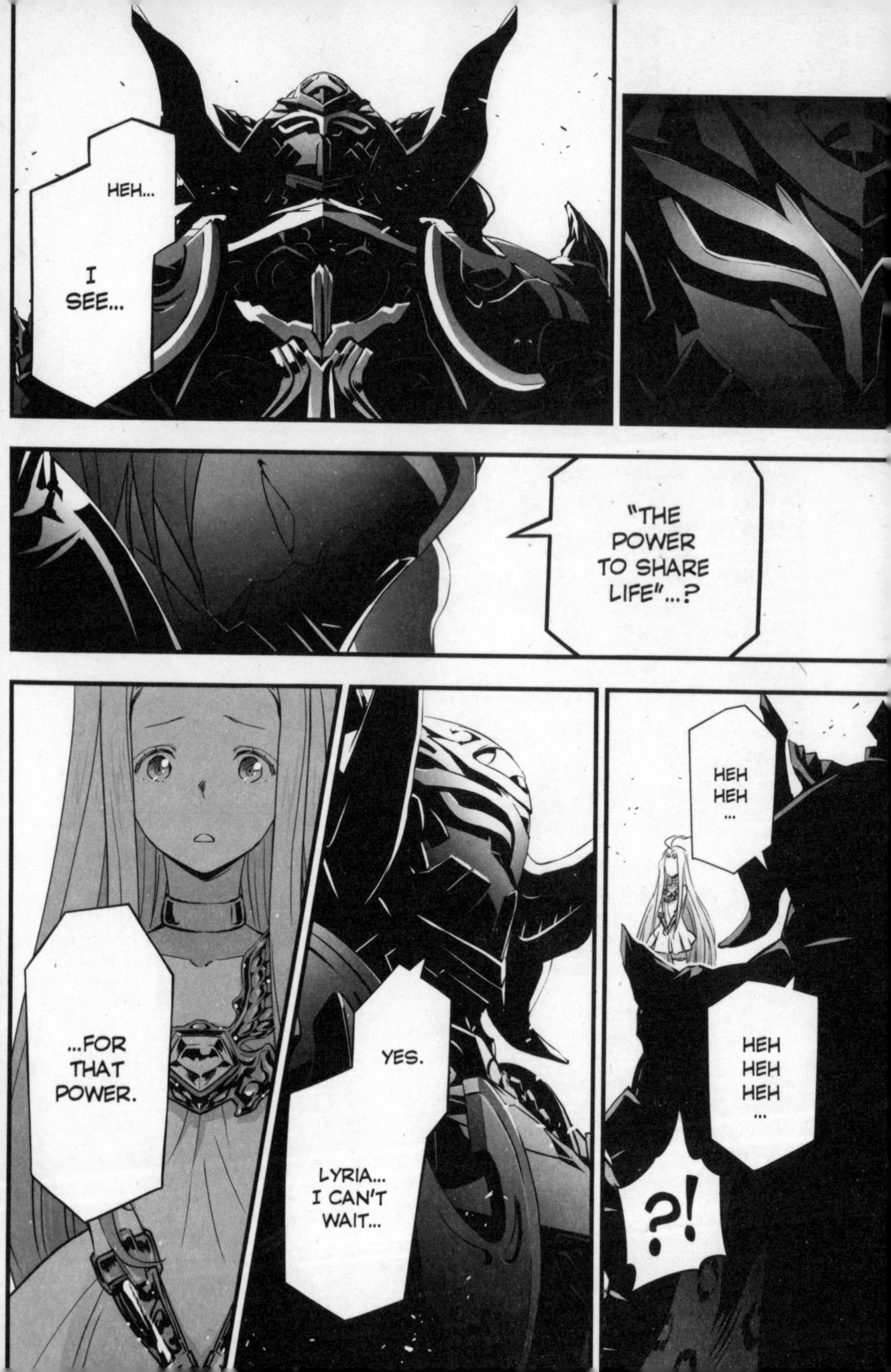
HEH...
I SEE...
"THE POWER TO SHARE LIFE"...?
HEH HEH ...
HEH HEH HEH ...
?!
YES.
LYRIA... I CAN'T WAIT...
...FOR THAT POWER.

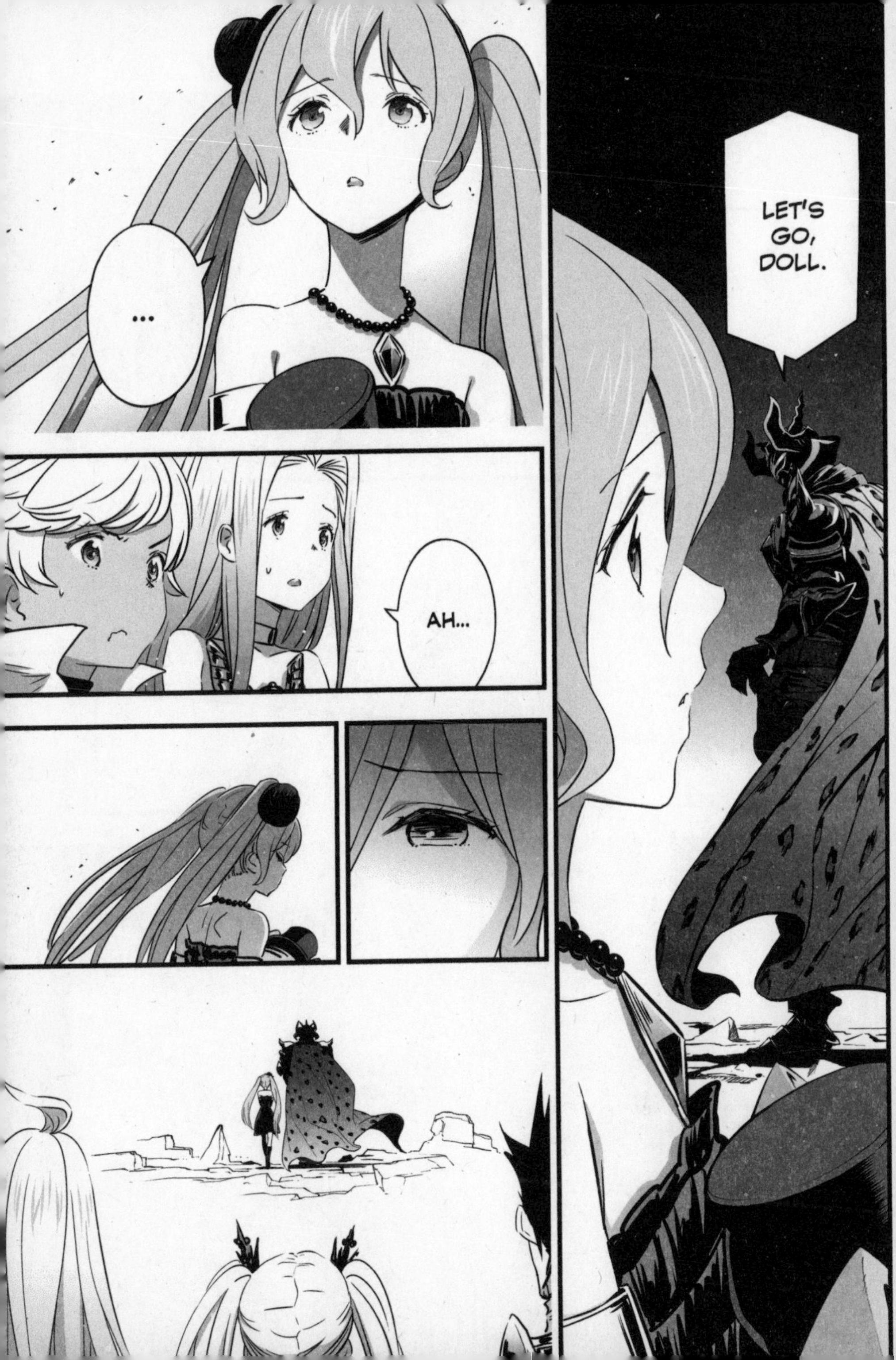
LET'S GO, DOLL.
...
AH...

THEY'RE GONE.

ろくっ SHAKE.

LOOKS LIKE LITTLE MISS ORCHIS COULDN'T HEAR YOU AFTER ALL...

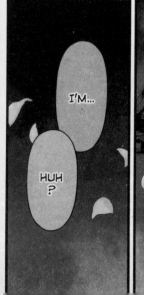

I'M...

HUH?

I KNOW SHE HEARD ME...

IN THAT MOMENT, SHE...

NO...

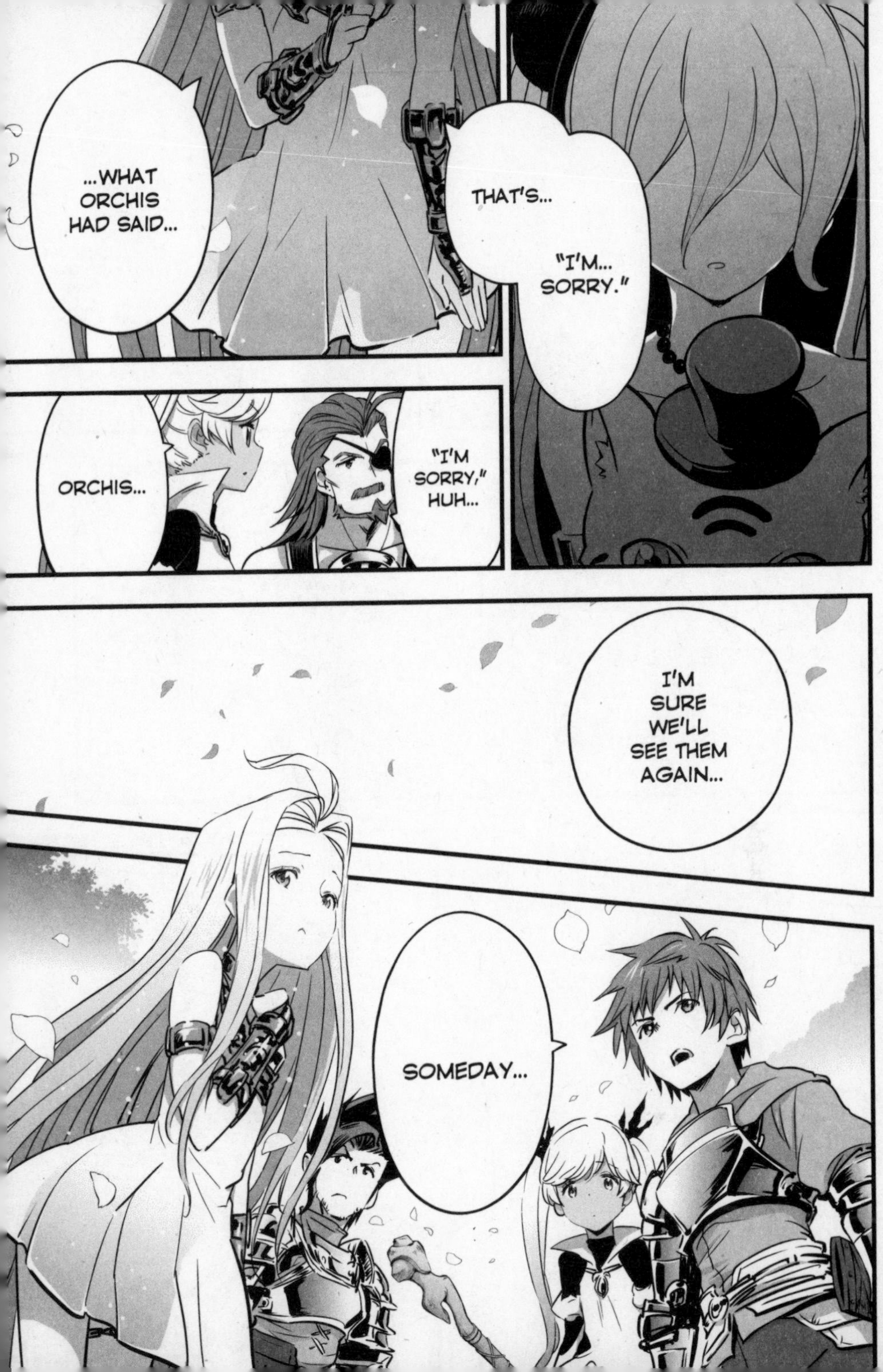
THAT'S...
"I'M... SORRY."
...WHAT ORCHIS HAD SAID...
"I'M SORRY," HUH...
ORCHIS...
I'M SURE WE'LL SEE THEM AGAIN...
SOMEDAY...

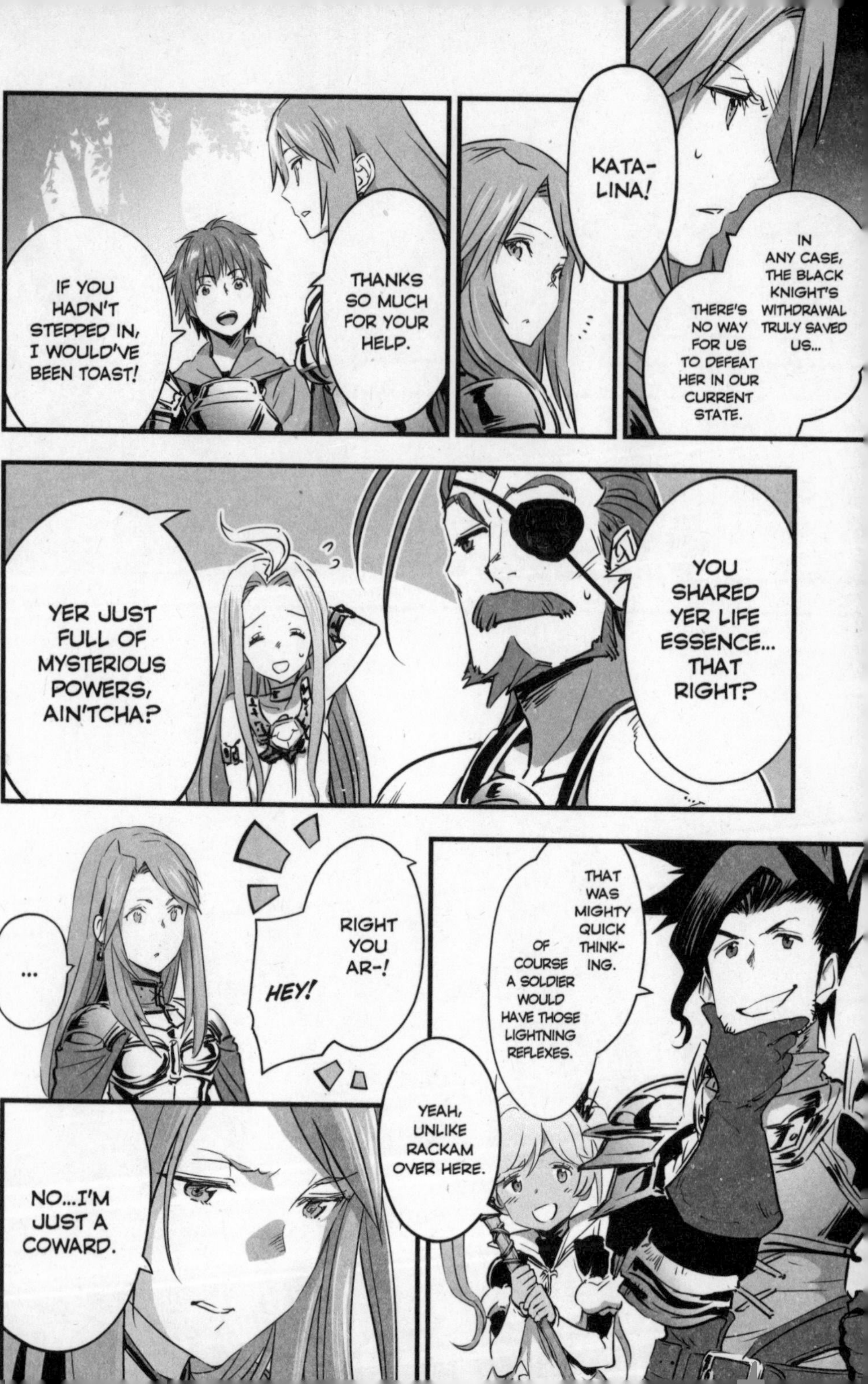

KATA-LINA!
IN ANY CASE, THE BLACK KNIGHT'S WITHDRAWAL TRULY SAVED US...
THERE'S NO WAY FOR US TO DEFEAT HER IN OUR CURRENT STATE.
...
THANKS SO MUCH FOR YOUR HELP.
IF YOU HADN'T STEPPED IN, I WOULD'VE BEEN TOAST!
YOU SHARED YER LIFE ESSENCE... THAT RIGHT?
YER JUST FULL OF MYSTERIOUS POWERS, AIN'TCHA?
THAT WAS MIGHTY QUICK THINKING.
OF COURSE A SOLDIER WOULD HAVE THOSE LIGHTNING REFLEXES.
YEAH, UNLIKE RACKAM OVER HERE.
RIGHT YOU AR-!
HEY!
...
NO...I'M JUST A COWARD.

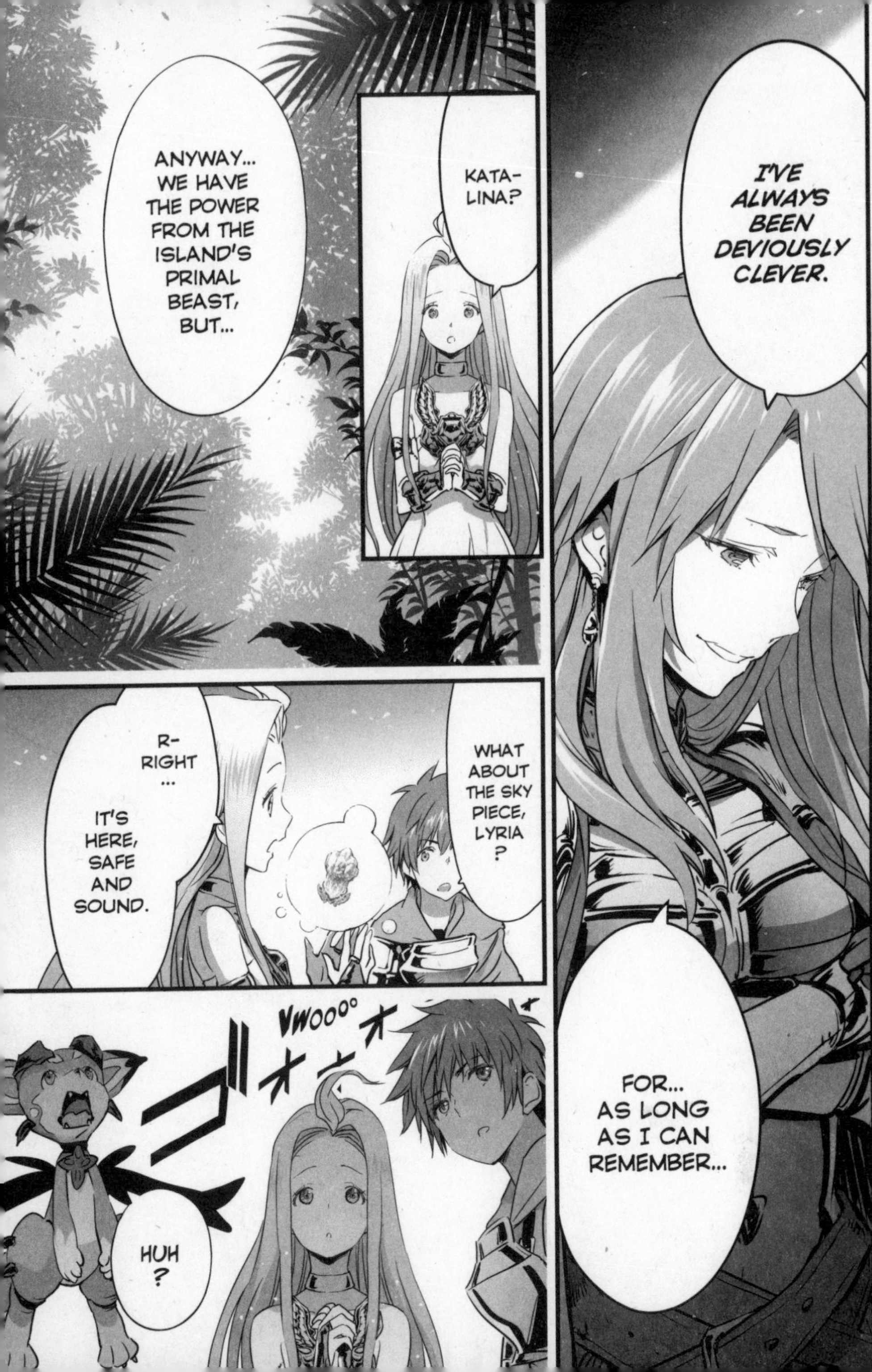

I'VE ALWAYS BEEN DEVIOUSLY CLEVER.
FOR... AS LONG AS I CAN REMEMBER...
KATA-LINA?
ANYWAY... WE HAVE THE POWER FROM THE ISLAND'S PRIMAL BEAST, BUT...
WHAT ABOUT THE SKY PIECE, LYRIA?
R-RIGHT...
IT'S HERE, SAFE AND SOUND.
VWOOO
HUH?

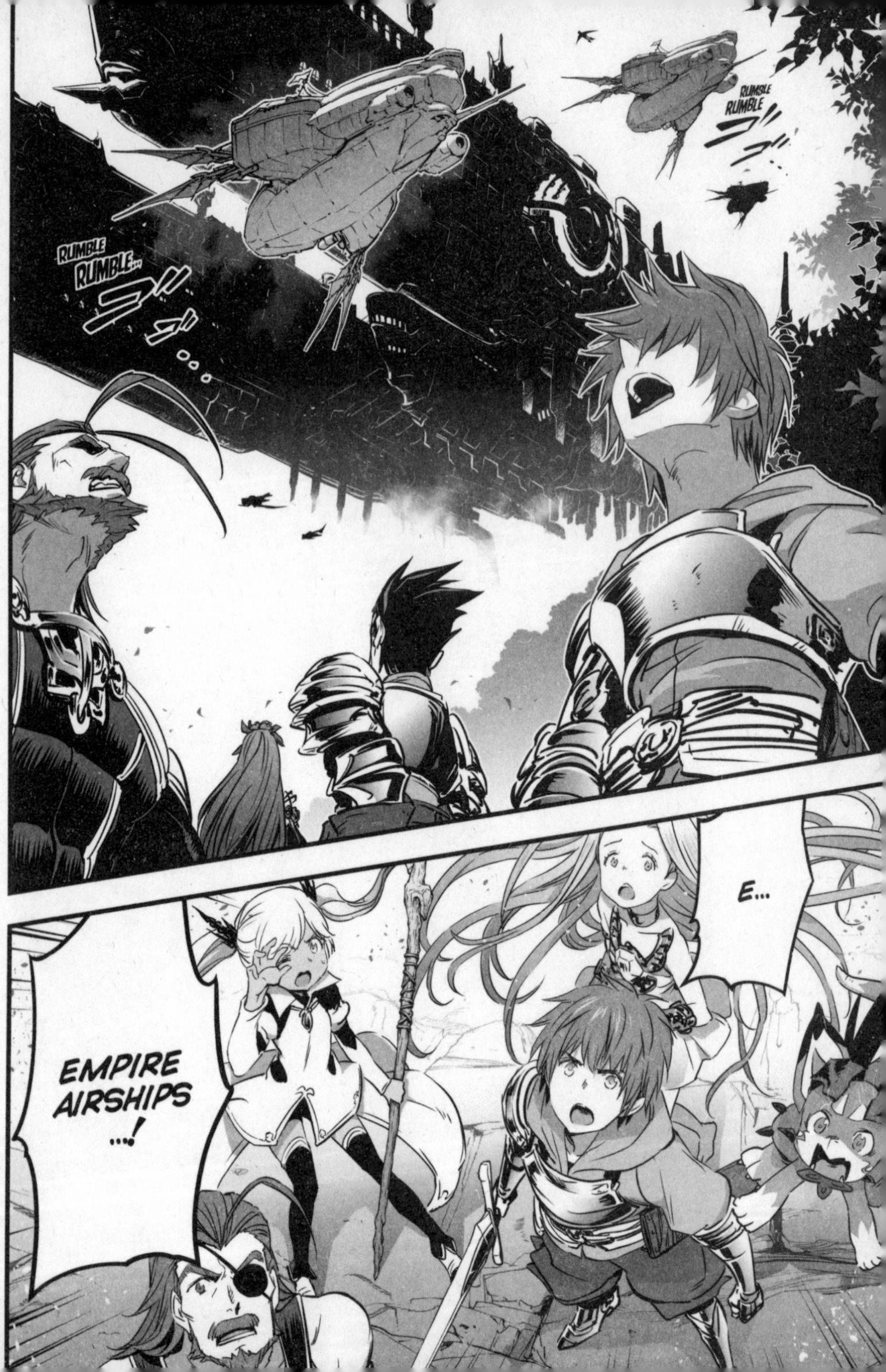
RUMBLE RUMBLE
RUMBLE RUMBLE...
E...
EMPIRE AIRSHIPS ...!

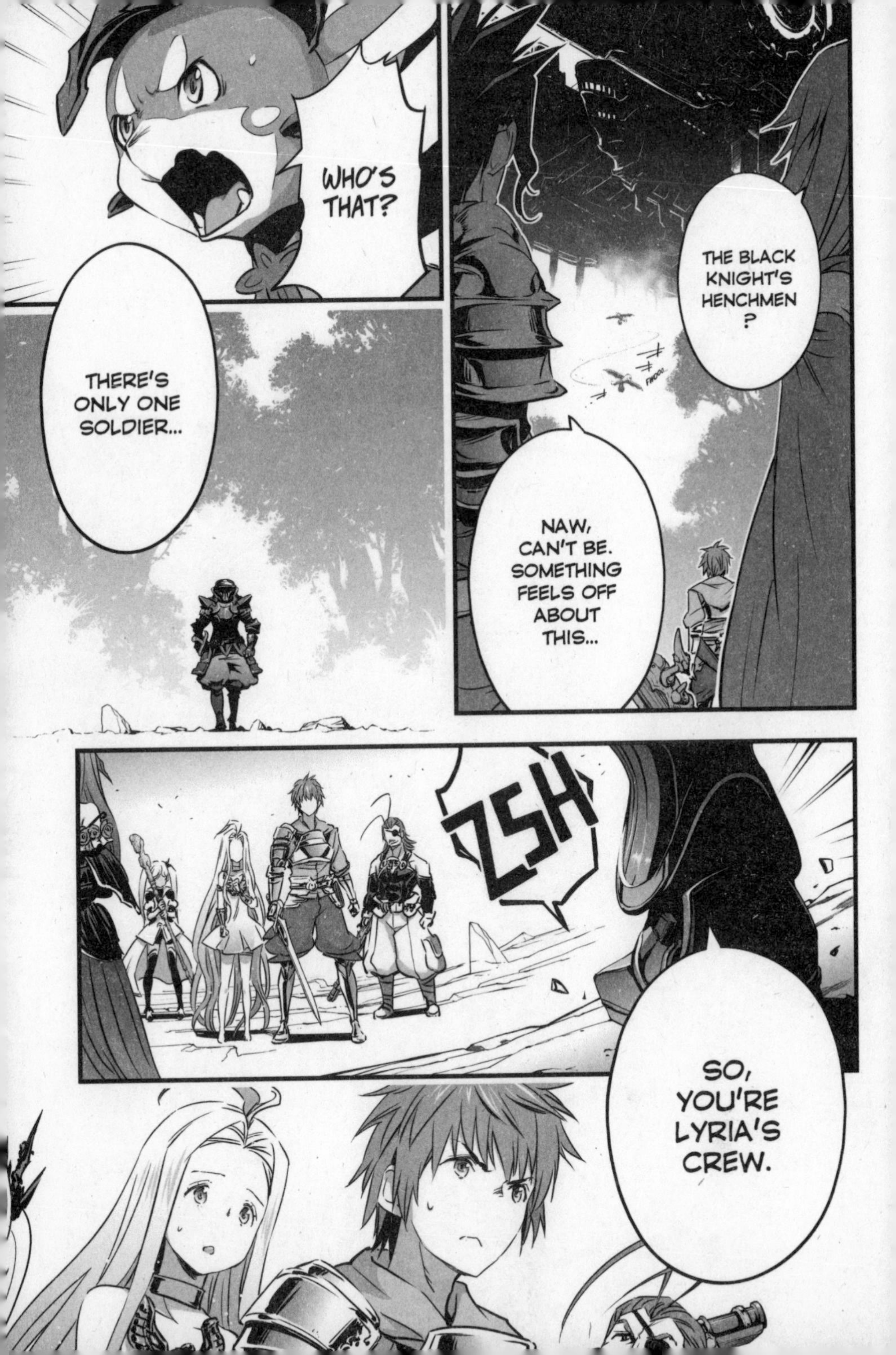
THE BLACK KNIGHT'S HENCHMEN?
NAW, CAN'T BE. SOMETHING FEELS OFF ABOUT THIS...
WHO'S THAT?
THERE'S ONLY ONE SOLDIER...
ZSH
SO, YOU'RE LYRIA'S CREW.

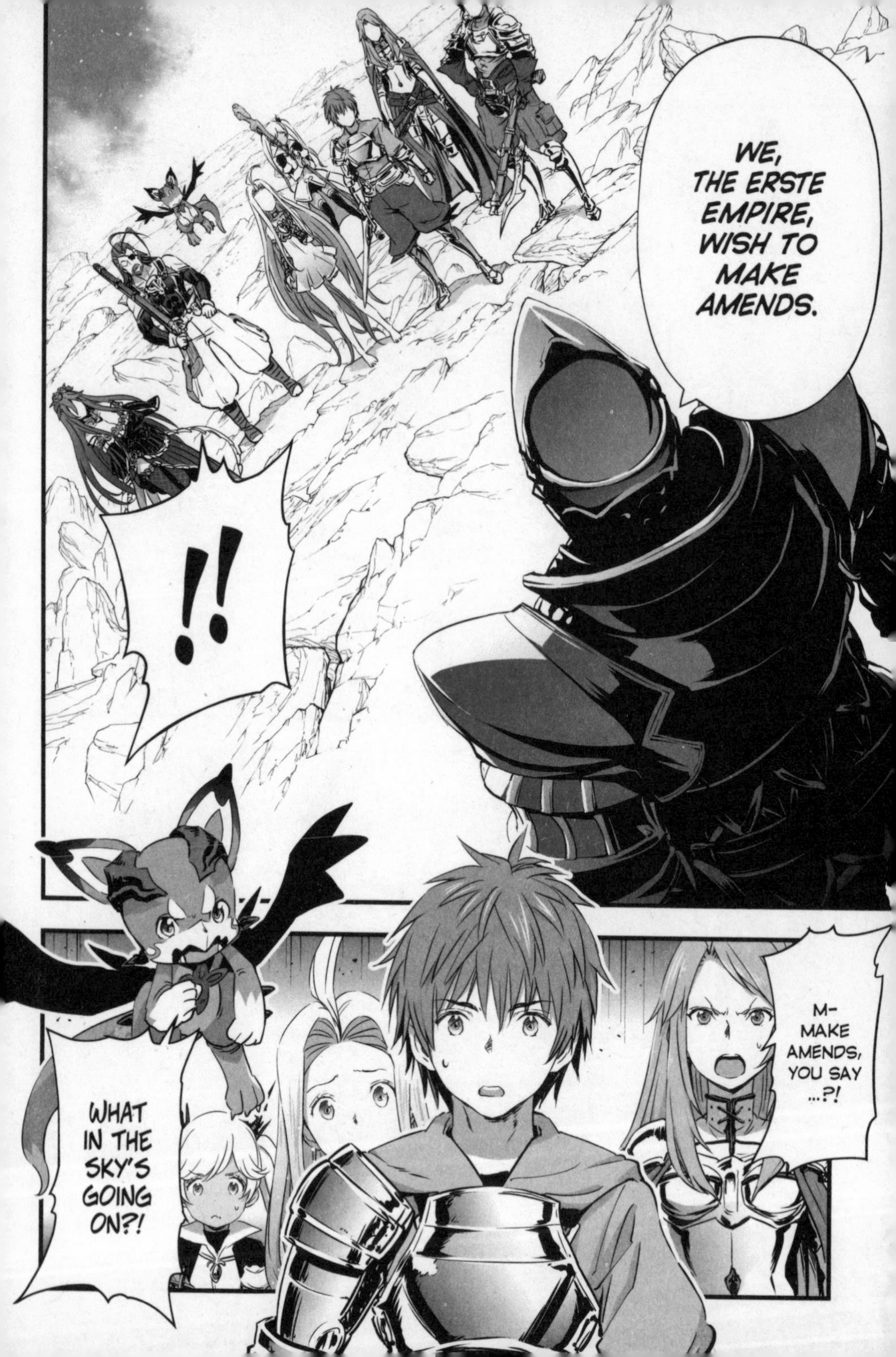
WE, THE ERSTE EMPIRE, WISH TO MAKE AMENDS.
!!
M-MAKE AMENDS, YOU SAY ...?!
WHAT IN THE SKY'S GOING ON?!

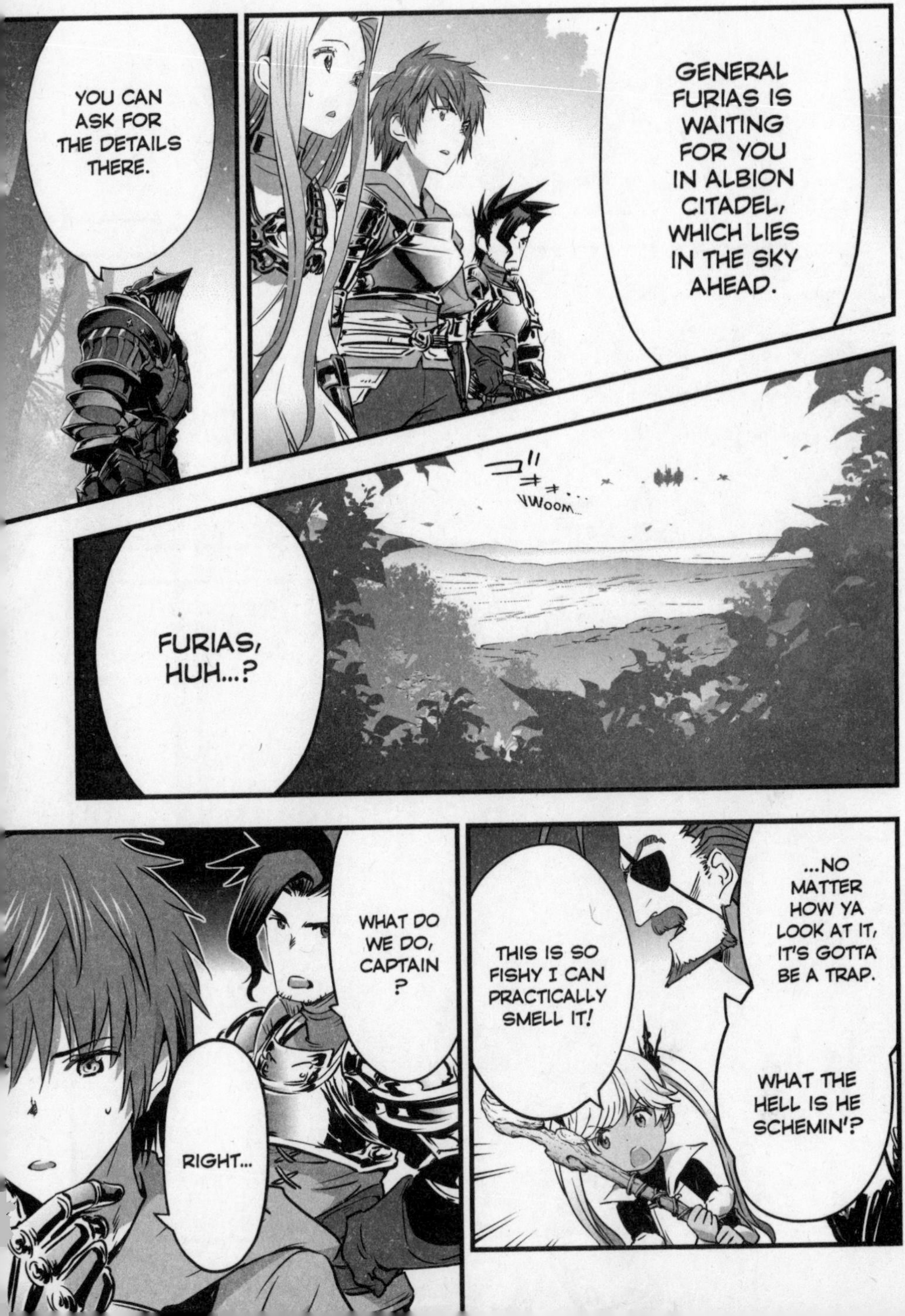
GENERAL FURIAS IS WAITING FOR YOU IN ALBION CITADEL, WHICH LIES IN THE SKY AHEAD.
YOU CAN ASK FOR THE DETAILS THERE.
VWOOM...
FURIAS, HUH...?
...NO MATTER HOW YA LOOK AT IT, IT'S GOTTA BE A TRAP.
THIS IS SO FISHY I CAN PRACTICALLY SMELL IT!
WHAT THE HELL IS HE SCHEMIN'?
WHAT DO WE DO, CAPTAIN?
RIGHT...

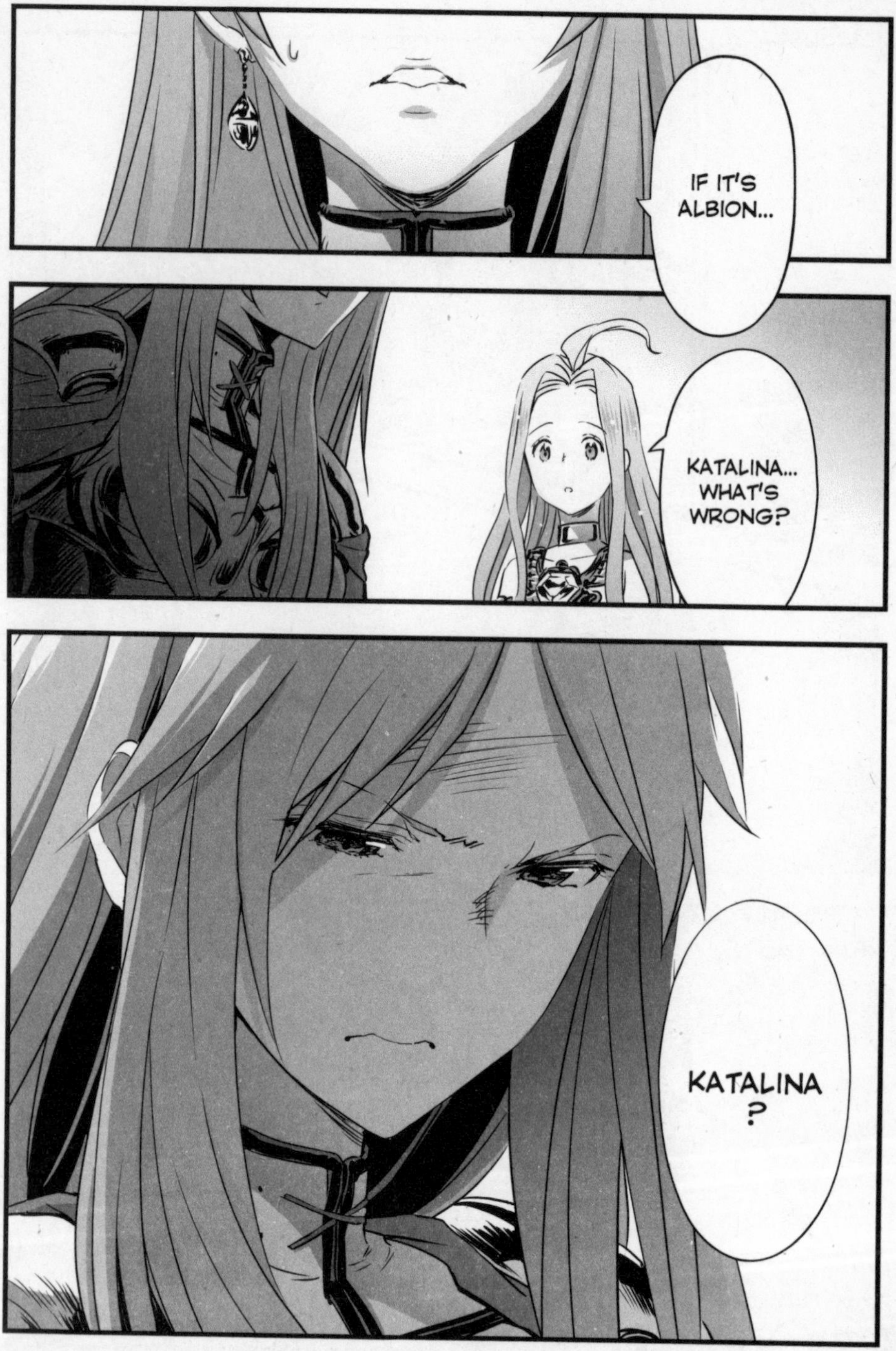
IF IT'S ALBION...
KATALINA... WHAT'S WRONG?
KATALINA ?

GRANBLUE FANTASY
グランブルーファンタジー

GRANBLUE FANTASY
グランブルーファンタジー

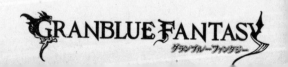

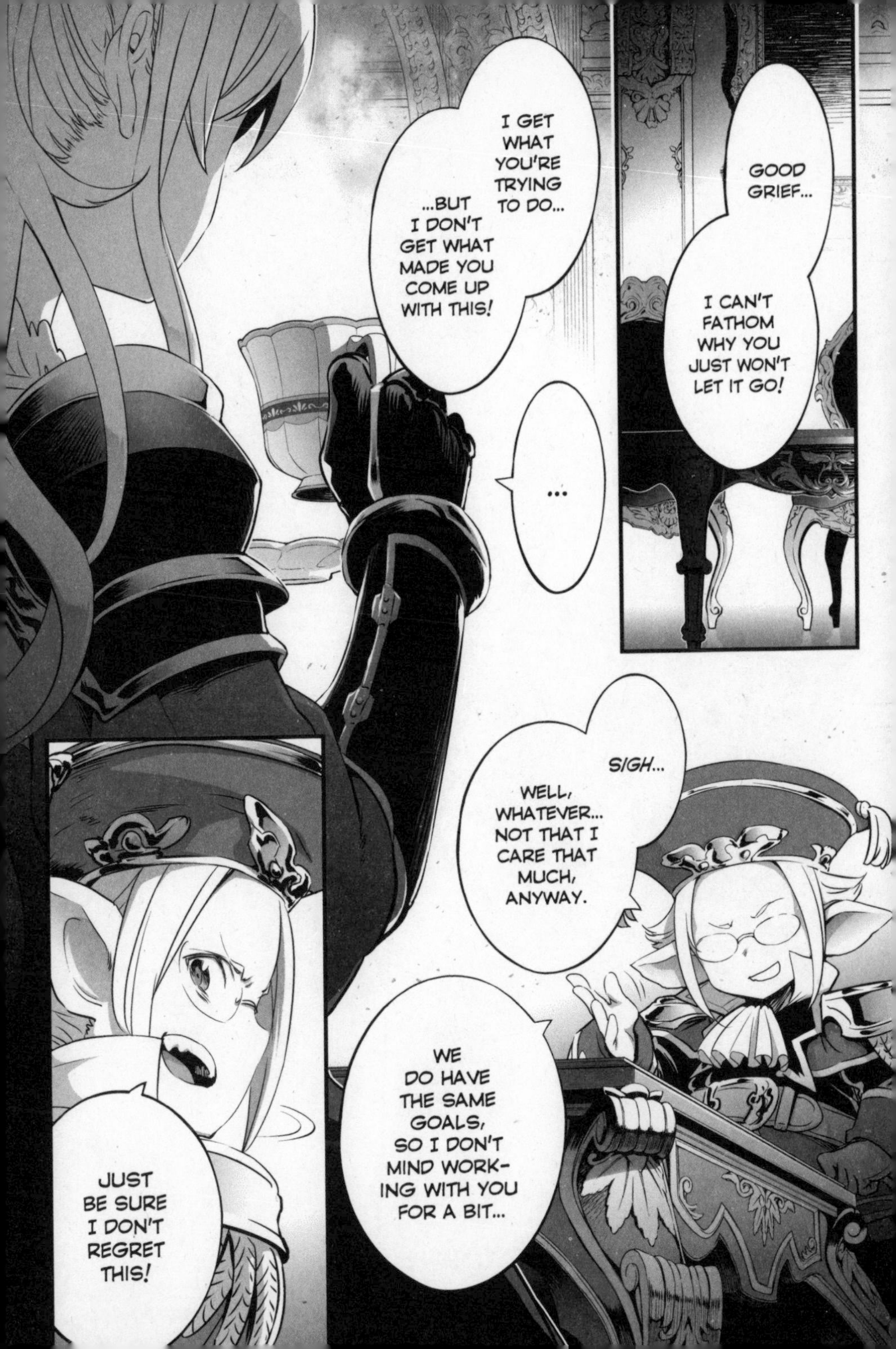
GOOD GRIEF...
I CAN'T FATHOM WHY YOU JUST WON'T LET IT GO!
I GET WHAT YOU'RE TRYING TO DO...
...BUT I DON'T GET WHAT MADE YOU COME UP WITH THIS!
...
SIGH...
WELL, WHATEVER... NOT THAT I CARE THAT MUCH, ANYWAY.
WE DO HAVE THE SAME GOALS, SO I DON'T MIND WORKING WITH YOU FOR A BIT...
JUST BE SURE I DON'T REGRET THIS!

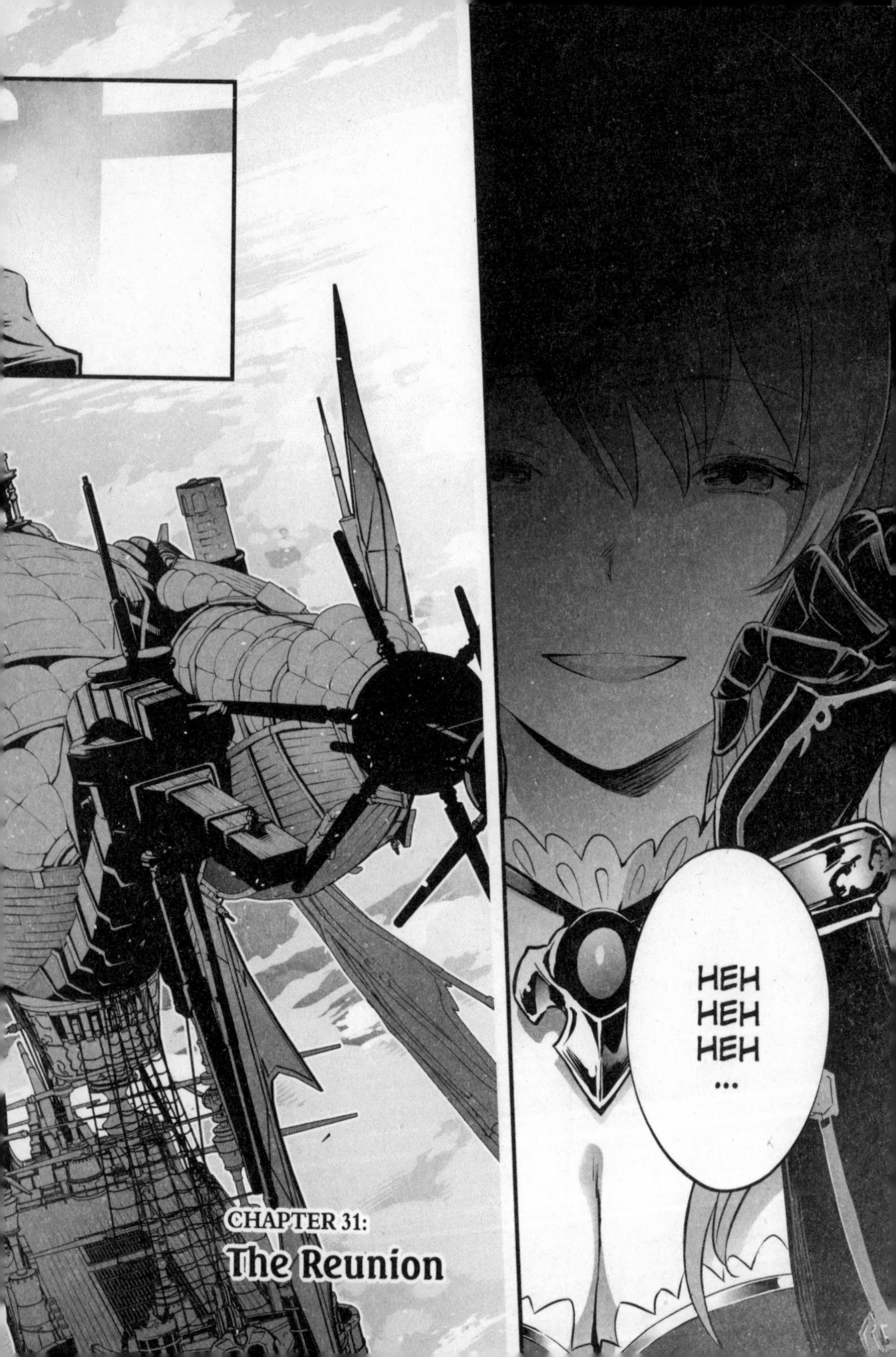
HEH HEH HEH ...
CHAPTER 31:
The Reunion

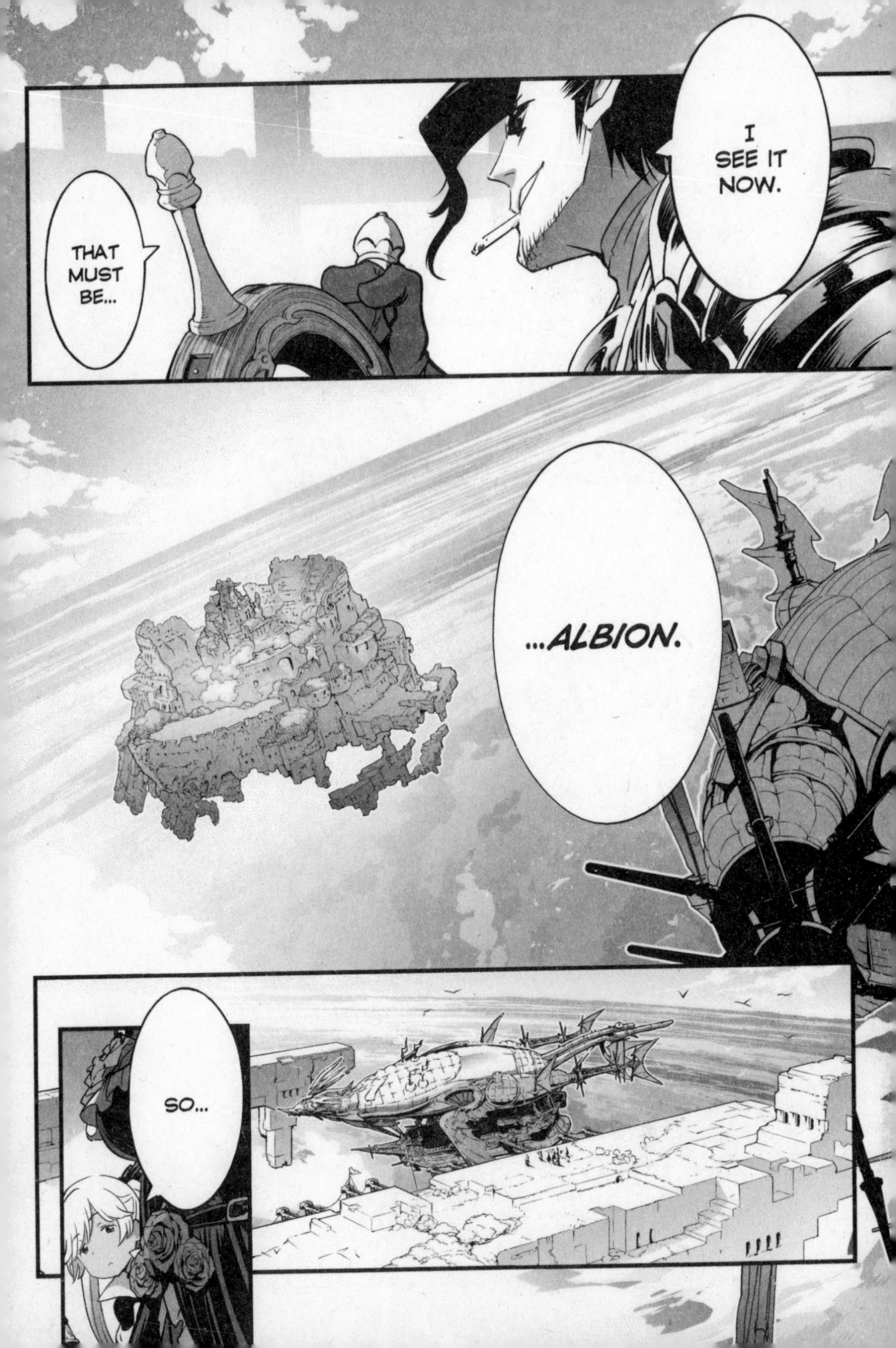
I SEE IT NOW.
THAT MUST BE...
...ALBION.
SO...

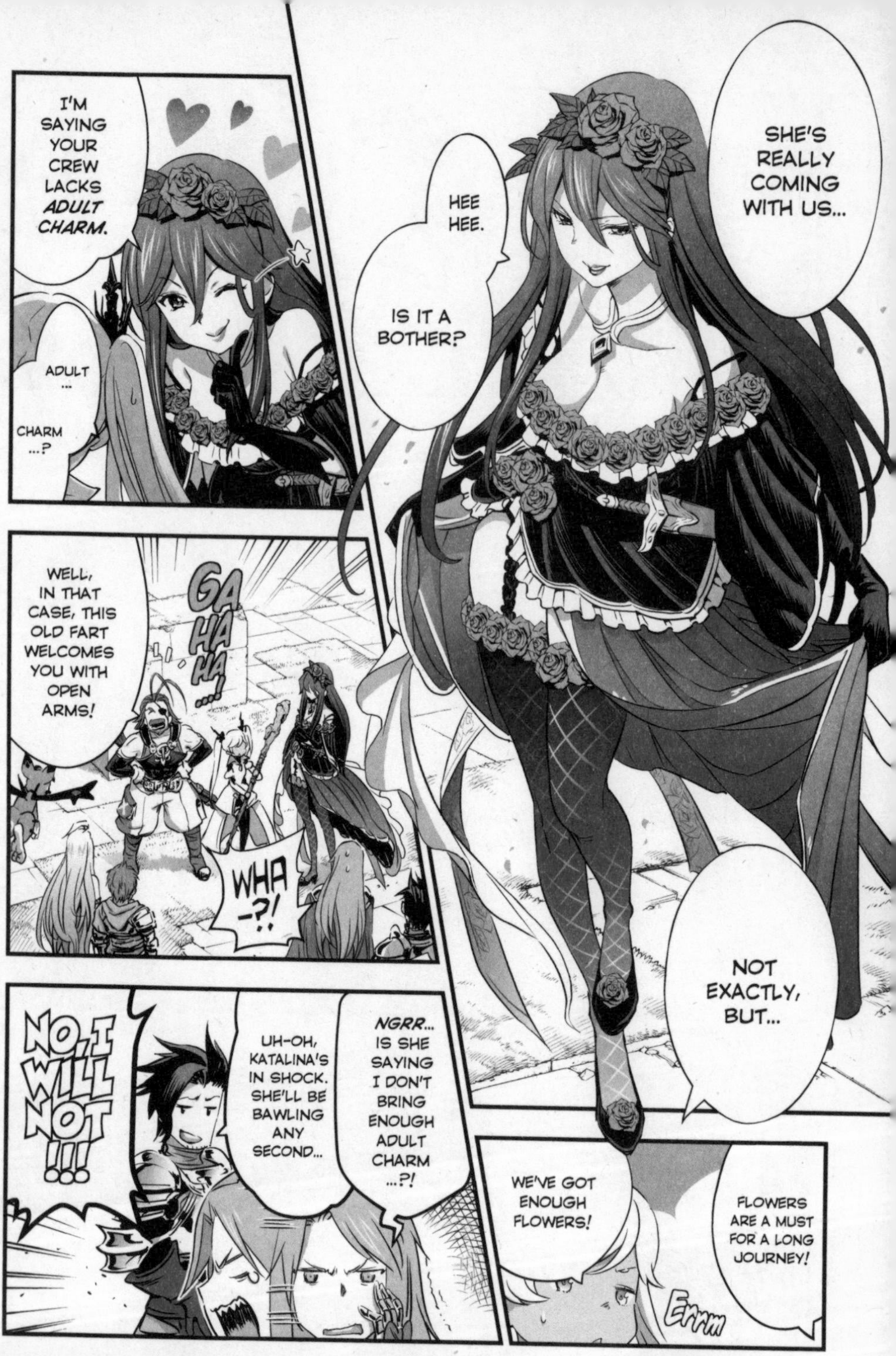
SHE'S REALLY COMING WITH US...
HEE HEE.
IS IT A BOTHER?
NOT EXACTLY, BUT...
I'M SAYING YOUR CREW LACKS ADULT CHARM.
ADULT ...
CHARM ...?
WELL, IN THAT CASE, THIS OLD FART WELCOMES YOU WITH OPEN ARMS!
GA HA HA...!
WHA-?!
FLOWERS ARE A MUST FOR A LONG JOURNEY!
WE'VE GOT ENOUGH FLOWERS!
Errm
NGRR... IS SHE SAYING I DON'T BRING ENOUGH ADULT CHARM...?!
UH-OH, KATALINA'S IN SHOCK. SHE'LL BE BAWLING ANY SECOND...
NO, I WILL NOT!!!

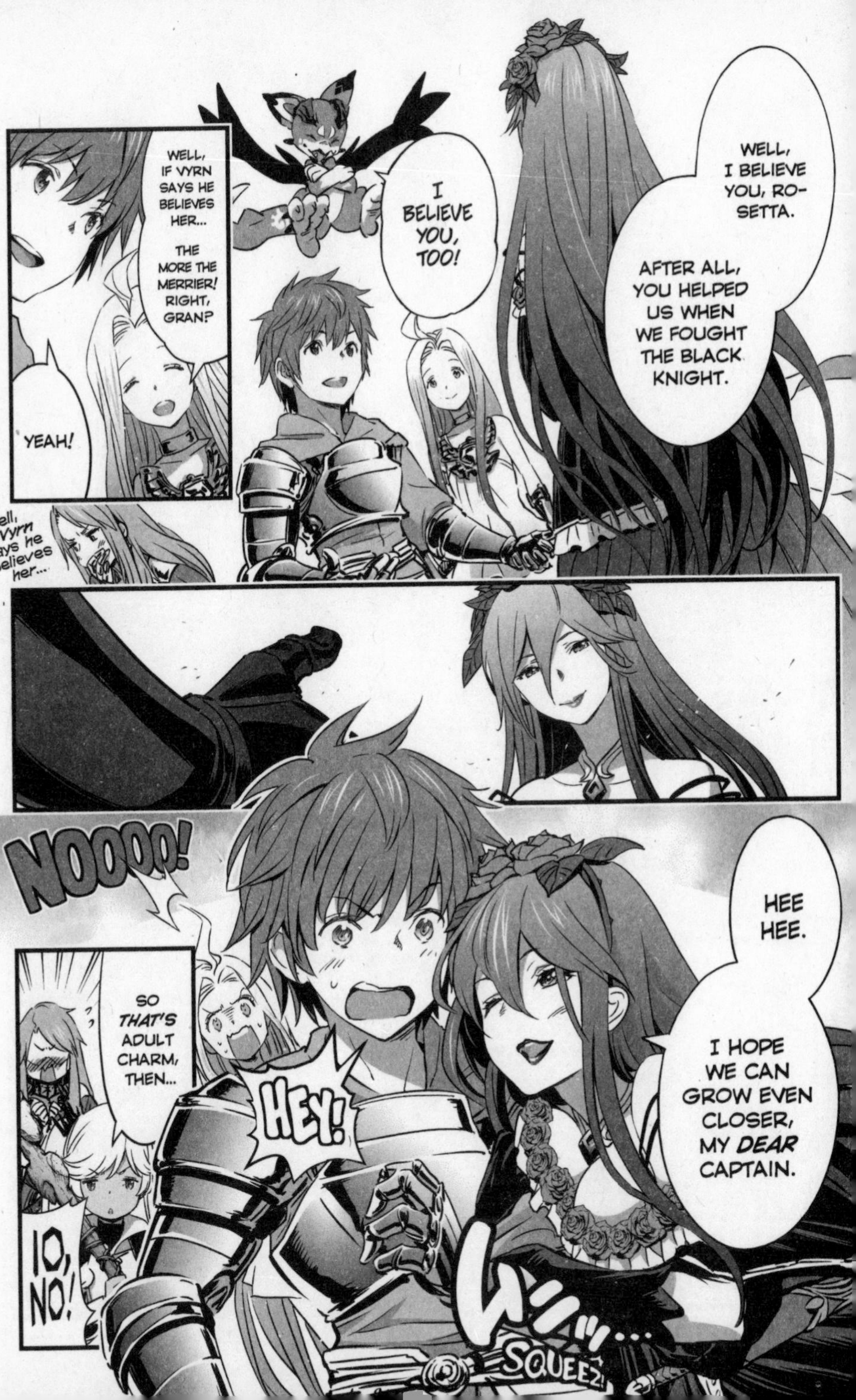
WELL, I BELIEVE YOU, RO-SETTA.
AFTER ALL, YOU HELPED US WHEN WE FOUGHT THE BLACK KNIGHT.
I BELIEVE YOU, TOO!
WELL, IF VYRN SAYS HE BELIEVES HER...
THE MORE THE MERRIER! RIGHT, GRAN?
YEAH!
Well, if Vyrn says he believes her...
HEE HEE.
I HOPE WE CAN GROW EVEN CLOSER, MY DEAR CAPTAIN.
NOOOO!
HEY!
SQUEEZ...
SO THAT'S ADULT CHARM, THEN...
IO, NO!

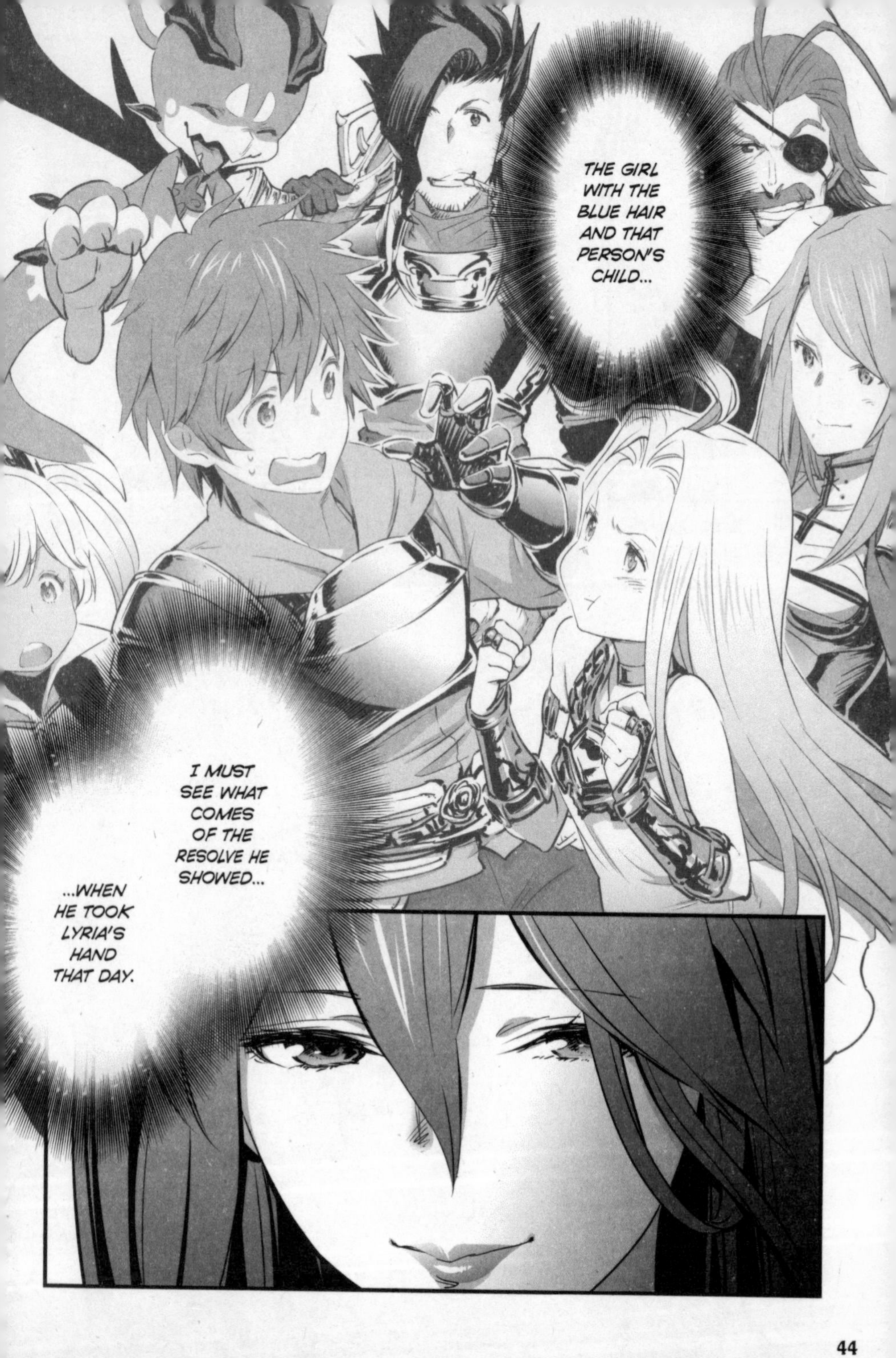
THE GIRL WITH THE BLUE HAIR AND THAT PERSON'S CHILD...
I MUST SEE WHAT COMES OF THE RESOLVE HE SHOWED...
...WHEN HE TOOK LYRIA'S HAND THAT DAY.

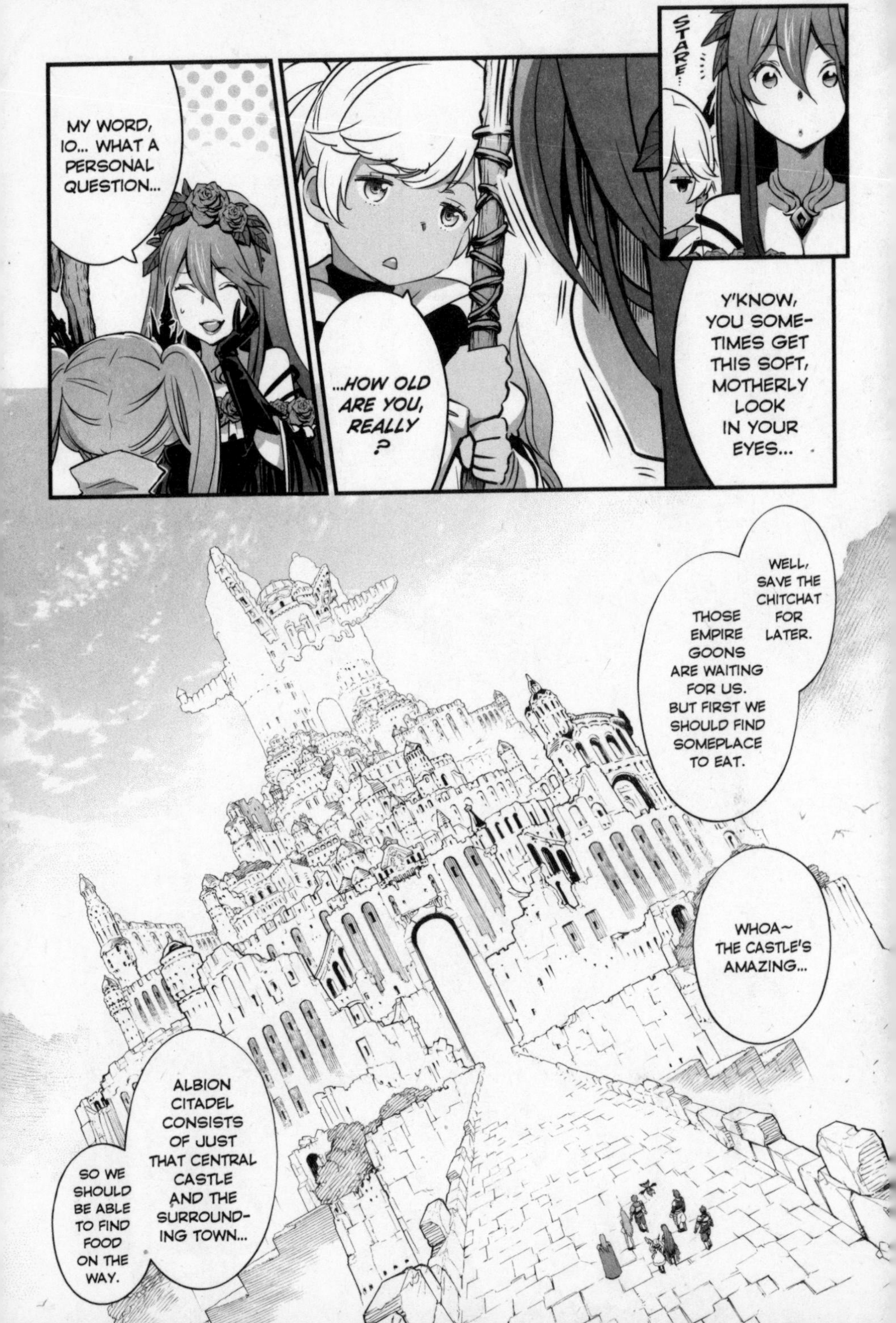
STARE...
Y'KNOW, YOU SOMETIMES GET THIS SOFT, MOTHERLY LOOK IN YOUR EYES...
...HOW OLD ARE YOU, REALLY?
MY WORD, IO... WHAT A PERSONAL QUESTION...
WELL, SAVE THE CHITCHAT FOR LATER.
THOSE EMPIRE GOONS ARE WAITING FOR US. BUT FIRST WE SHOULD FIND SOMEPLACE TO EAT.
WHOA~ THE CASTLE'S AMAZING...
ALBION CITADEL CONSISTS OF JUST THAT CENTRAL CASTLE AND THE SURROUNDING TOWN...
SO WE SHOULD BE ABLE TO FIND FOOD ON THE WAY.

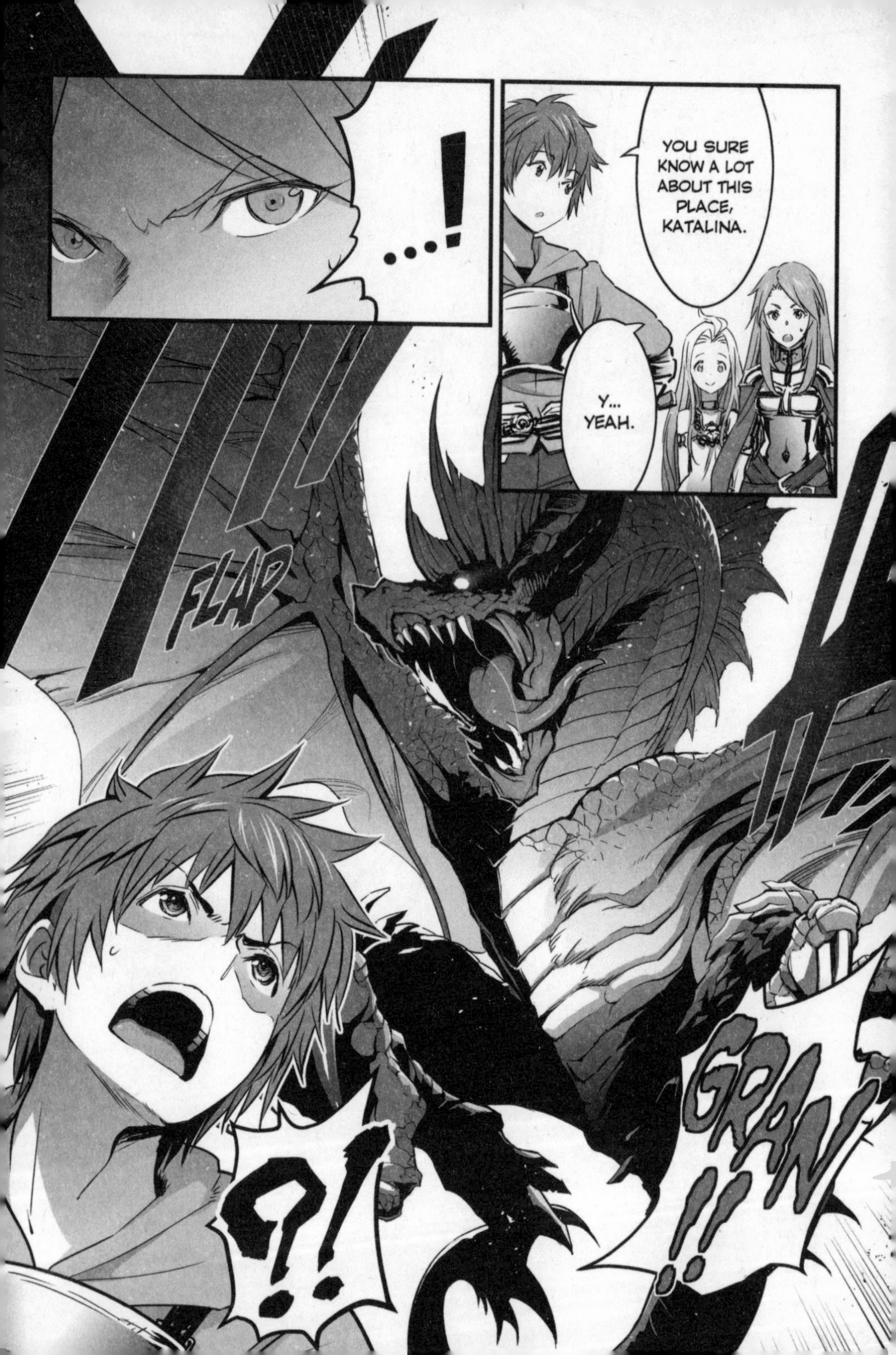
YOU SURE KNOW A LOT ABOUT THIS PLACE, KATALINA.
Y... YEAH.
...!
FLAP
GRAN!!
?!

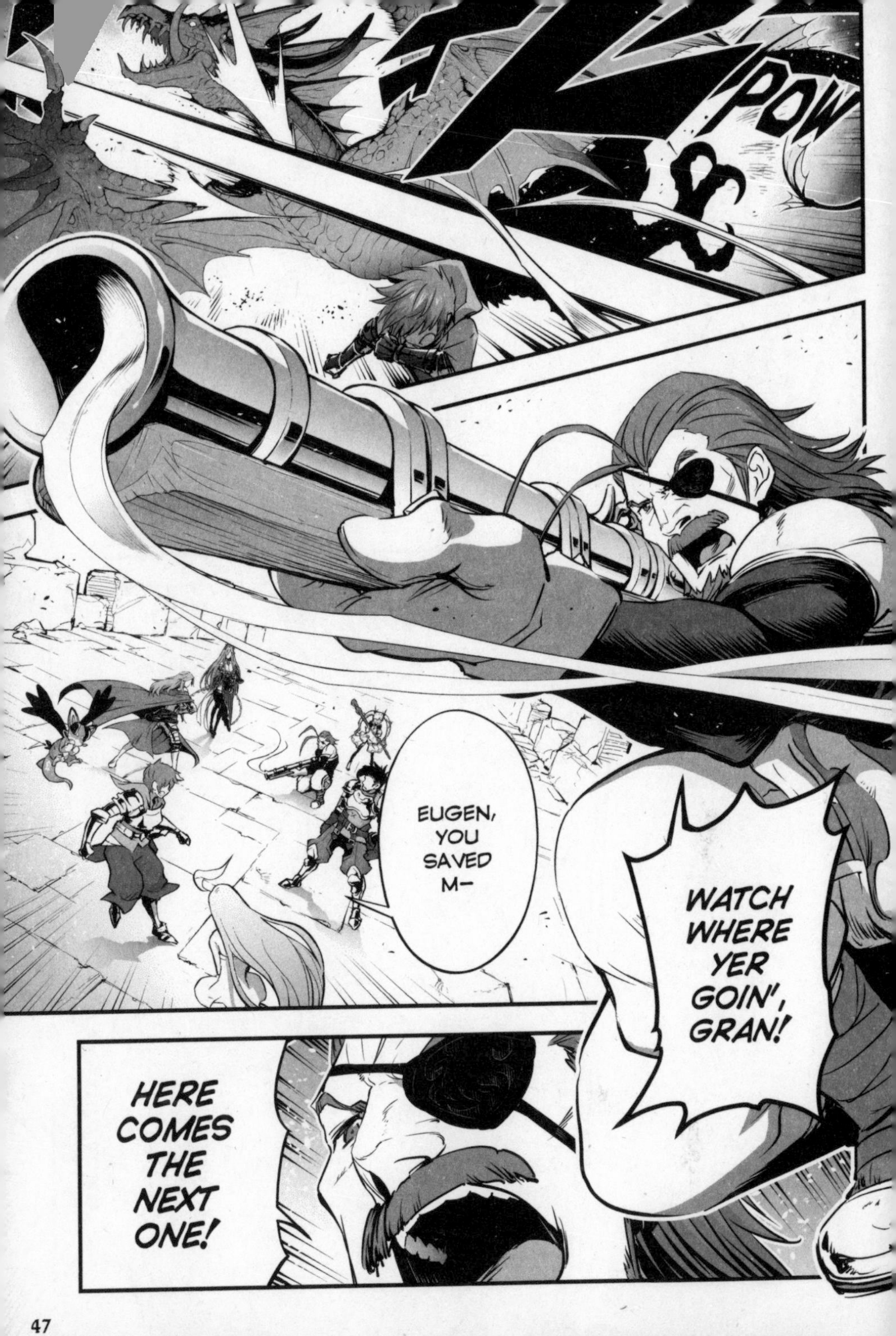
POW
EUGEN, YOU SAVED M—
WATCH WHERE YER GOIN', GRAN!
HERE COMES THE NEXT ONE!

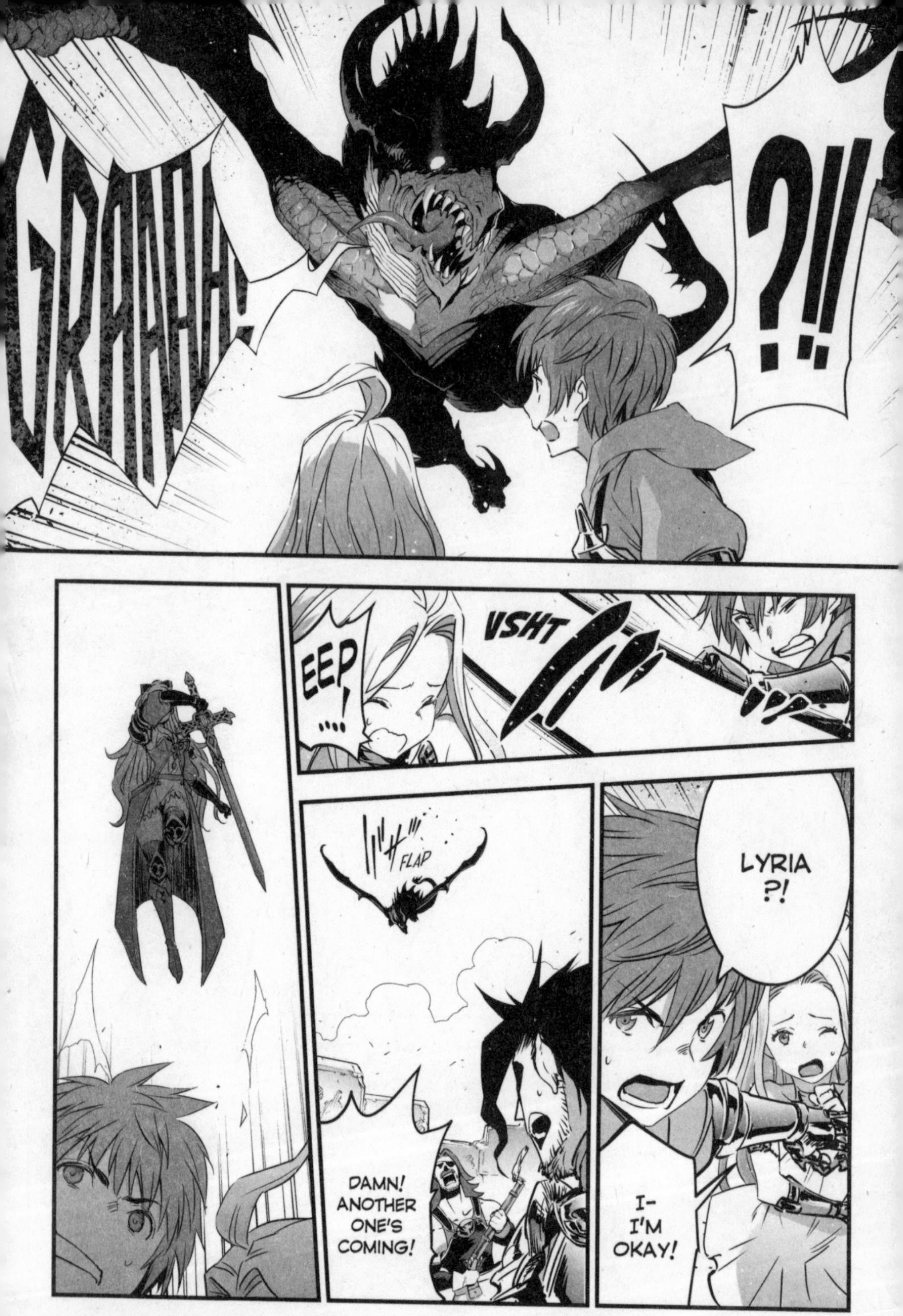
?!!
GRAAAH!
VSHT
EEP...!
LYRIA ?!
I- I'M OKAY!
FLAP
DAMN! ANOTHER ONE'S COMING!

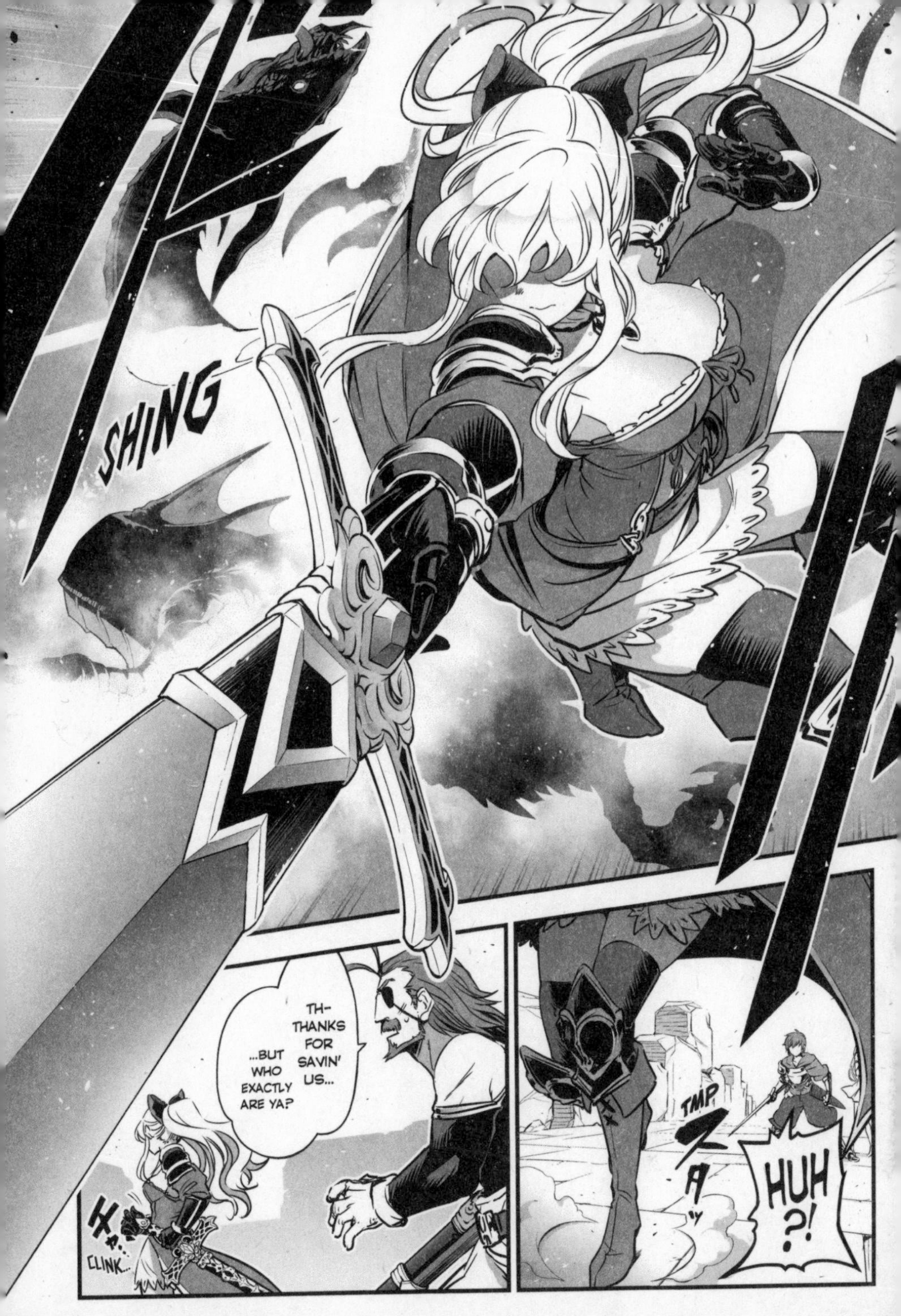
SHING
TMP
HUH?!
TH-THANKS FOR SAVIN' US...
...BUT WHO EXACTLY ARE YA?
CLINK...

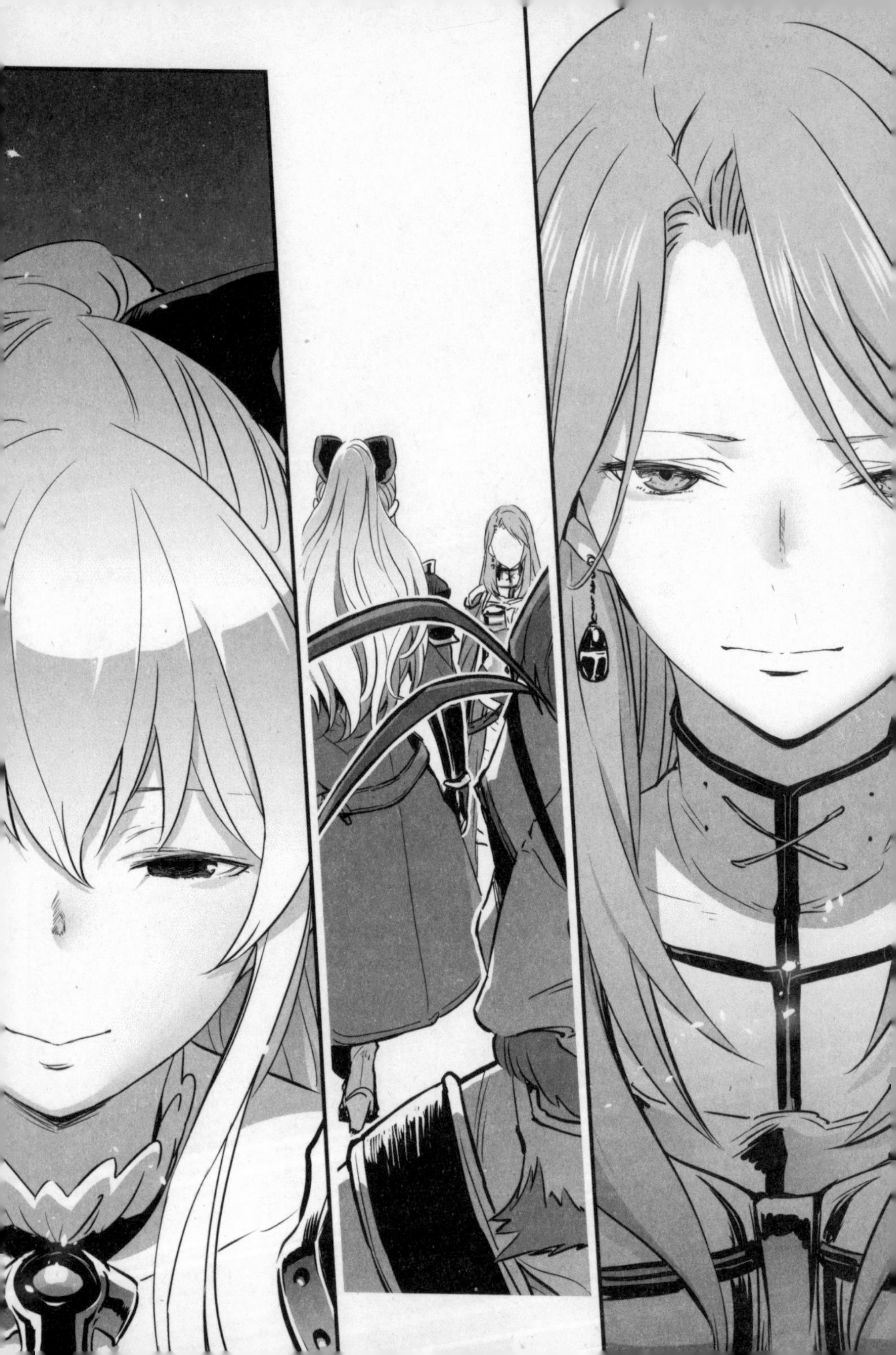

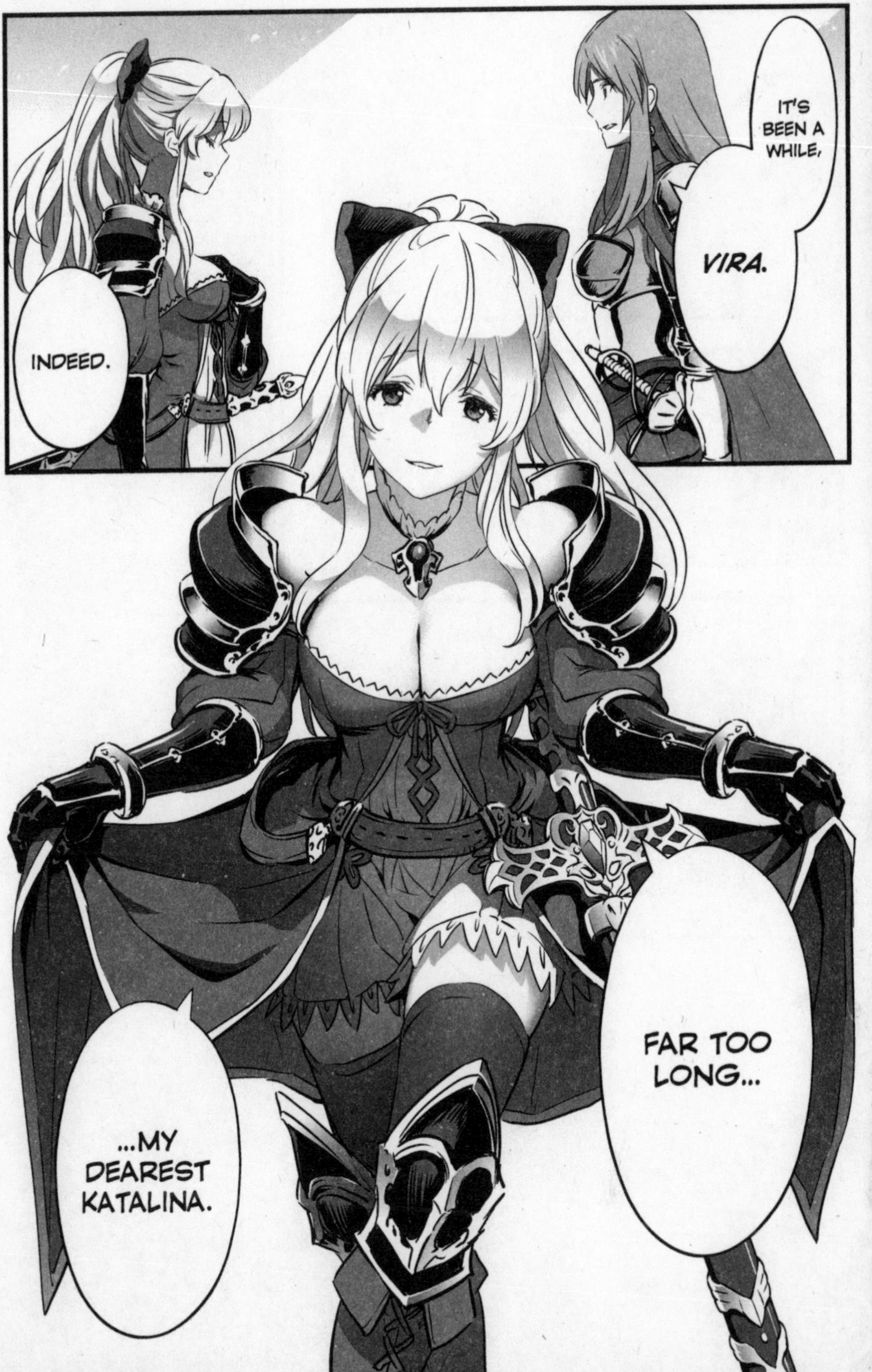
IT'S BEEN A WHILE,
VIRA.
INDEED.
FAR TOO LONG...
...MY DEAREST KATALINA.

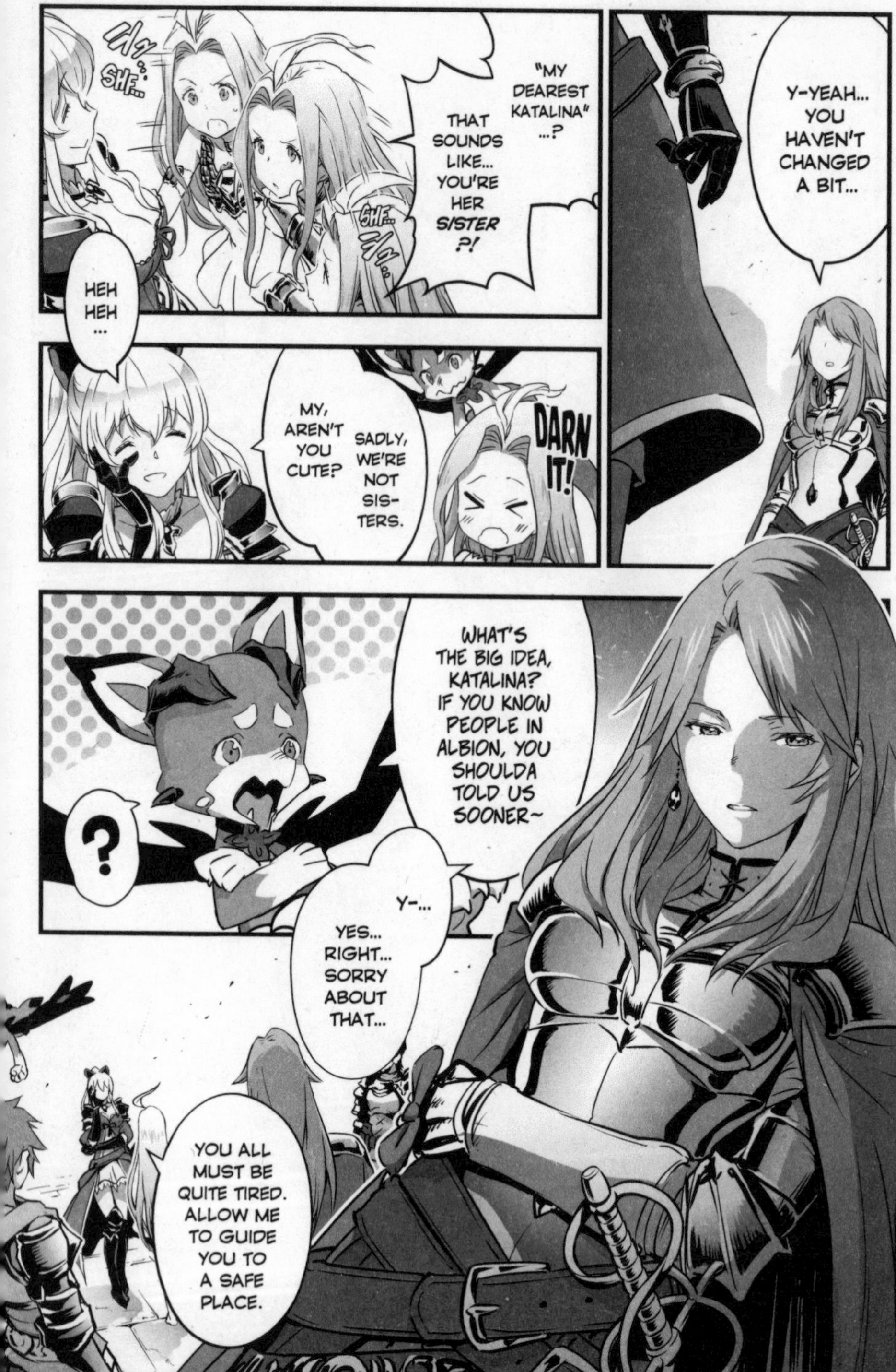
Y-YEAH... YOU HAVEN'T CHANGED A BIT...
SHF...
"MY DEAREST KATALINA" ...?
THAT SOUNDS LIKE... YOU'RE HER *SISTER* ?!
SHF...
HEH HEH ...
MY, AREN'T YOU CUTE?
SADLY, WE'RE NOT SIS-TERS.
DARN IT!
WHAT'S THE BIG IDEA, KATALINA? IF YOU KNOW PEOPLE IN ALBION, YOU SHOULDA TOLD US SOONER~
?
Y-...
YES... RIGHT... SORRY ABOUT THAT...
YOU ALL MUST BE QUITE TIRED. ALLOW ME TO GUIDE YOU TO A SAFE PLACE.

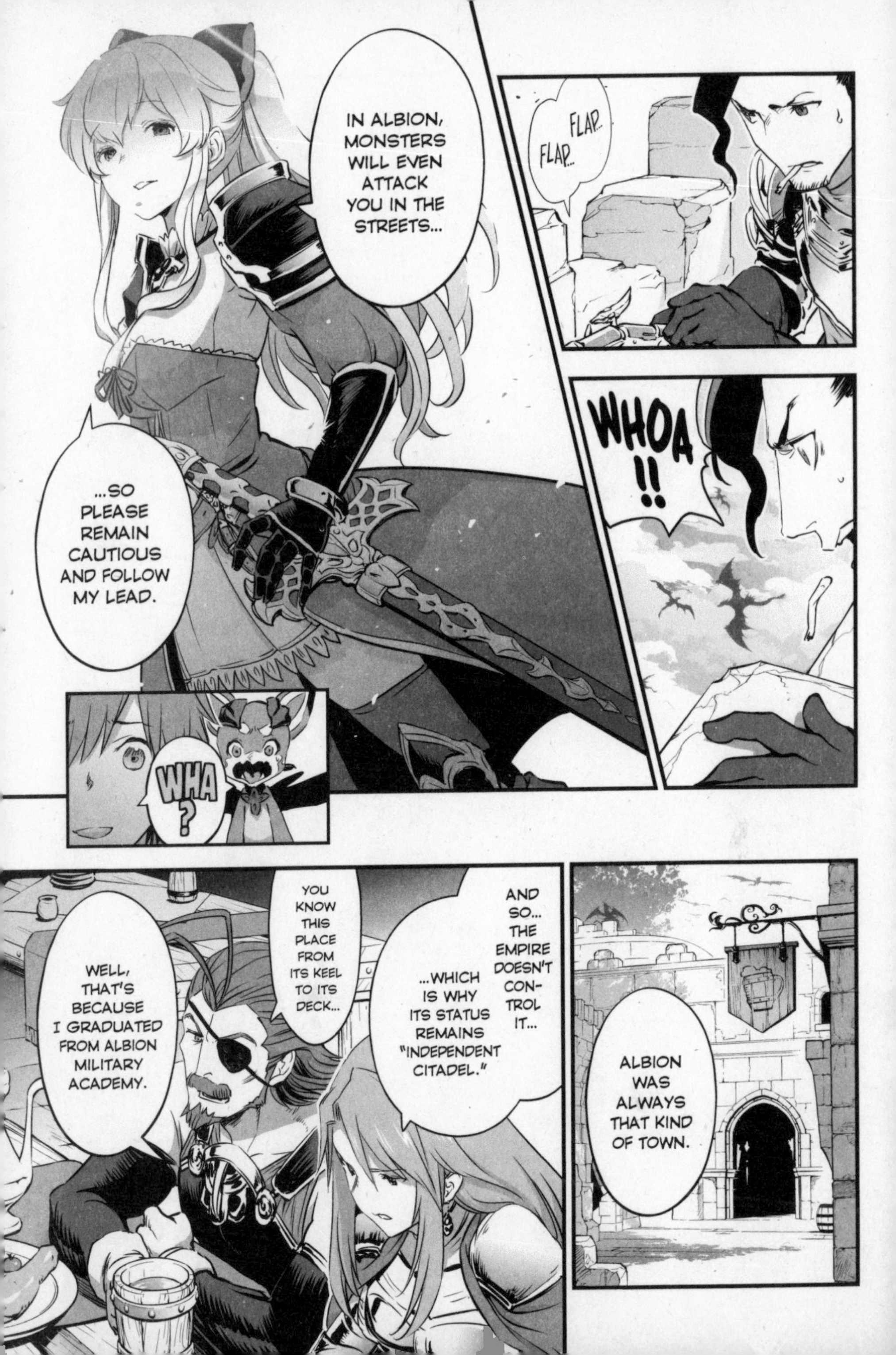
FLAP... FLAP...
WHOA!!
IN ALBION, MONSTERS WILL EVEN ATTACK YOU IN THE STREETS...
...SO PLEASE REMAIN CAUTIOUS AND FOLLOW MY LEAD.
WHA?
ALBION WAS ALWAYS THAT KIND OF TOWN.
AND SO... THE EMPIRE DOESN'T CON-TROL IT...
...WHICH IS WHY ITS STATUS REMAINS "INDEPENDENT CITADEL."
YOU KNOW THIS PLACE FROM ITS KEEL TO ITS DECK...
WELL, THAT'S BECAUSE I GRADUATED FROM ALBION MILITARY ACADEMY.

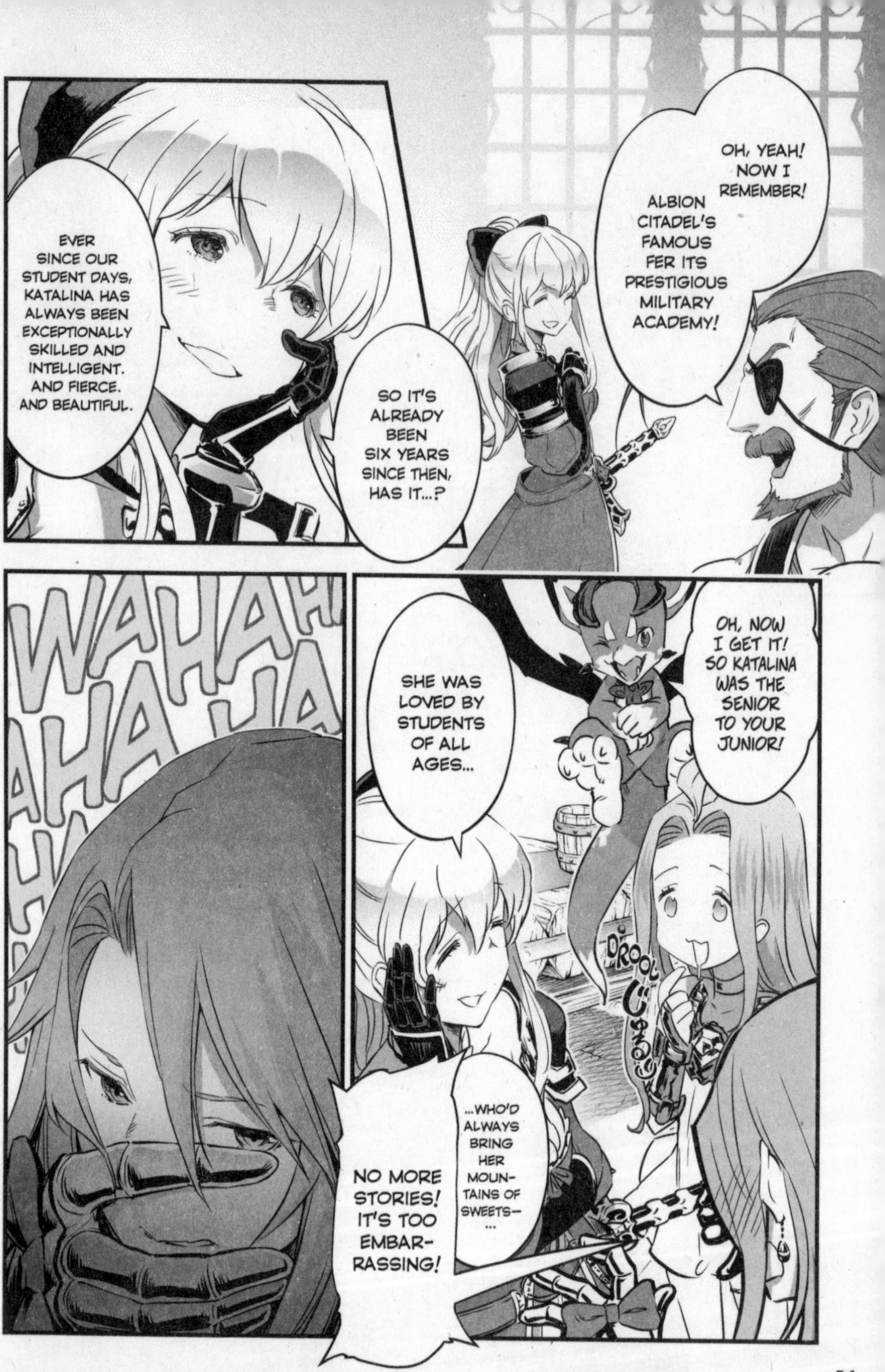
OH, YEAH! NOW I REMEMBER!
ALBION CITADEL'S FAMOUS FER ITS PRESTIGIOUS MILITARY ACADEMY!
SO IT'S ALREADY BEEN SIX YEARS SINCE THEN, HAS IT...?
EVER SINCE OUR STUDENT DAYS, KATALINA HAS ALWAYS BEEN EXCEPTIONALLY SKILLED AND INTELLIGENT. AND FIERCE. AND BEAUTIFUL.
OH, NOW I GET IT! SO KATALINA WAS THE SENIOR TO YOUR JUNIOR!
SHE WAS LOVED BY STUDENTS OF ALL AGES...
DROOL
...WHO'D ALWAYS BRING HER MOUNTAINS OF SWEETS—...
NO MORE STORIES! IT'S TOO EMBARRASSING!
WAHAHAHAHA

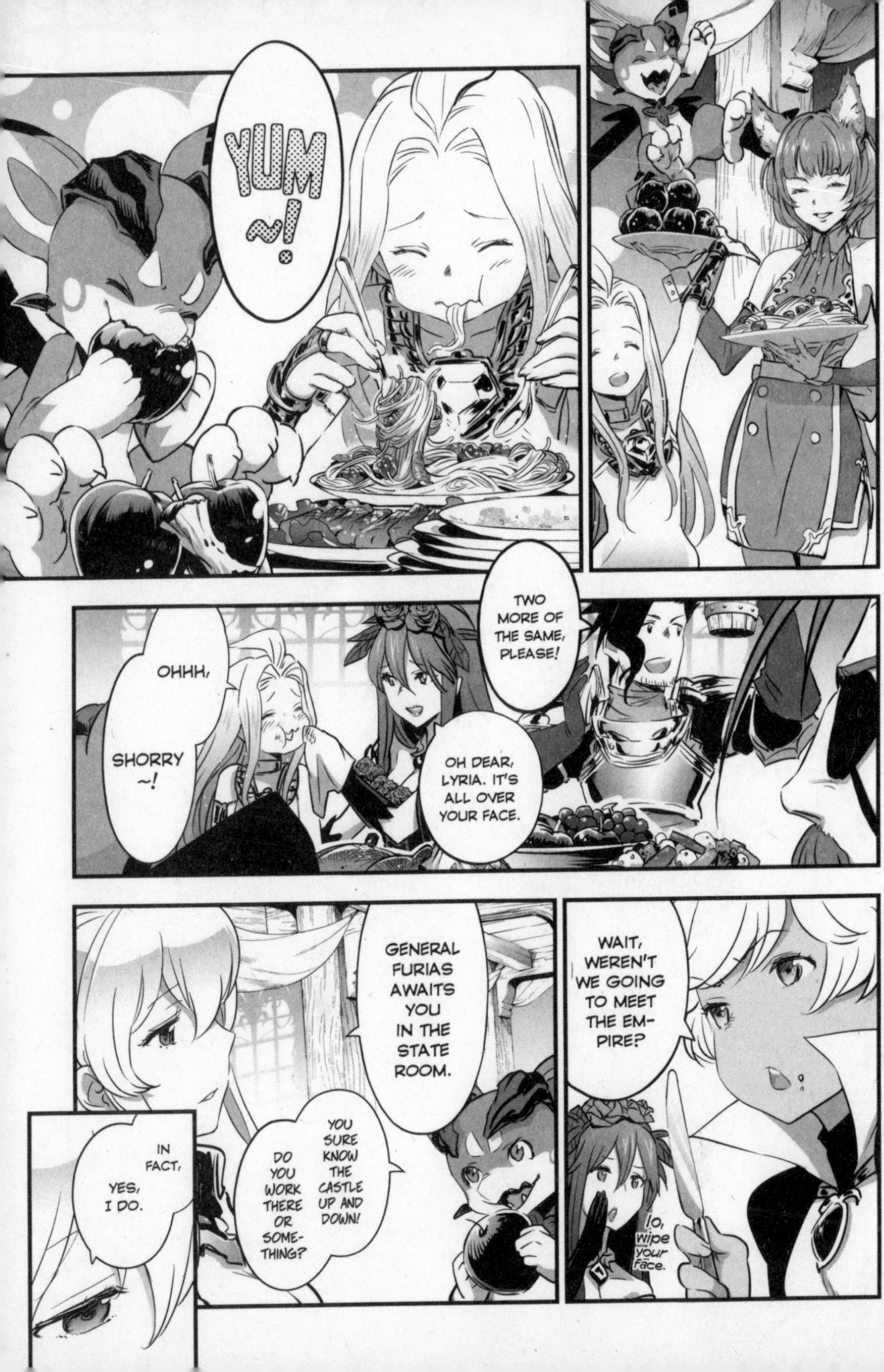
YUM~!
TWO MORE OF THE SAME, PLEASE!
OH DEAR, LYRIA. IT'S ALL OVER YOUR FACE.
OHHH, SHORRY~!
WAIT, WEREN'T WE GOING TO MEET THE EMPIRE?
Io, wipe your face.
GENERAL FURIAS AWAITS YOU IN THE STATE ROOM.
YOU SURE KNOW THE CASTLE UP AND DOWN!
DO YOU WORK THERE OR SOMETHING?
IN FACT, YES, I DO.

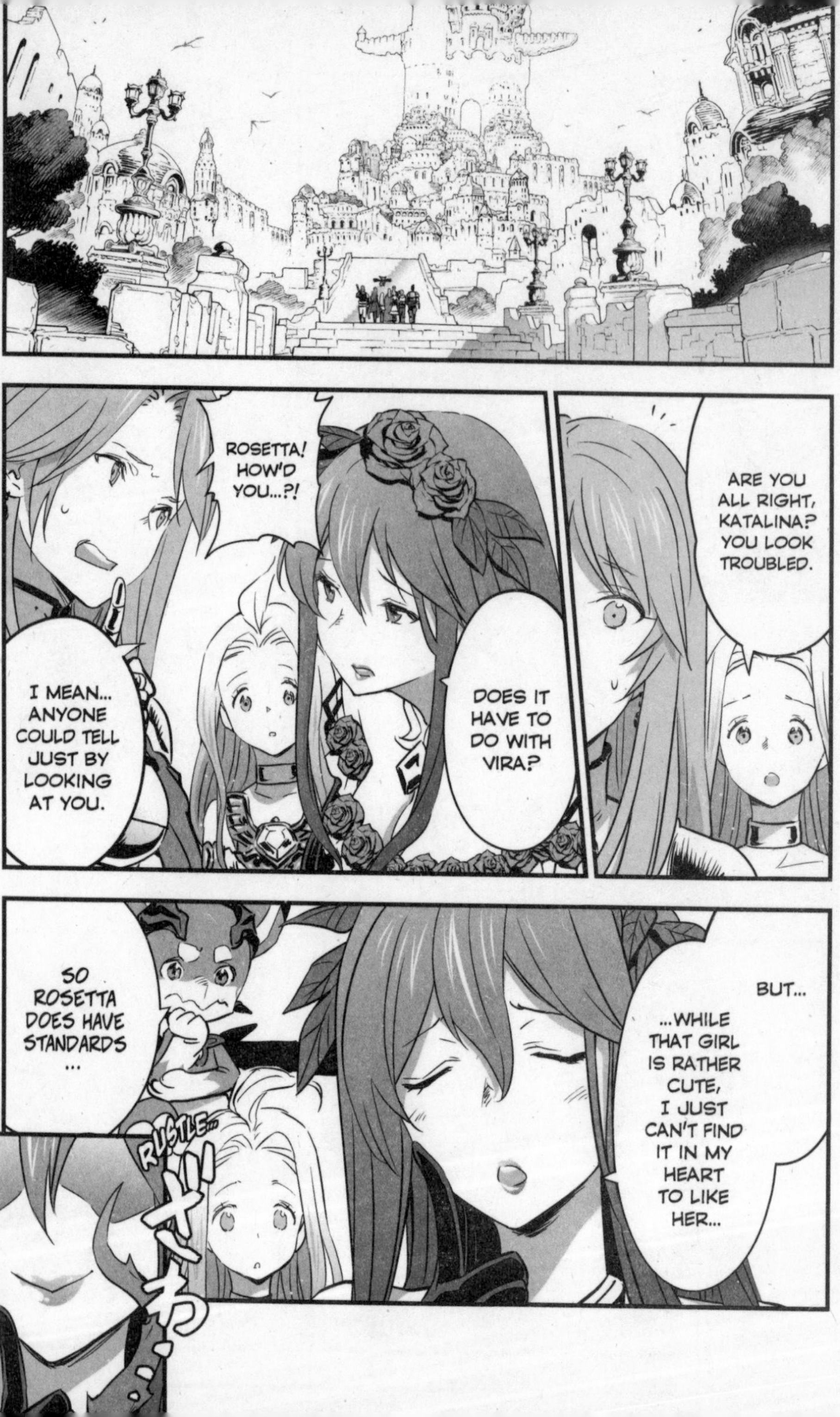
ARE YOU ALL RIGHT, KATALINA? YOU LOOK TROUBLED.
ROSETTA! HOW'D YOU...?!
DOES IT HAVE TO DO WITH VIRA?
I MEAN... ANYONE COULD TELL JUST BY LOOKING AT YOU.
BUT...
...WHILE THAT GIRL IS RATHER CUTE, I JUST CAN'T FIND IT IN MY HEART TO LIKE HER...
SO ROSETTA DOES HAVE STANDARDS ...
RUSTLE...

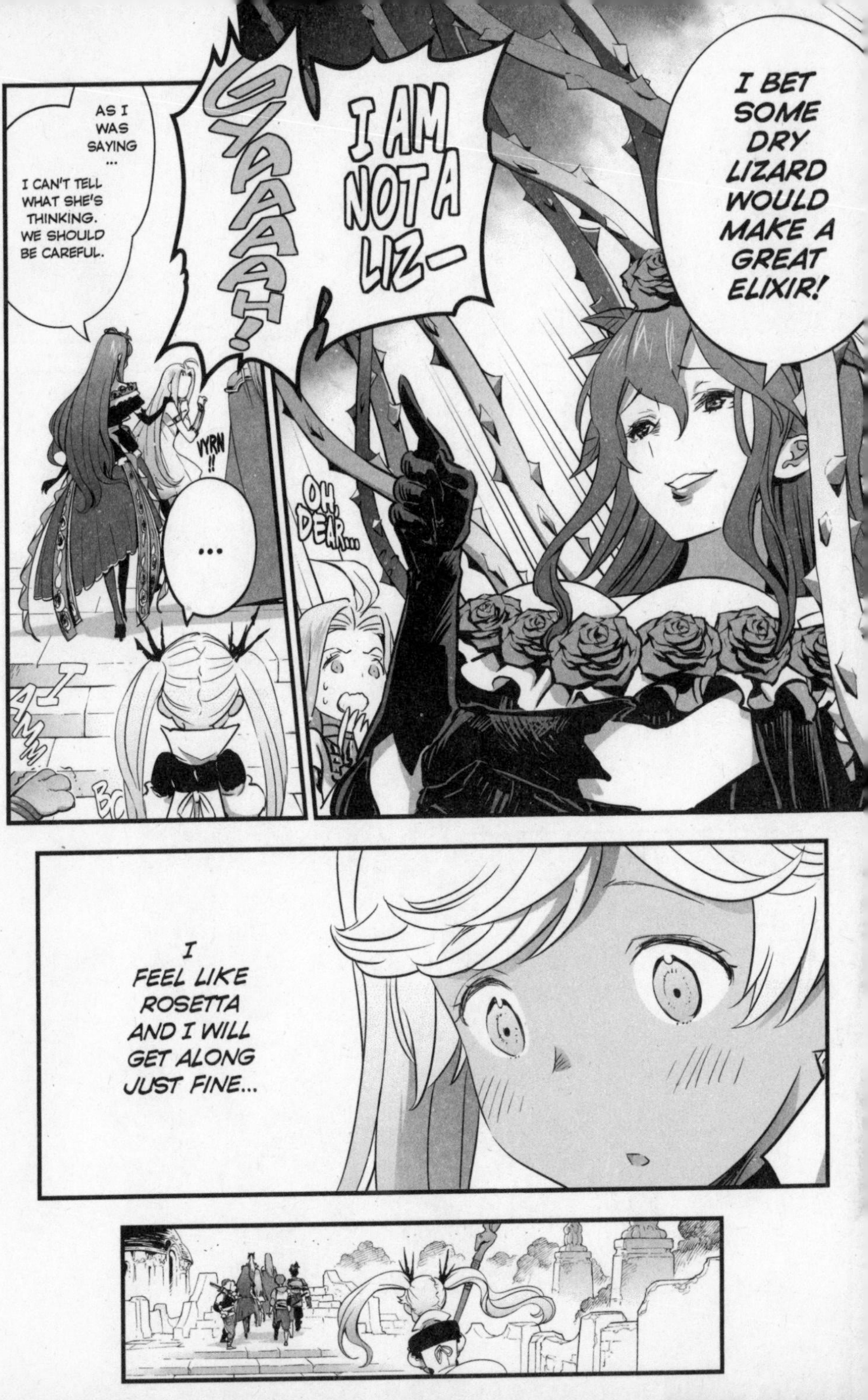
I BET SOME DRY LIZARD WOULD MAKE A GREAT ELIXIR!
I AM NOT A LIZ–
GYAAAAH!
OH, DEAR...
AS I WAS SAYING ... I CAN'T TELL WHAT SHE'S THINKING. WE SHOULD BE CAREFUL.
VYRN !!
...
I AMM
I FEEL LIKE ROSETTA AND I WILL GET ALONG JUST FINE...

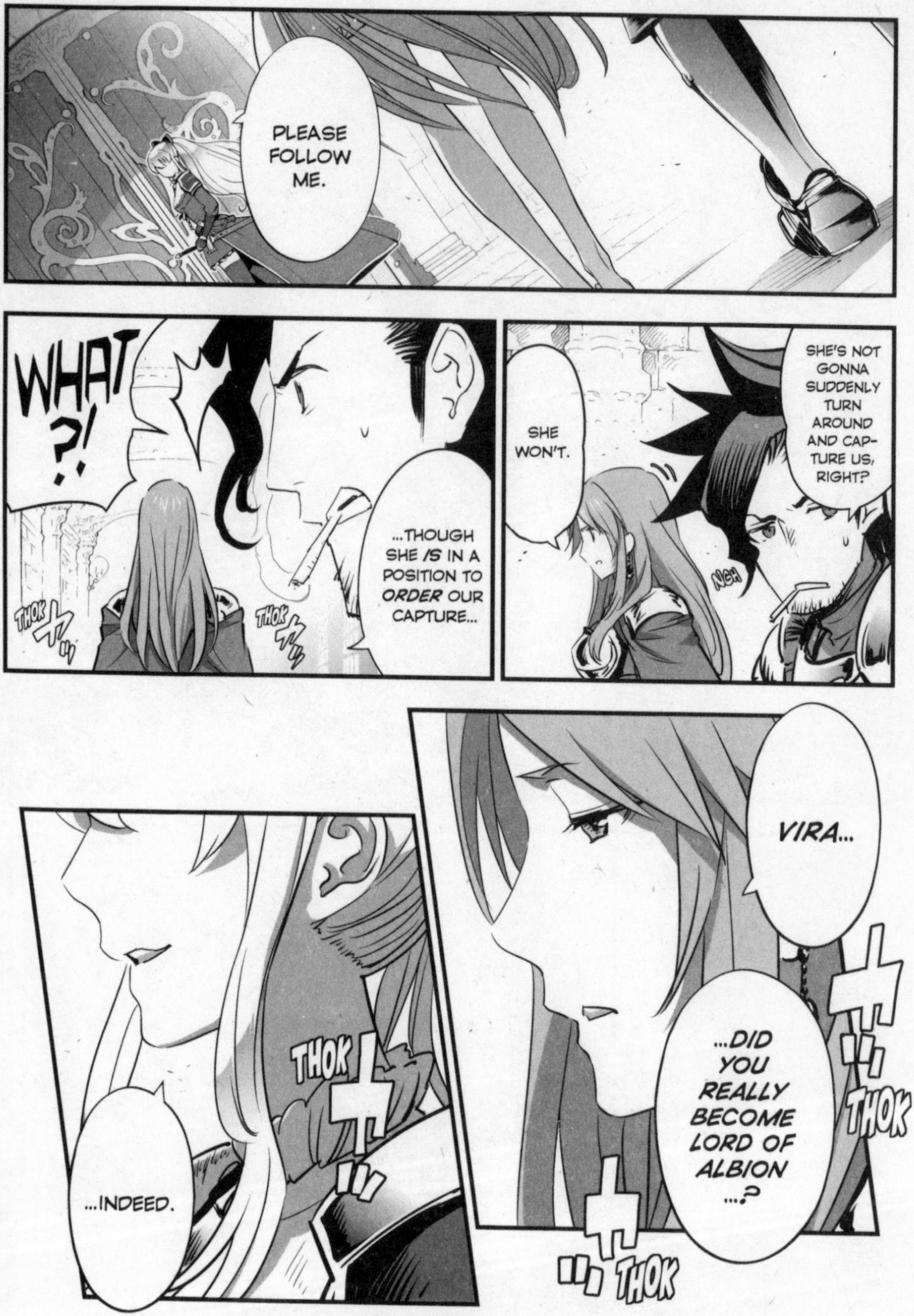
PLEASE FOLLOW ME.
SHE'S NOT GONNA SUDDENLY TURN AROUND AND CAP-TURE US, RIGHT?
NGH
SHE WON'T.
...THOUGH SHE *IS* IN A POSITION TO *ORDER* OUR CAPTURE...
THOK
WHAT?!
THOK
VIRA...
...DID YOU REALLY BECOME LORD OF ALBION ...?
THOK
THOK
THOK
...INDEED.

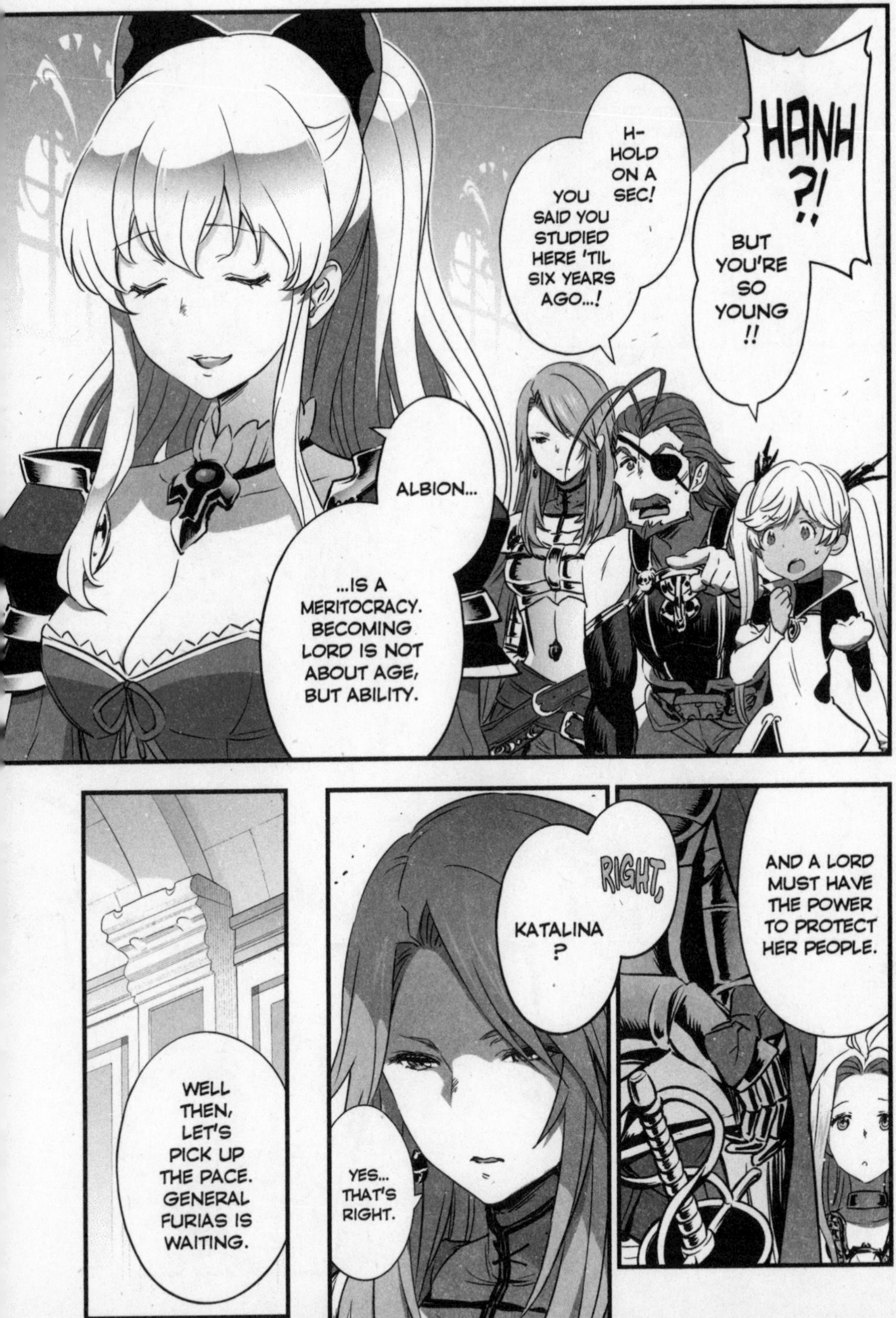
HANH ?!
BUT YOU'RE SO YOUNG !!
H-HOLD ON A SEC!
YOU SAID YOU STUDIED HERE 'TIL SIX YEARS AGO...!
ALBION...
...IS A MERITOCRACY. BECOMING LORD IS NOT ABOUT AGE, BUT ABILITY.
AND A LORD MUST HAVE THE POWER TO PROTECT HER PEOPLE.
RIGHT,
KATALINA ?
YES... THAT'S RIGHT.
WELL THEN, LET'S PICK UP THE PACE. GENERAL FURIAS IS WAITING.

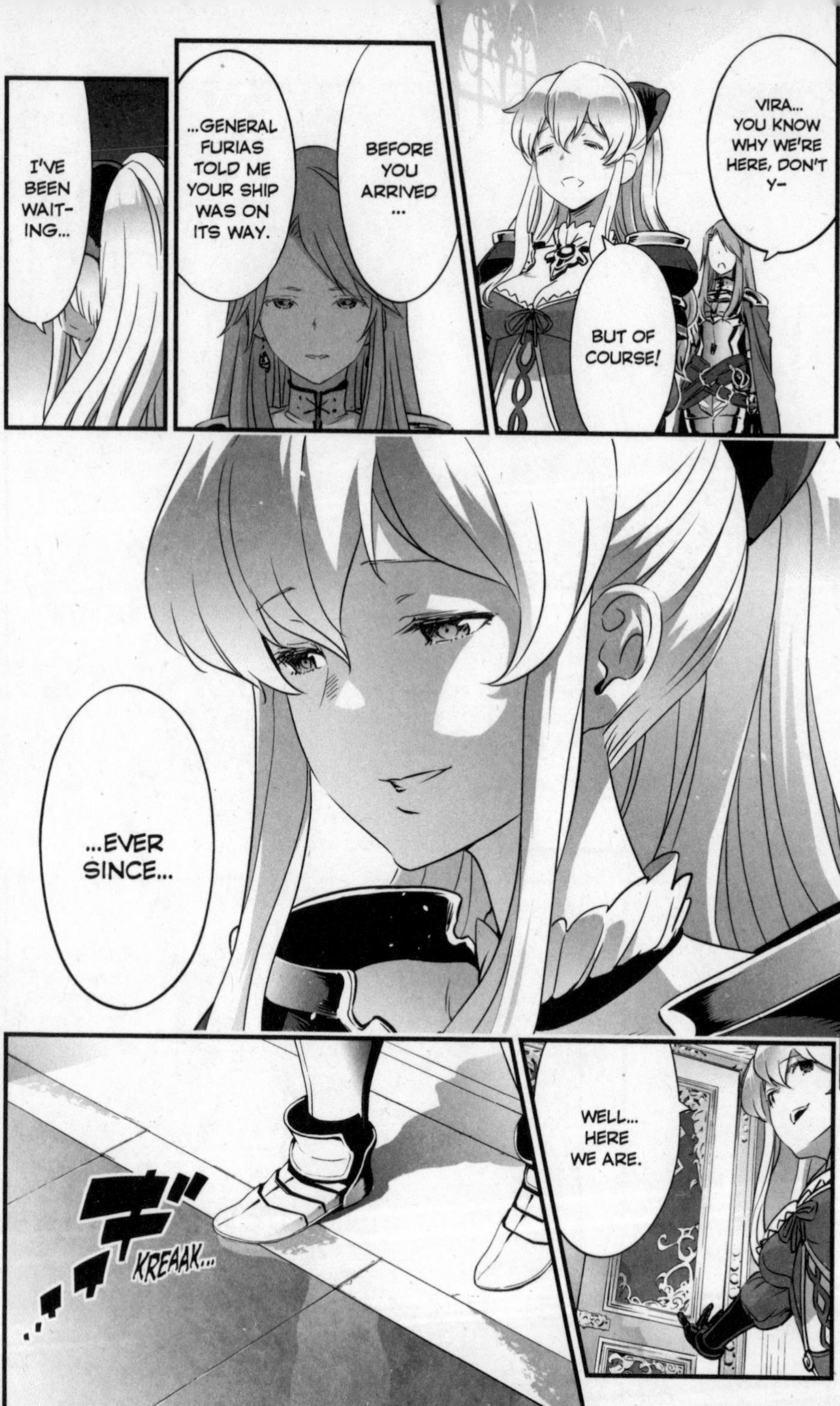
VIRA... YOU KNOW WHY WE'RE HERE, DON'T Y-
BUT OF COURSE!
BEFORE YOU ARRIVED...
...GENERAL FURIAS TOLD ME YOUR SHIP WAS ON ITS WAY.
I'VE BEEN WAIT-ING...
...EVER SINCE...
WELL... HERE WE ARE.
KREAAK...

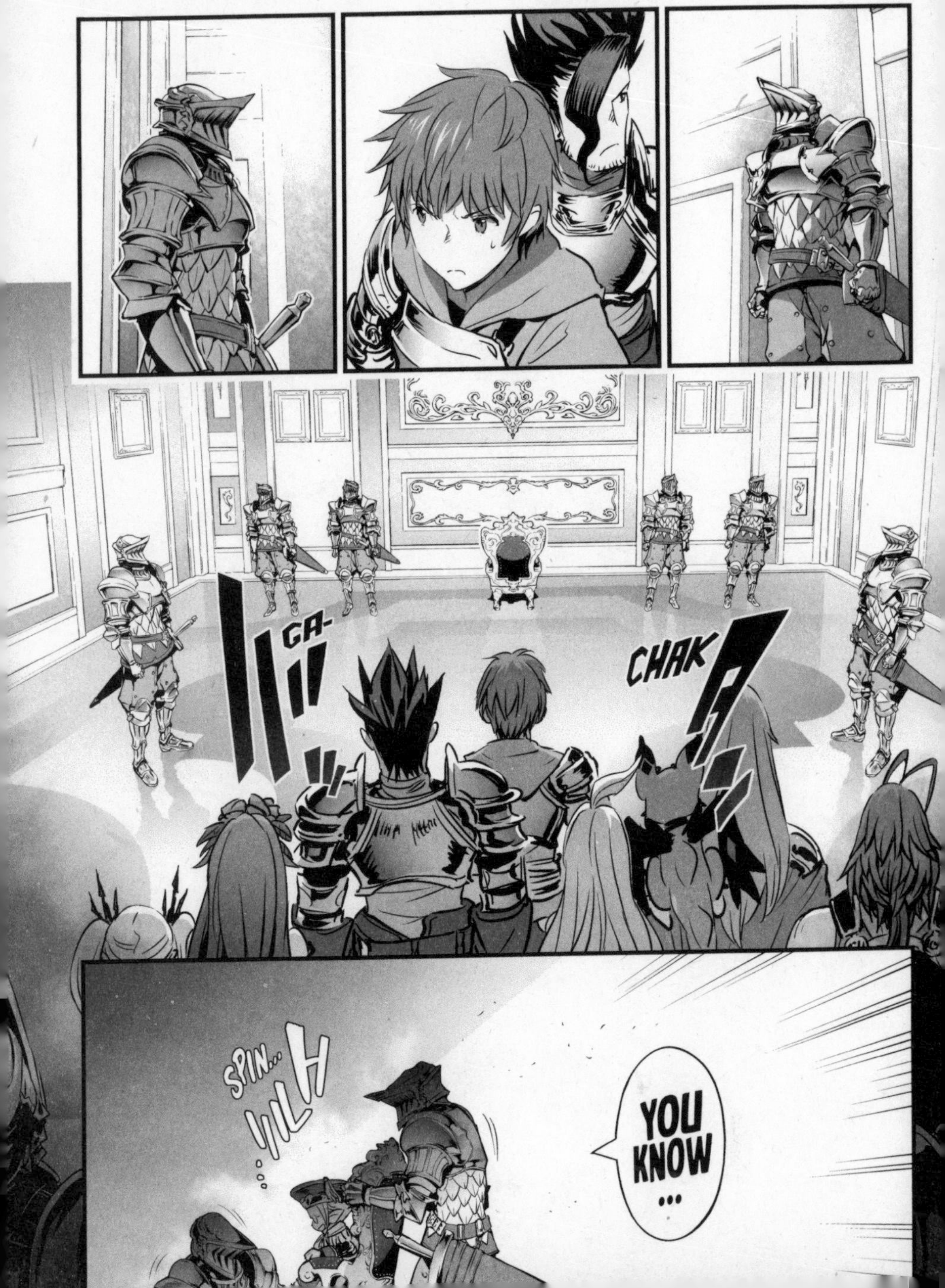
CHAK
GA-
YOU KNOW...
SPIN...

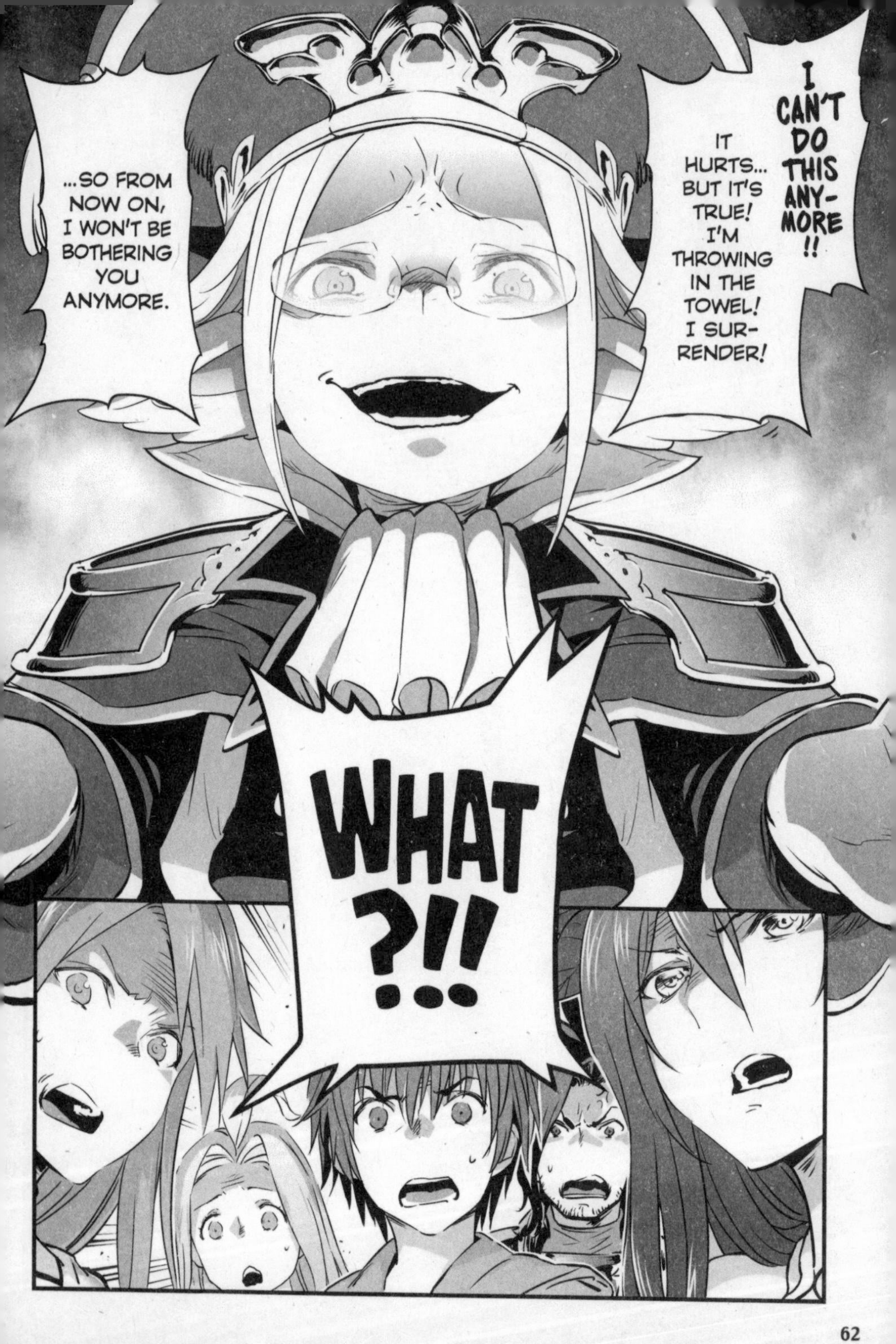

I CAN'T DO THIS ANY-MORE!!
IT HURTS... BUT IT'S TRUE! I'M THROWING IN THE TOWEL! I SUR-RENDER!
...SO FROM NOW ON, I WON'T BE BOTHERING YOU ANYMORE.
WHAT?!!...

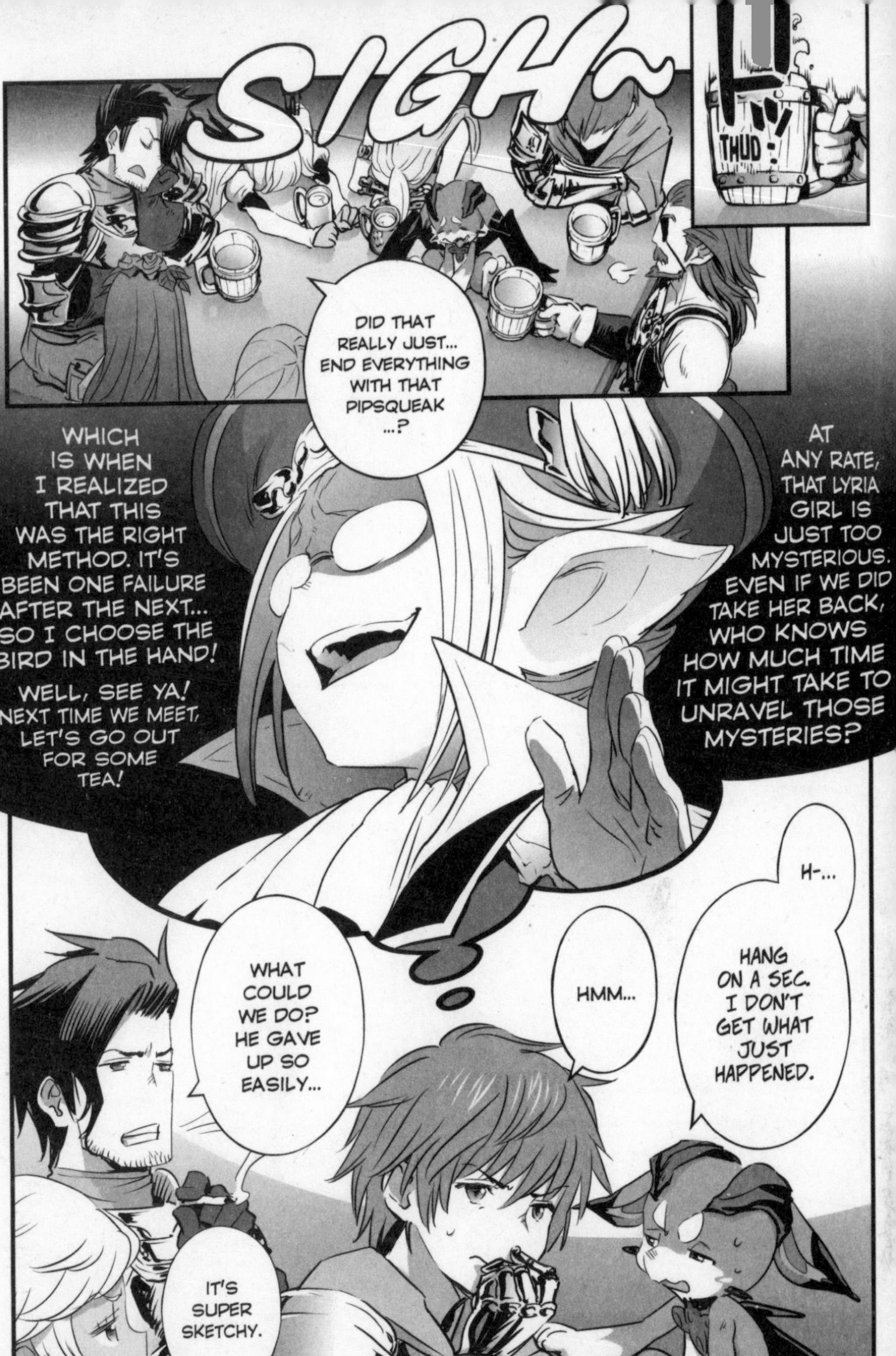

THUD
SIGH~
DID THAT REALLY JUST... END EVERYTHING WITH THAT PIPSQUEAK ...?
AT ANY RATE, THAT LYRIA GIRL IS JUST TOO MYSTERIOUS. EVEN IF WE DID TAKE HER BACK, WHO KNOWS HOW MUCH TIME IT MIGHT TAKE TO UNRAVEL THOSE MYSTERIES?
WHICH IS WHEN I REALIZED THAT THIS WAS THE RIGHT METHOD. IT'S BEEN ONE FAILURE AFTER THE NEXT... SO I CHOOSE THE BIRD IN THE HAND!
WELL, SEE YA! NEXT TIME WE MEET, LET'S GO OUT FOR SOME TEA!
H-...
HANG ON A SEC. I DON'T GET WHAT JUST HAPPENED.
HMM...
WHAT COULD WE DO? HE GAVE UP SO EASILY...
IT'S SUPER SKETCHY.

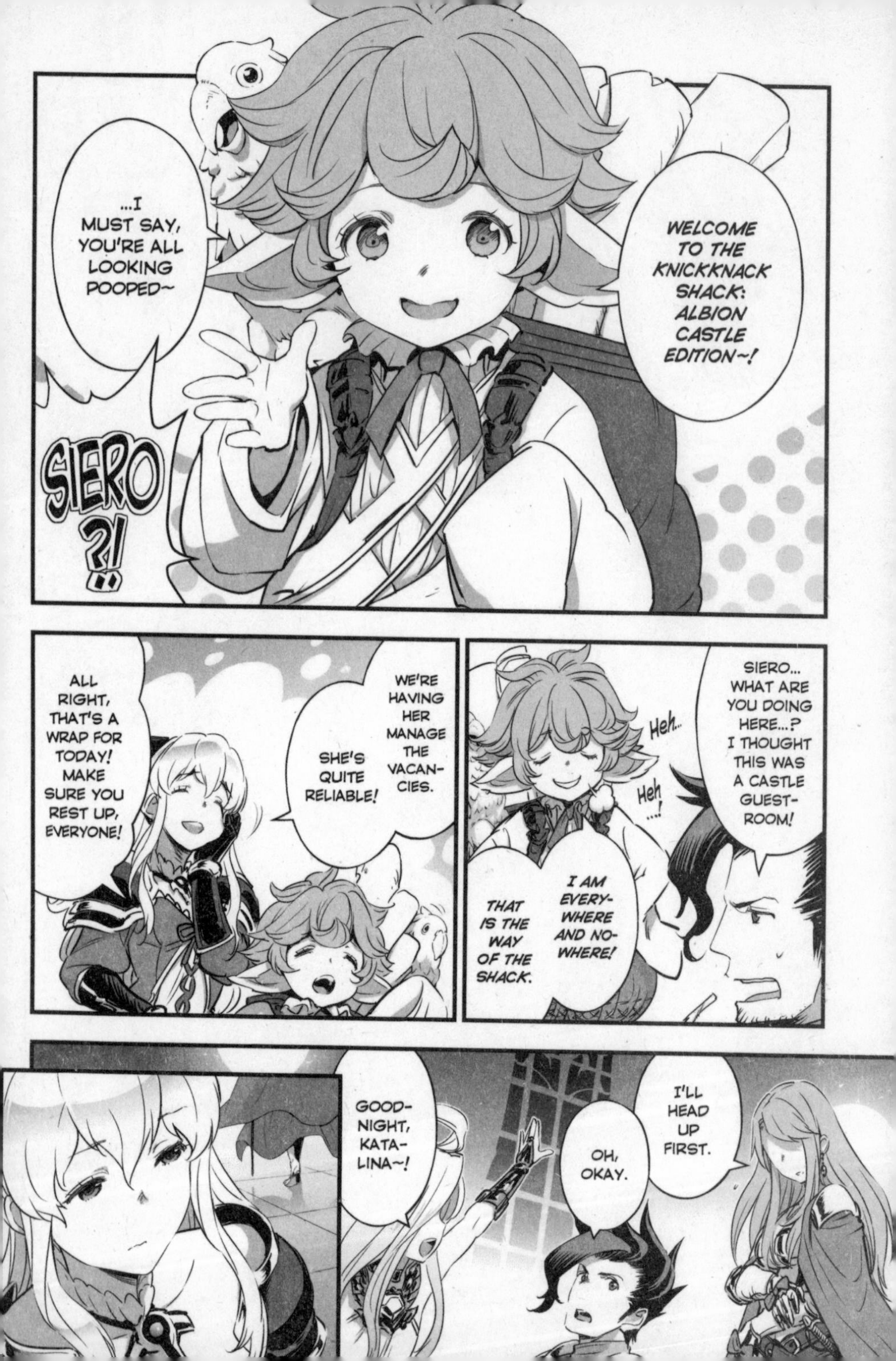
WELCOME TO THE KNICKKNACK SHACK: ALBION CASTLE EDITION~!
...I MUST SAY, YOU'RE ALL LOOKING POOPED~
SIERO?!
SIERO... WHAT ARE YOU DOING HERE...? I THOUGHT THIS WAS A CASTLE GUEST-ROOM!
Heh...
Heh...!
I AM EVERY-WHERE AND NO-WHERE!
THAT IS THE WAY OF THE SHACK.
WE'RE HAVING HER MANAGE THE VACAN-CIES.
SHE'S QUITE RELIABLE!
ALL RIGHT, THAT'S A WRAP FOR TODAY! MAKE SURE YOU REST UP, EVERYONE!
I'LL HEAD UP FIRST.
OH, OKAY.
GOOD-NIGHT, KATA-LINA~!

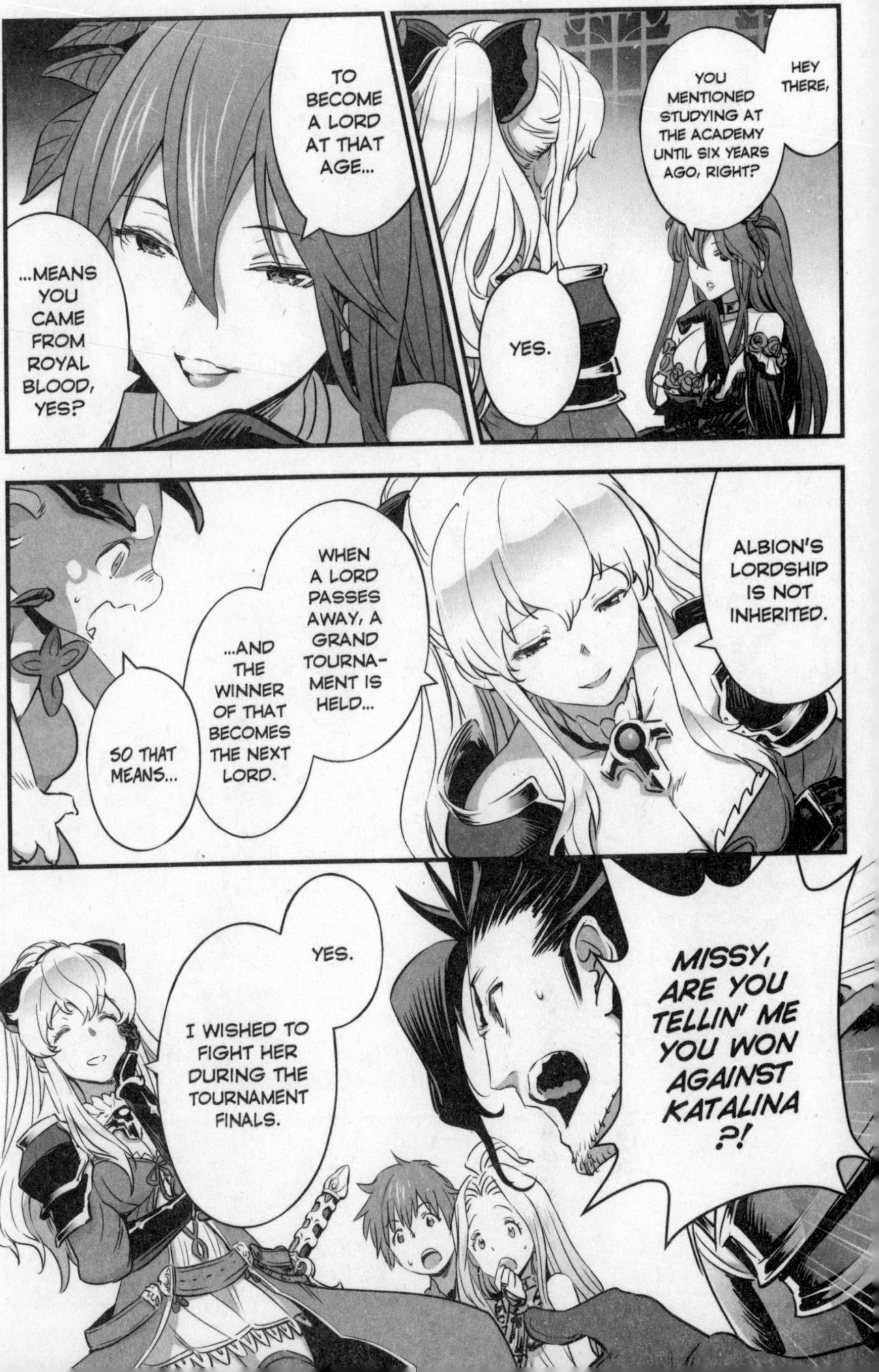
HEY THERE,
YOU MENTIONED STUDYING AT THE ACADEMY UNTIL SIX YEARS AGO, RIGHT?
YES.
TO BECOME A LORD AT THAT AGE...
...MEANS YOU CAME FROM ROYAL BLOOD, YES?
ALBION'S LORDSHIP IS NOT INHERITED.
WHEN A LORD PASSES AWAY, A GRAND TOURNA-MENT IS HELD...
...AND THE WINNER OF THAT BECOMES THE NEXT LORD.
SO THAT MEANS...
MISSY, ARE YOU TELLIN' ME YOU WON AGAINST KATALINA?!
YES.
I WISHED TO FIGHT HER DURING THE TOURNAMENT FINALS.

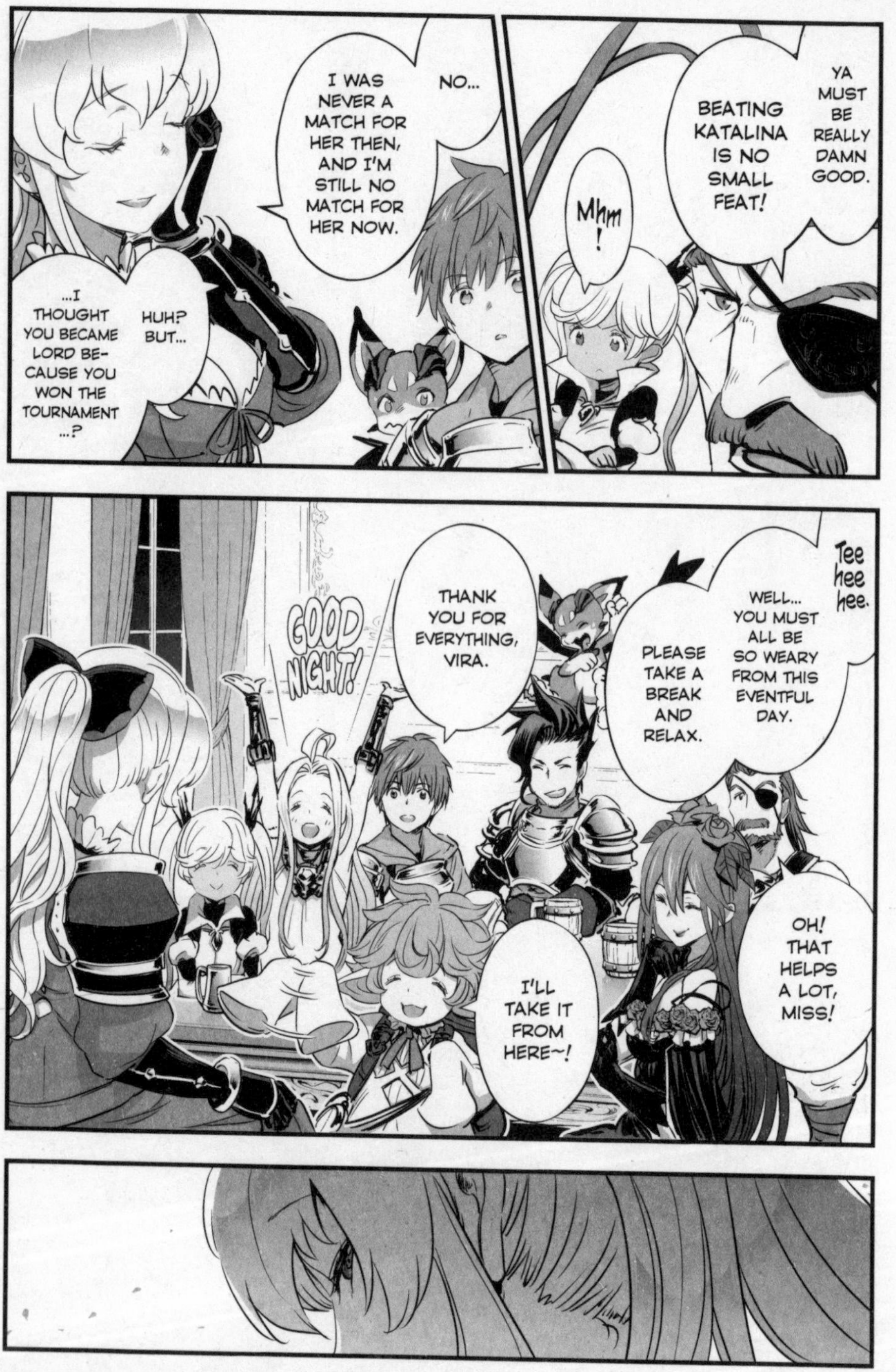
YA MUST BE REALLY DAMN GOOD.
BEATING KATALINA IS NO SMALL FEAT!
Mhm!
NO...
I WAS NEVER A MATCH FOR HER THEN, AND I'M STILL NO MATCH FOR HER NOW.
HUH? BUT...
...I THOUGHT YOU BECAME LORD BE-CAUSE YOU WON THE TOURNAMENT ...?
Tee hee hee.
WELL... YOU MUST ALL BE SO WEARY FROM THIS EVENTFUL DAY.
PLEASE TAKE A BREAK AND RELAX.
THANK YOU FOR EVERYTHING, VIRA.
GOOD NIGHT!
OH! THAT HELPS A LOT, MISS!
I'LL TAKE IT FROM HERE~!

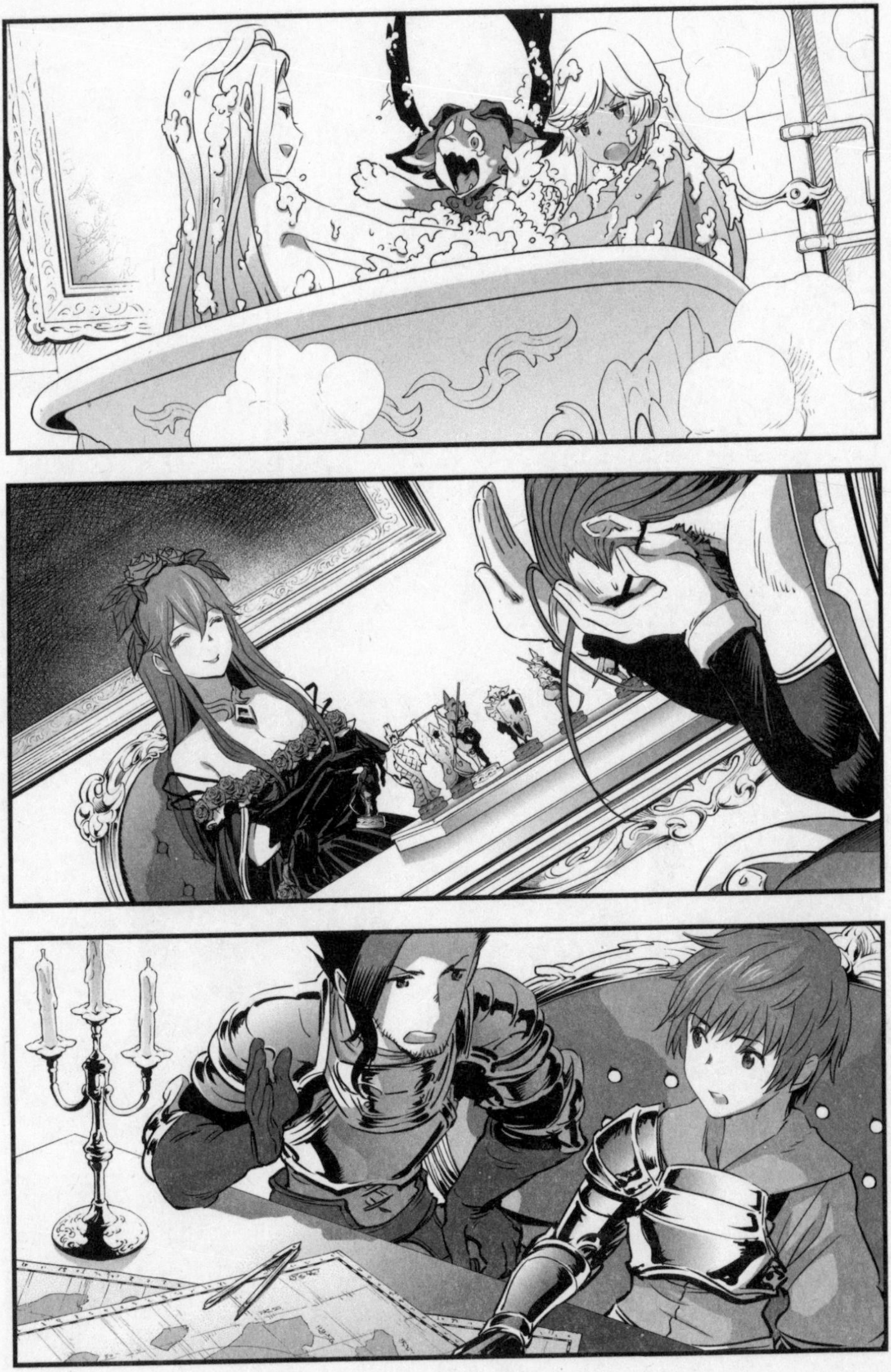

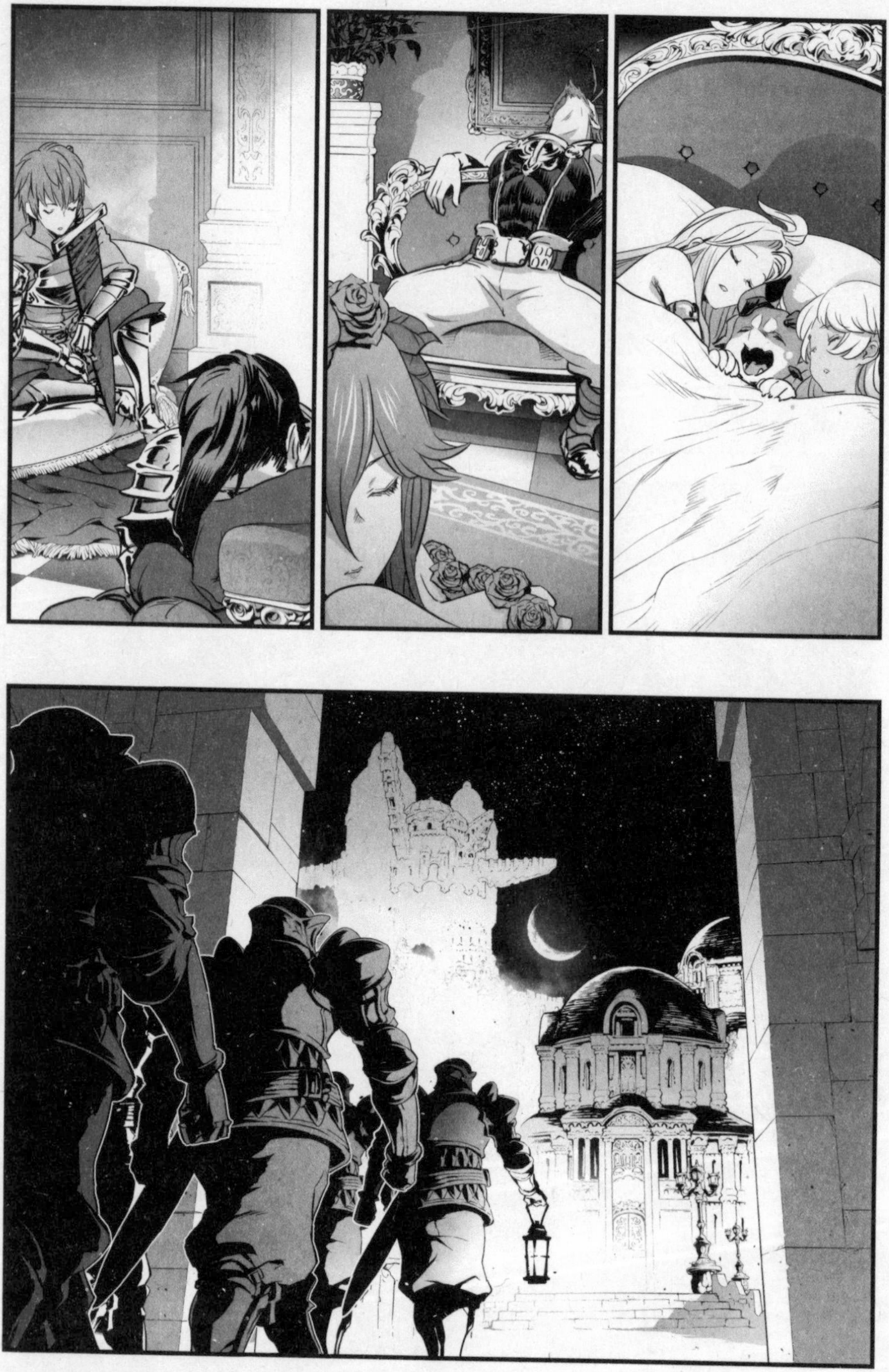

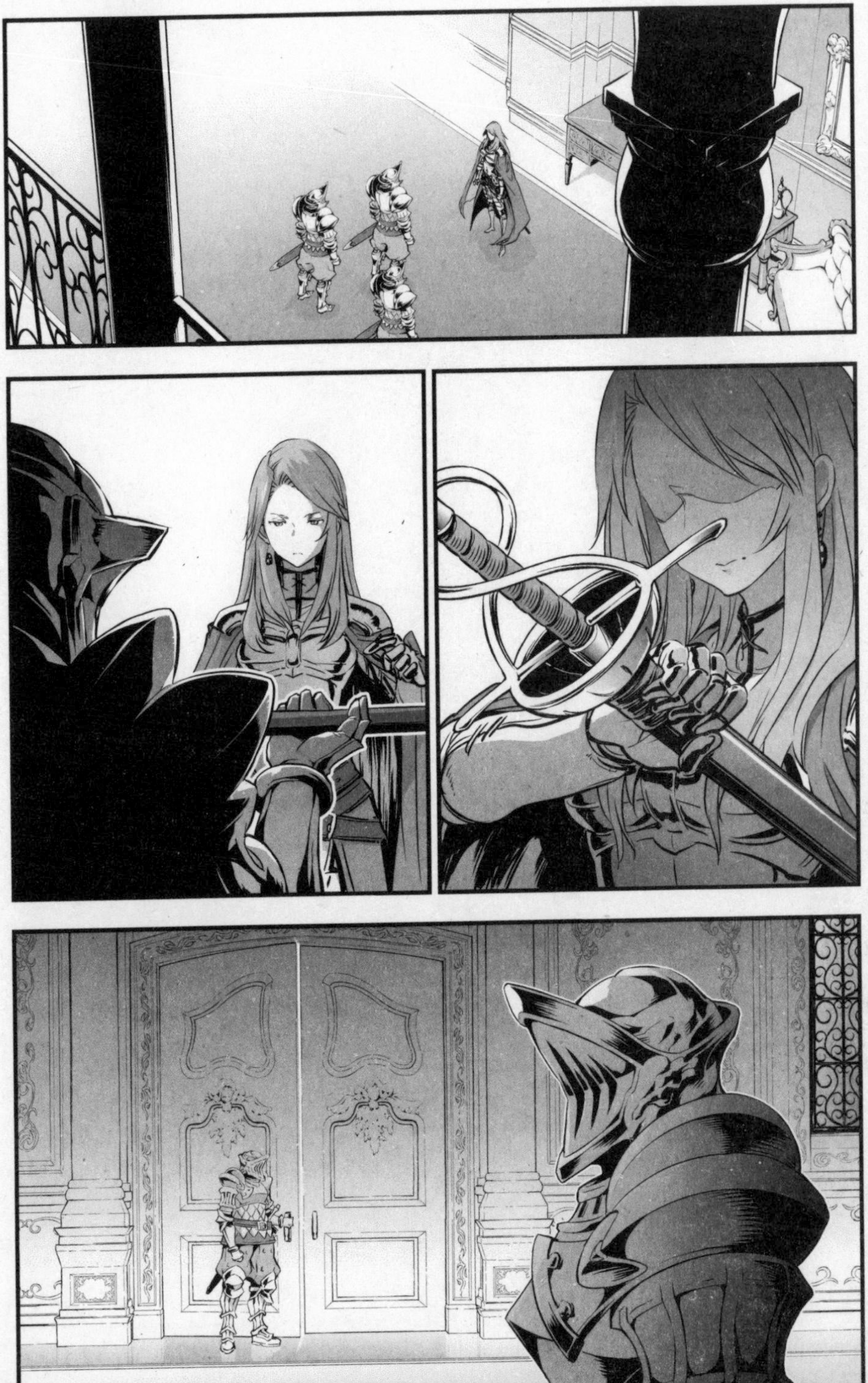

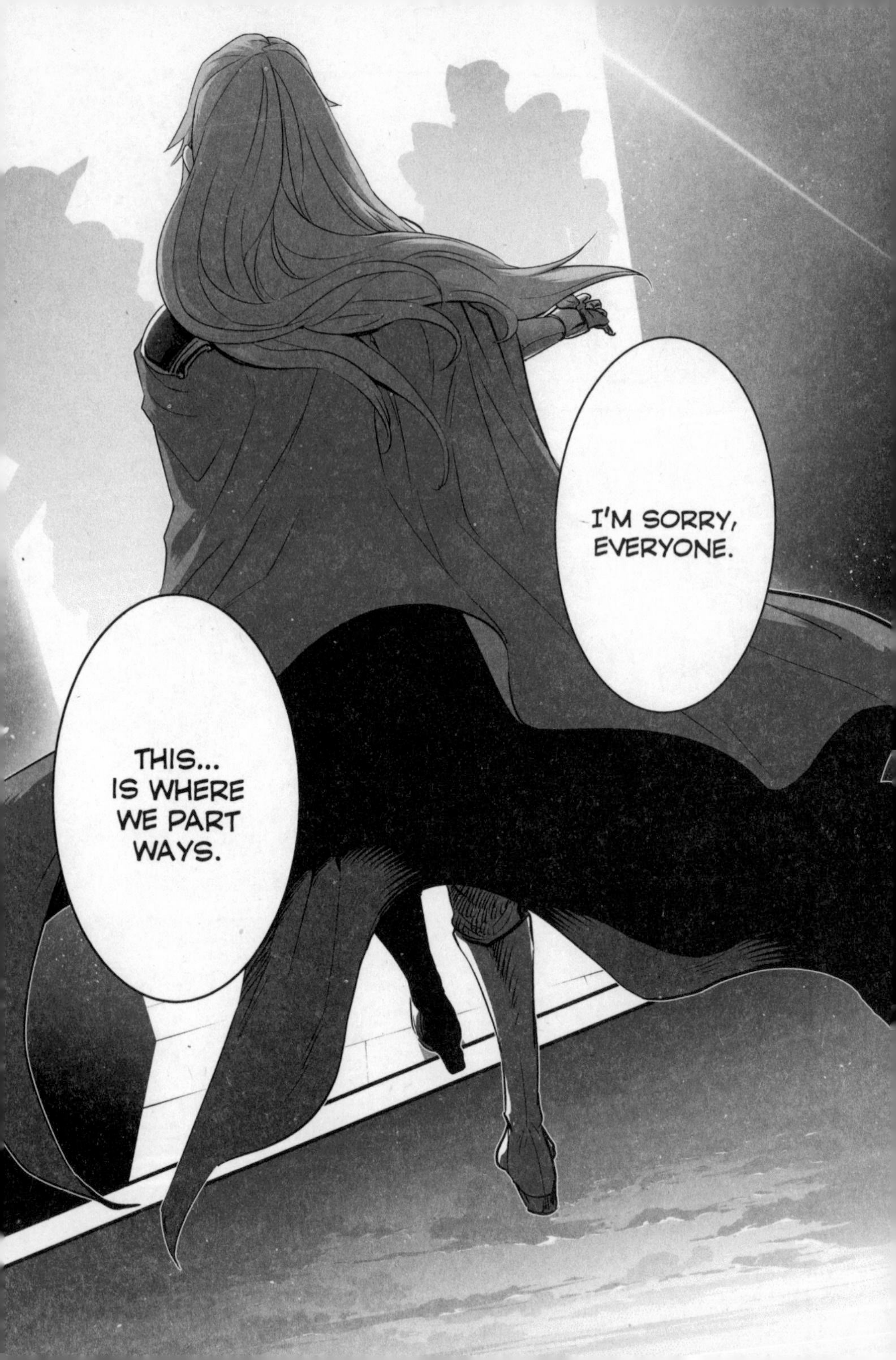
I'M SORRY, EVERYONE.
THIS... IS WHERE WE PART WAYS.

GRANBLUE FANTASY
グランブルーファンタジー

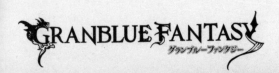

GRANBLUE FANTASY
グランブルーファンタジー

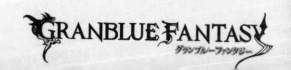

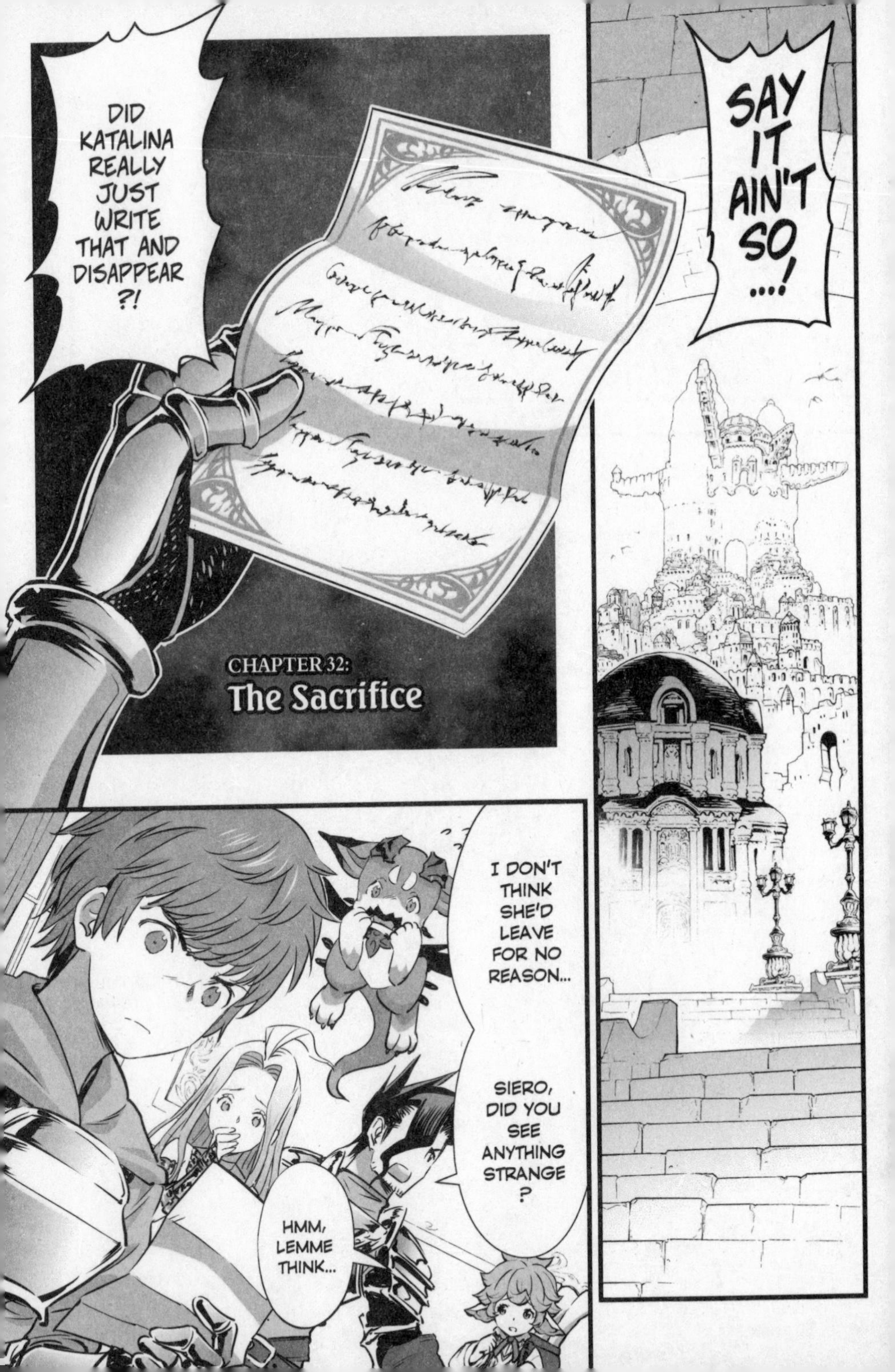
SAY IT AIN'T SO....!
DID KATALINA REALLY JUST WRITE THAT AND DISAPPEAR ?!
CHAPTER 32:
The Sacrifice
I DON'T THINK SHE'D LEAVE FOR NO REASON...
SIERO, DID YOU SEE ANYTHING STRANGE ?
HMM, LEMME THINK...

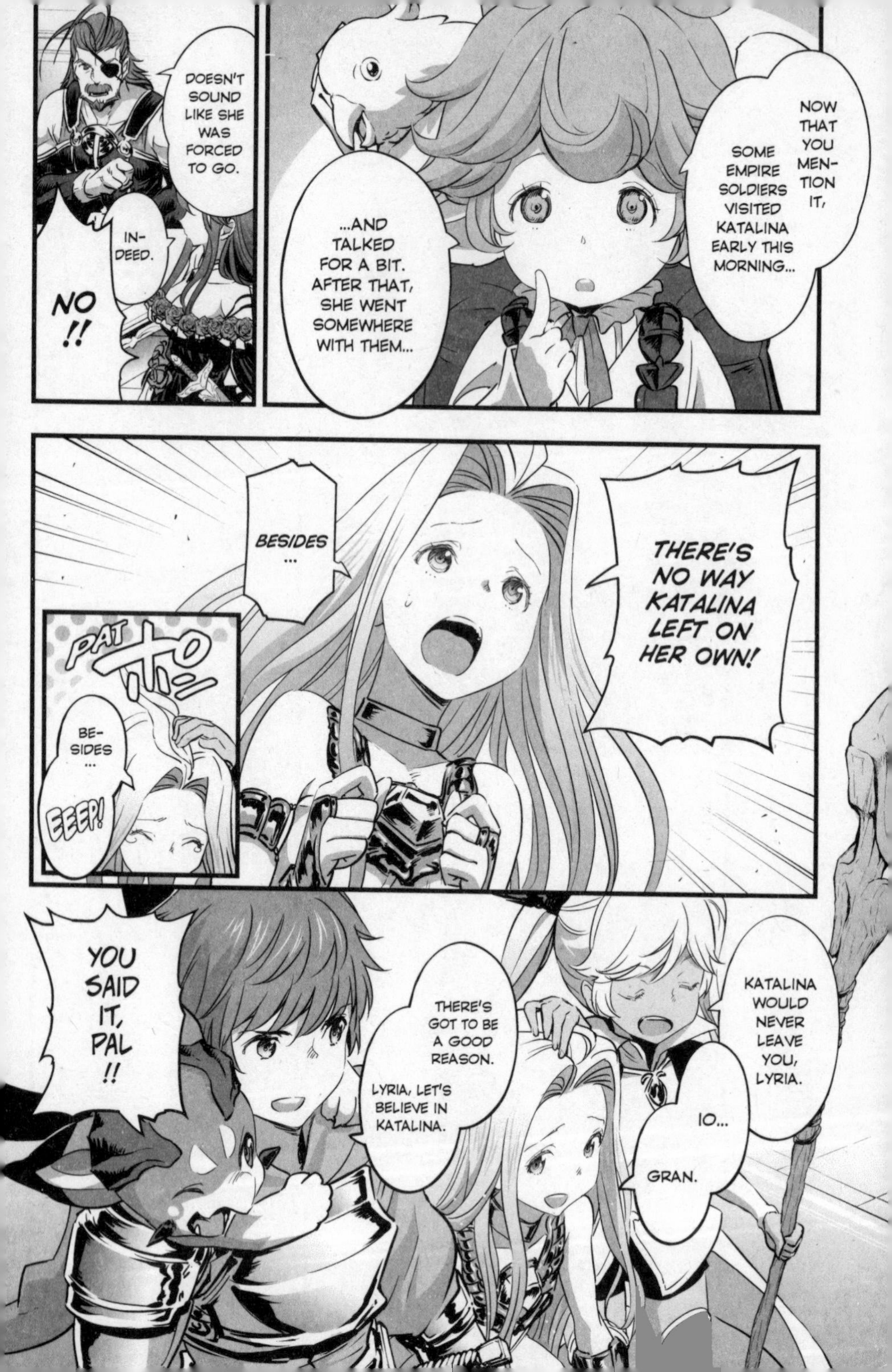
NOW THAT YOU MENTION IT,
SOME EMPIRE SOLDIERS VISITED KATALINA EARLY THIS MORNING...
...AND TALKED FOR A BIT. AFTER THAT, SHE WENT SOMEWHERE WITH THEM...
DOESN'T SOUND LIKE SHE WAS FORCED TO GO.
IN-DEED.
NO !!
THERE'S NO WAY KATALINA LEFT ON HER OWN!
BESIDES ...
PAT
BE-SIDES ...
EEEP!
KATALINA WOULD NEVER LEAVE YOU, LYRIA.
IO...
THERE'S GOT TO BE A GOOD REASON.
LYRIA, LET'S BELIEVE IN KATALINA.
GRAN.
YOU SAID IT, PAL !!

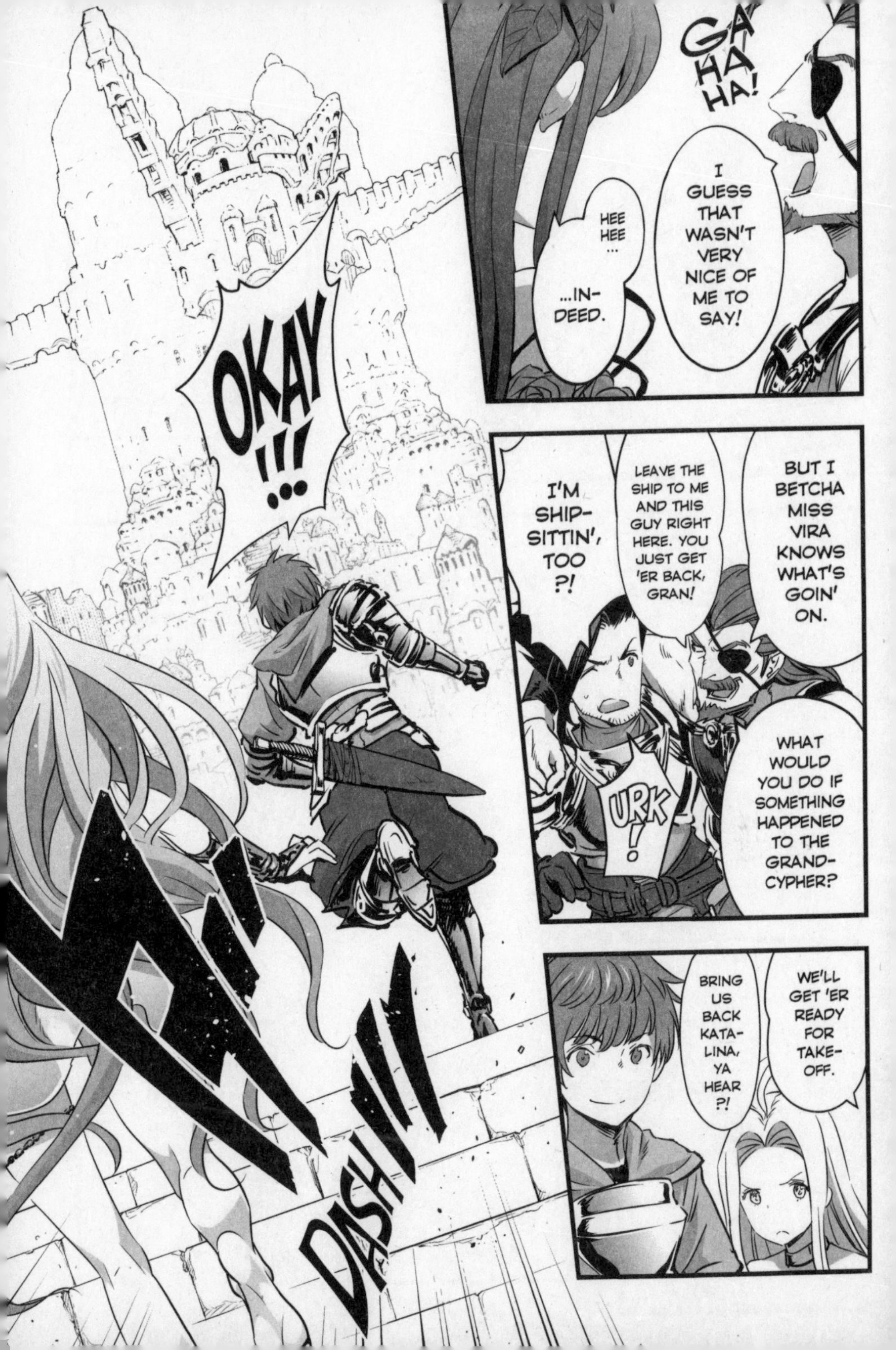
GA HA HA!
I GUESS THAT WASN'T VERY NICE OF ME TO SAY!
HEE HEE ... ...IN-DEED.
BUT I BETCHA MISS VIRA KNOWS WHAT'S GOIN' ON.
LEAVE THE SHIP TO ME AND THIS GUY RIGHT HERE. YOU JUST GET 'ER BACK, GRAN!
I'M SHIP-SITTIN', TOO?!
WHAT WOULD YOU DO IF SOMETHING HAPPENED TO THE GRAND-CYPHER?
URK!
WE'LL GET 'ER READY FOR TAKE-OFF.
BRING US BACK KATA-LINA, YA HEAR?!
OKAY!!!...
DASH!!!

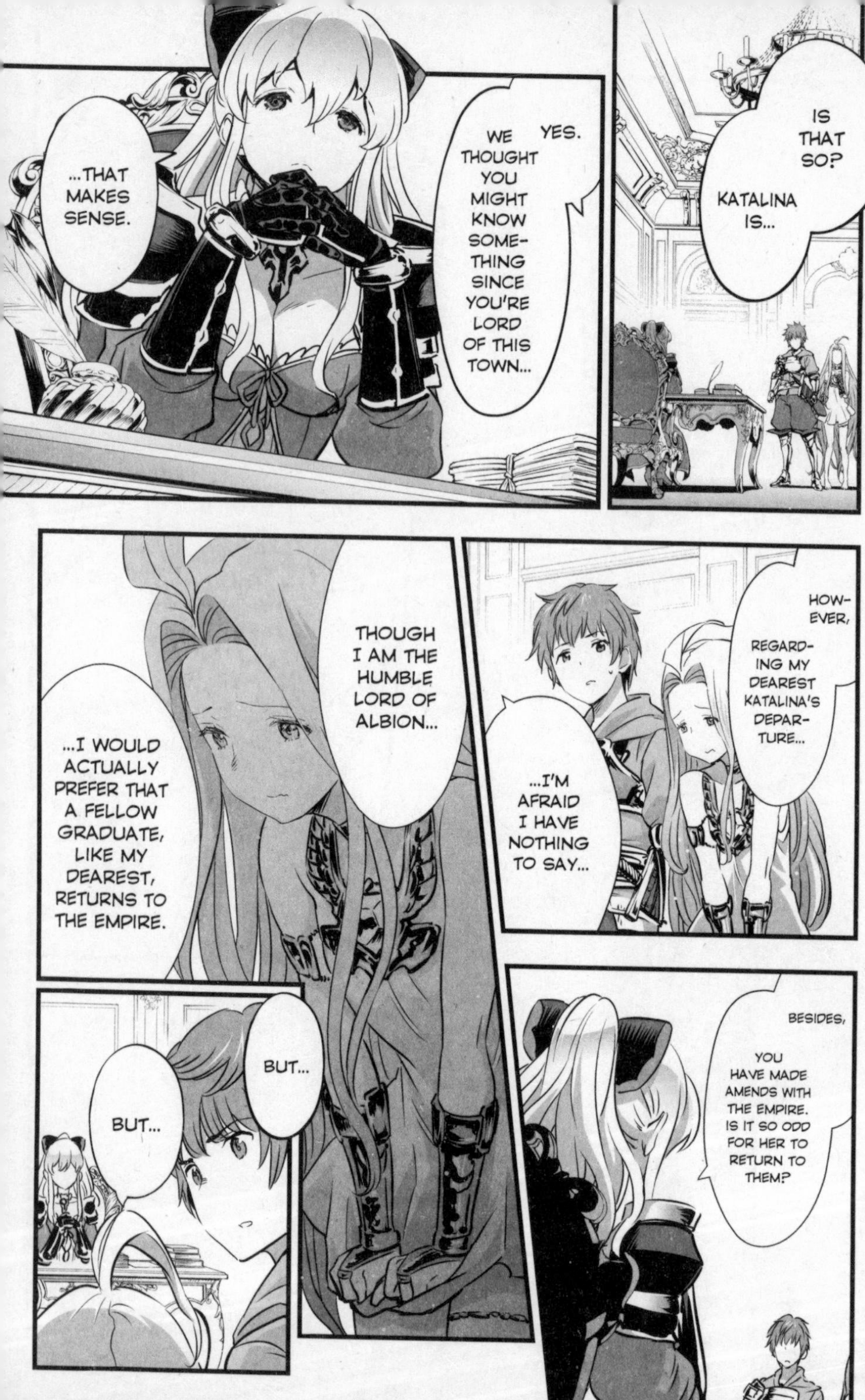
IS THAT SO?
KATALINA IS...
YES.
WE THOUGHT YOU MIGHT KNOW SOMETHING SINCE YOU'RE LORD OF THIS TOWN...
...THAT MAKES SENSE.
HOWEVER, REGARDING MY DEAREST KATALINA'S DEPARTURE...
...I'M AFRAID I HAVE NOTHING TO SAY...
THOUGH I AM THE HUMBLE LORD OF ALBION...
...I WOULD ACTUALLY PREFER THAT A FELLOW GRADUATE, LIKE MY DEAREST, RETURNS TO THE EMPIRE.
BESIDES,
YOU HAVE MADE AMENDS WITH THE EMPIRE. IS IT SO ODD FOR HER TO RETURN TO THEM?
BUT...
BUT...

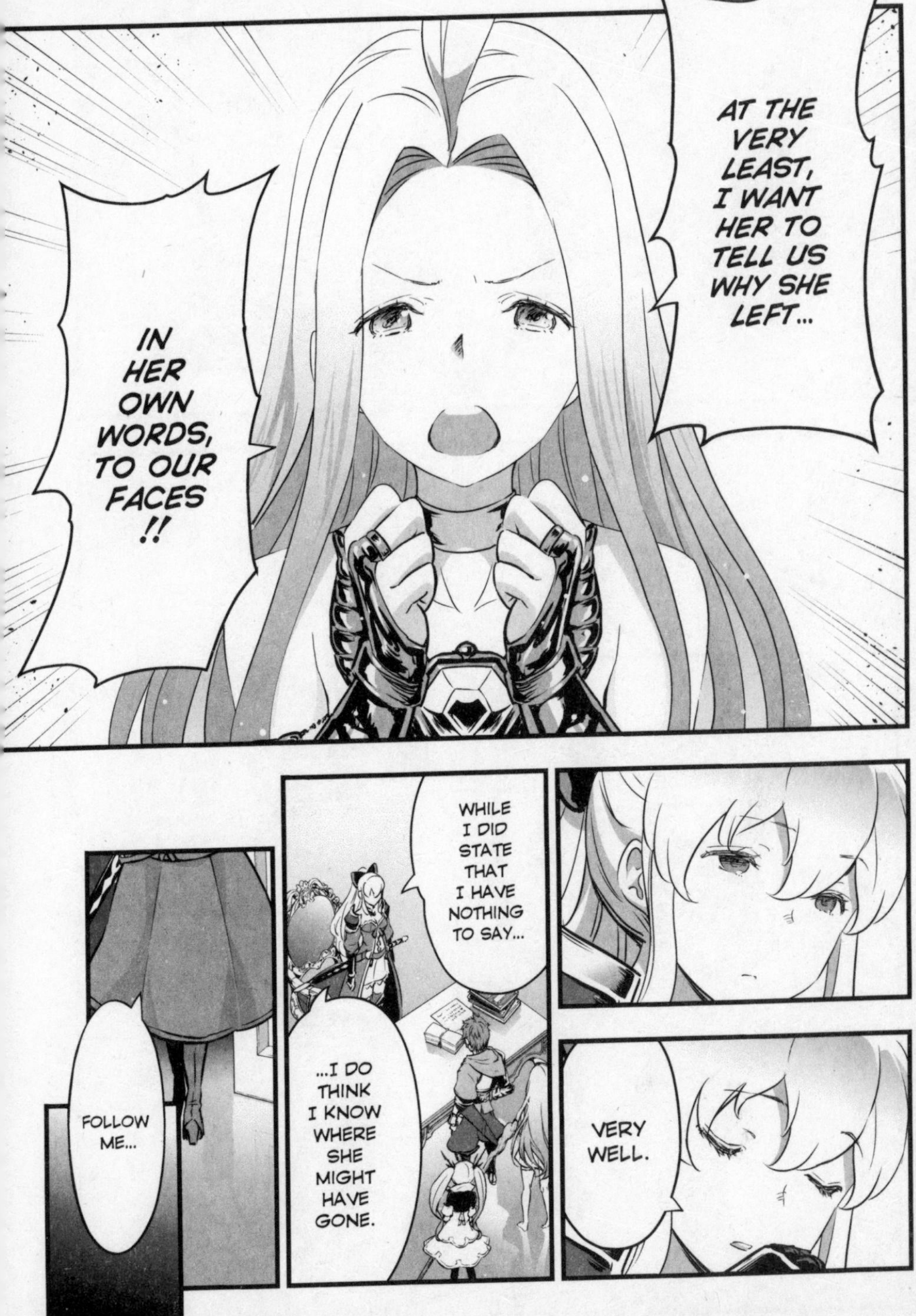
AT THE VERY LEAST, I WANT HER TO TELL US WHY SHE LEFT...
IN HER OWN WORDS, TO OUR FACES!!
VERY WELL.
WHILE I DID STATE THAT I HAVE NOTHING TO SAY...
...I DO THINK I KNOW WHERE SHE MIGHT HAVE GONE.
FOLLOW ME...

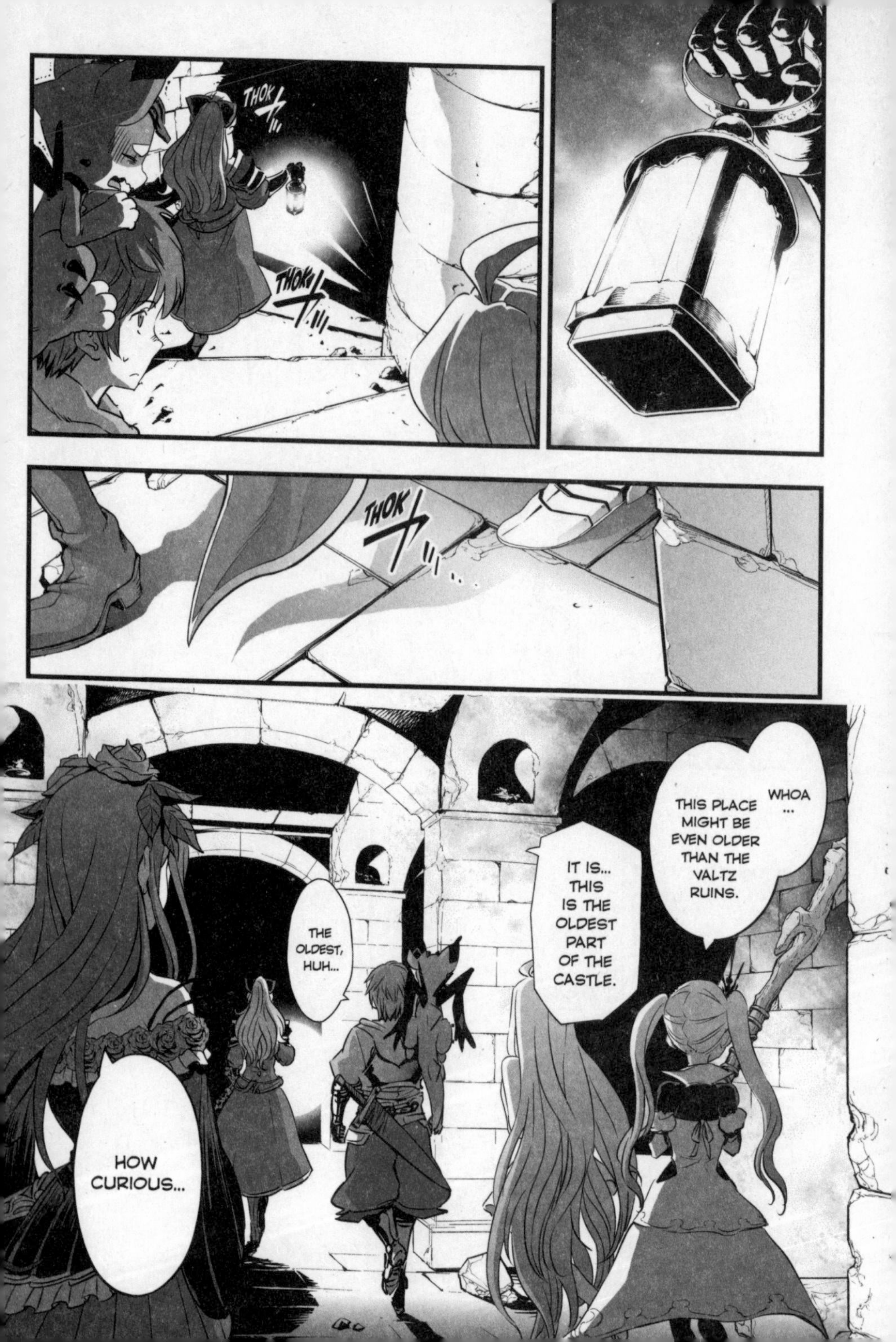
THOK
THOK
THOK
WHOA...
THIS PLACE MIGHT BE EVEN OLDER THAN THE VALTZ RUINS.
IT IS... THIS IS THE OLDEST PART OF THE CASTLE.
THE OLDEST, HUH...
HOW CURIOUS...

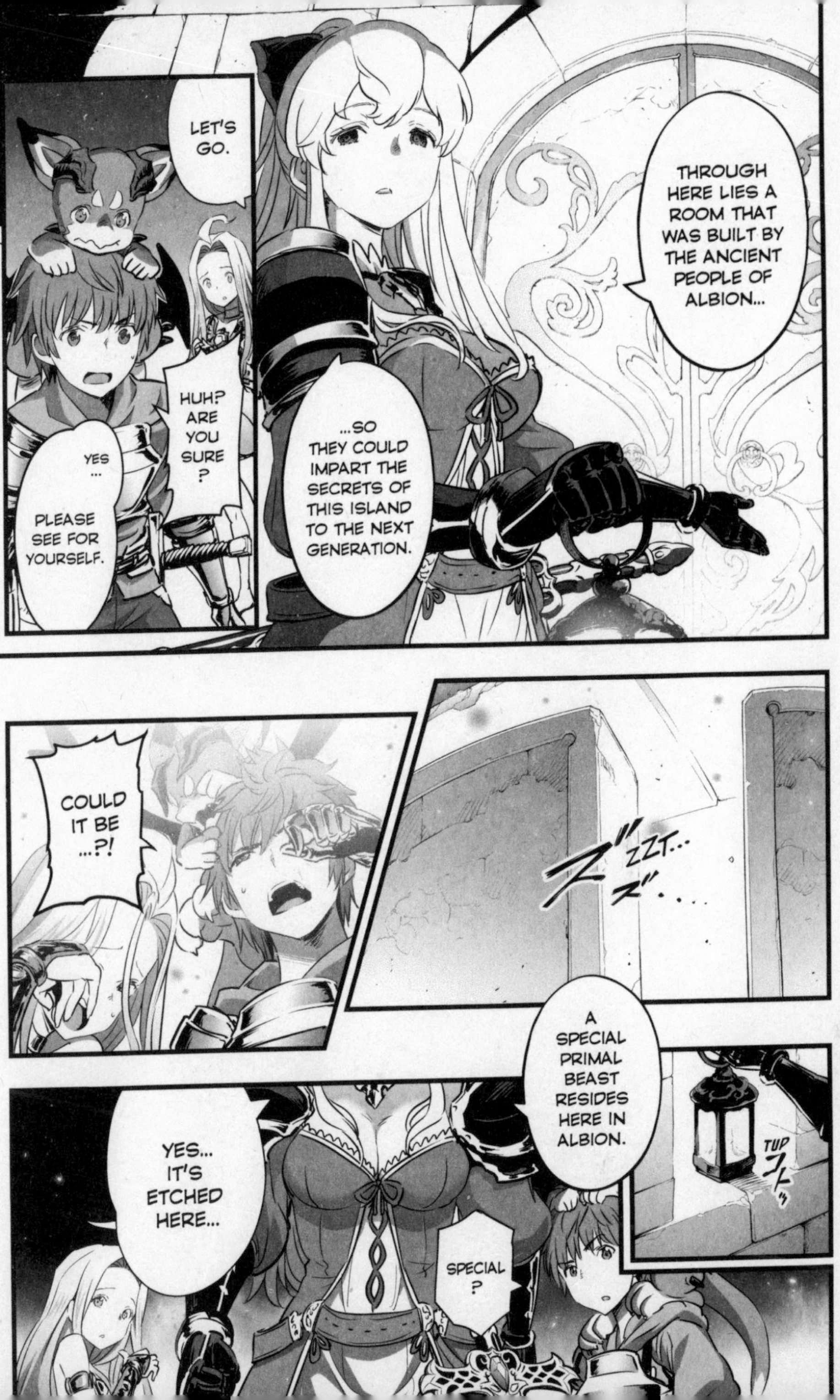
THROUGH HERE LIES A ROOM THAT WAS BUILT BY THE ANCIENT PEOPLE OF ALBION...
...SO THEY COULD IMPART THE SECRETS OF THIS ISLAND TO THE NEXT GENERATION.
LET'S GO.
HUH? ARE YOU SURE?
YES...
PLEASE SEE FOR YOURSELF.
ZZZT...
COULD IT BE ...?!
TUP
A SPECIAL PRIMAL BEAST RESIDES HERE IN ALBION.
SPECIAL?
YES... IT'S ETCHED HERE...

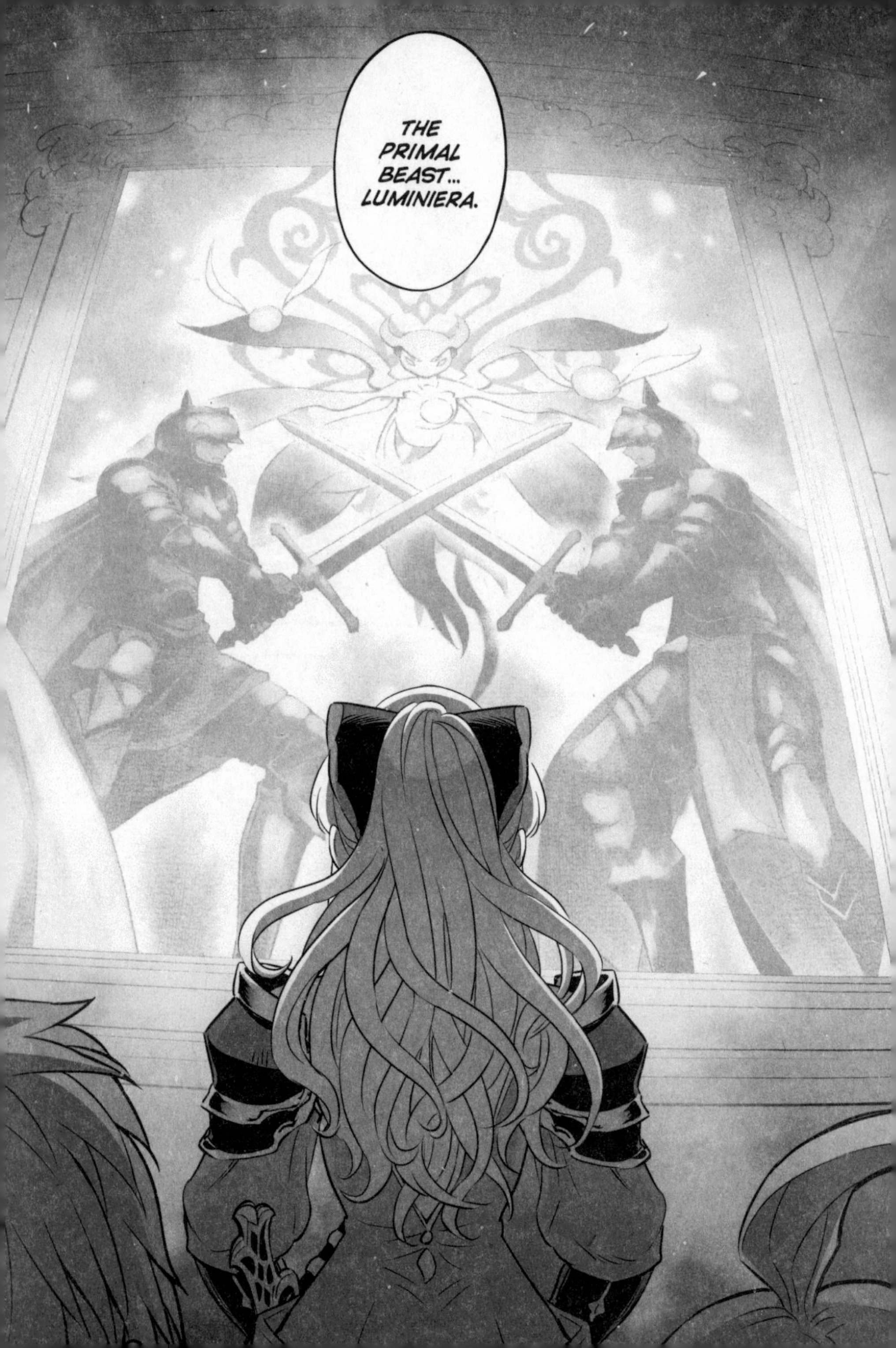
THE PRIMAL BEAST... LUMINIERA.

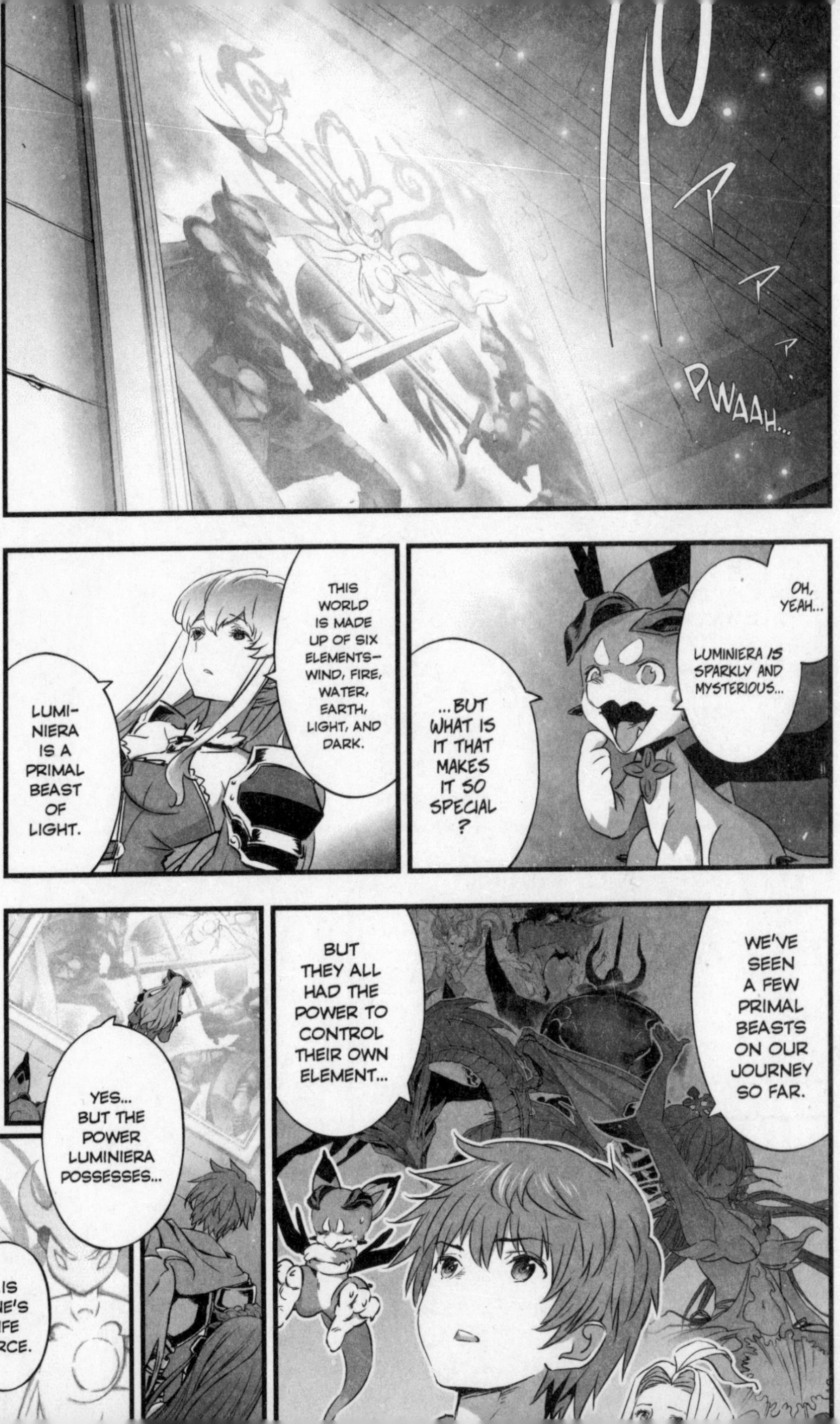
PWAAH...
OH, YEAH...
LUMINIERA IS SPARKLY AND MYSTERIOUS...
...BUT WHAT IS IT THAT MAKES IT SO SPECIAL?
THIS WORLD IS MADE UP OF SIX ELEMENTS—WIND, FIRE, WATER, EARTH, LIGHT, AND DARK.
LUMINIERA IS A PRIMAL BEAST OF LIGHT.
WE'VE SEEN A FEW PRIMAL BEASTS ON OUR JOURNEY SO FAR.
BUT THEY ALL HAD THE POWER TO CONTROL THEIR OWN ELEMENT...
YES... BUT THE POWER LUMINIERA POSSESSES...
...IS ONE'S LIFE FORCE.

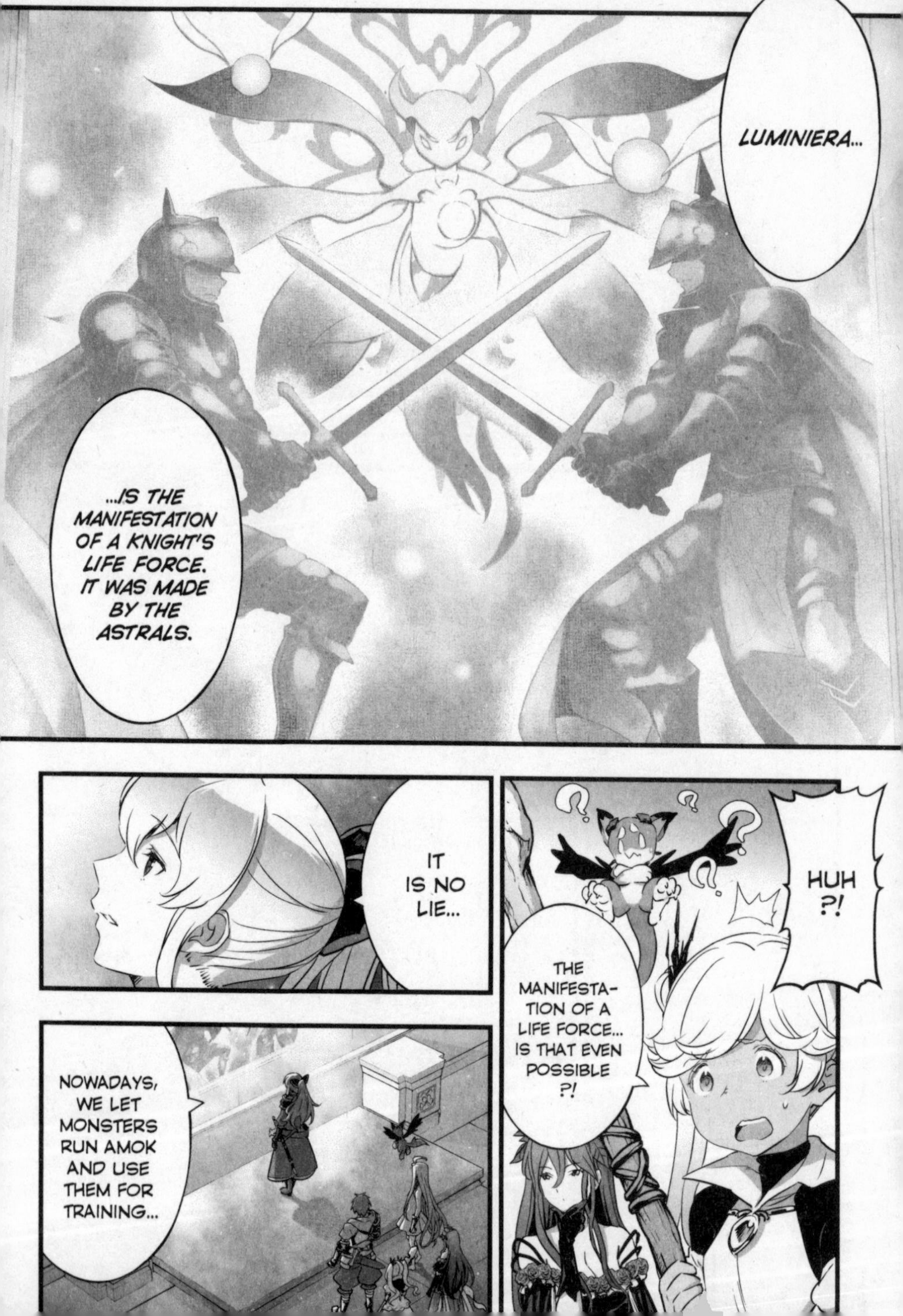
LUMINIERA...
...IS THE MANIFESTATION OF A KNIGHT'S LIFE FORCE. IT WAS MADE BY THE ASTRALS.
HUH ?!
THE MANIFESTA-TION OF A LIFE FORCE... IS THAT EVEN POSSIBLE ?!
IT IS NO LIE...
NOWADAYS, WE LET MONSTERS RUN AMOK AND USE THEM FOR TRAINING...

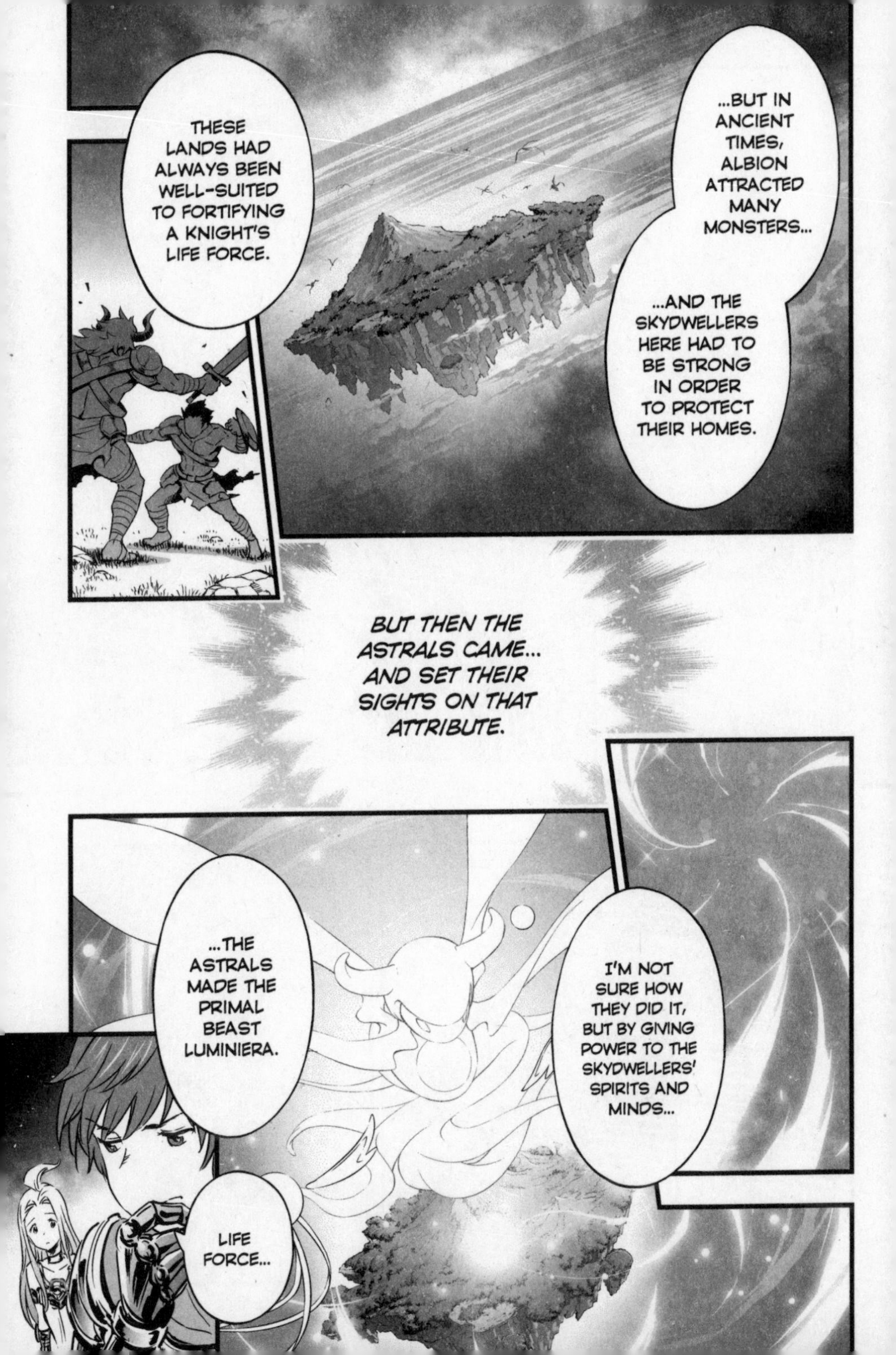
...BUT IN ANCIENT TIMES, ALBION ATTRACTED MANY MONSTERS...
...AND THE SKYDWELLERS HERE HAD TO BE STRONG IN ORDER TO PROTECT THEIR HOMES.
THESE LANDS HAD ALWAYS BEEN WELL-SUITED TO FORTIFYING A KNIGHT'S LIFE FORCE.
BUT THEN THE ASTRALS CAME... AND SET THEIR SIGHTS ON THAT ATTRIBUTE.
I'M NOT SURE HOW THEY DID IT, BUT BY GIVING POWER TO THE SKYDWELLERS' SPIRITS AND MINDS...
...THE ASTRALS MADE THE PRIMAL BEAST LUMINIERA.
LIFE FORCE...

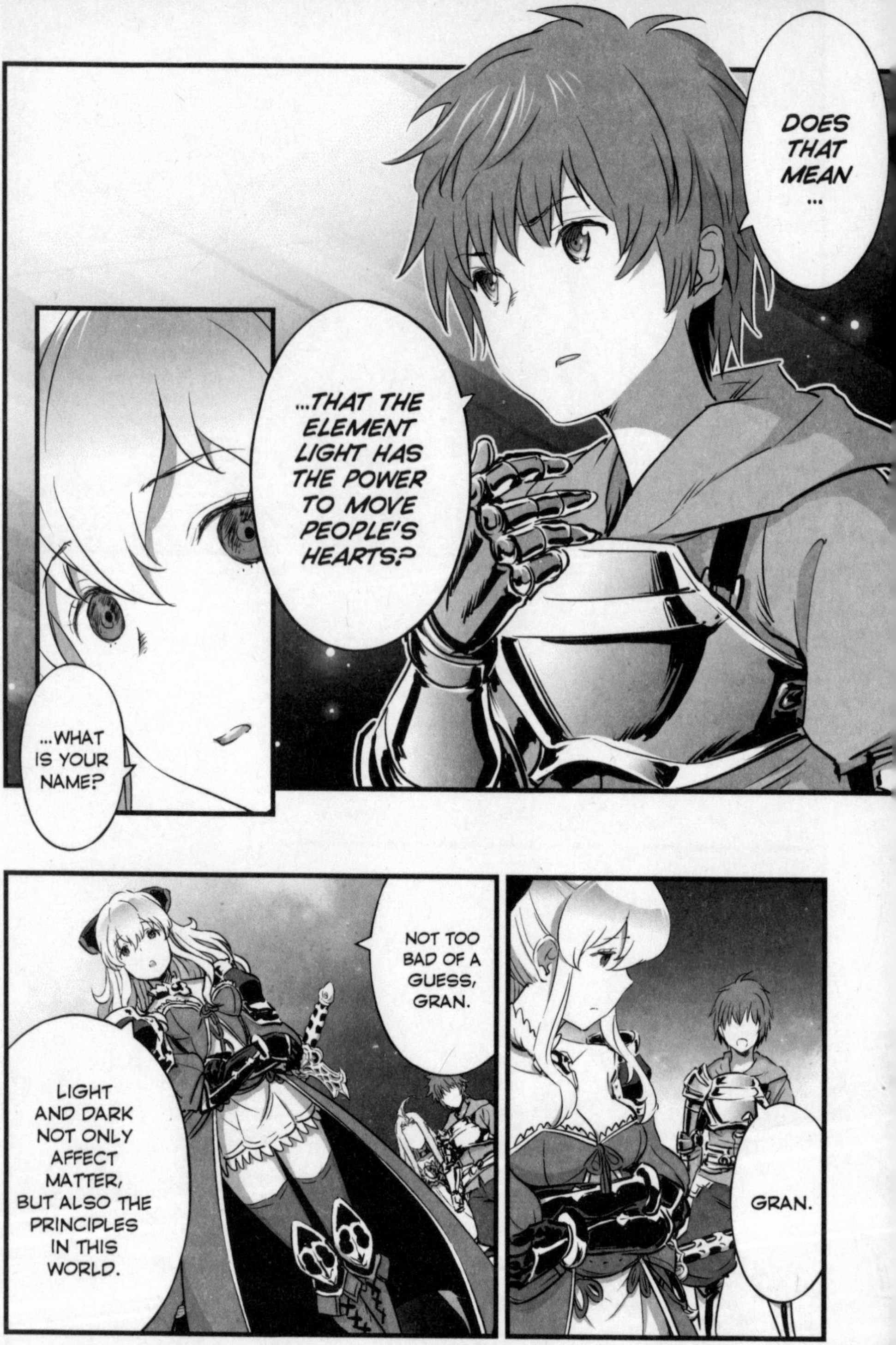
DOES THAT MEAN ...
...THAT THE ELEMENT LIGHT HAS THE POWER TO MOVE PEOPLE'S HEARTS?
...WHAT IS YOUR NAME?
GRAN.
NOT TOO BAD OF A GUESS, GRAN.
LIGHT AND DARK NOT ONLY AFFECT MATTER, BUT ALSO THE PRINCIPLES IN THIS WORLD.

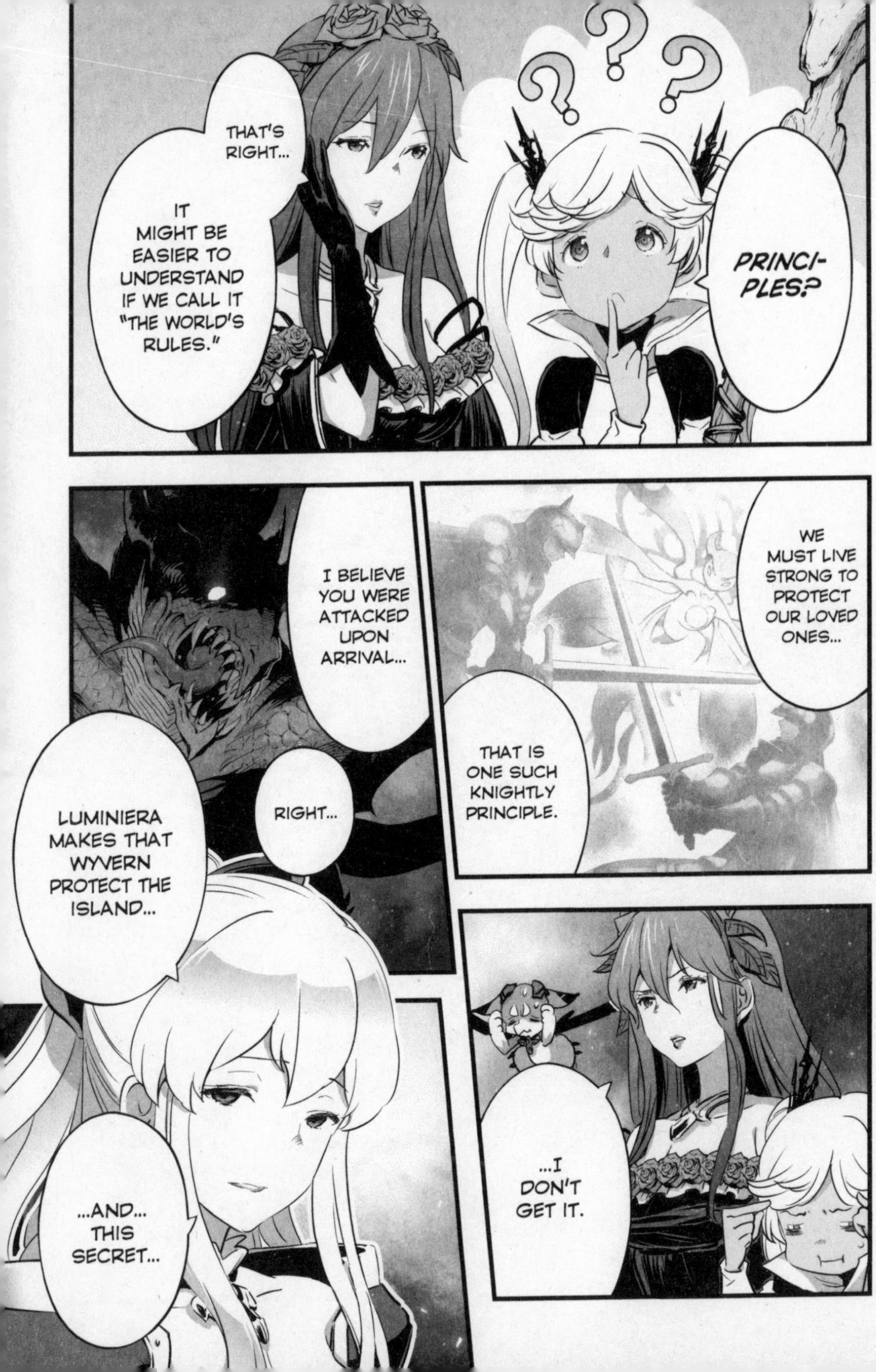
PRINCIPLES?
THAT'S RIGHT...
IT MIGHT BE EASIER TO UNDERSTAND IF WE CALL IT "THE WORLD'S RULES."
WE MUST LIVE STRONG TO PROTECT OUR LOVED ONES...
THAT IS ONE SUCH KNIGHTLY PRINCIPLE.
I BELIEVE YOU WERE ATTACKED UPON ARRIVAL...
RIGHT...
LUMINIERA MAKES THAT WYVERN PROTECT THE ISLAND...
...I DON'T GET IT.
...AND... THIS SECRET...

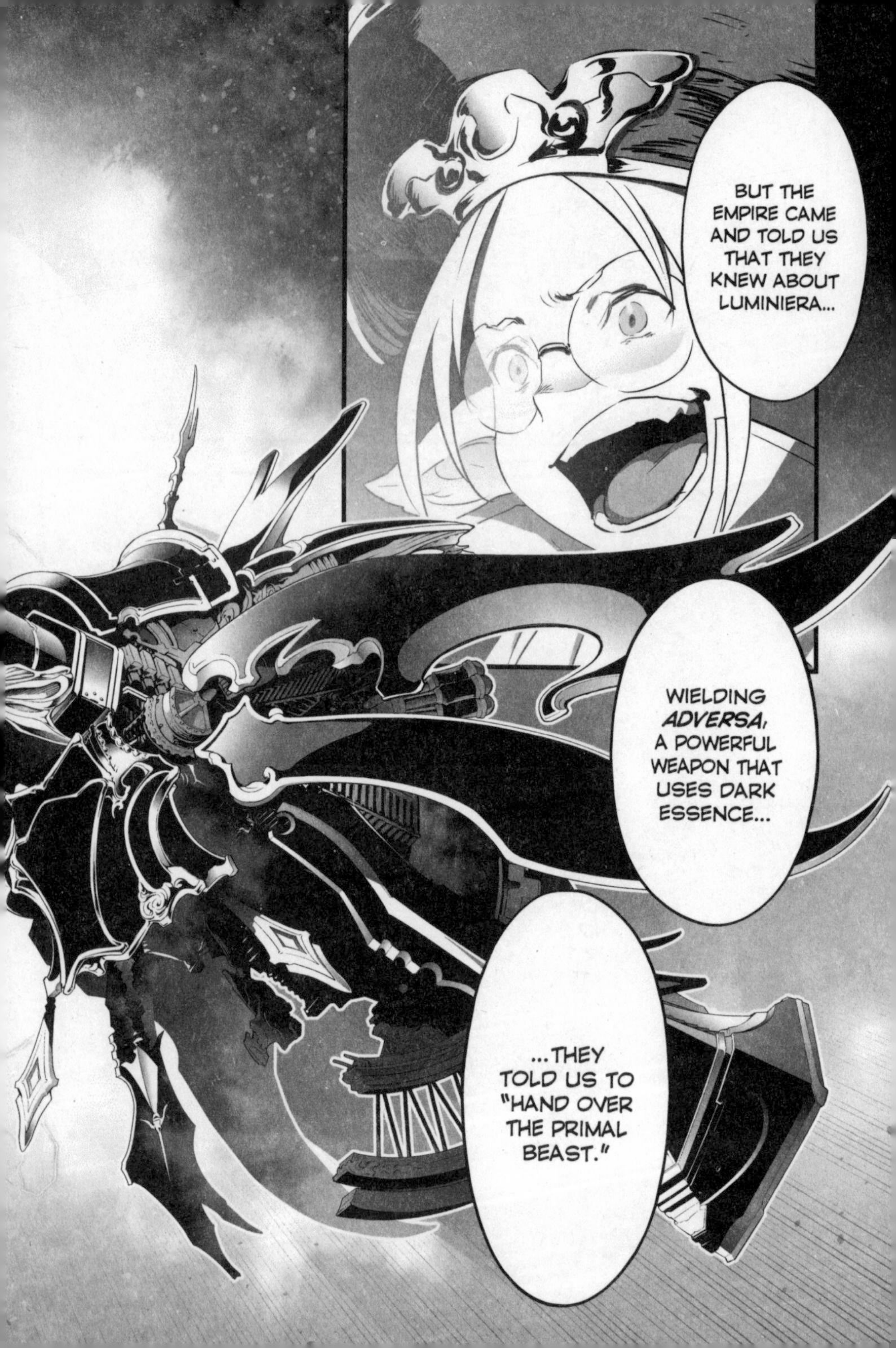
BUT THE EMPIRE CAME AND TOLD US THAT THEY KNEW ABOUT LUMINIERA...
WIELDING *ADVERSA*, A POWERFUL WEAPON THAT USES DARK ESSENCE...
...THEY TOLD US TO "HAND OVER THE PRIMAL BEAST."

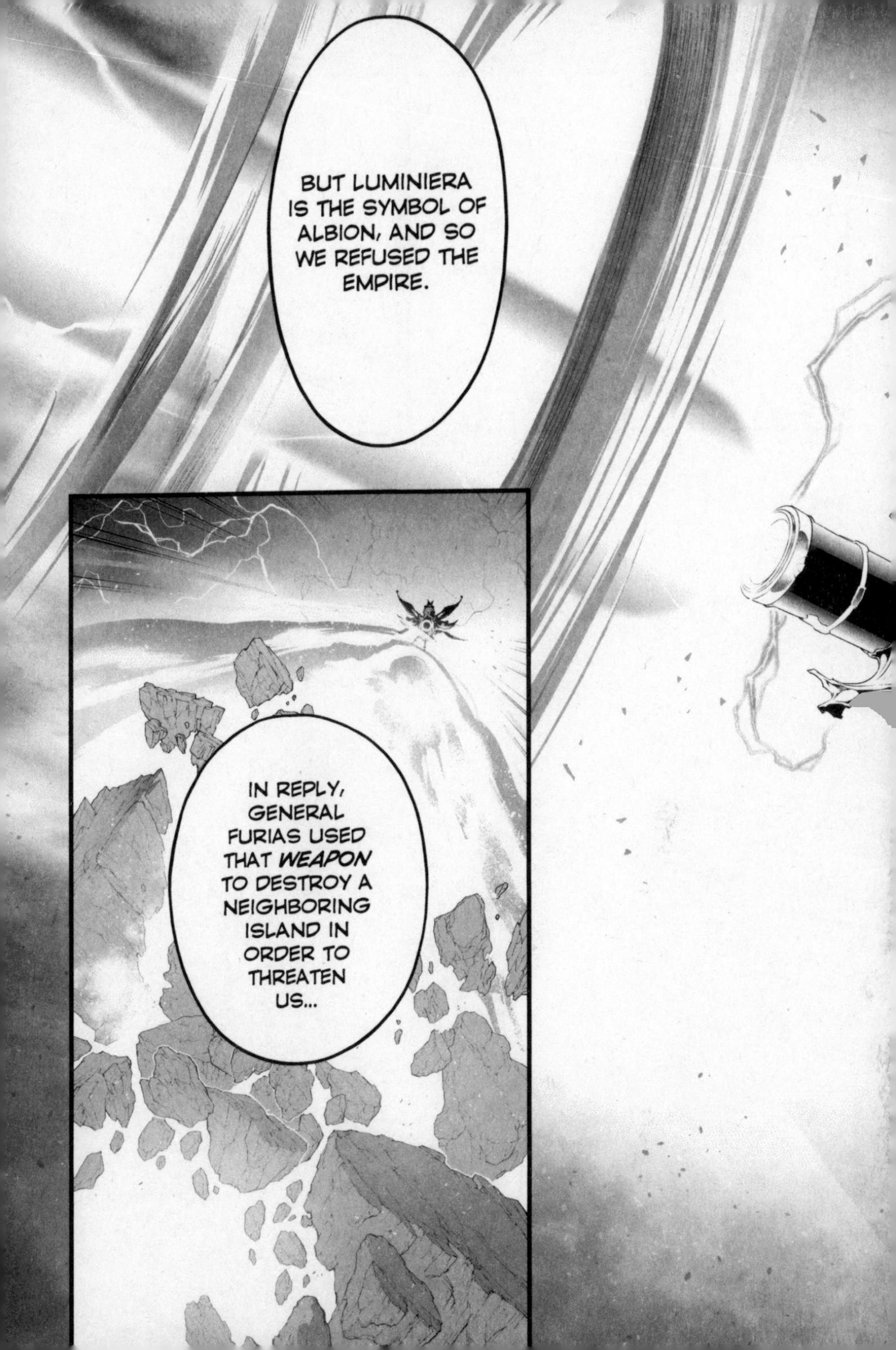
BUT LUMINIERA IS THE SYMBOL OF ALBION, AND SO WE REFUSED THE EMPIRE.
IN REPLY, GENERAL FURIAS USED THAT *WEAPON* TO DESTROY A NEIGHBORING ISLAND IN ORDER TO THREATEN US...

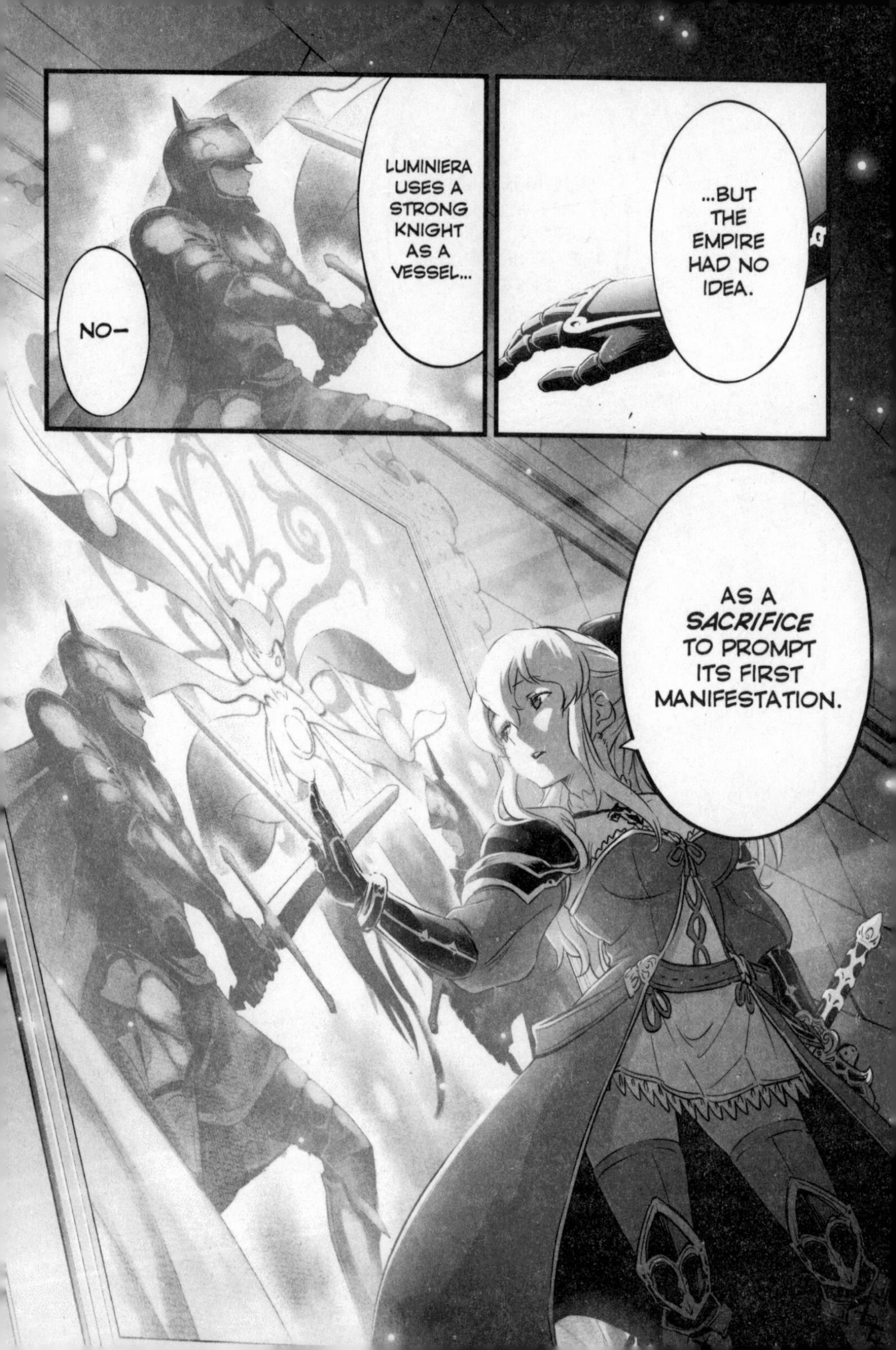
...BUT THE EMPIRE HAD NO IDEA.
LUMINIERA USES A STRONG KNIGHT AS A VESSEL...
NO—
AS A *SACRIFICE* TO PROMPT ITS FIRST MANIFESTATION.

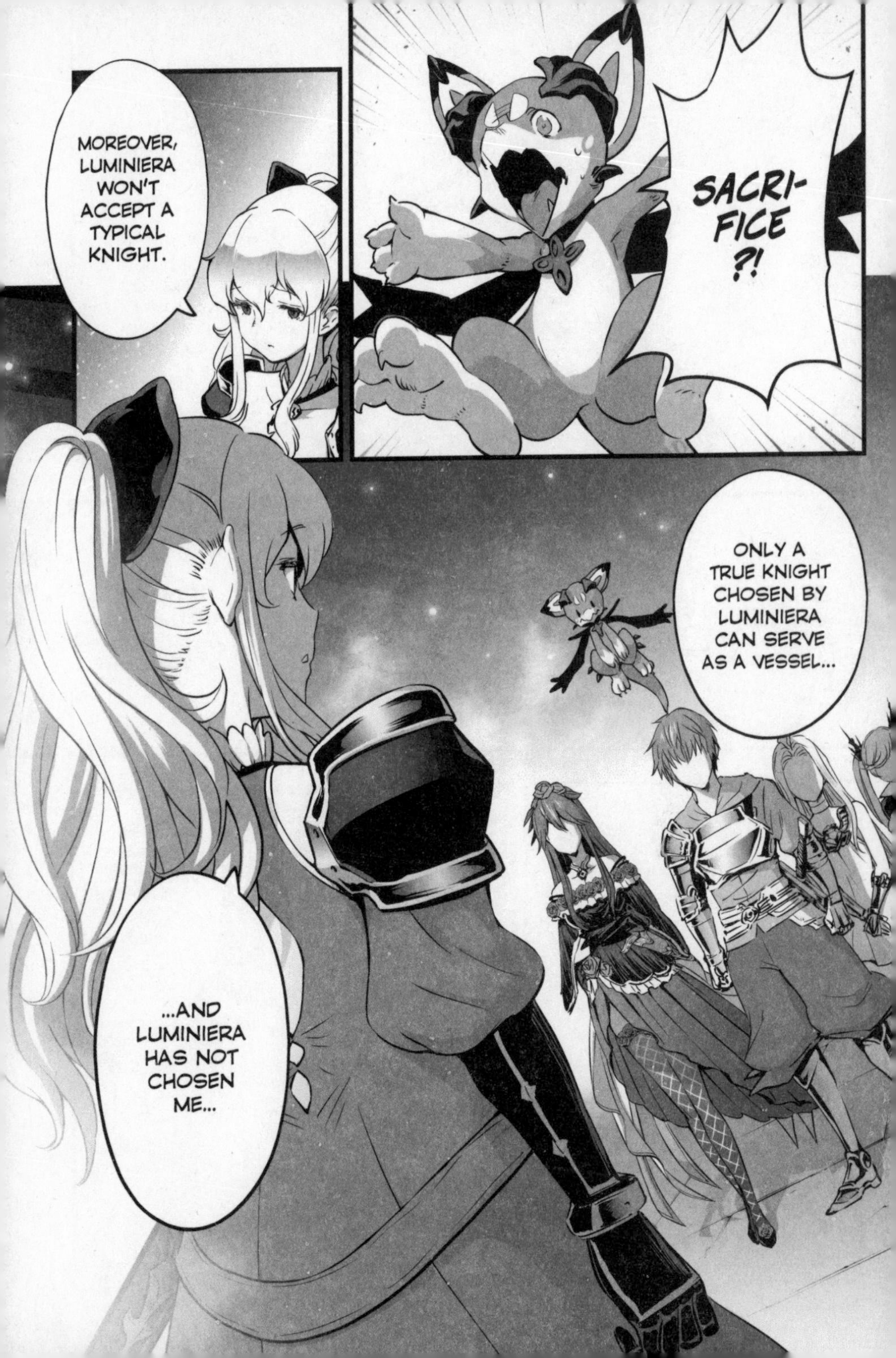
SACRI-FICE ?!
MOREOVER, LUMINIERA WON'T ACCEPT A TYPICAL KNIGHT.
ONLY A TRUE KNIGHT CHOSEN BY LUMINIERA CAN SERVE AS A VESSEL...
...AND LUMINIERA HAS NOT CHOSEN ME...

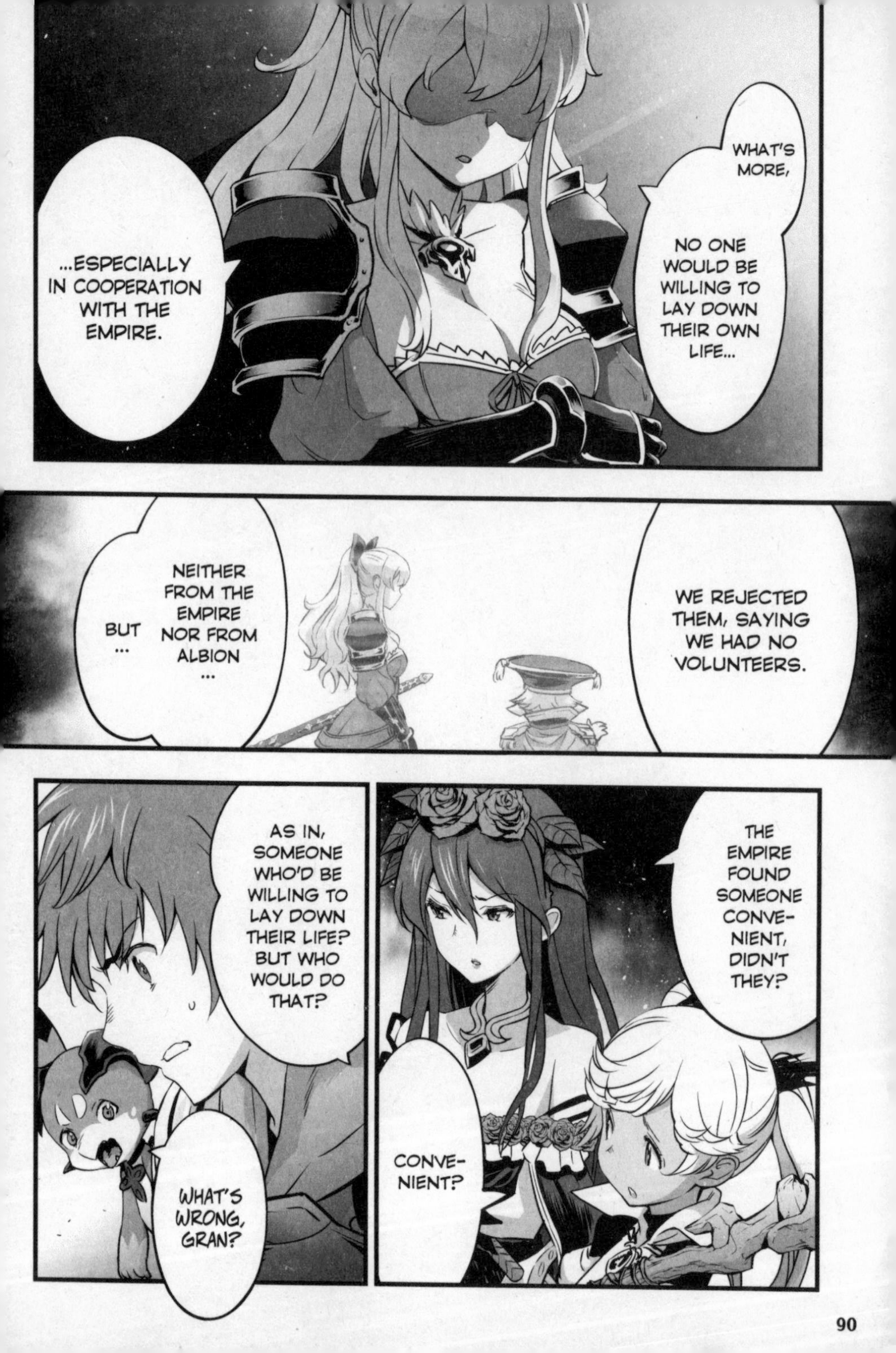
WHAT'S MORE,
NO ONE WOULD BE WILLING TO LAY DOWN THEIR OWN LIFE...
...ESPECIALLY IN COOPERATION WITH THE EMPIRE.
WE REJECTED THEM, SAYING WE HAD NO VOLUNTEERS.
NEITHER FROM THE EMPIRE NOR FROM ALBION ...
BUT ...
THE EMPIRE FOUND SOMEONE CONVE-NIENT, DIDN'T THEY?
CONVE-NIENT?
AS IN, SOMEONE WHO'D BE WILLING TO LAY DOWN THEIR LIFE? BUT WHO WOULD DO THAT?
WHAT'S WRONG, GRAN?

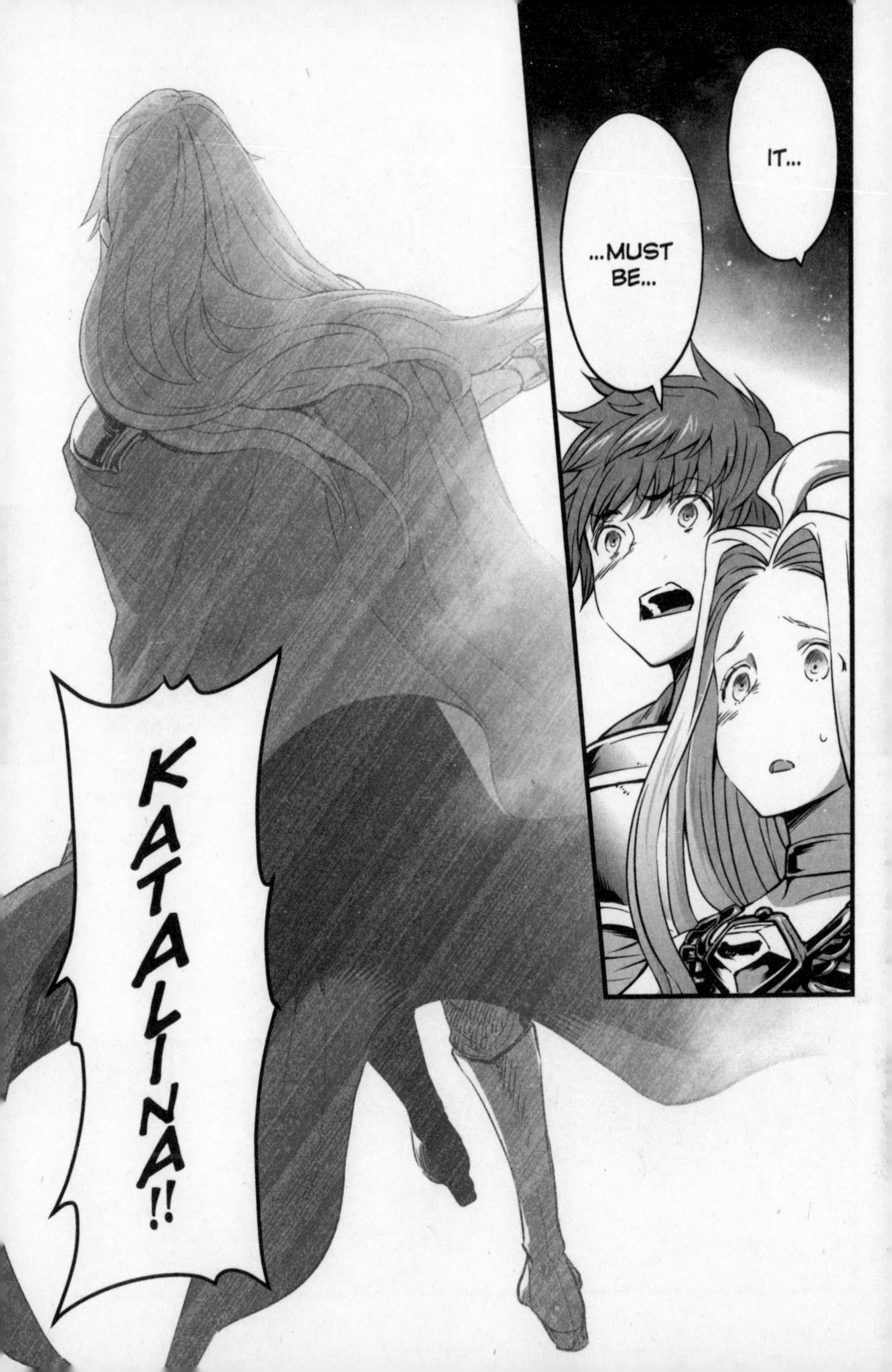
IT...
...MUST BE...
KATALINA!!

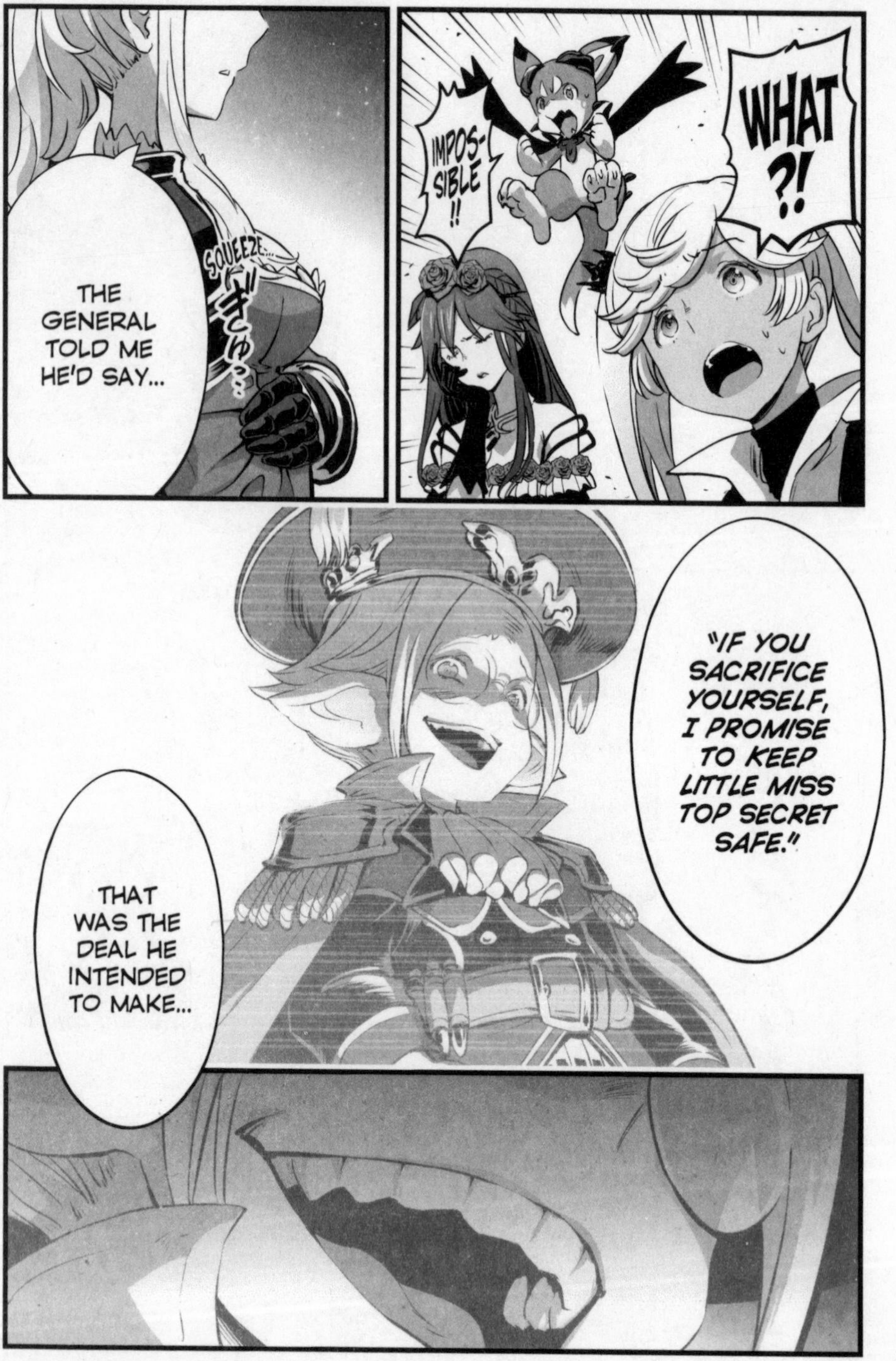
WHAT ?!
IMPOS-SIBLE !!
SQUEEZE...
ぎゅっ...
THE GENERAL TOLD ME HE'D SAY...
"IF YOU SACRIFICE YOURSELF, I PROMISE TO KEEP LITTLE MISS TOP SECRET SAFE."
THAT WAS THE DEAL HE INTENDED TO MAKE...

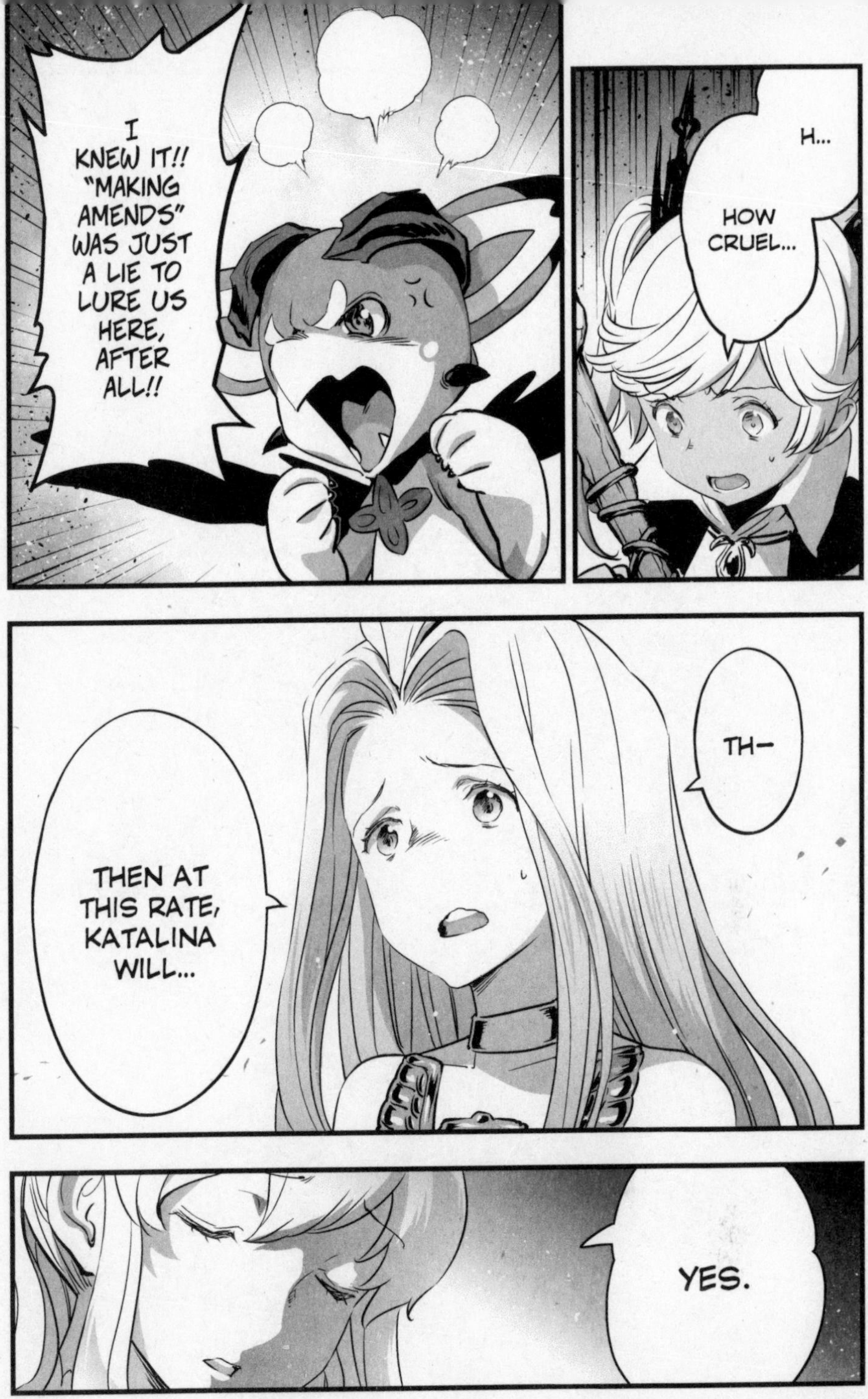
H...
HOW CRUEL...
I KNEW IT!! "MAKING AMENDS" WAS JUST A LIE TO LURE US HERE, AFTER ALL!!
TH—
THEN AT THIS RATE, KATALINA WILL...
YES.

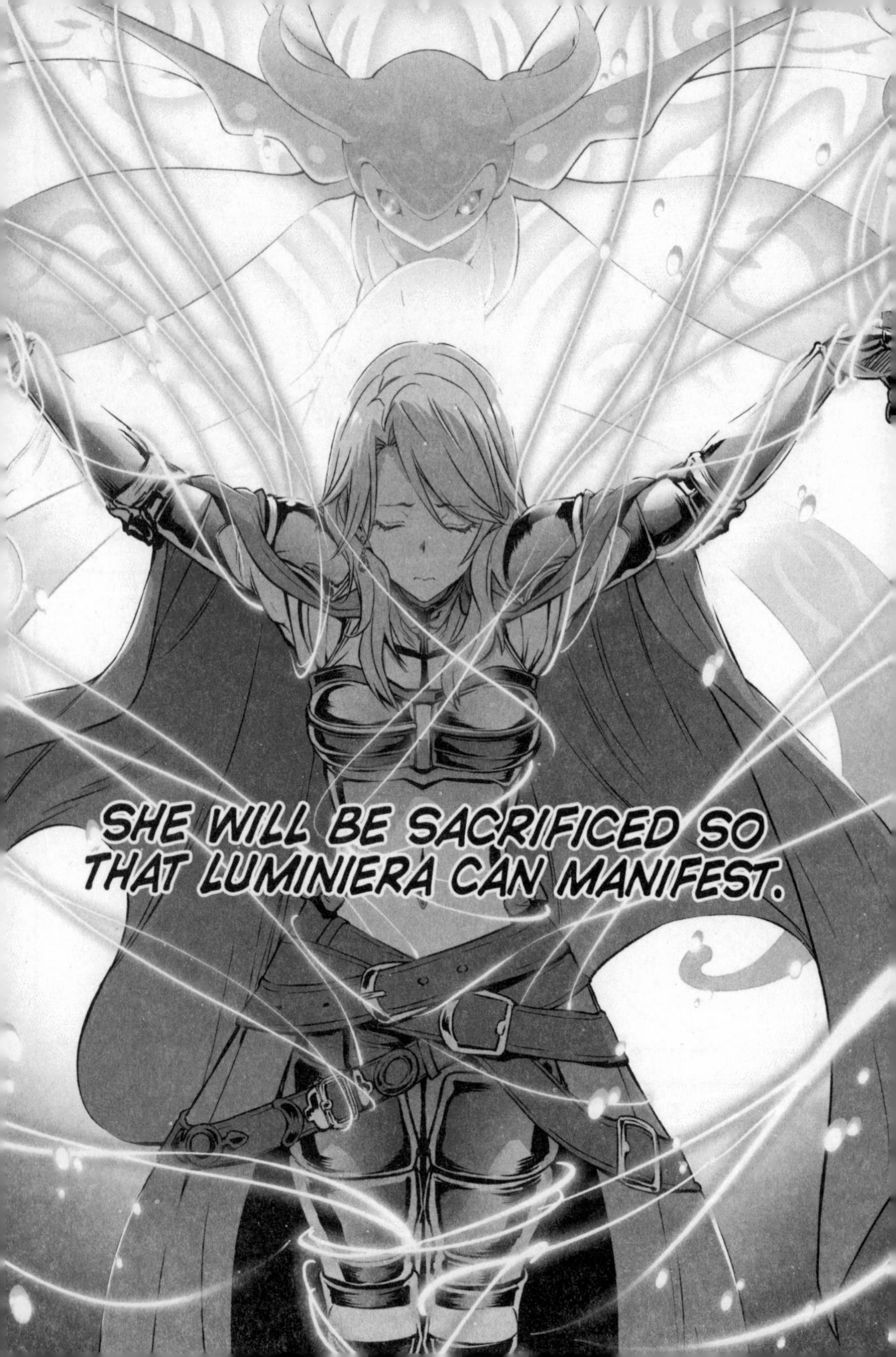
SHE WILL BE SACRIFICED SO THAT LUMINIERA CAN MANIFEST.

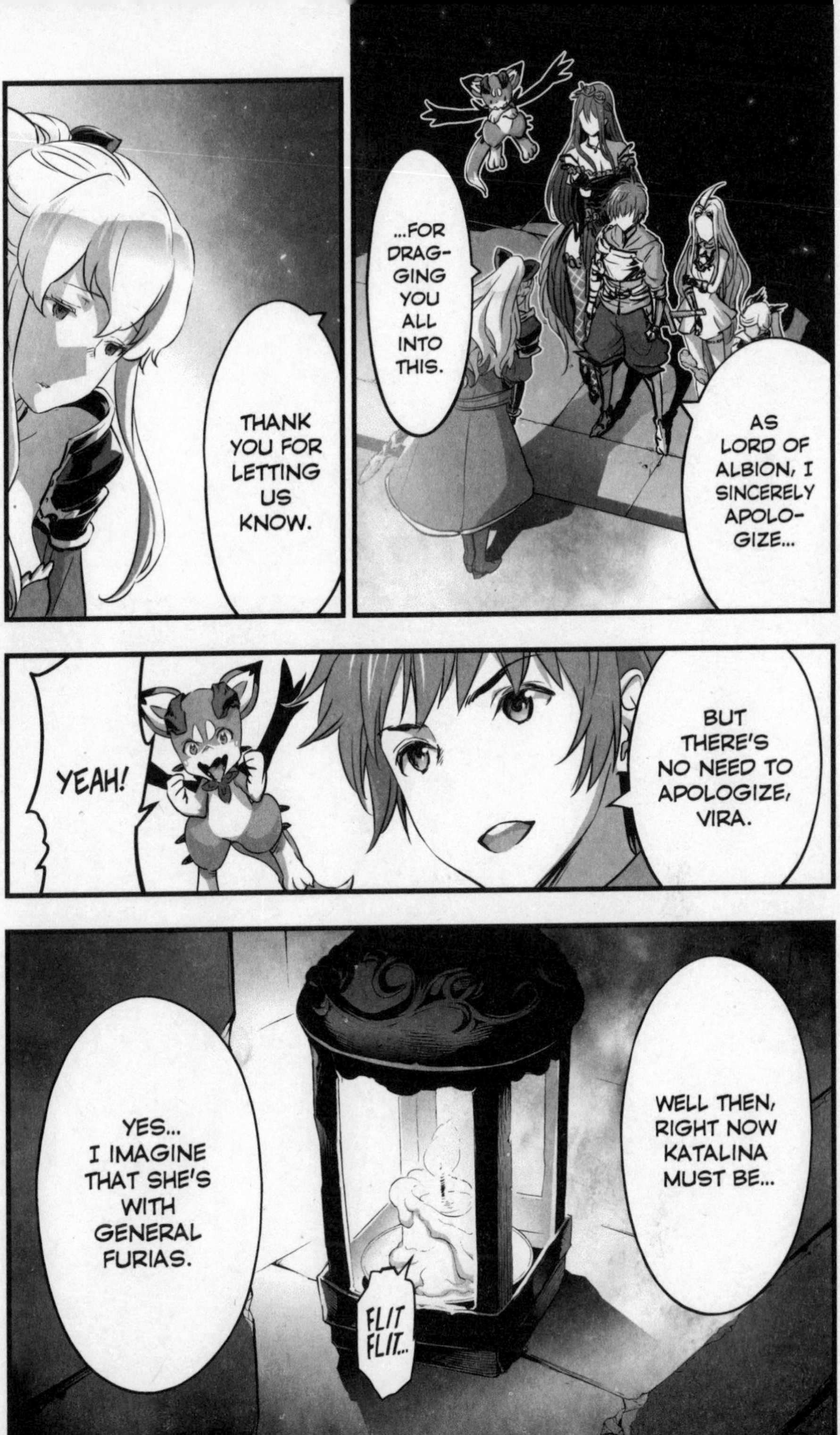
AS LORD OF ALBION, I SINCERELY APOLOGIZE...
...FOR DRAGGING YOU ALL INTO THIS.
THANK YOU FOR LETTING US KNOW.
BUT THERE'S NO NEED TO APOLOGIZE, VIRA.
YEAH!
WELL THEN, RIGHT NOW KATALINA MUST BE...
FLIT FLIT...
YES... I IMAGINE THAT SHE'S WITH GENERAL FURIAS.

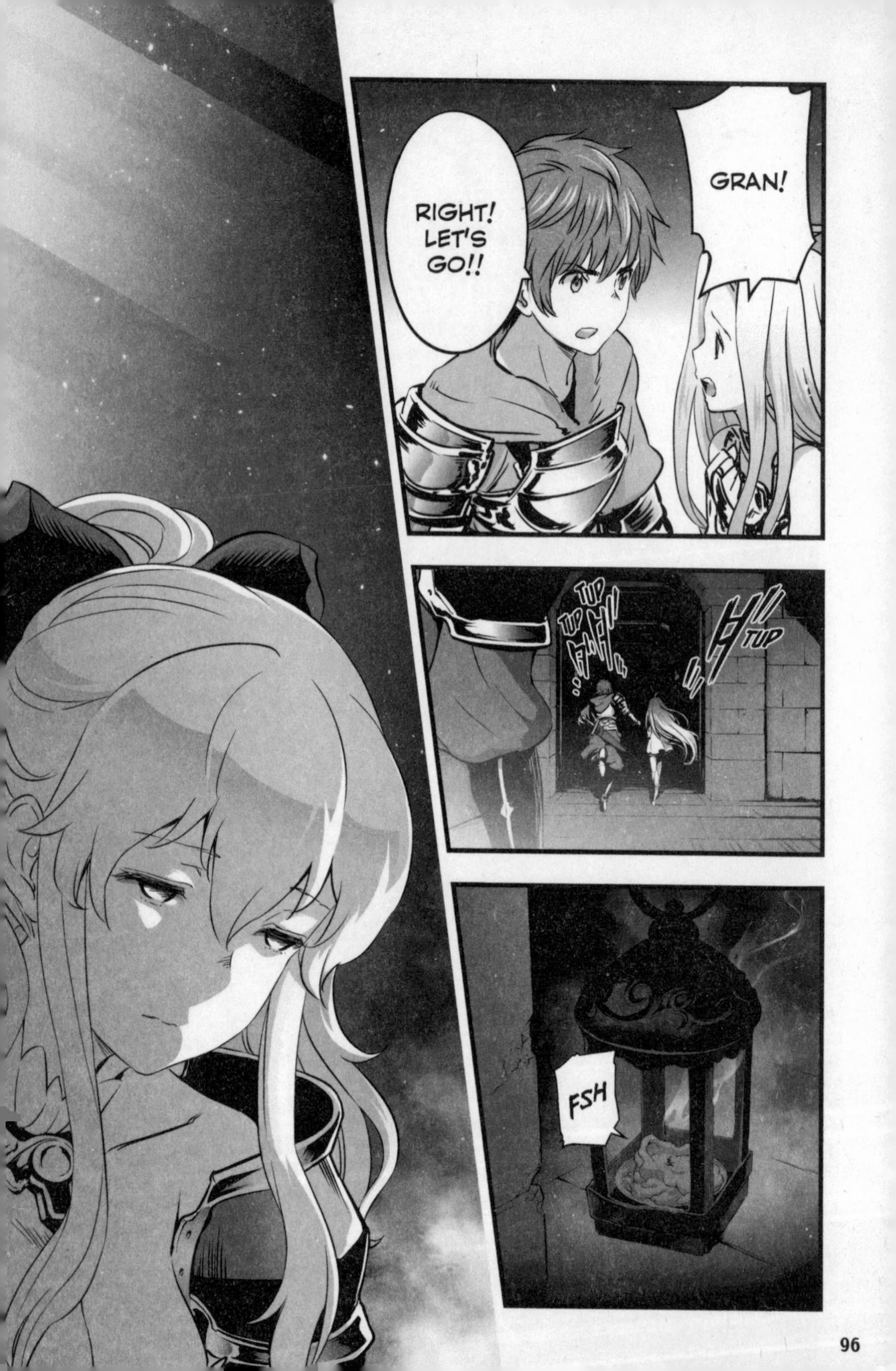
GRAN!
RIGHT! LET'S GO!!
TUP
TUP
TUP
FSH

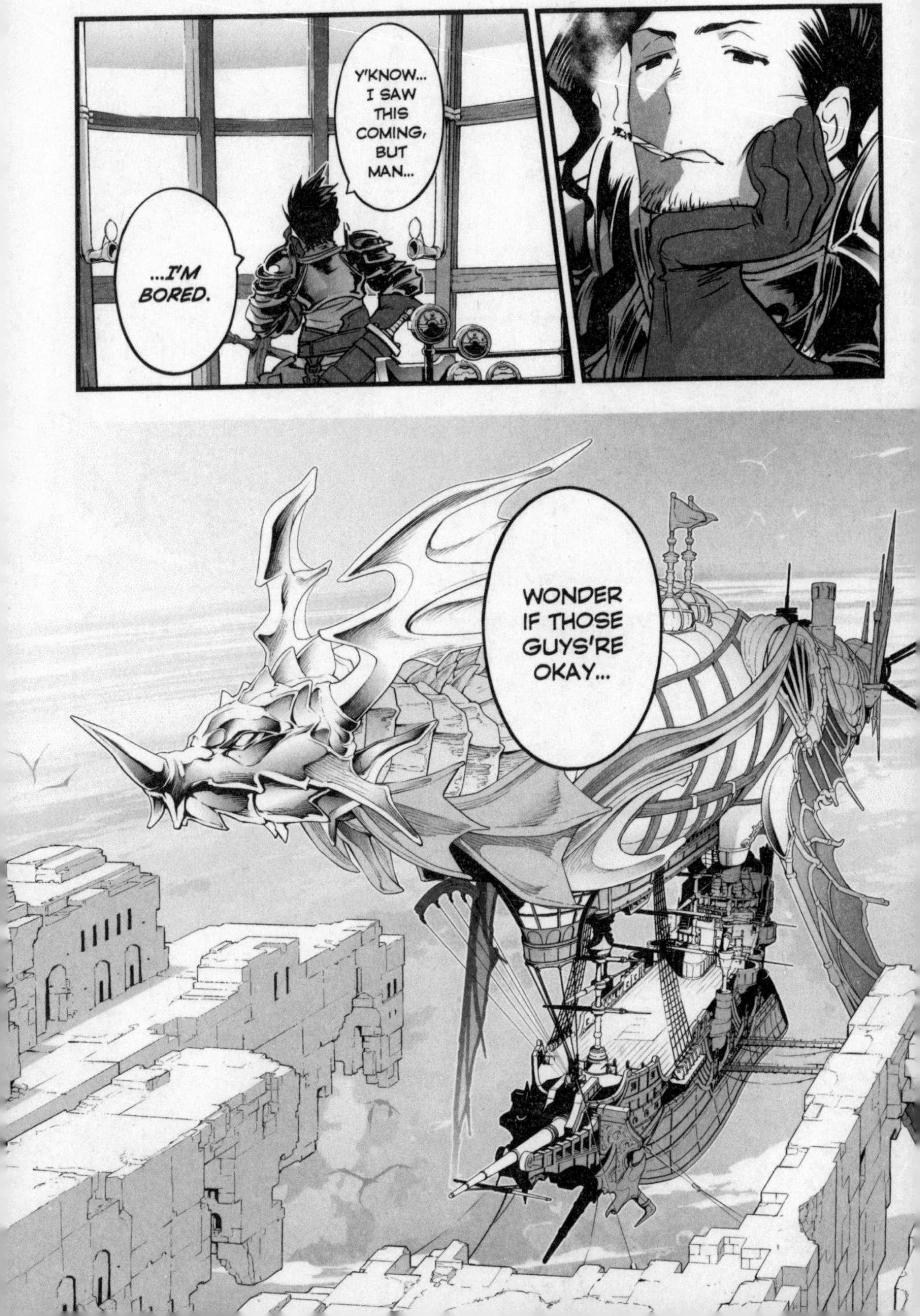
Y'KNOW... I SAW THIS COMING, BUT MAN...
...I'M BORED.
WONDER IF THOSE GUYS'RE OKAY...

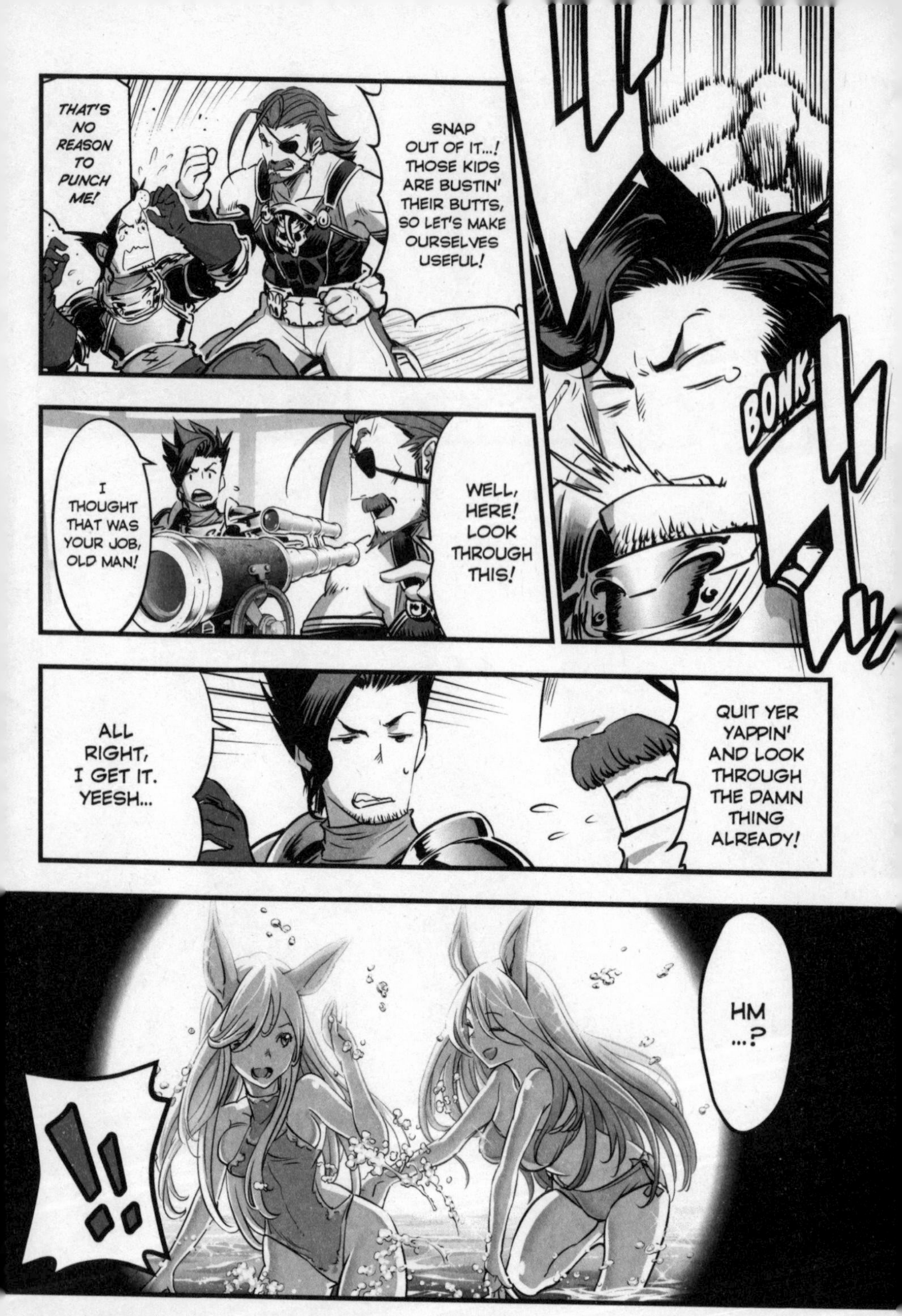
BONK!!
SNAP OUT OF IT...! THOSE KIDS ARE BUSTIN' THEIR BUTTS, SO LET'S MAKE OURSELVES USEFUL!
THAT'S NO REASON TO PUNCH ME!
WELL, HERE! LOOK THROUGH THIS!
I THOUGHT THAT WAS YOUR JOB, OLD MAN!
QUIT YER YAPPIN' AND LOOK THROUGH THE DAMN THING ALREADY!
ALL RIGHT, I GET IT. YEESH...
HM ...?
!!

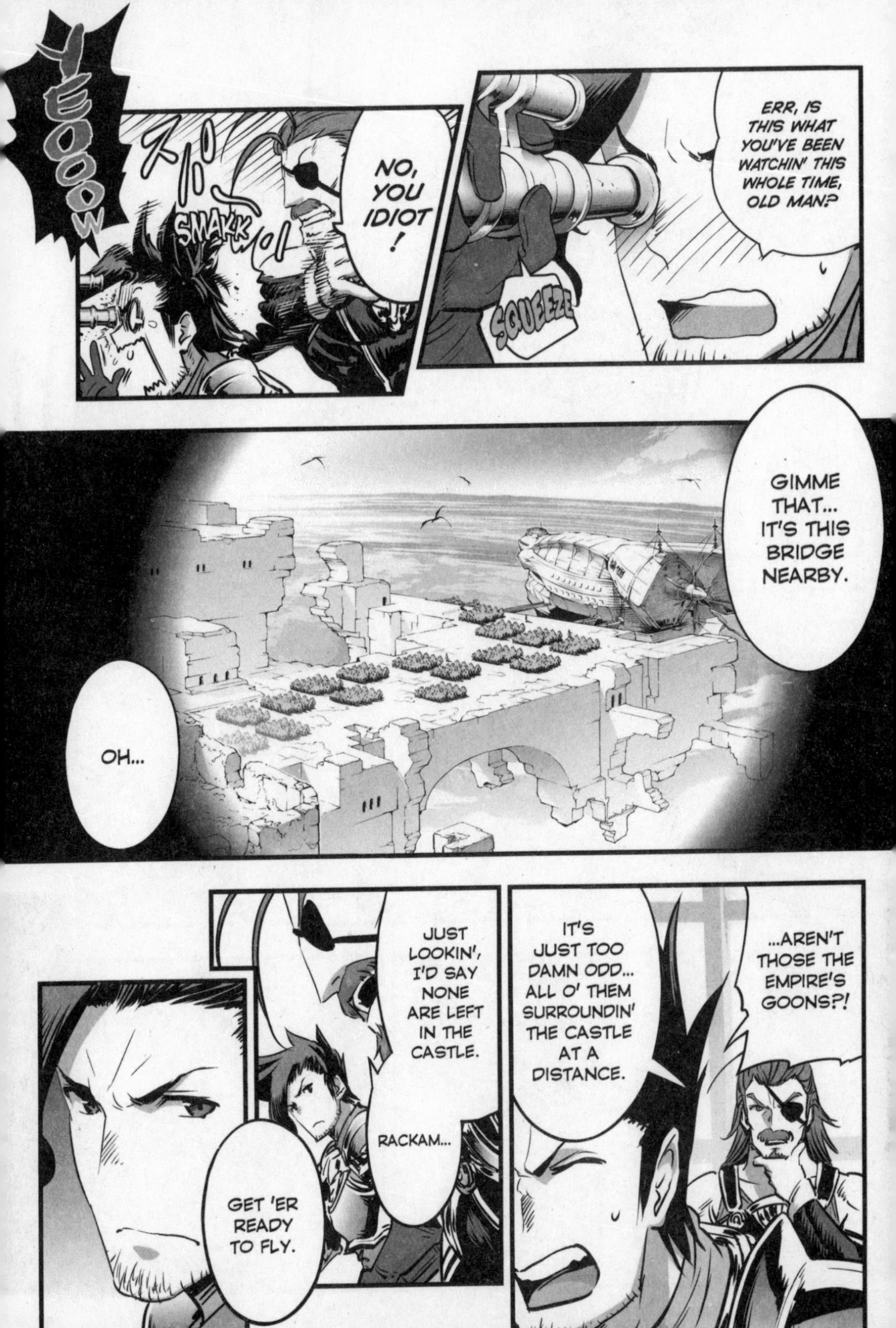
ERR, IS THIS WHAT YOU'VE BEEN WATCHIN' THIS WHOLE TIME, OLD MAN?
SQUEEZE
NO, YOU IDIOT!
SMAKK
YEOOOOW
GIMME THAT... IT'S THIS BRIDGE NEARBY.
OH...
...AREN'T THOSE THE EMPIRE'S GOONS?!
IT'S JUST TOO DAMN ODD... ALL O' THEM SURROUNDIN' THE CASTLE AT A DISTANCE.
JUST LOOKIN', I'D SAY NONE ARE LEFT IN THE CASTLE.
RACKAM...
GET 'ER READY TO FLY.

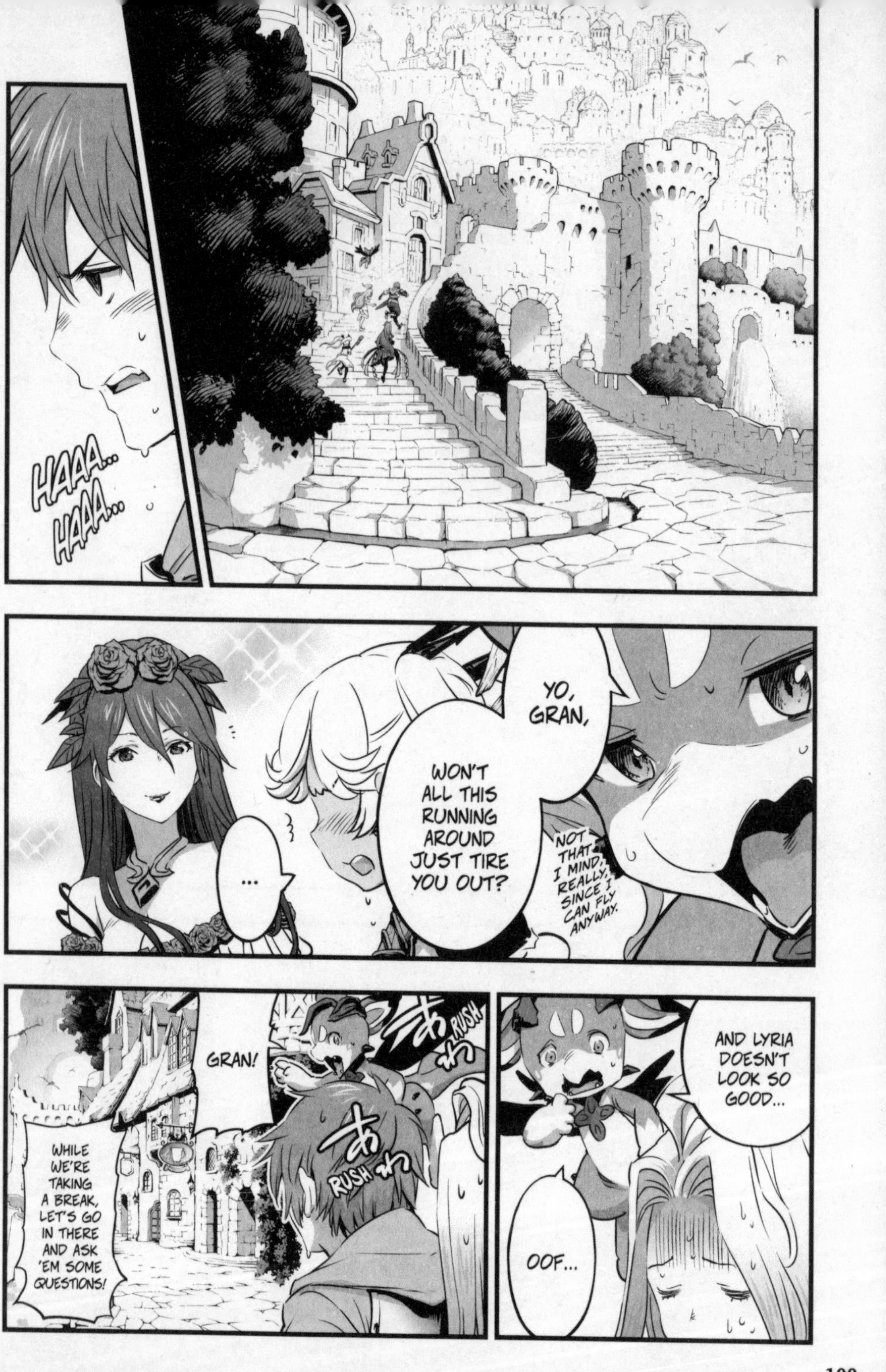
HAAA... HAAA...
YO, GRAN,
WON'T ALL THIS RUNNING AROUND JUST TIRE YOU OUT?
NOT THAT I MIND, REALLY, SINCE I CAN FLY ANYWAY.
...
AND LYRIA DOESN'T LOOK SO GOOD...
OOF...
RUSH
RUSH
GRAN!
WHILE WE'RE TAKING A BREAK, LET'S GO IN THERE AND ASK 'EM SOME QUESTIONS!

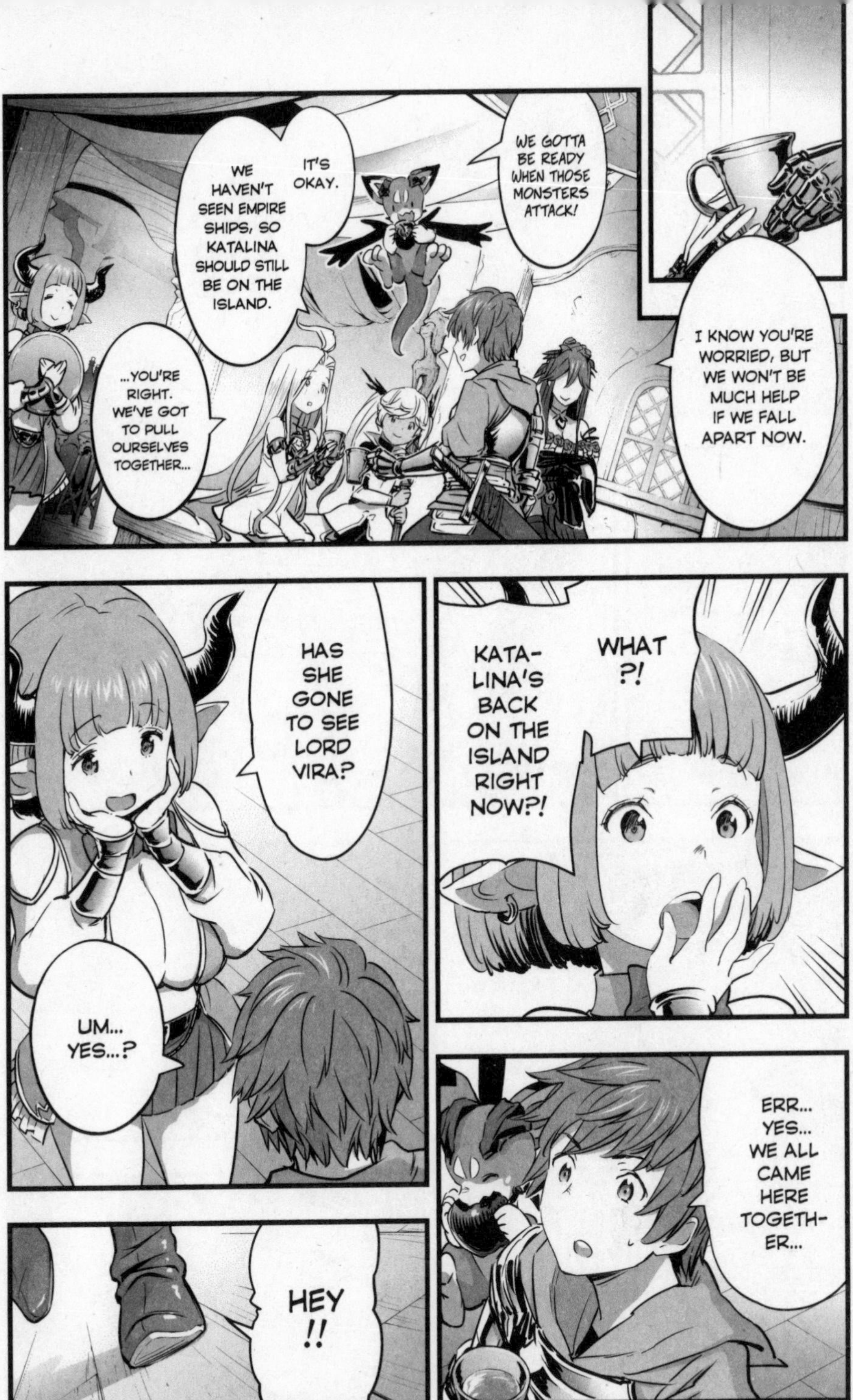
WE GOTTA BE READY WHEN THOSE MONSTERS ATTACK!
I KNOW YOU'RE WORRIED, BUT WE WON'T BE MUCH HELP IF WE FALL APART NOW.
IT'S OKAY. WE HAVEN'T SEEN EMPIRE SHIPS, SO KATALINA SHOULD STILL BE ON THE ISLAND.
...YOU'RE RIGHT. WE'VE GOT TO PULL OURSELVES TOGETHER...
WHAT?!
KATA-LINA'S BACK ON THE ISLAND RIGHT NOW?!
HAS SHE GONE TO SEE LORD VIRA?
UM... YES...?
ERR... YES... WE ALL CAME HERE TOGETH-ER...
HEY!!

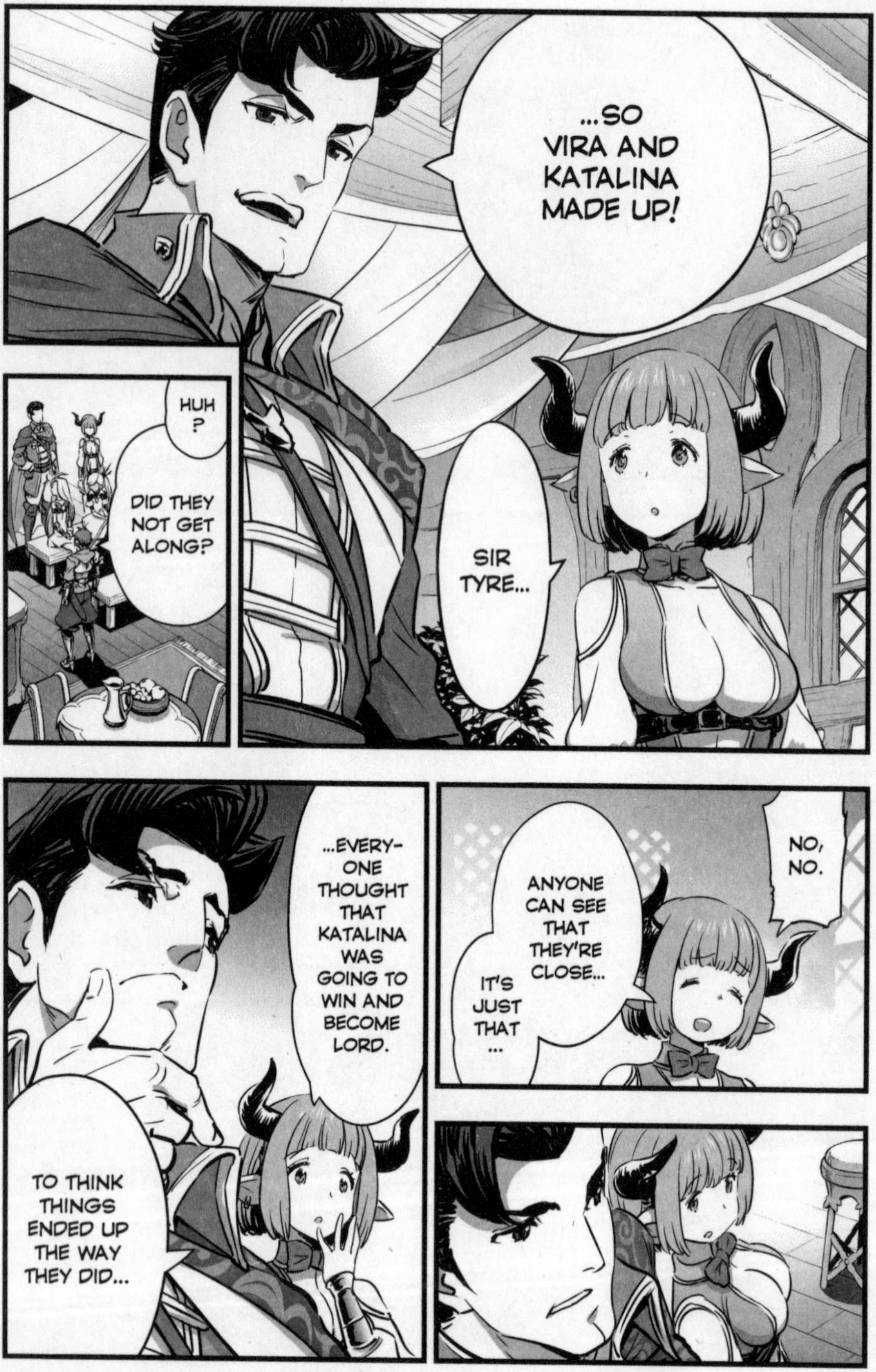
...SO VIRA AND KATALINA MADE UP!
SIR TYRE...
HUH?
DID THEY NOT GET ALONG?
NO, NO.
ANYONE CAN SEE THAT THEY'RE CLOSE...
IT'S JUST THAT ...
...EVERY-ONE THOUGHT THAT KATALINA WAS GOING TO WIN AND BECOME LORD.
TO THINK THINGS ENDED UP THE WAY THEY DID...

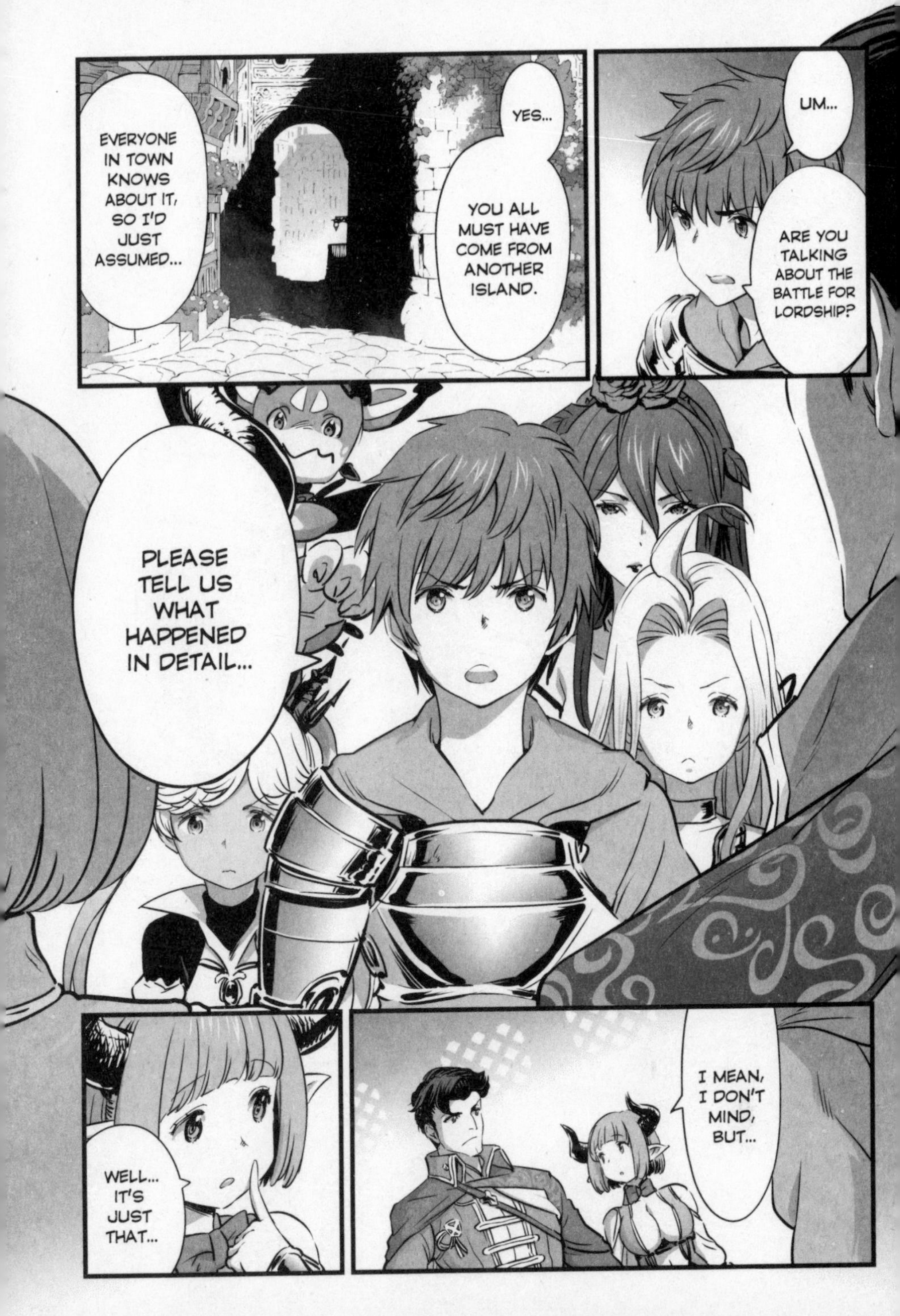
UM...
ARE YOU TALKING ABOUT THE BATTLE FOR LORDSHIP?
YES...
YOU ALL MUST HAVE COME FROM ANOTHER ISLAND.
EVERYONE IN TOWN KNOWS ABOUT IT, SO I'D JUST ASSUMED...
PLEASE TELL US WHAT HAPPENED IN DETAIL...
I MEAN, I DON'T MIND, BUT...
WELL... IT'S JUST THAT...

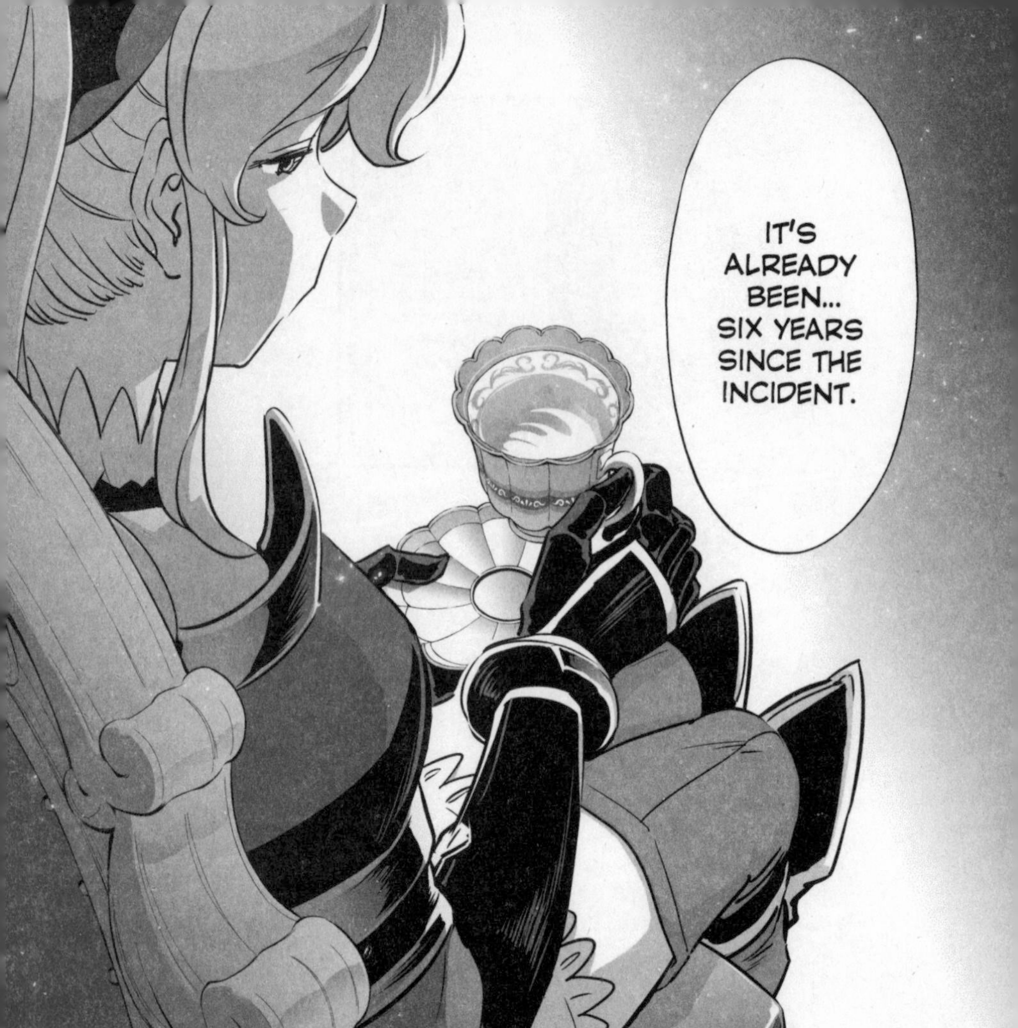
IT'S ALREADY BEEN... SIX YEARS SINCE THE INCIDENT.
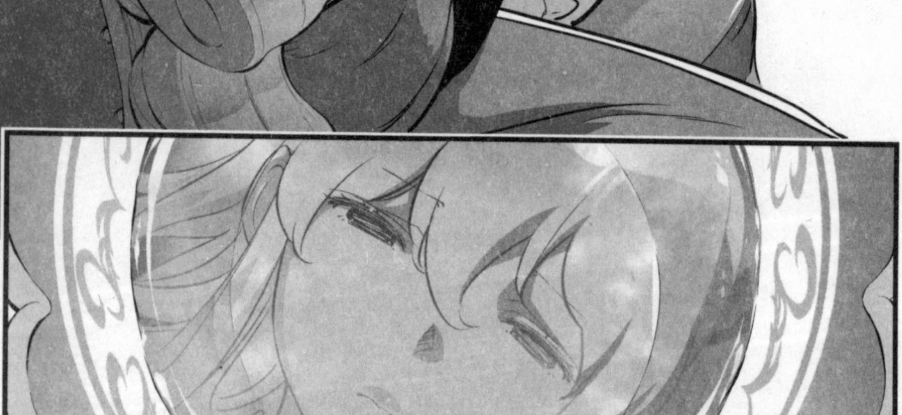

GRANBLUE FANTASY
グランブルーファンタジー

GRANBLUE FANTASY
グランブルーファンタジー

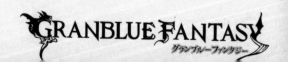

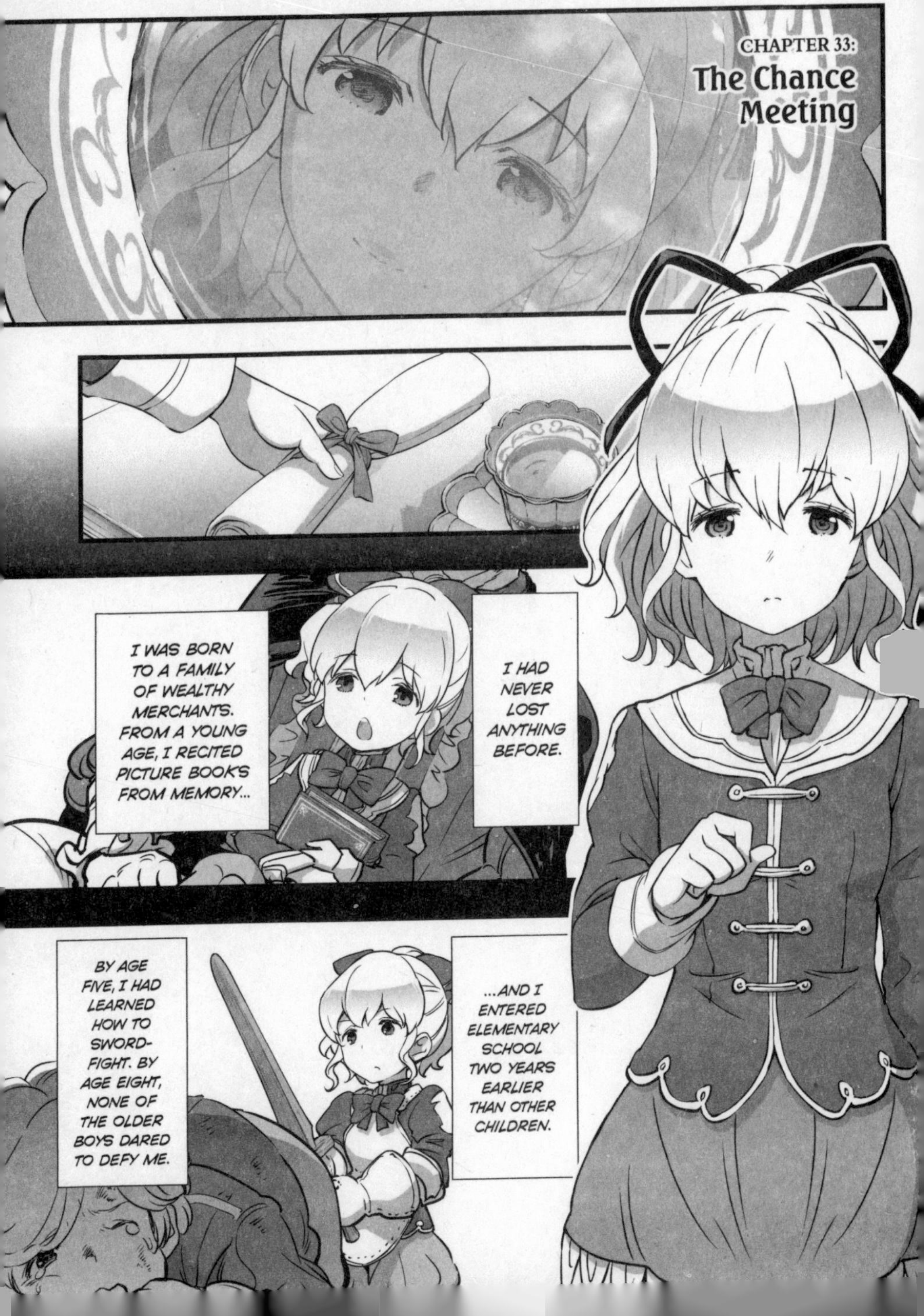

CHAPTER 33:
The Chance Meeting
I HAD NEVER LOST ANYTHING BEFORE.
I WAS BORN TO A FAMILY OF WEALTHY MERCHANTS. FROM A YOUNG AGE, I RECITED PICTURE BOOKS FROM MEMORY...
...AND I ENTERED ELEMENTARY SCHOOL TWO YEARS EARLIER THAN OTHER CHILDREN.
BY AGE FIVE, I HAD LEARNED HOW TO SWORD-FIGHT. BY AGE EIGHT, NONE OF THE OLDER BOYS DARED TO DEFY ME.

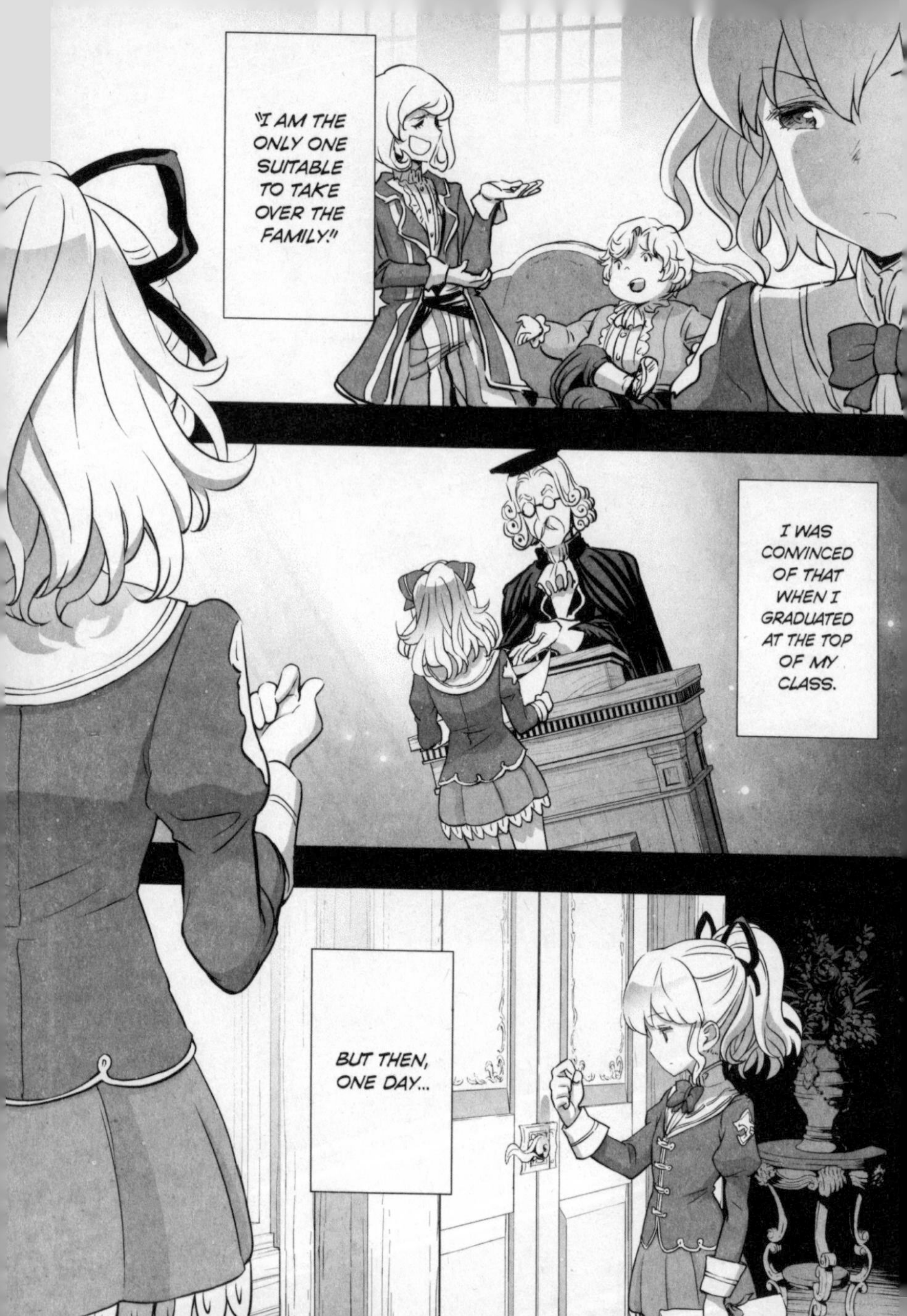
"I AM THE ONLY ONE SUITABLE TO TAKE OVER THE FAMILY!"
I WAS CONVINCED OF THAT WHEN I GRADUATED AT THE TOP OF MY CLASS.
BUT THEN, ONE DAY...

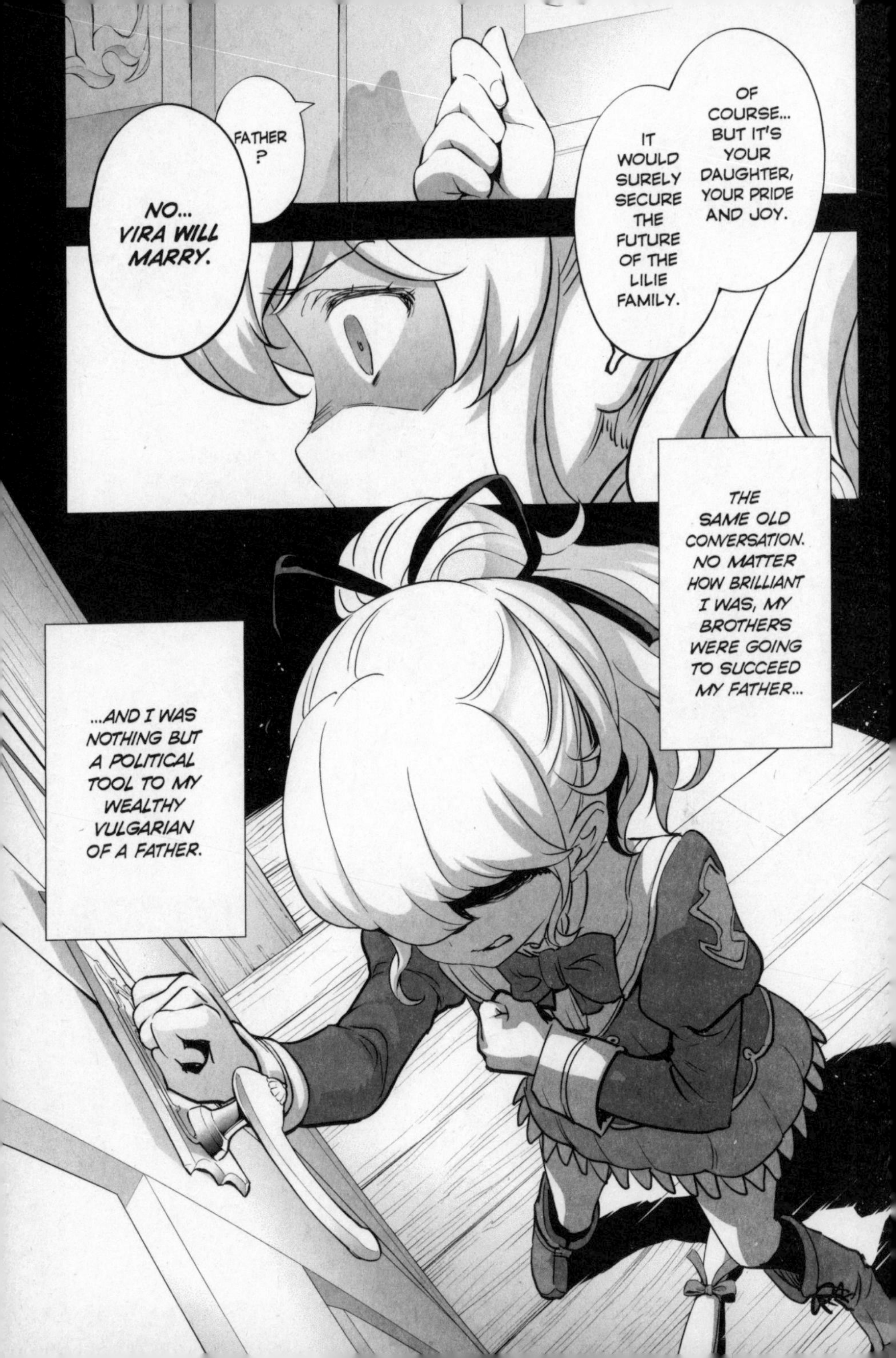
OF COURSE... BUT IT'S YOUR DAUGHTER, YOUR PRIDE AND JOY.
IT WOULD SURELY SECURE THE FUTURE OF THE LILIE FAMILY.
FATHER?
NO... VIRA WILL MARRY.
THE SAME OLD CONVERSATION. NO MATTER HOW BRILLIANT I WAS, MY BROTHERS WERE GOING TO SUCCEED MY FATHER...
...AND I WAS NOTHING BUT A POLITICAL TOOL TO MY WEALTHY VULGARIAN OF A FATHER.

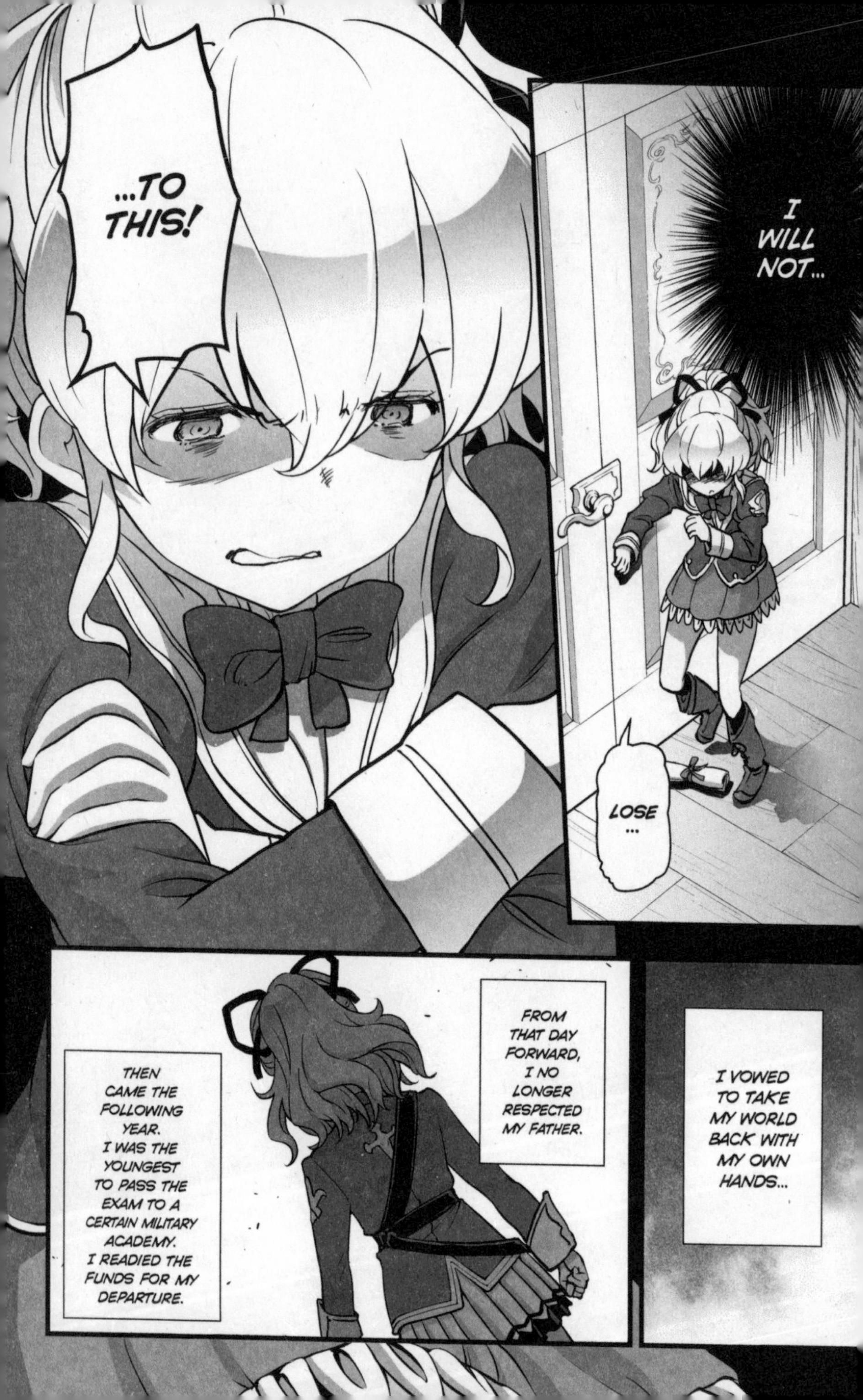
I WILL NOT...
LOSE ...
...TO THIS!
I VOWED TO TAKE MY WORLD BACK WITH MY OWN HANDS...
FROM THAT DAY FORWARD, I NO LONGER RESPECTED MY FATHER.
THEN CAME THE FOLLOWING YEAR. I WAS THE YOUNGEST TO PASS THE EXAM TO A CERTAIN MILITARY ACADEMY. I READIED THE FUNDS FOR MY DEPARTURE.

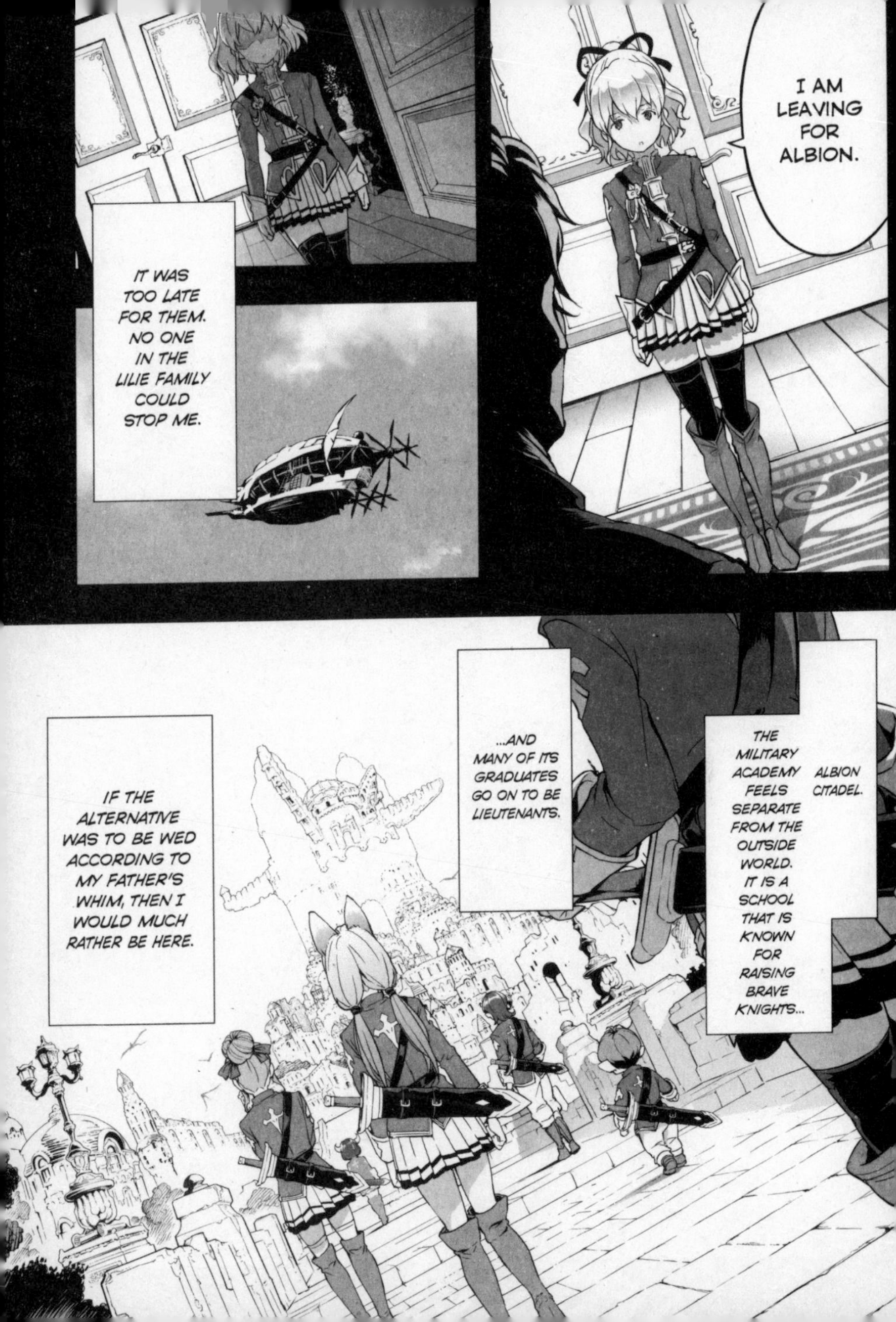

I AM LEAVING FOR ALBION.
IT WAS TOO LATE FOR THEM. NO ONE IN THE LILIE FAMILY COULD STOP ME.
ALBION CITADEL.
THE MILITARY ACADEMY FEELS SEPARATE FROM THE OUTSIDE WORLD. IT IS A SCHOOL THAT IS KNOWN FOR RAISING BRAVE KNIGHTS...
...AND MANY OF ITS GRADUATES GO ON TO BE LIEUTENANTS.
IF THE ALTERNATIVE WAS TO BE WED ACCORDING TO MY FATHER'S WHIM, THEN I WOULD MUCH RATHER BE HERE.

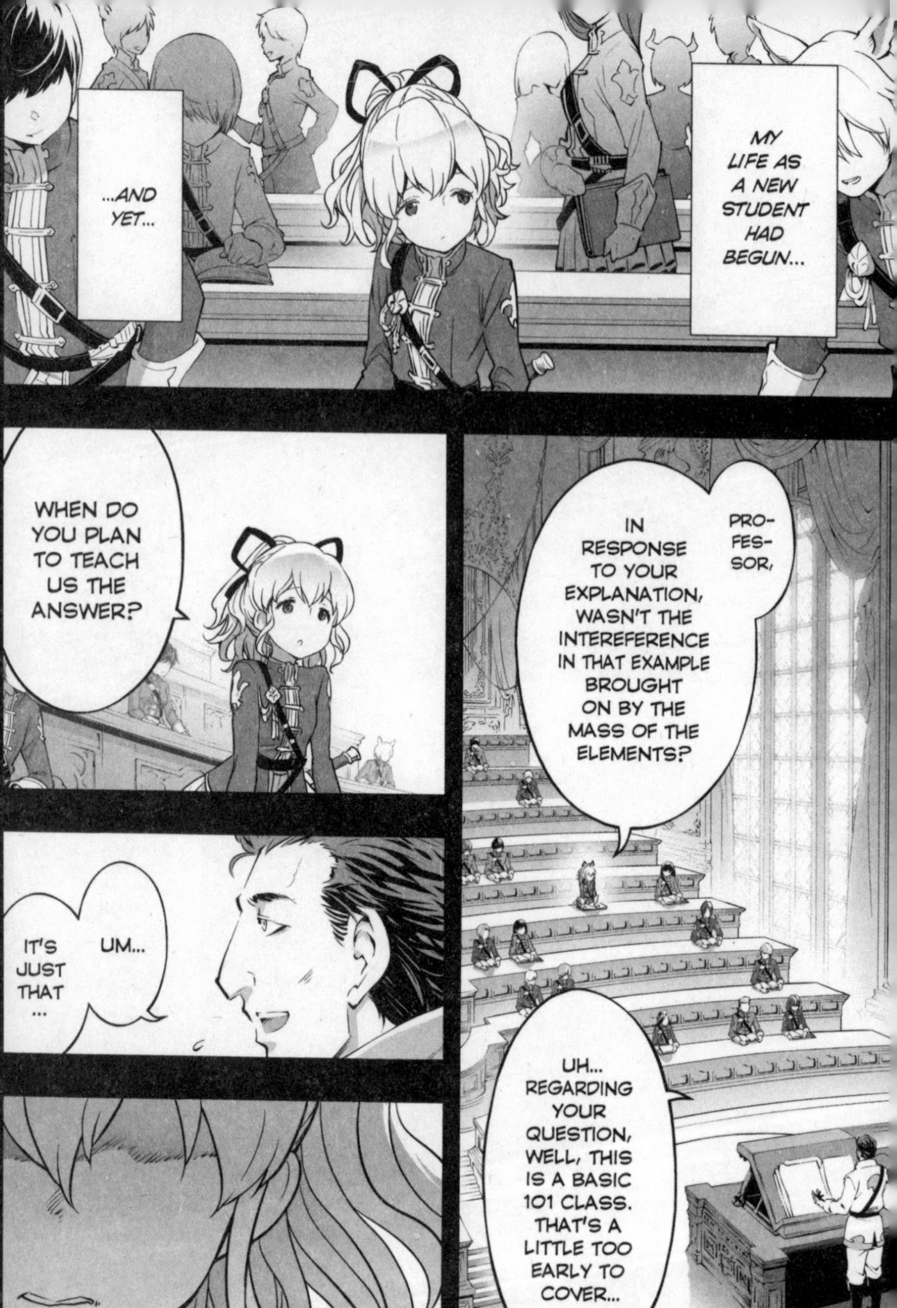
MY LIFE AS A NEW STUDENT HAD BEGUN...
...AND YET...
PRO-FES-SOR,
IN RESPONSE TO YOUR EXPLANATION, WASN'T THE INTEREFERENCE IN THAT EXAMPLE BROUGHT ON BY THE MASS OF THE ELEMENTS?
UH... REGARDING YOUR QUESTION, WELL, THIS IS A BASIC 101 CLASS. THAT'S A LITTLE TOO EARLY TO COVER...
WHEN DO YOU PLAN TO TEACH US THE ANSWER?
UM...
IT'S JUST THAT ...

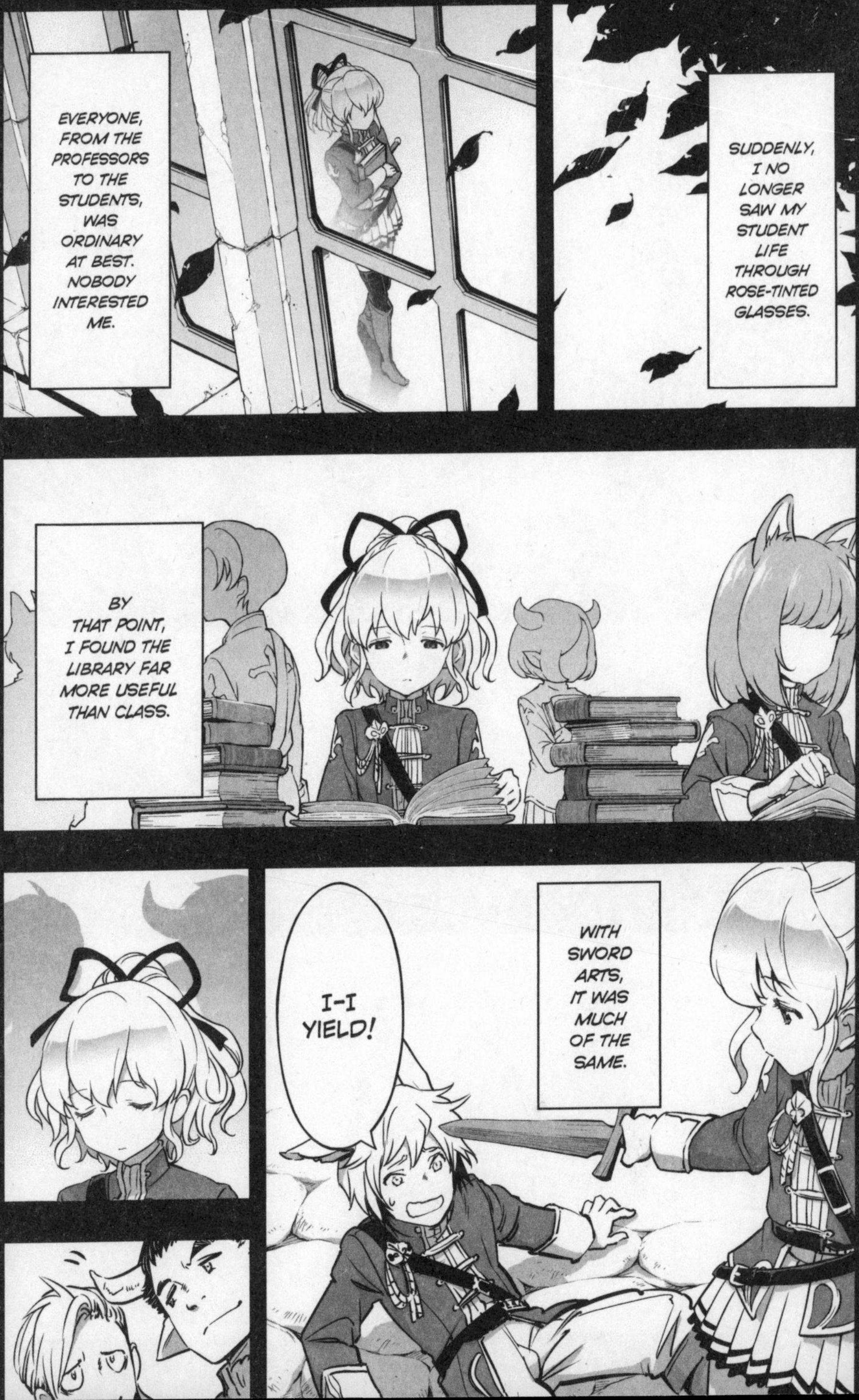
SUDDENLY, I NO LONGER SAW MY STUDENT LIFE THROUGH ROSE-TINTED GLASSES.
EVERYONE, FROM THE PROFESSORS TO THE STUDENTS, WAS ORDINARY AT BEST. NOBODY INTERESTED ME.
BY THAT POINT, I FOUND THE LIBRARY FAR MORE USEFUL THAN CLASS.
WITH SWORD ARTS, IT WAS MUCH OF THE SAME.
I-I YIELD!

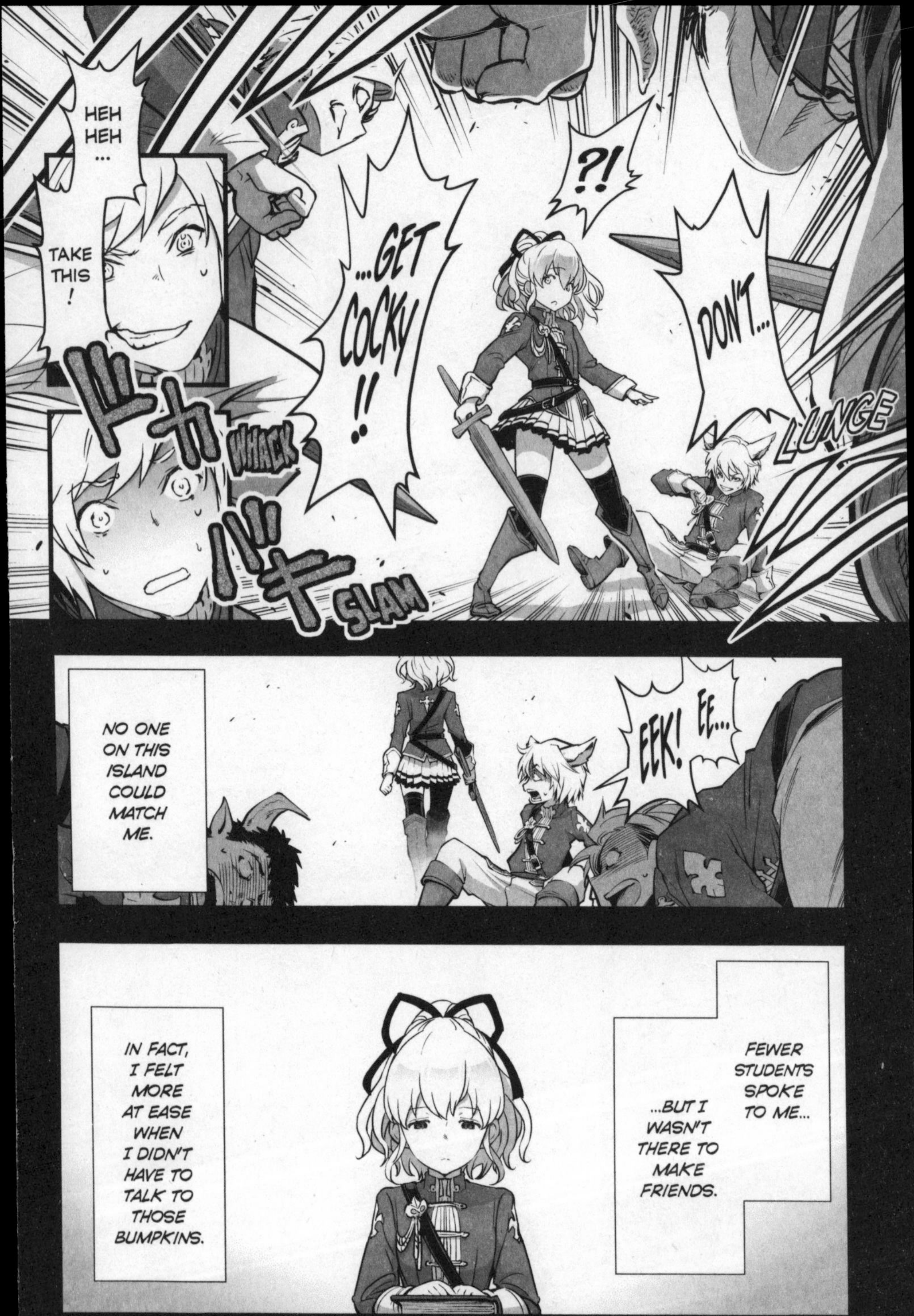
?!
DON'T...
LUNGE
...GET COCKY!!
HEH HEH ...
TAKE THIS!
ドカ WHACK
バキ SLAM
EEK! EE...
NO ONE ON THIS ISLAND COULD MATCH ME.
FEWER STUDENTS SPOKE TO ME...
...BUT I WASN'T THERE TO MAKE FRIENDS.
IN FACT, I FELT MORE AT EASE WHEN I DIDN'T HAVE TO TALK TO THOSE BUMPKINS.

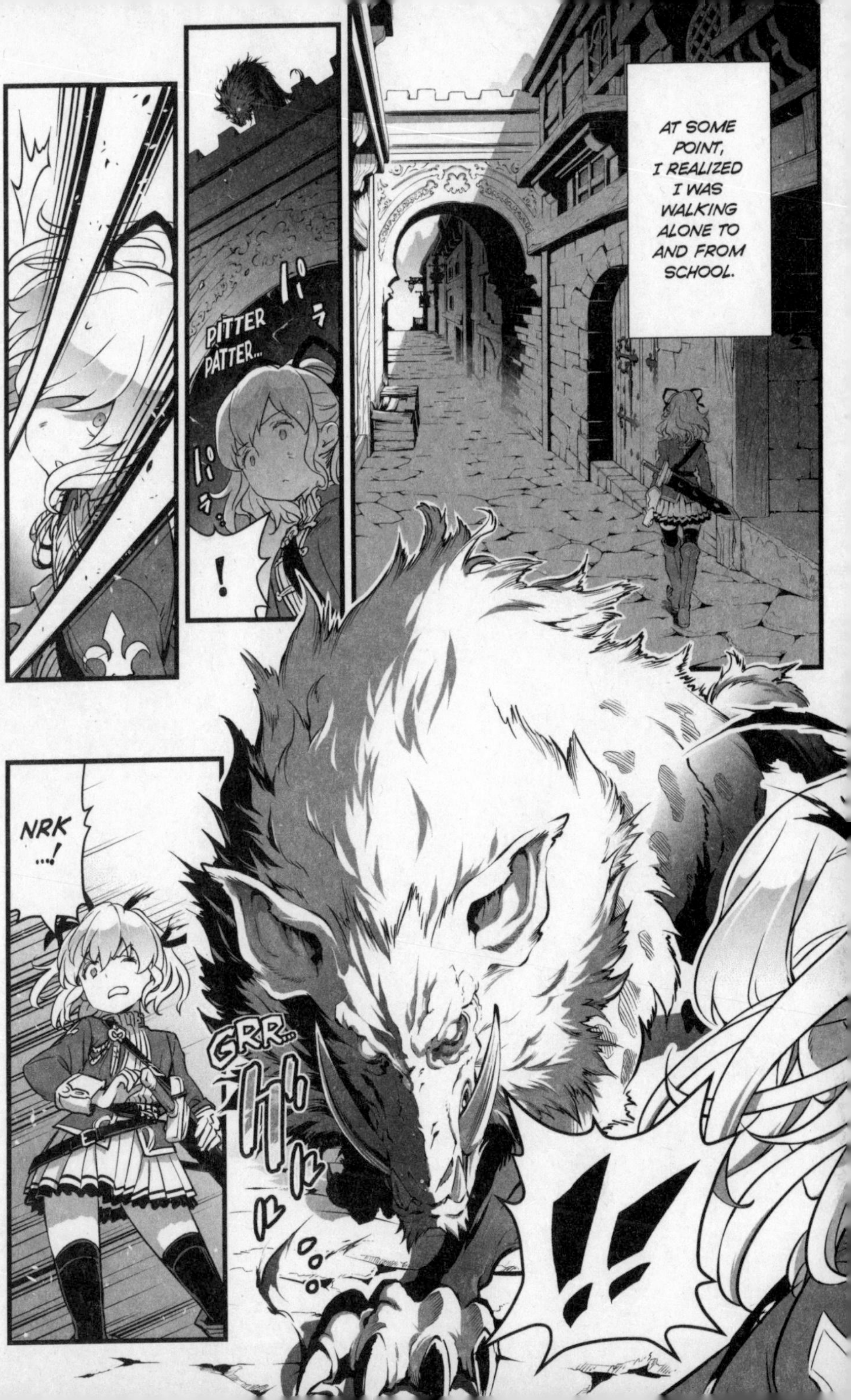

AT SOME POINT, I REALIZED I WAS WALKING ALONE TO AND FROM SCHOOL.
PITTER PATTER...
パラ
パラ
!
GRR...
!!
NRK ...!

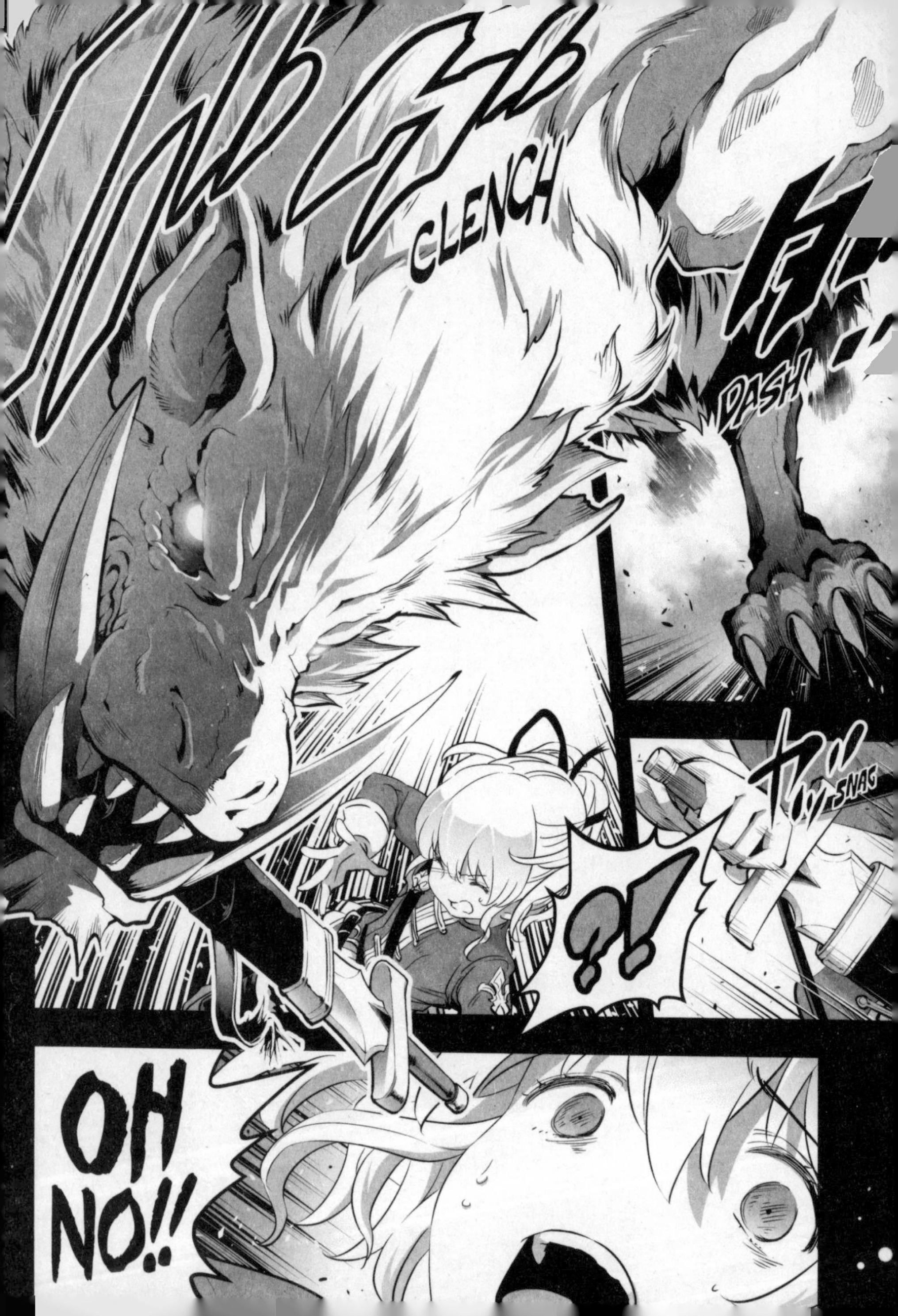
DASH
CLENCH
SNAG
?!
OH NO!!

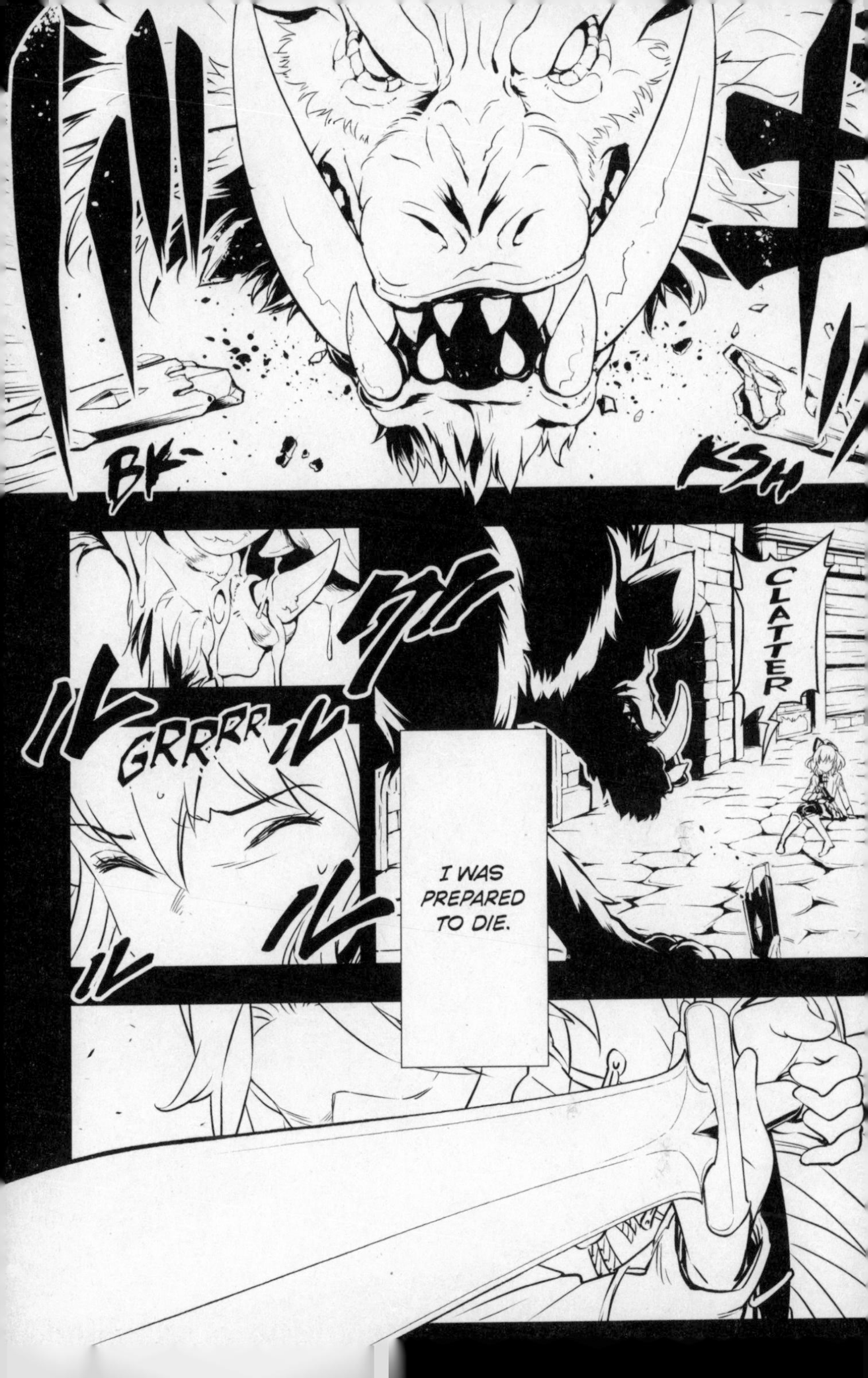
BK-
KSH
CLATTER
I WAS PREPARED TO DIE.
GRRRR

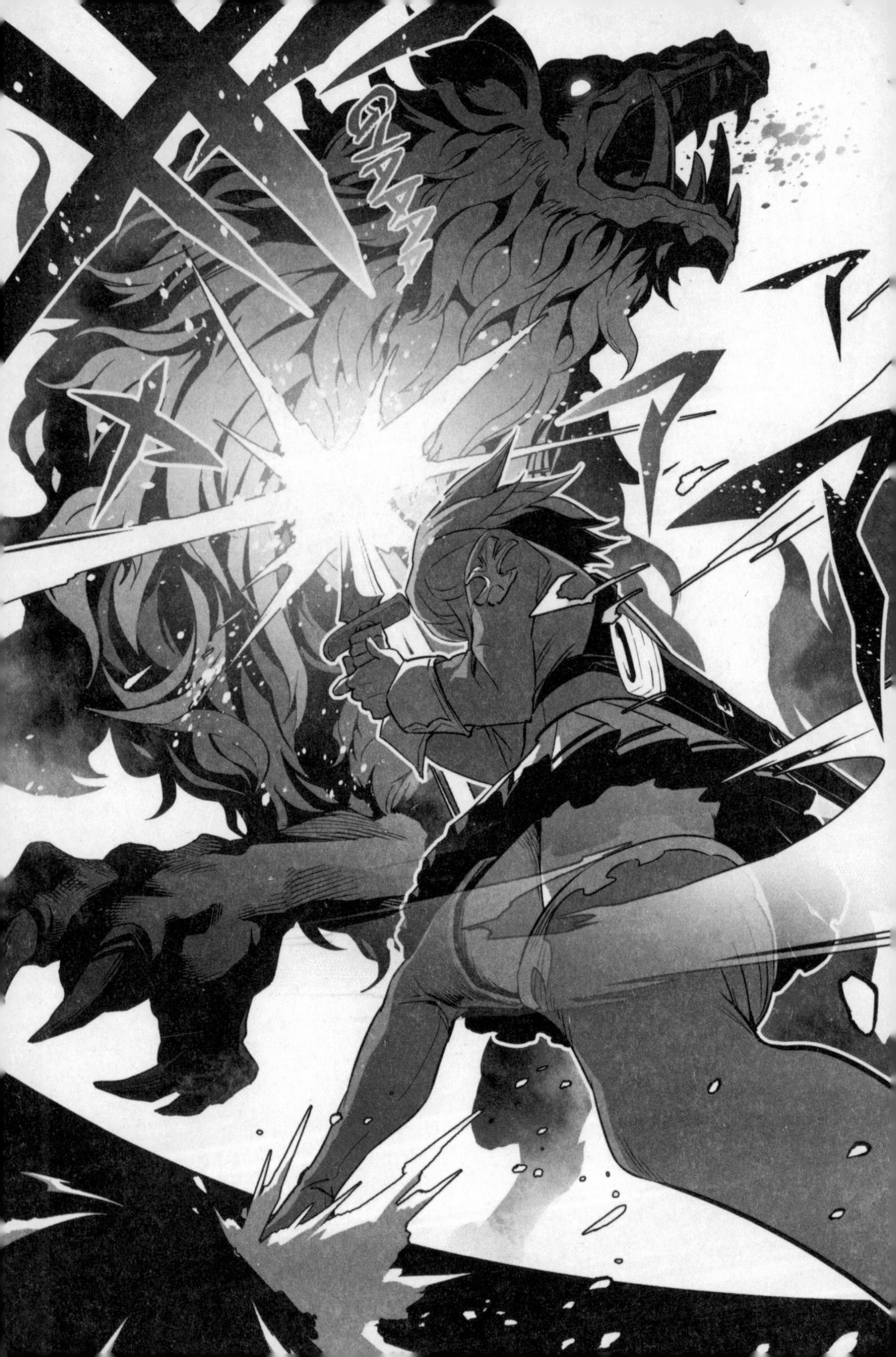
GNAAAA

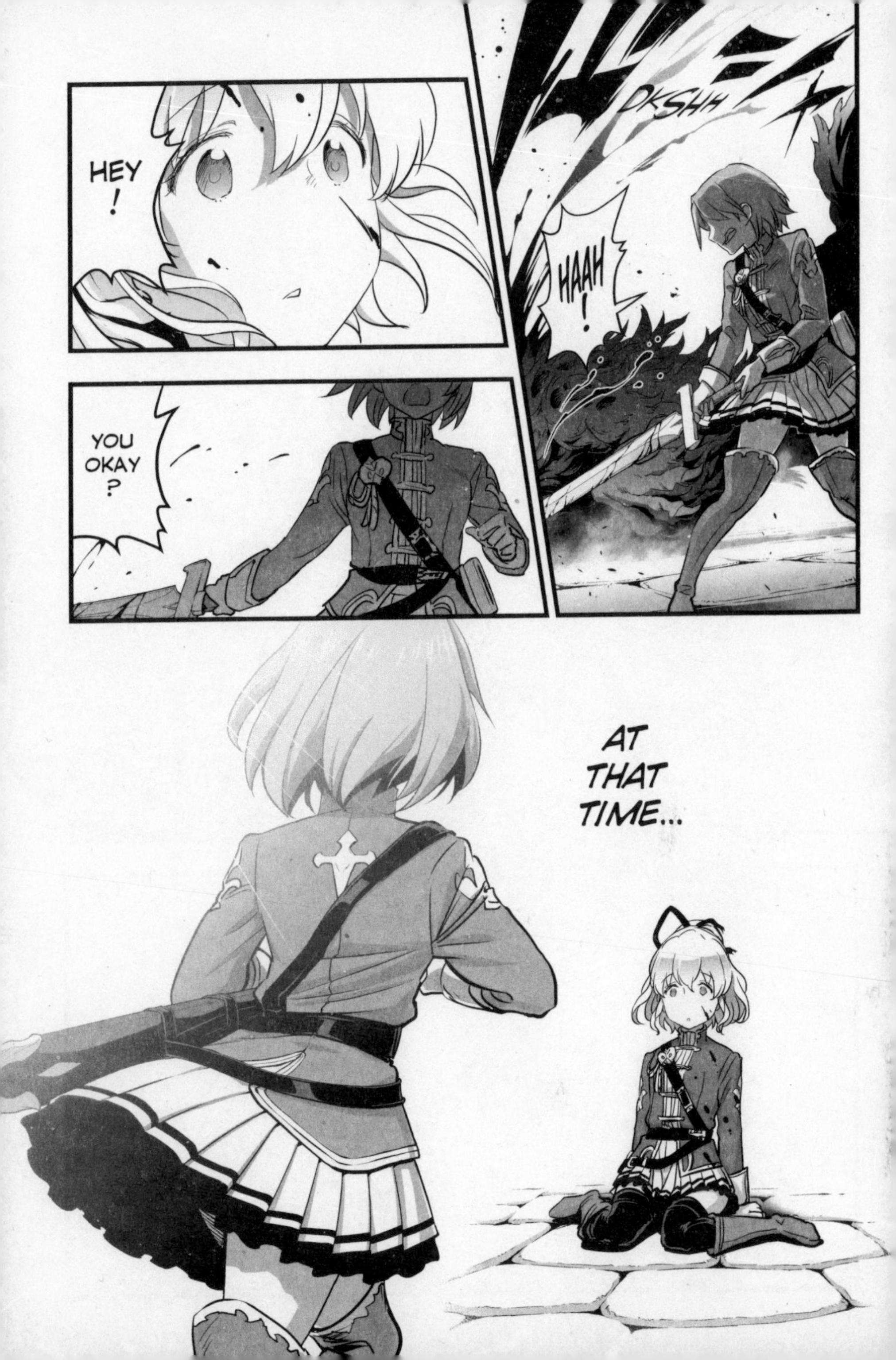
DKSHH
HAAH!
HEY!
YOU OKAY?
AT THAT TIME...

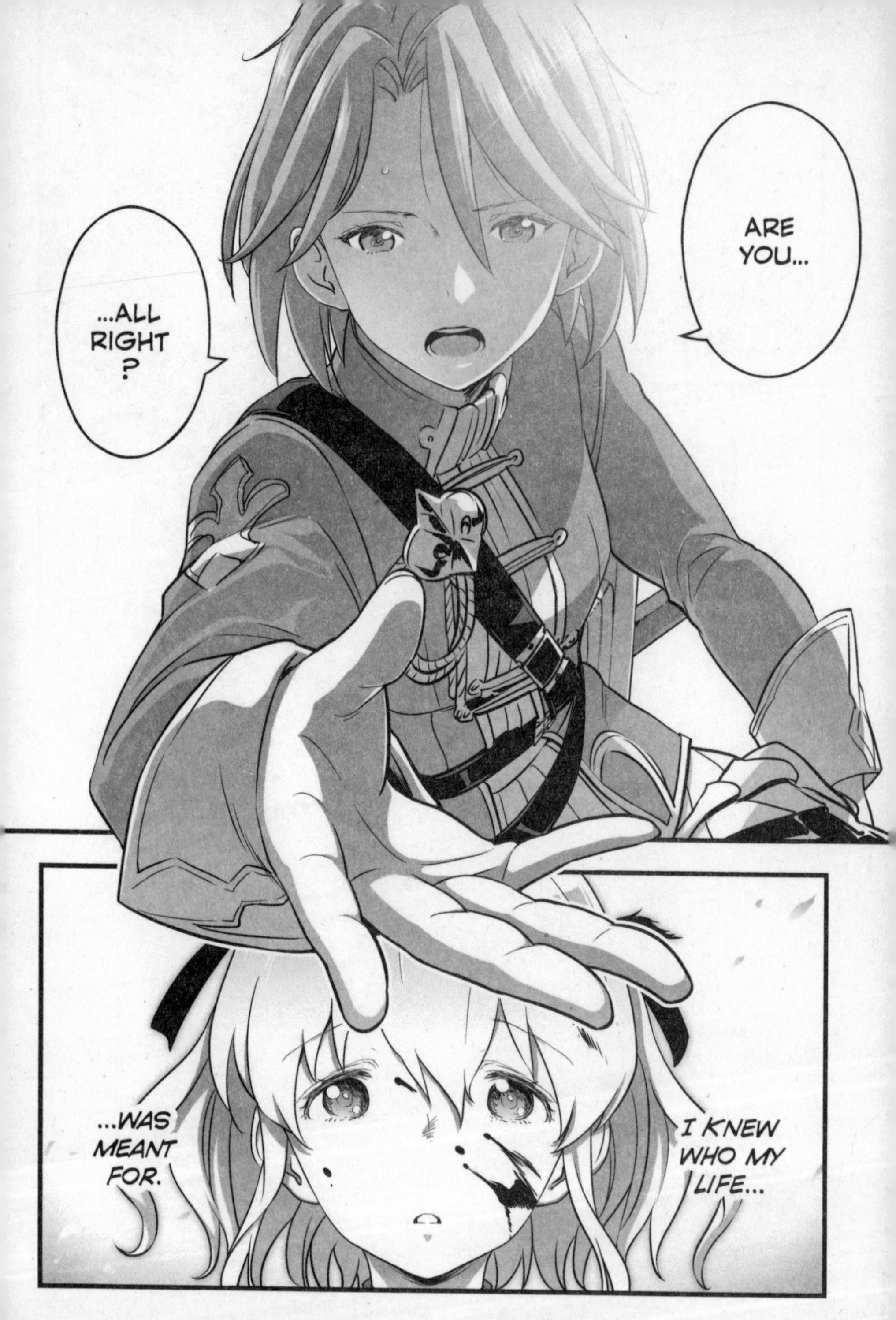
ARE YOU...
...ALL RIGHT?
I KNEW WHO MY LIFE...
...WAS MEANT FOR.

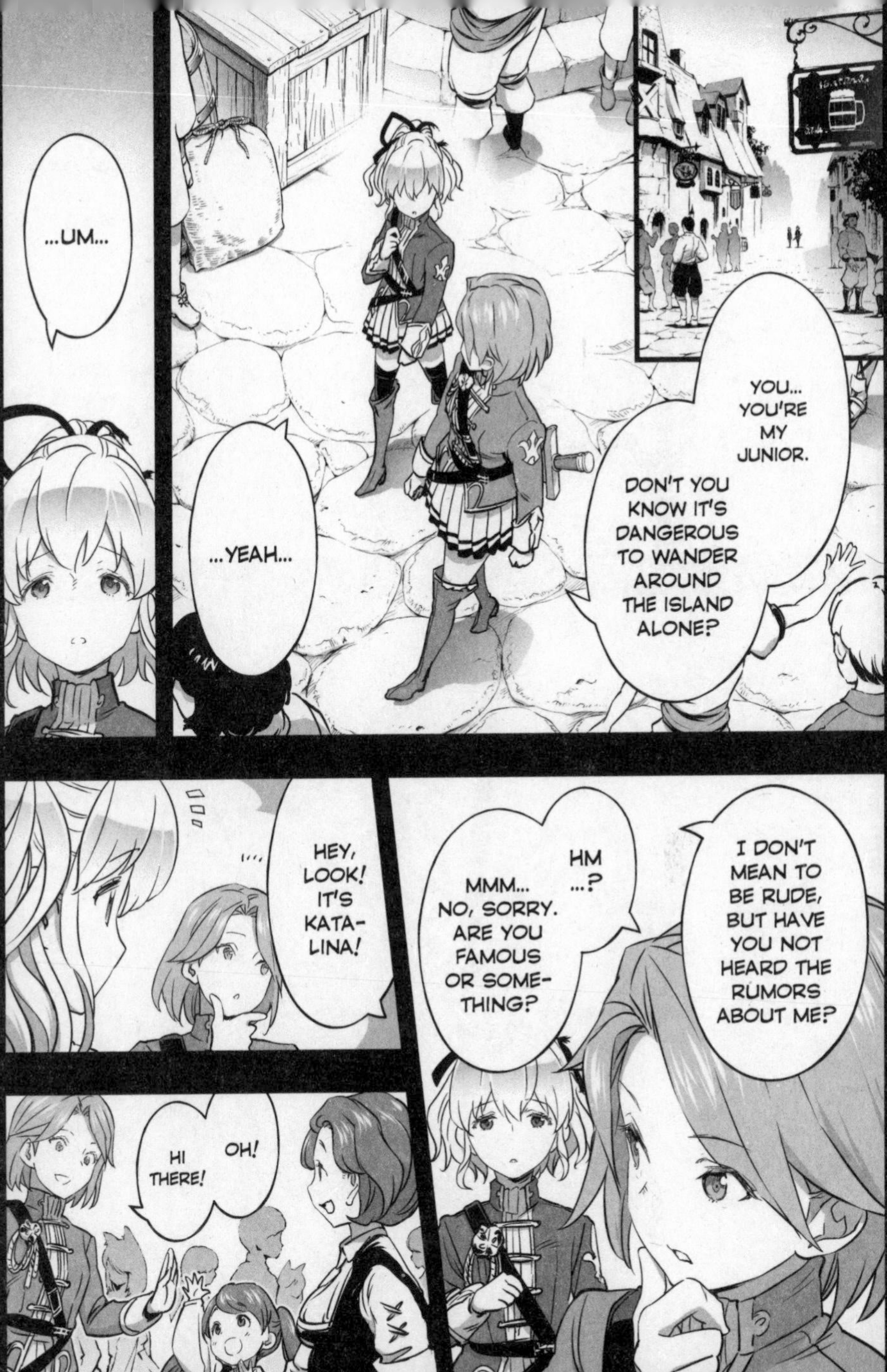
YOU... YOU'RE MY JUNIOR.
DON'T YOU KNOW IT'S DANGEROUS TO WANDER AROUND THE ISLAND ALONE?
...YEAH...
...UM...
I DON'T MEAN TO BE RUDE, BUT HAVE YOU NOT HEARD THE RUMORS ABOUT ME?
HM ...?
MMM... NO, SORRY. ARE YOU FAMOUS OR SOME-THING?
HEY, LOOK! IT'S KATA-LINA!
OH!
HI THERE!

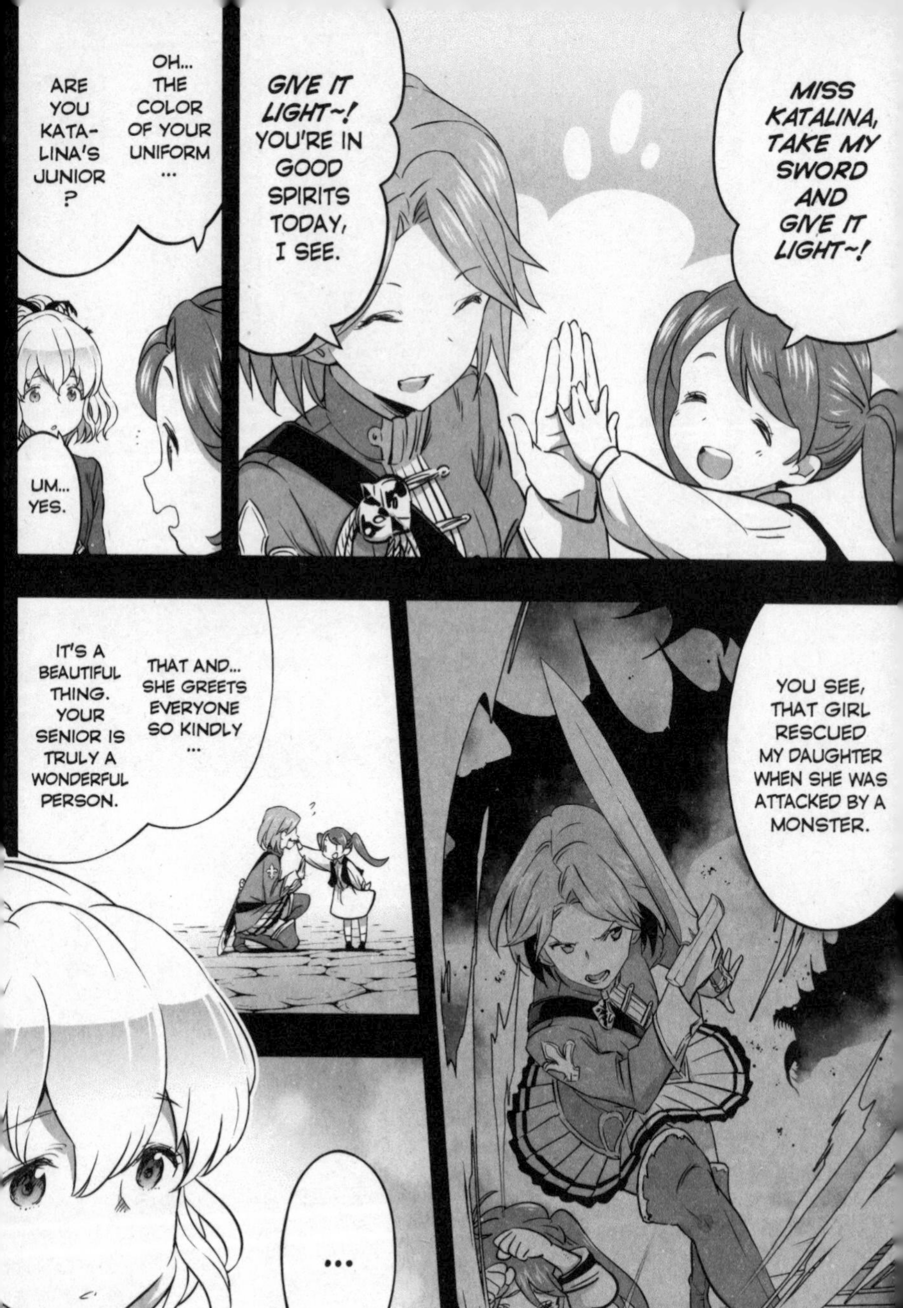
MISS KATALINA, TAKE MY SWORD AND GIVE IT LIGHT~!
GIVE IT LIGHT~! YOU'RE IN GOOD SPIRITS TODAY, I SEE.
OH... THE COLOR OF YOUR UNIFORM ...
ARE YOU KATA-LINA'S JUNIOR ?
UM... YES.
YOU SEE, THAT GIRL RESCUED MY DAUGHTER WHEN SHE WAS ATTACKED BY A MONSTER.
THAT AND... SHE GREETS EVERYONE SO KINDLY ...
IT'S A BEAUTIFUL THING. YOUR SENIOR IS TRULY A WONDERFUL PERSON.
...

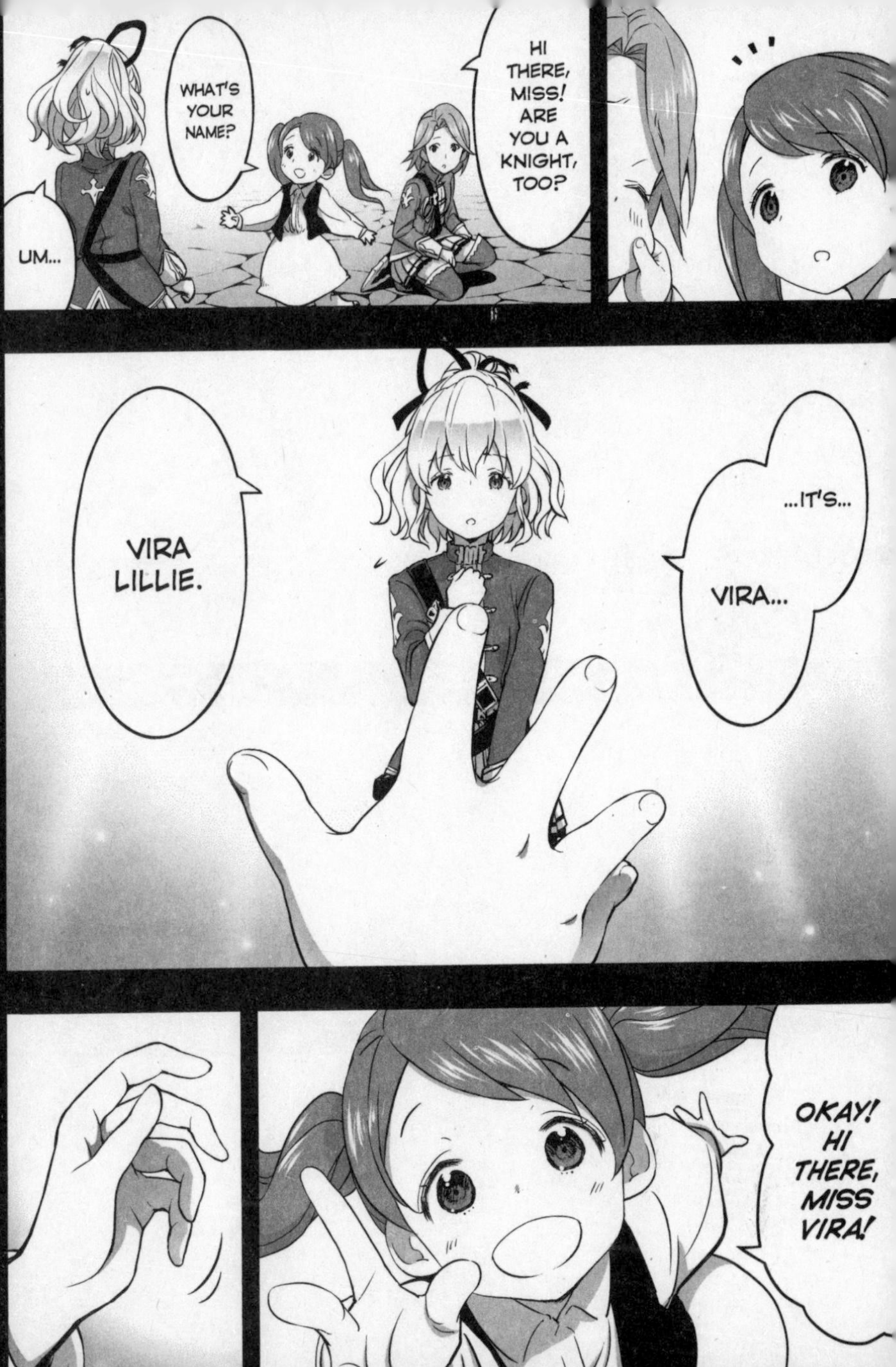
HI THERE, MISS! ARE YOU A KNIGHT, TOO?
WHAT'S YOUR NAME?
UM...
...IT'S...
VIRA...
VIRA LILLIE.
OKAY! HI THERE, MISS VIRA!

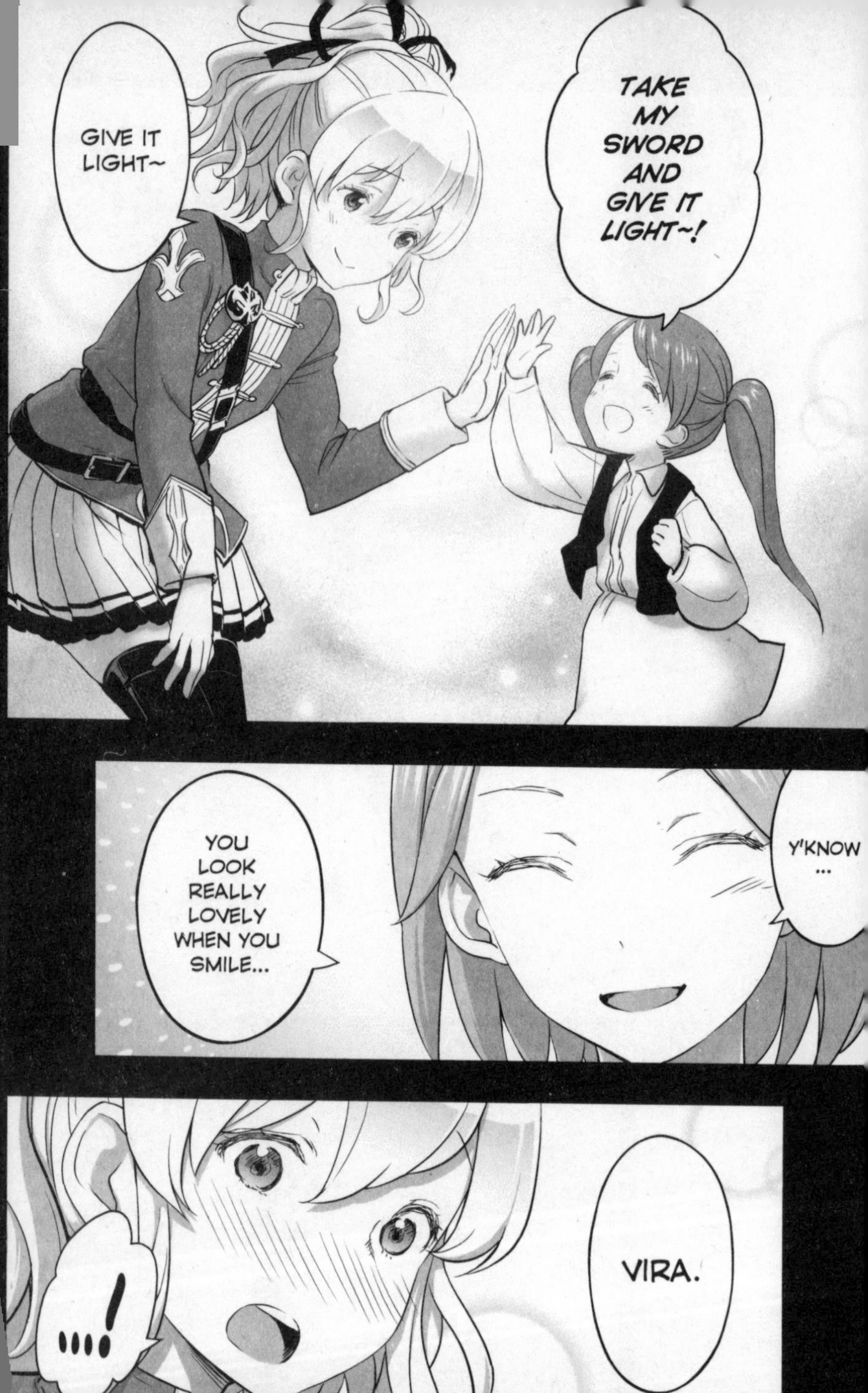
TAKE MY SWORD AND GIVE IT LIGHT~!
GIVE IT LIGHT~
Y'KNOW ...
YOU LOOK REALLY LOVELY WHEN YOU SMILE...
VIRA.
....!

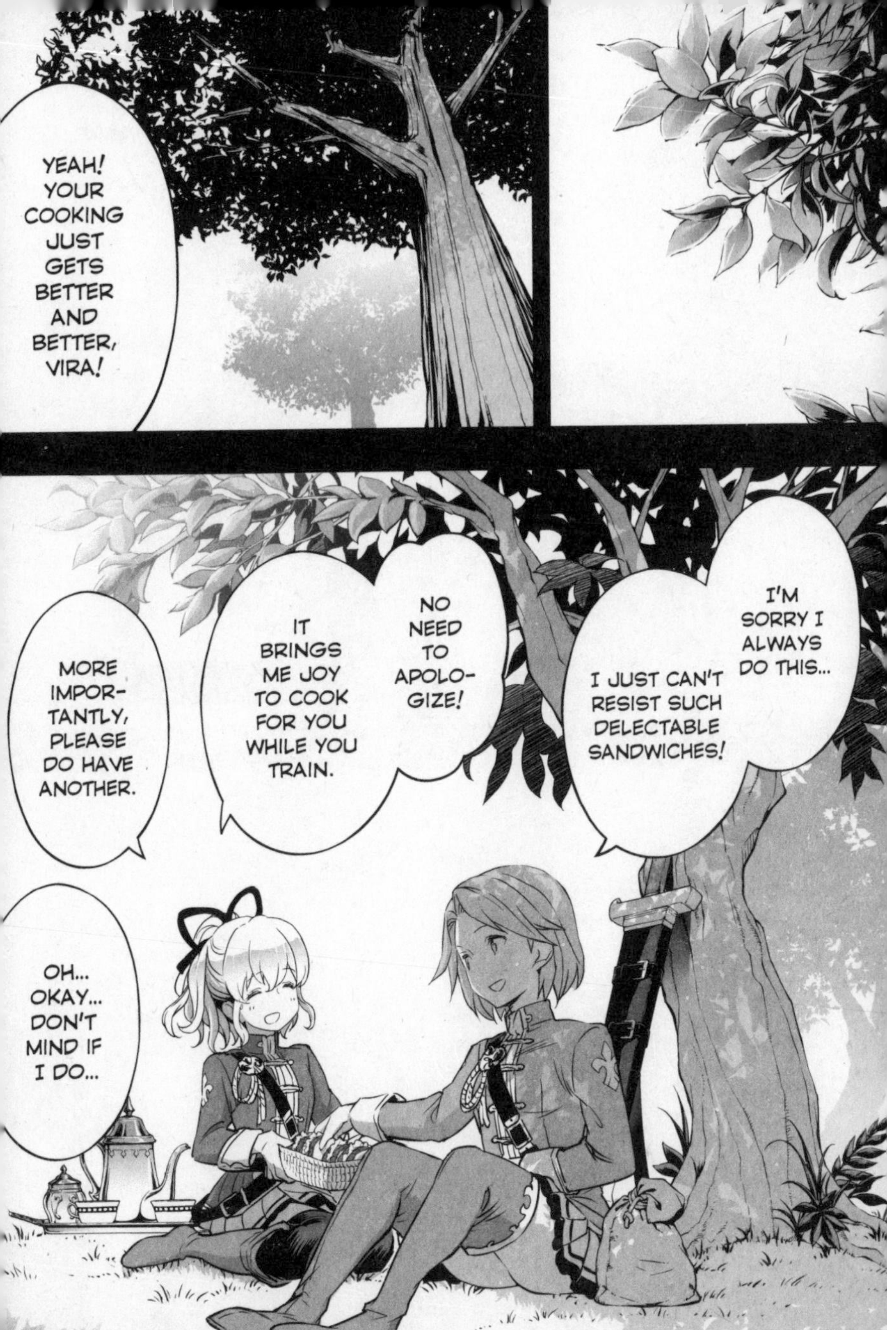
YEAH! YOUR COOKING JUST GETS BETTER AND BETTER, VIRA!
I'M SORRY I ALWAYS DO THIS...
I JUST CAN'T RESIST SUCH DELECTABLE SANDWICHES!
NO NEED TO APOLOGIZE!
IT BRINGS ME JOY TO COOK FOR YOU WHILE YOU TRAIN.
MORE IMPORTANTLY, PLEASE DO HAVE ANOTHER.
OH... OKAY... DON'T MIND IF I DO...

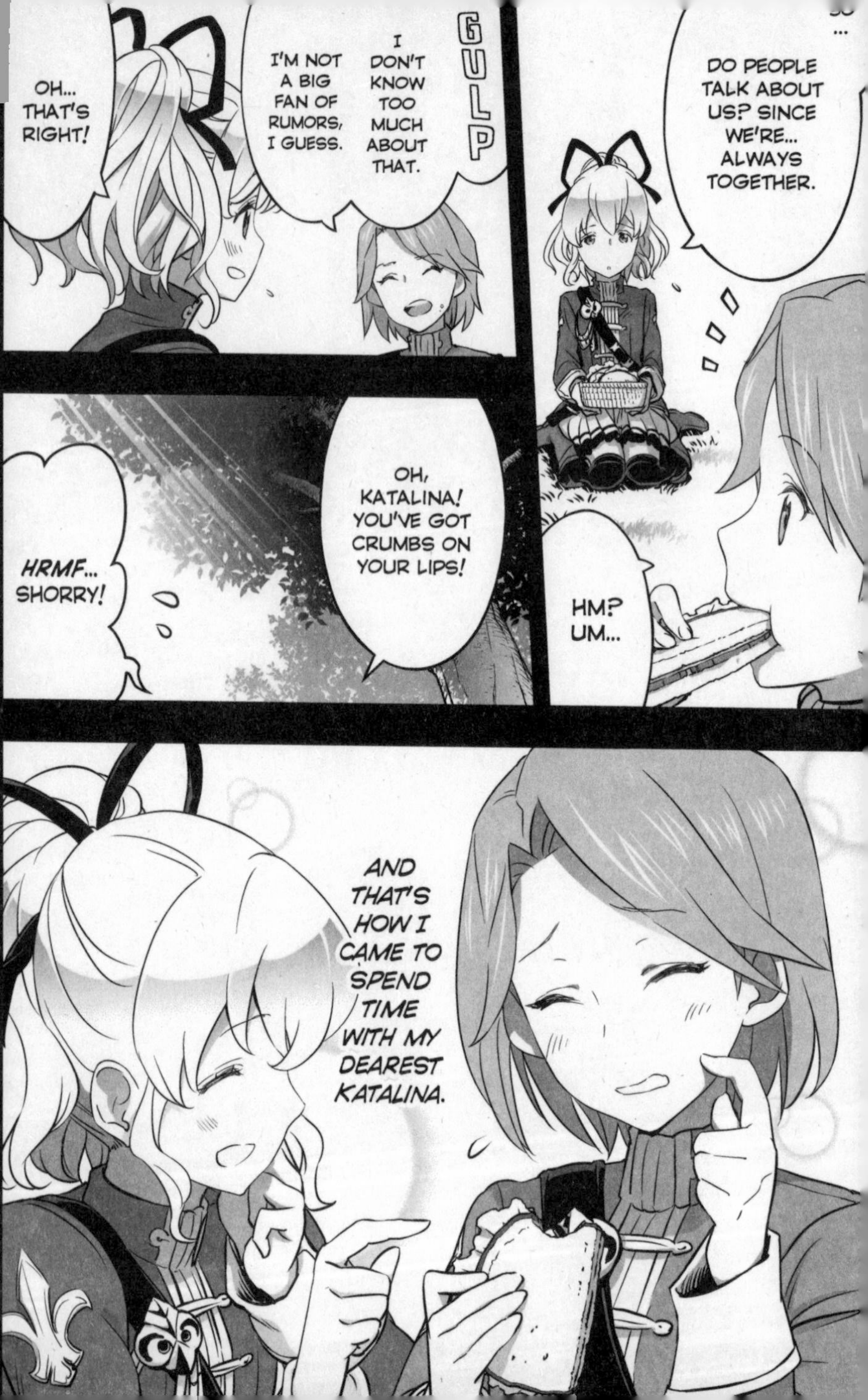

DO PEOPLE TALK ABOUT US? SINCE WE'RE... ALWAYS TOGETHER.
HM? UM...
GULP
I DON'T KNOW TOO MUCH ABOUT THAT.
I'M NOT A BIG FAN OF RUMORS, I GUESS.
OH... THAT'S RIGHT!
OH, KATALINA! YOU'VE GOT CRUMBS ON YOUR LIPS!
HRMF... SHORRY!
AND THAT'S HOW I CAME TO SPEND TIME WITH MY DEAREST KATALINA.

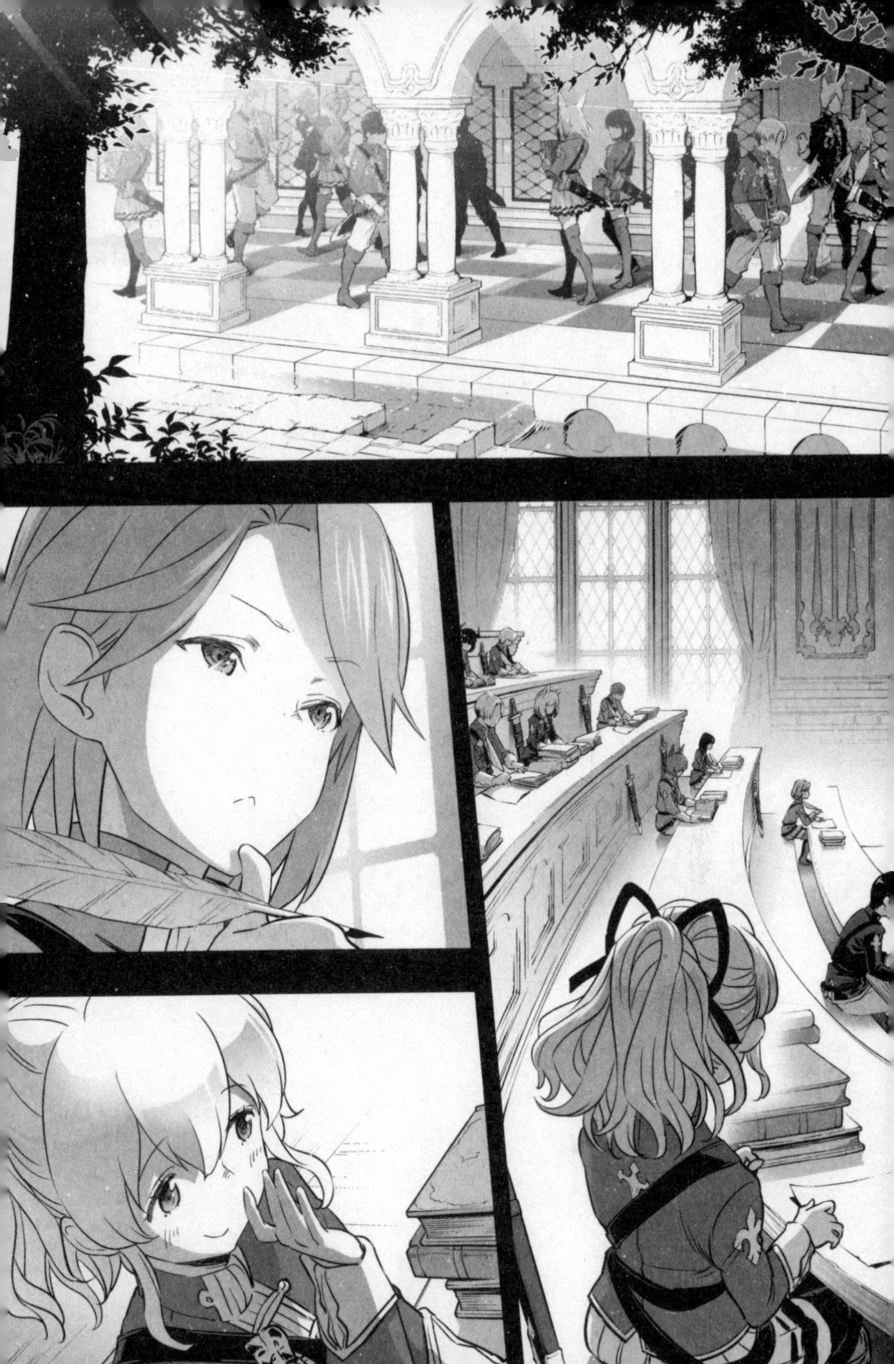

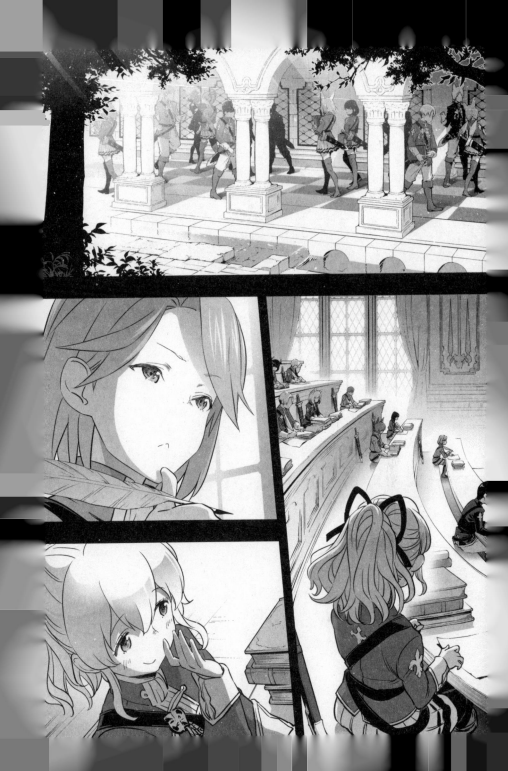

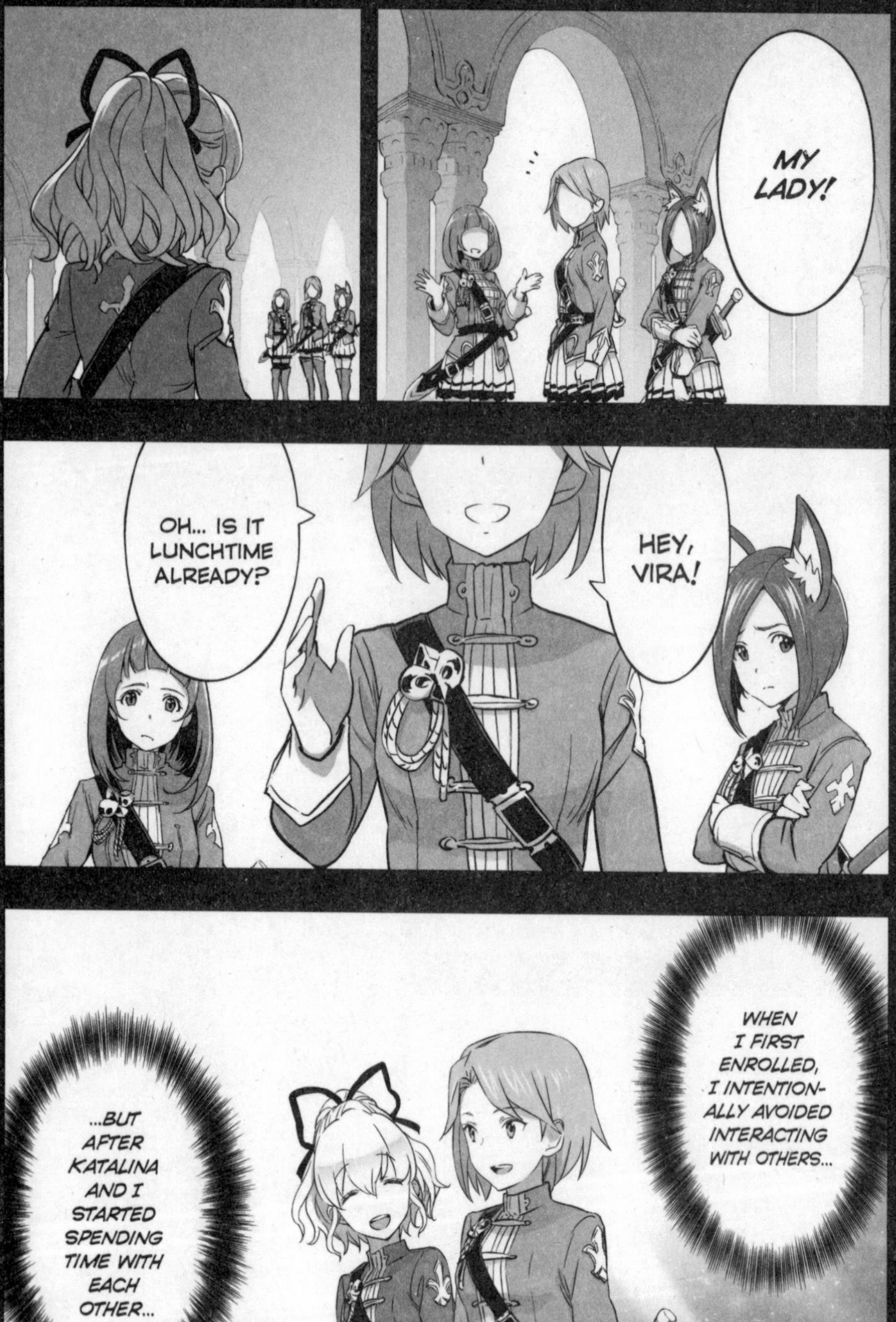
MY LADY!
HEY, VIRA!
OH... IS IT LUNCHTIME ALREADY?
WHEN I FIRST ENROLLED, I INTENTION-ALLY AVOIDED INTERACTING WITH OTHERS...
...BUT AFTER KATALINA AND I STARTED SPENDING TIME WITH EACH OTHER...

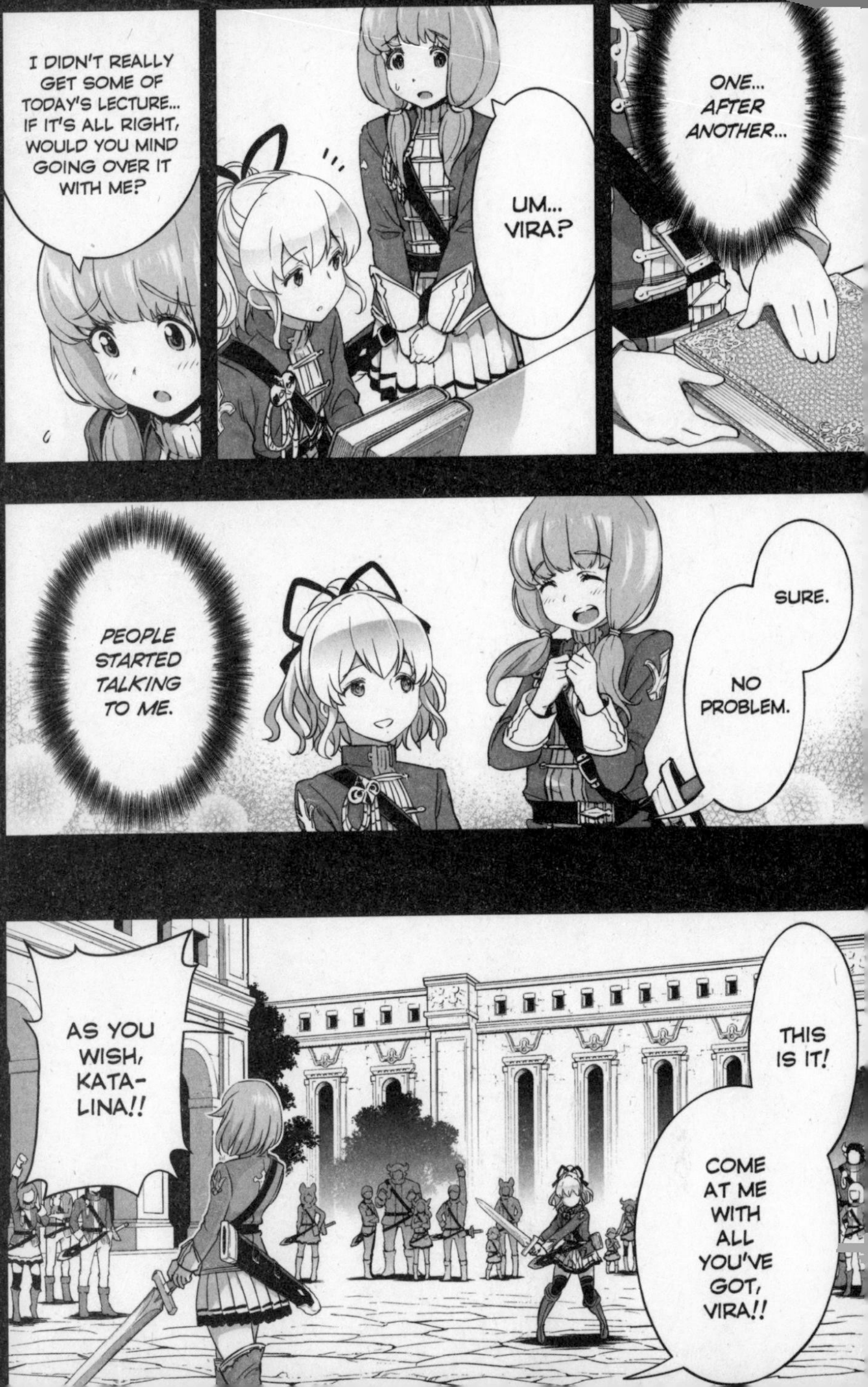
ONE... AFTER ANOTHER...
UM... VIRA?
I DIDN'T REALLY GET SOME OF TODAY'S LECTURE... IF IT'S ALL RIGHT, WOULD YOU MIND GOING OVER IT WITH ME?
SURE.
NO PROBLEM.
PEOPLE STARTED TALKING TO ME.
THIS IS IT!
COME AT ME WITH ALL YOU'VE GOT, VIRA!!
AS YOU WISH, KATA-LINA!!

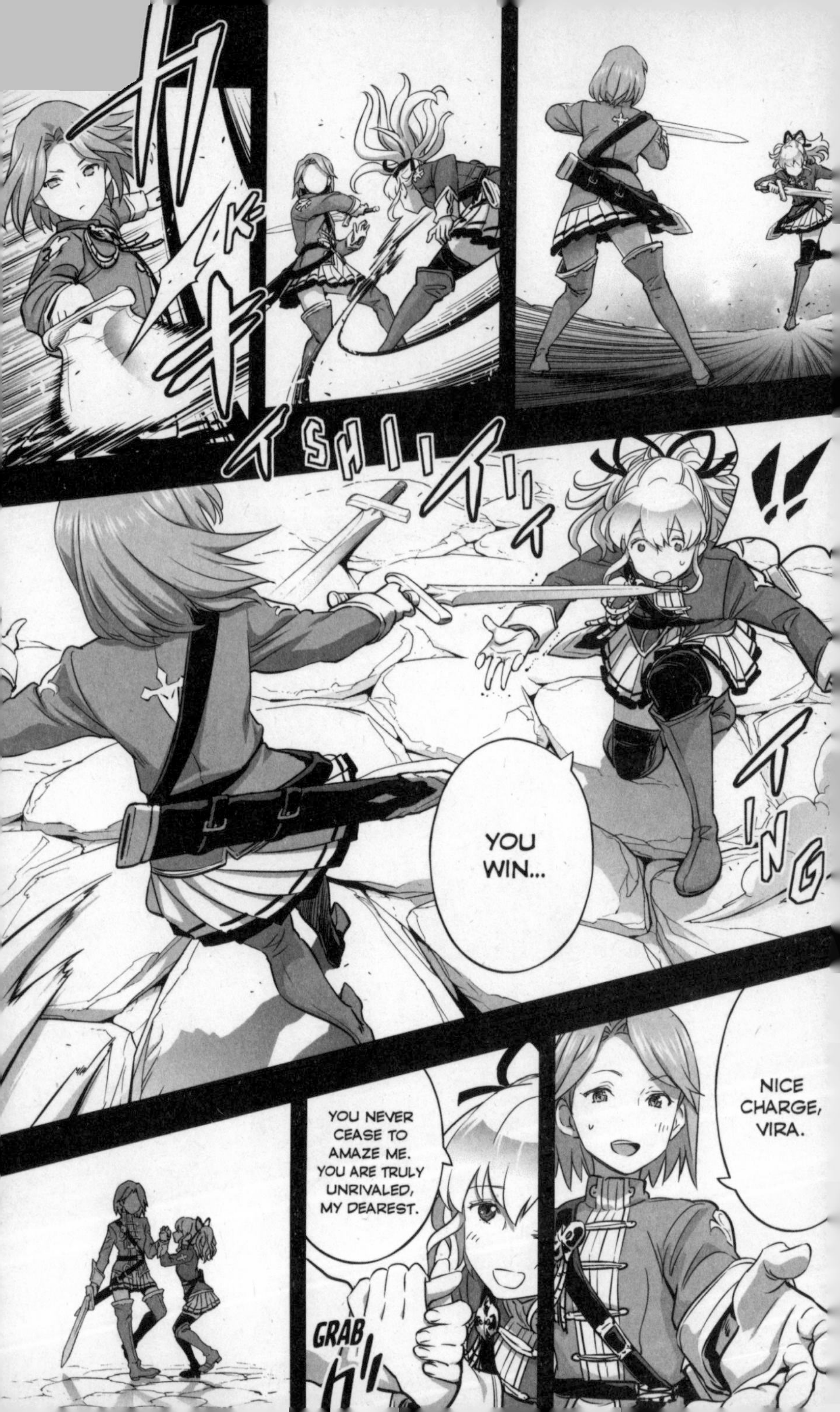
K
SHII
!!
TING
YOU WIN...
NICE CHARGE, VIRA.
YOU NEVER CEASE TO AMAZE ME. YOU ARE TRULY UNRIVALED, MY DEAREST.
GRAB

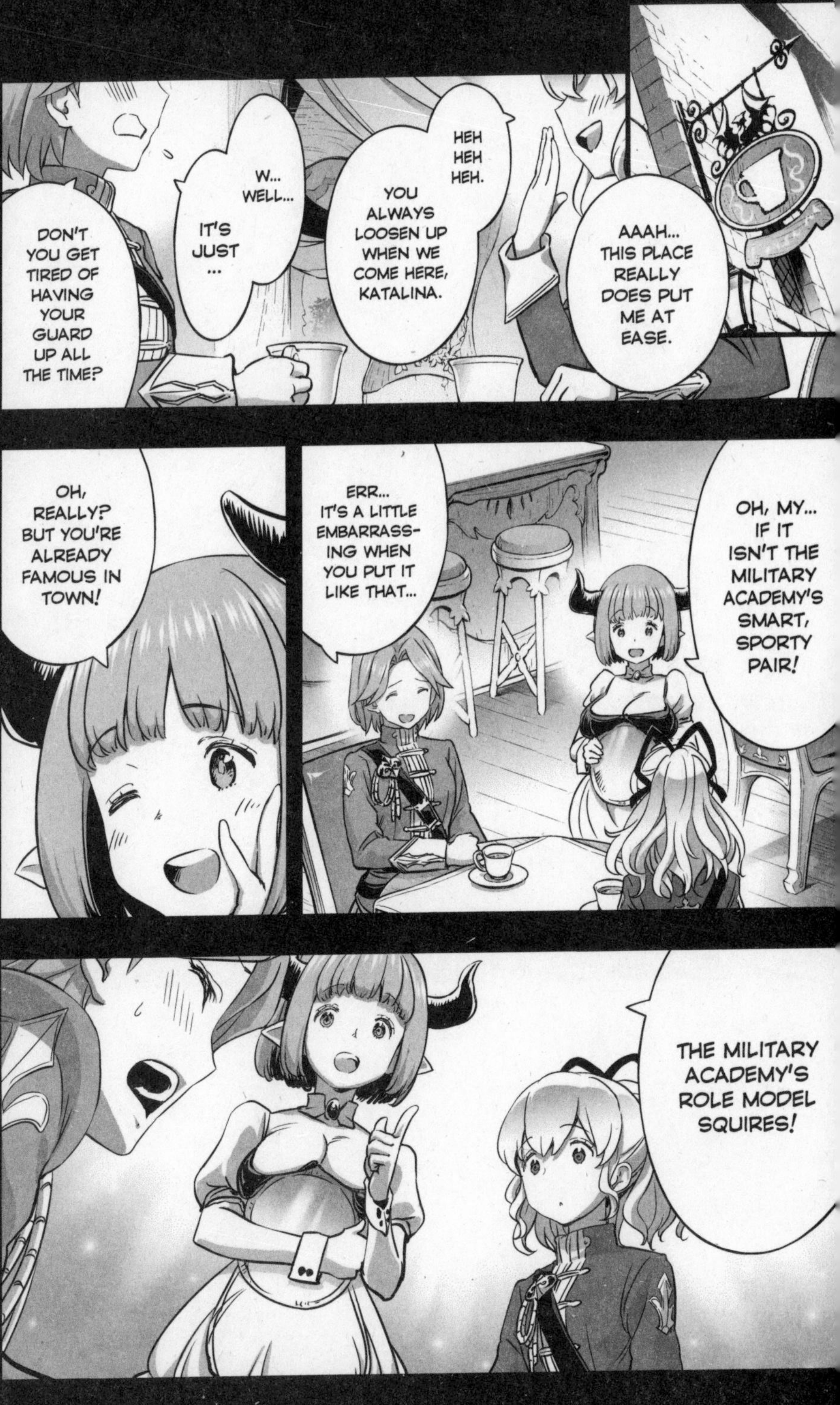
AAAH... THIS PLACE REALLY DOES PUT ME AT EASE.
HEH HEH HEH.
YOU ALWAYS LOOSEN UP WHEN WE COME HERE, KATALINA.
W... WELL...
IT'S JUST ...
DON'T YOU GET TIRED OF HAVING YOUR GUARD UP ALL THE TIME?
OH, MY... IF IT ISN'T THE MILITARY ACADEMY'S SMART, SPORTY PAIR!
ERR... IT'S A LITTLE EMBARRASS-ING WHEN YOU PUT IT LIKE THAT...
OH, REALLY? BUT YOU'RE ALREADY FAMOUS IN TOWN!
THE MILITARY ACADEMY'S ROLE MODEL SQUIRES!

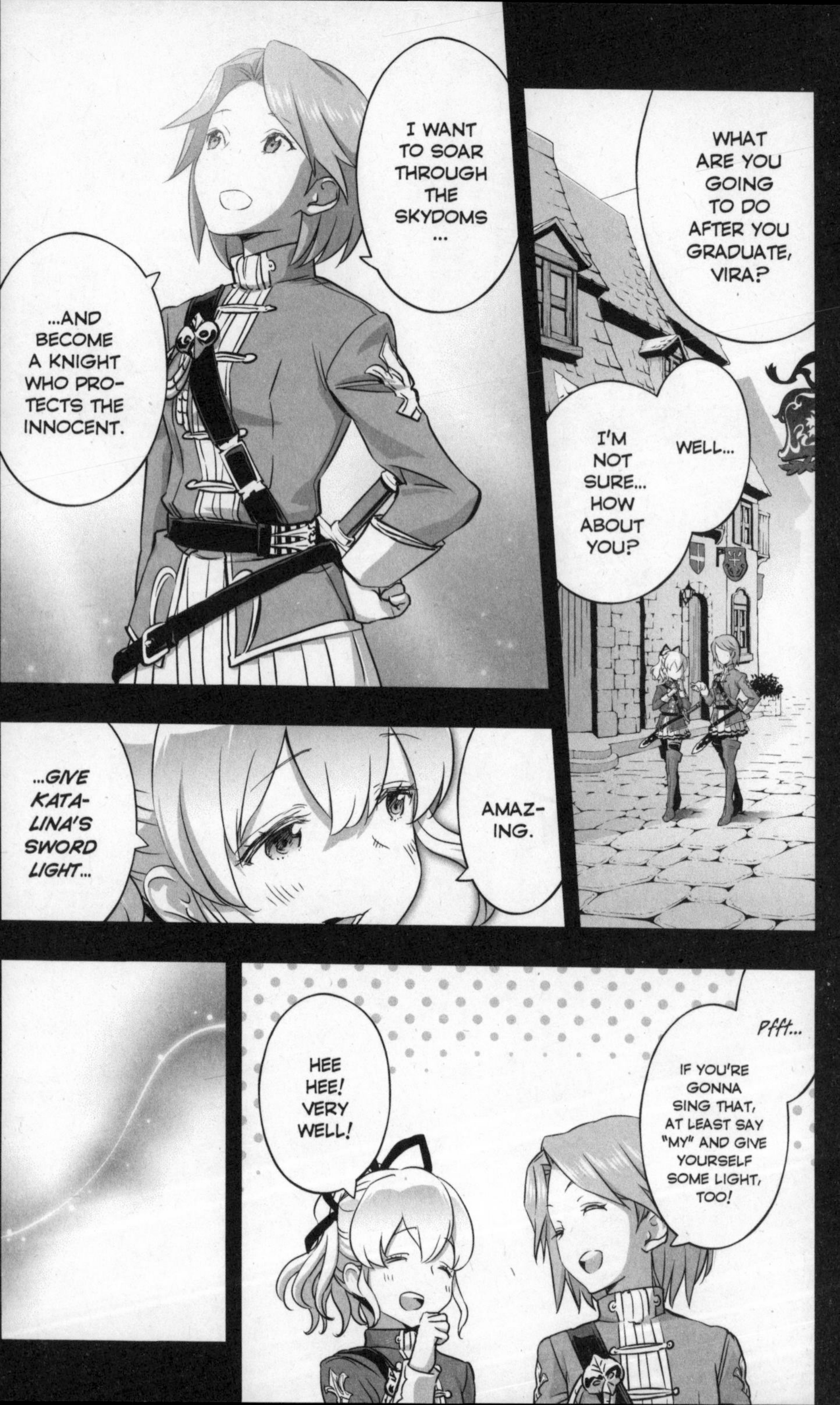
WHAT ARE YOU GOING TO DO AFTER YOU GRADUATE, VIRA?
WELL...
I'M NOT SURE... HOW ABOUT YOU?
I WANT TO SOAR THROUGH THE SKYDOMS...
...AND BECOME A KNIGHT WHO PROTECTS THE INNOCENT.
AMAZ-ING.
...GIVE KATA-LINA'S SWORD LIGHT...
Pfft...
IF YOU'RE GONNA SING THAT, AT LEAST SAY "MY" AND GIVE YOURSELF SOME LIGHT, TOO!
HEE HEE! VERY WELL!

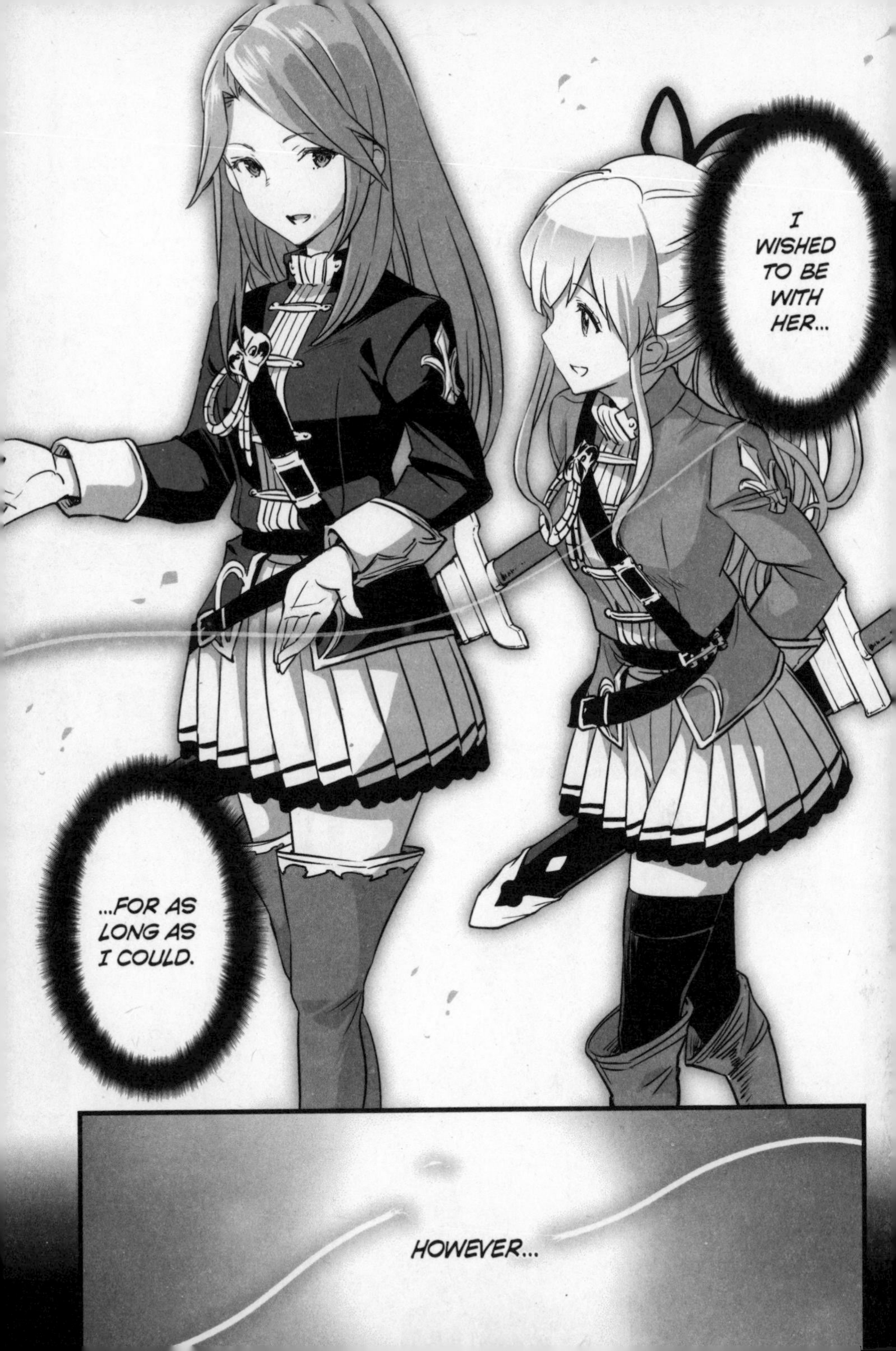
I WISHED TO BE WITH HER...
...FOR AS LONG AS I COULD.
HOWEVER...

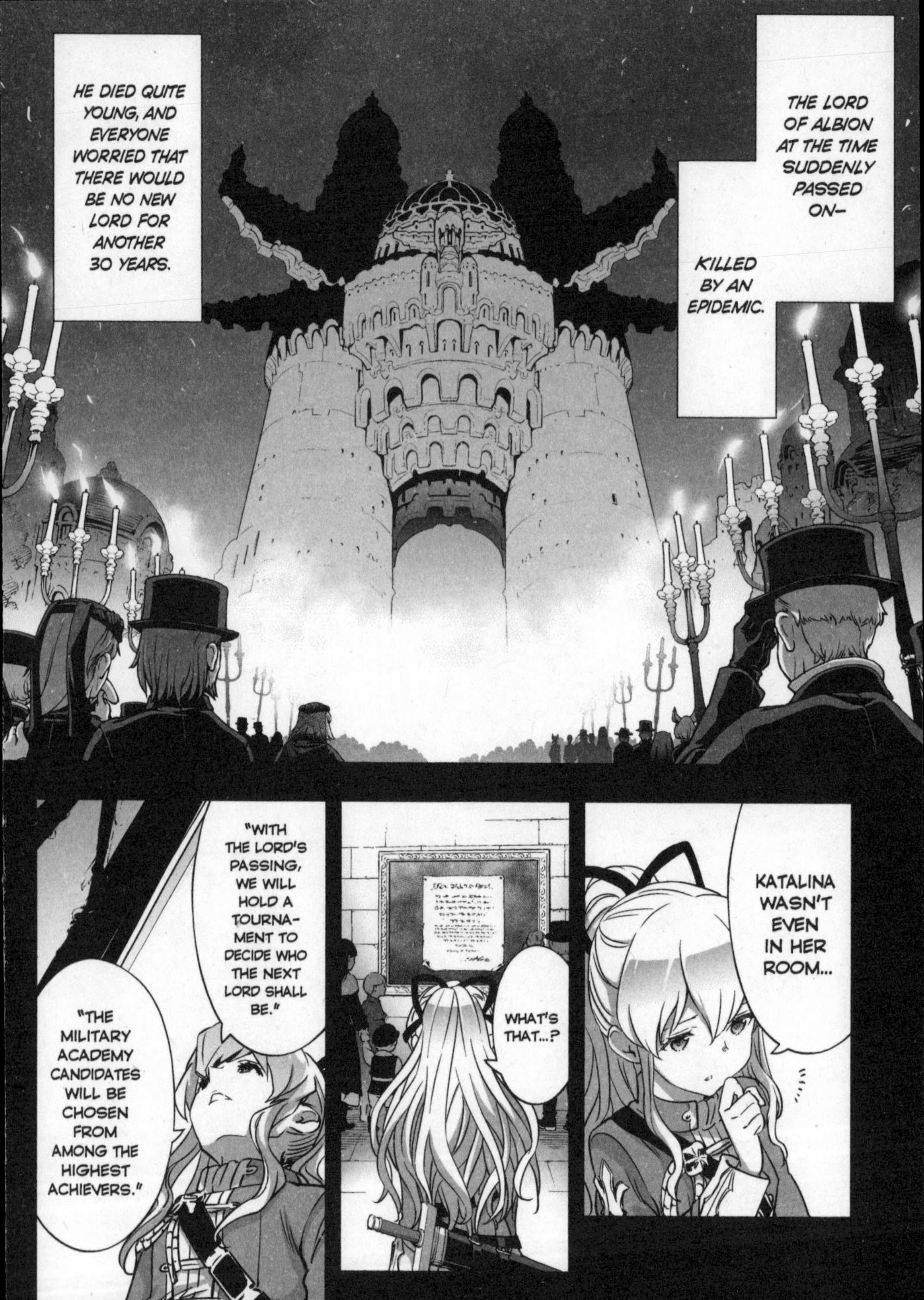
THE LORD OF ALBION AT THE TIME SUDDENLY PASSED ON—
KILLED BY AN EPIDEMIC.
HE DIED QUITE YOUNG, AND EVERYONE WORRIED THAT THERE WOULD BE NO NEW LORD FOR ANOTHER 30 YEARS.
KATALINA WASN'T EVEN IN HER ROOM...
WHAT'S THAT...?
"WITH THE LORD'S PASSING, WE WILL HOLD A TOURNA-MENT TO DECIDE WHO THE NEXT LORD SHALL BE."
"THE MILITARY ACADEMY CANDIDATES WILL BE CHOSEN FROM AMONG THE HIGHEST ACHIEVERS."

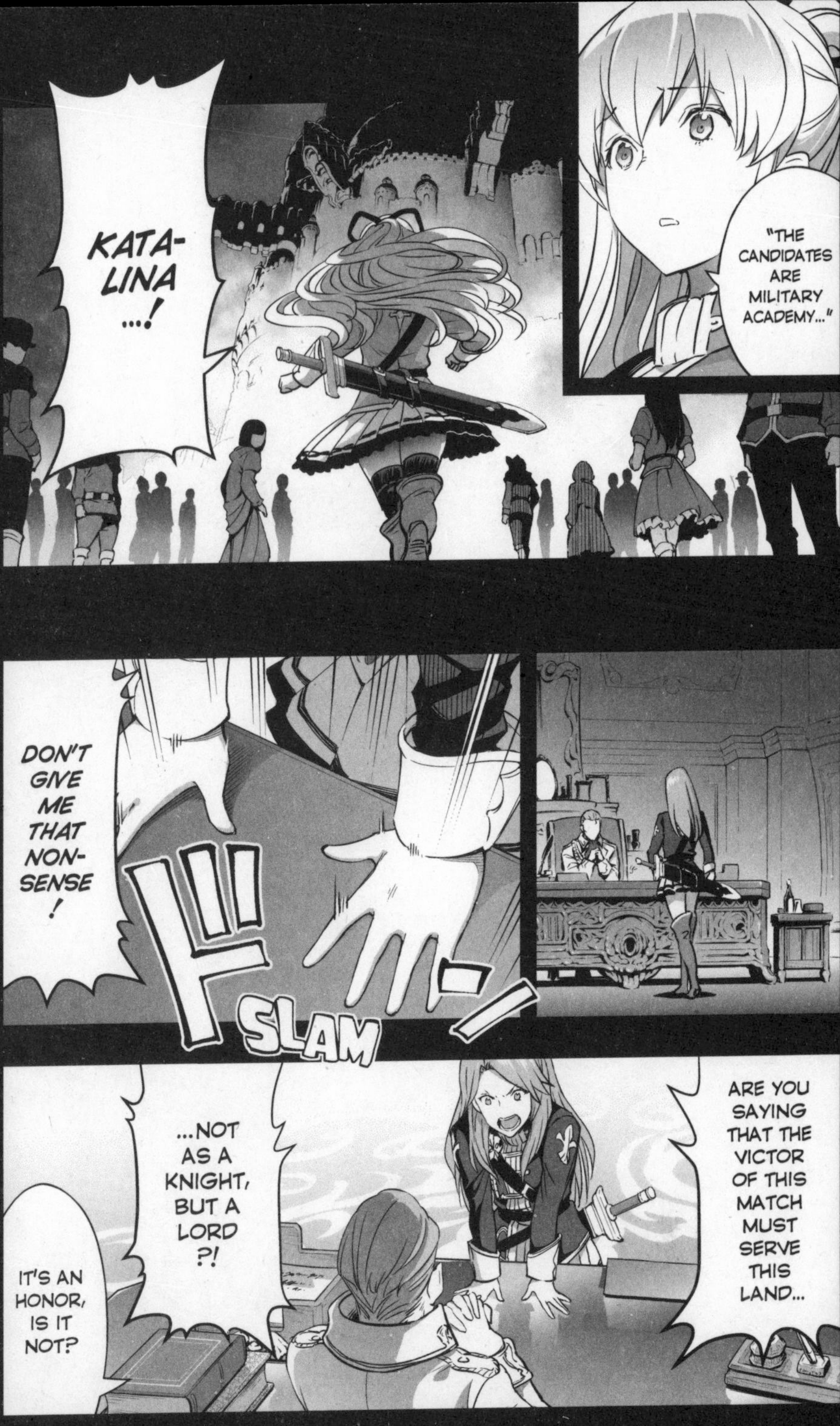
"THE CANDIDATES ARE MILITARY ACADEMY..."
KATA-LINA ...!
DON'T GIVE ME THAT NON-SENSE!
SLAM
ARE YOU SAYING THAT THE VICTOR OF THIS MATCH MUST SERVE THIS LAND...
...NOT AS A KNIGHT, BUT A LORD?!
IT'S AN HONOR, IS IT NOT?

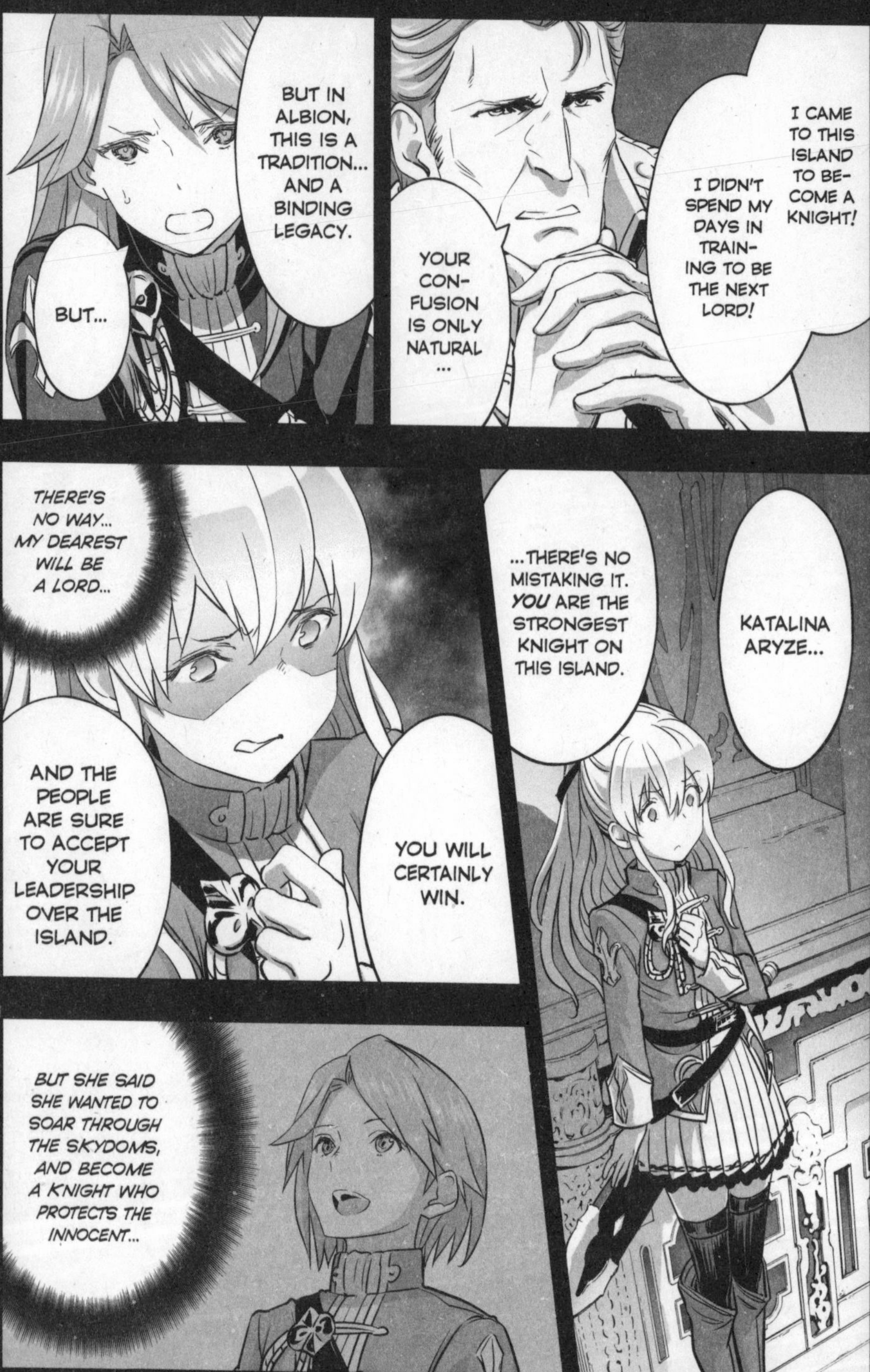
I CAME TO THIS ISLAND TO BECOME A KNIGHT!
I DIDN'T SPEND MY DAYS IN TRAINING TO BE THE NEXT LORD!
YOUR CONFUSION IS ONLY NATURAL...
BUT IN ALBION, THIS IS A TRADITION... AND A BINDING LEGACY.
BUT...
KATALINA ARYZE...
...THERE'S NO MISTAKING IT. *YOU* ARE THE STRONGEST KNIGHT ON THIS ISLAND.
YOU WILL CERTAINLY WIN.
AND THE PEOPLE ARE SURE TO ACCEPT YOUR LEADERSHIP OVER THE ISLAND.
THERE'S NO WAY... MY DEAREST WILL BE A LORD...
BUT SHE SAID SHE WANTED TO SOAR THROUGH THE SKYDOMS, AND BECOME A KNIGHT WHO PROTECTS THE INNOCENT...

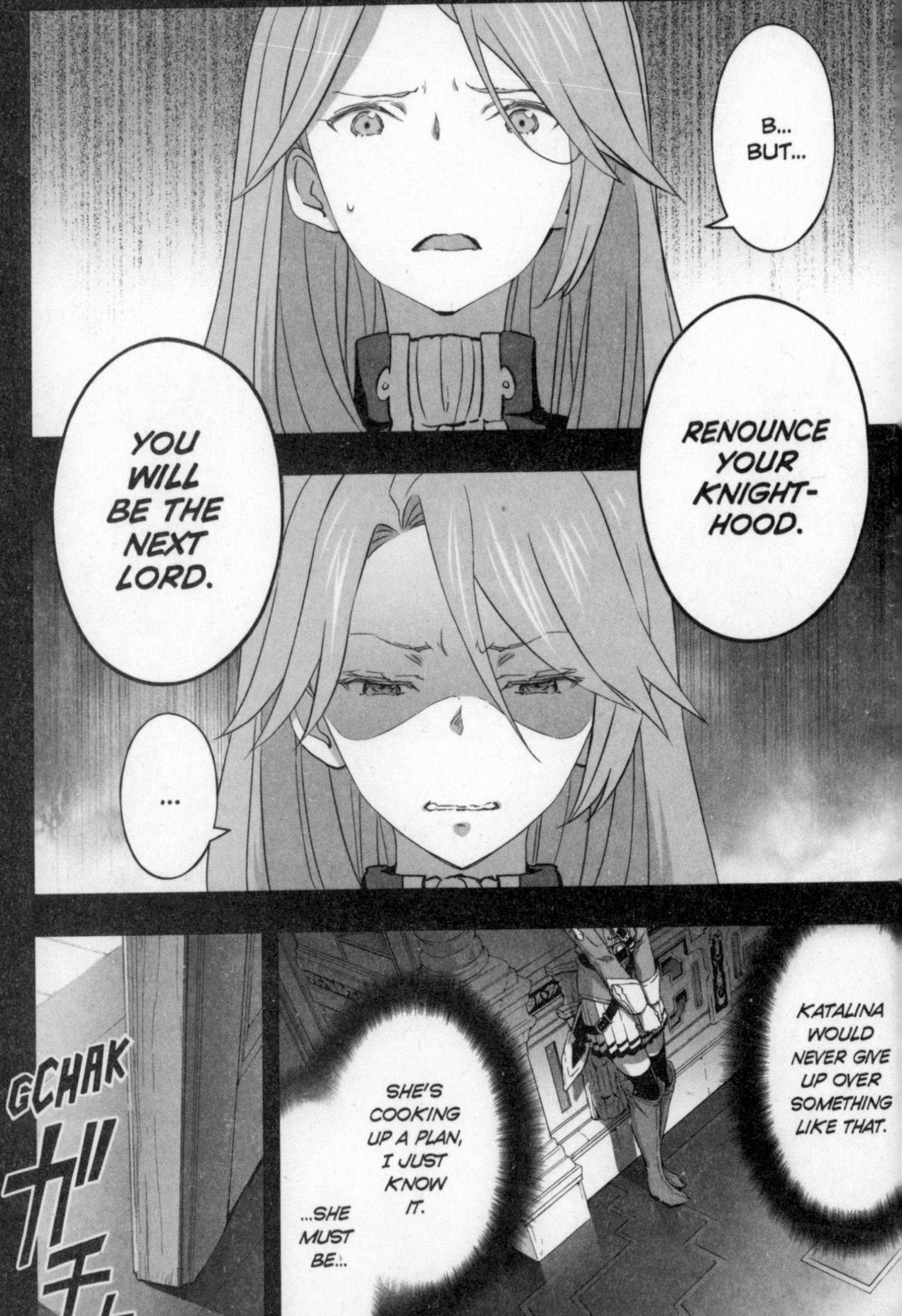
B... BUT...
RENOUNCE YOUR KNIGHT-HOOD.
YOU WILL BE THE NEXT LORD.
...
KATALINA WOULD NEVER GIVE UP OVER SOMETHING LIKE THAT.
SHE'S COOKING UP A PLAN, I JUST KNOW IT.
...SHE MUST BE...
GCHAK
ガチャ

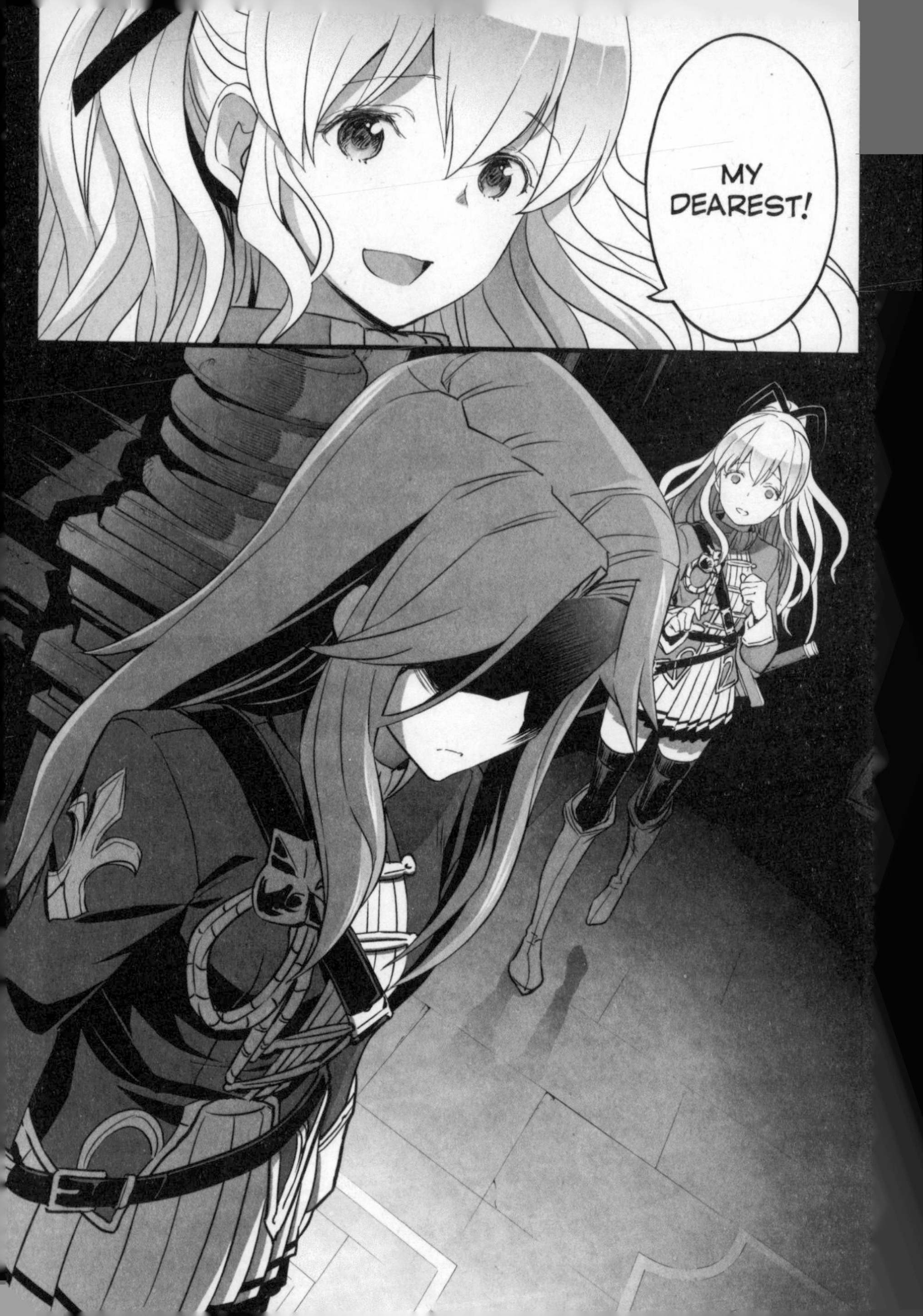
MY DEAREST!

...MY DEAREST...
カッ
THOK
カッ
THOK
IF THIS IS WHAT YOU DESIRE...
カッ
THOK
...THEN...
SQEEZE...

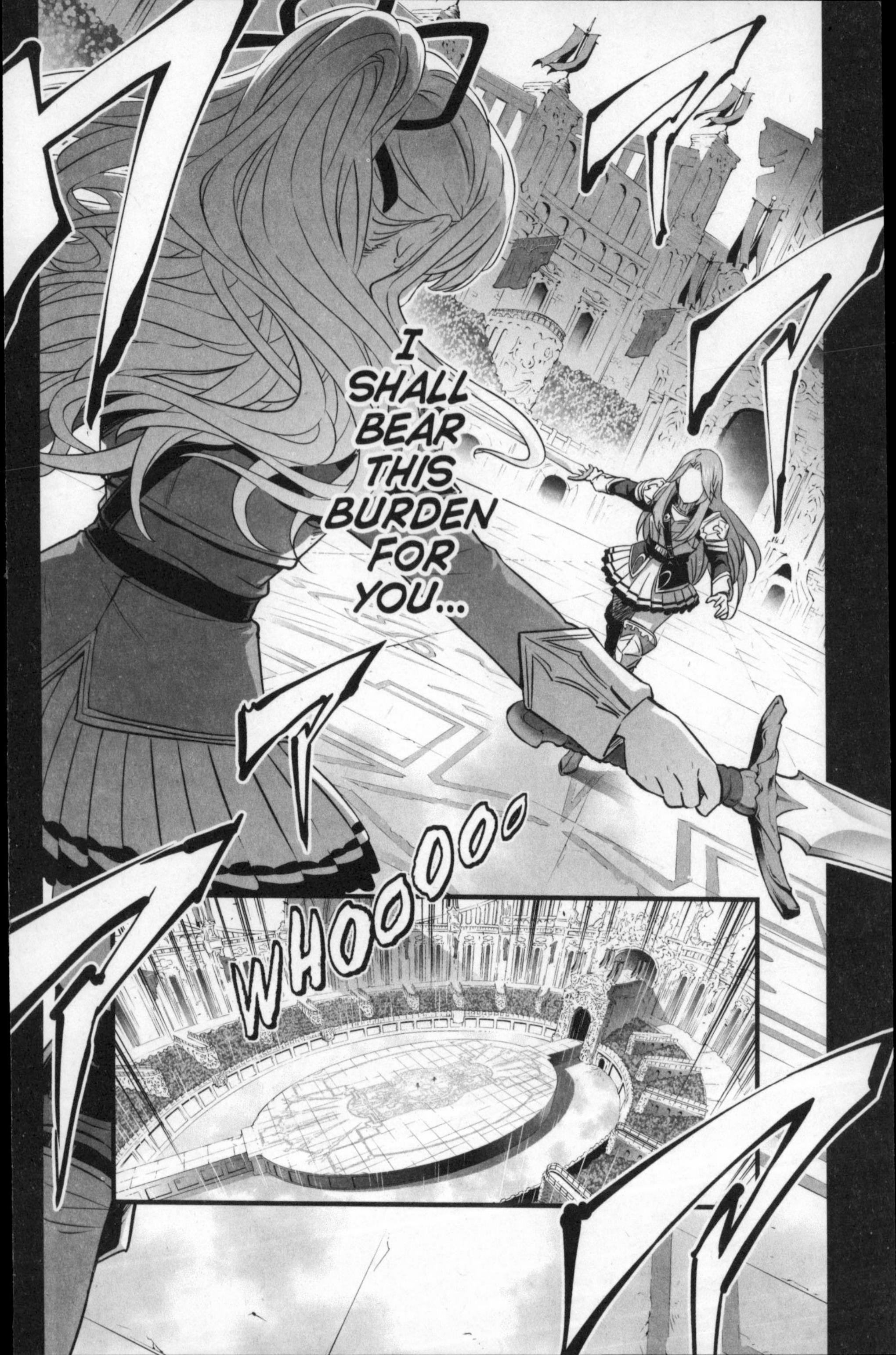
I SHALL BEAR THIS BURDEN FOR YOU...
WHOOOOO

GRANBLUE FANTASY
グランブルーファンタジー

GRANBLUE FANTASY
グランブルーファンタジー

CHAPTER 34: The Duel

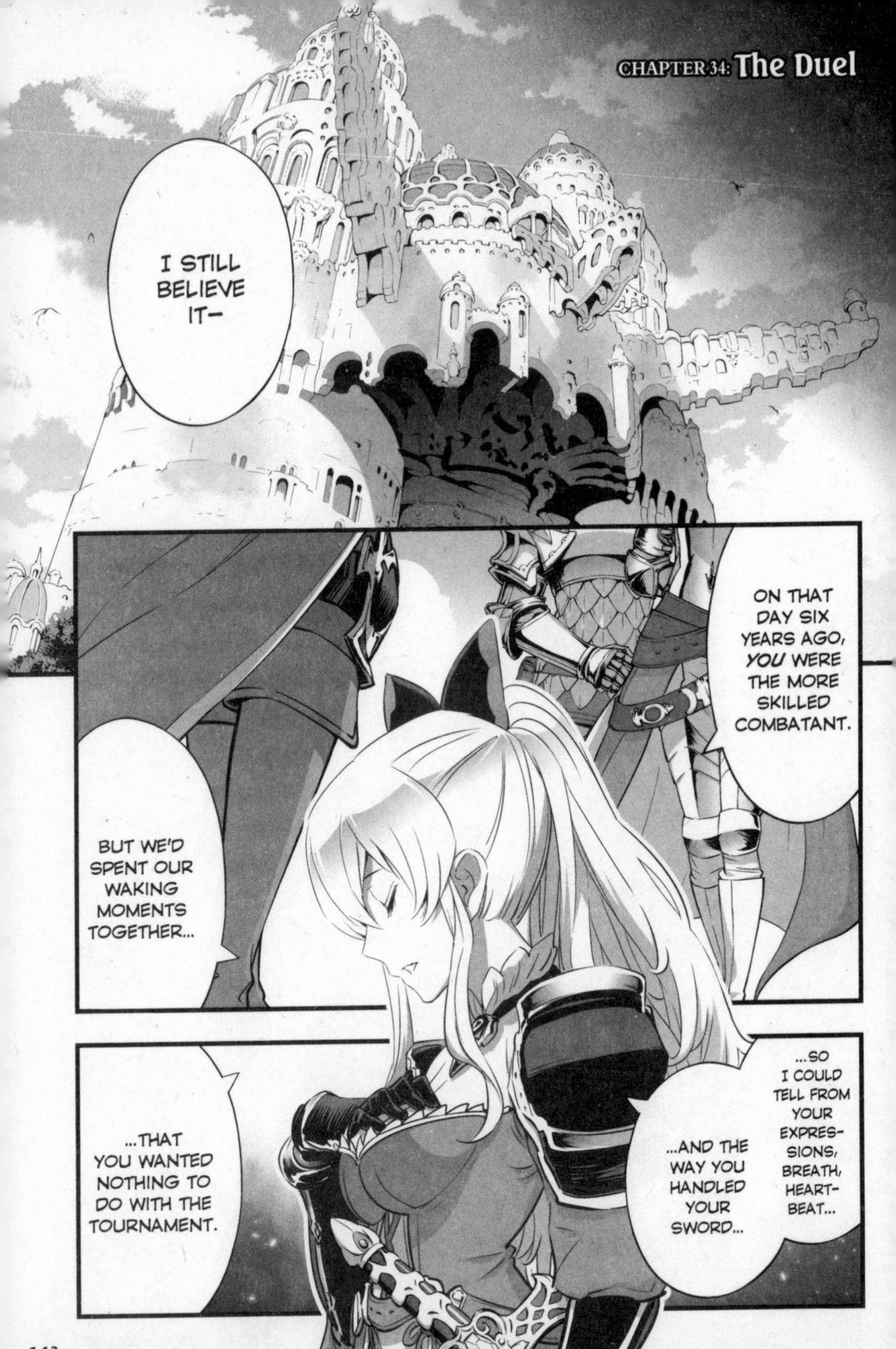
I STILL BELIEVE IT—
ON THAT DAY SIX YEARS AGO, *YOU* WERE THE MORE SKILLED COMBATANT.
BUT WE'D SPENT OUR WAKING MOMENTS TOGETHER...
...SO I COULD TELL FROM YOUR EXPRESSIONS, BREATH, HEART-BEAT...
...AND THE WAY YOU HANDLED YOUR SWORD...
...THAT YOU WANTED NOTHING TO DO WITH THE TOURNAMENT.

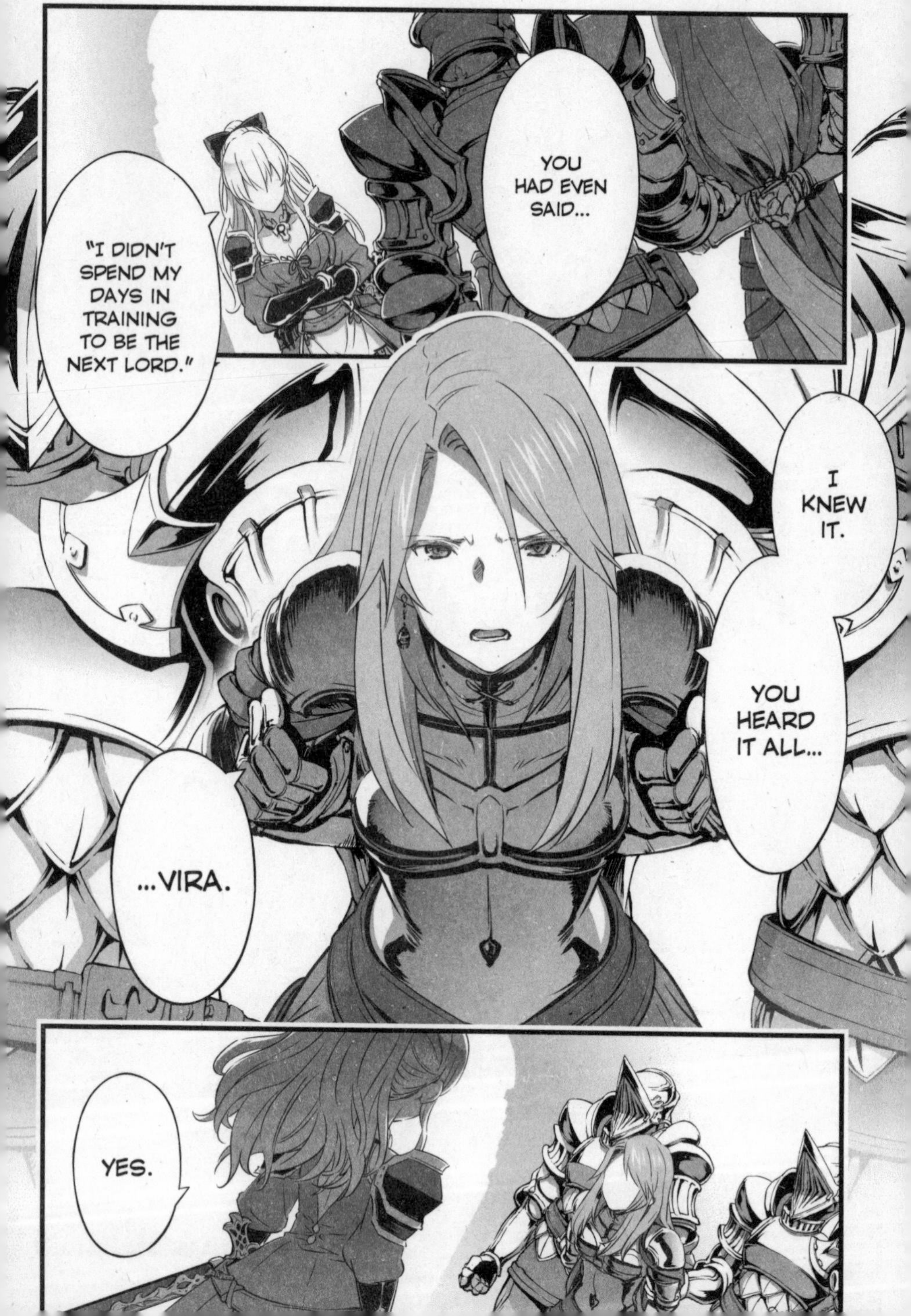
YOU HAD EVEN SAID...
"I DIDN'T SPEND MY DAYS IN TRAINING TO BE THE NEXT LORD."
I KNEW IT.
YOU HEARD IT ALL...
...VIRA.
YES.

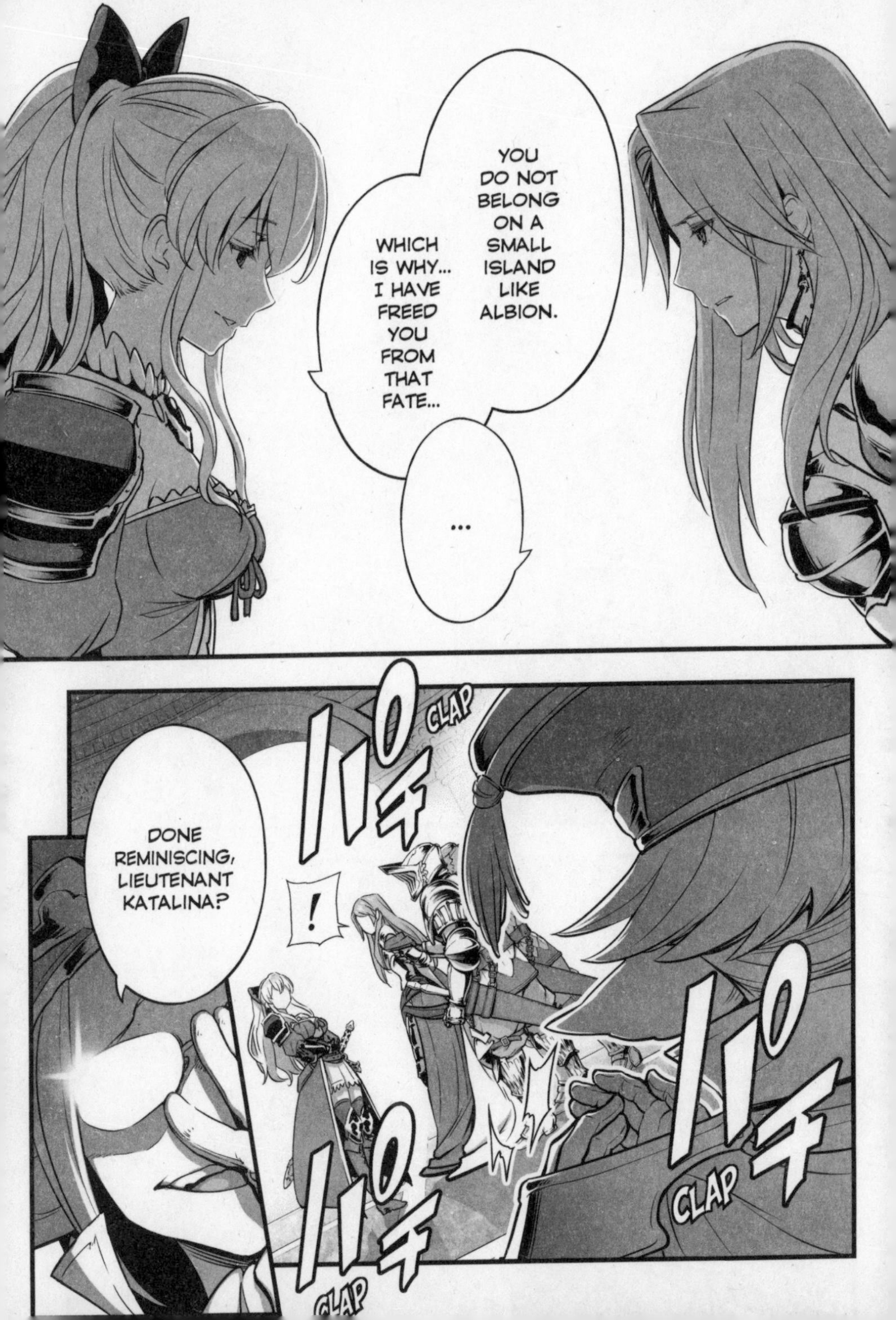
YOU DO NOT BELONG ON A SMALL ISLAND LIKE ALBION.
WHICH IS WHY... I HAVE FREED YOU FROM THAT FATE...
...
パチ
CLAP
DONE REMINISCING, LIEUTENANT KATALINA?
!
パチ
CLAP
パチ
CLAP

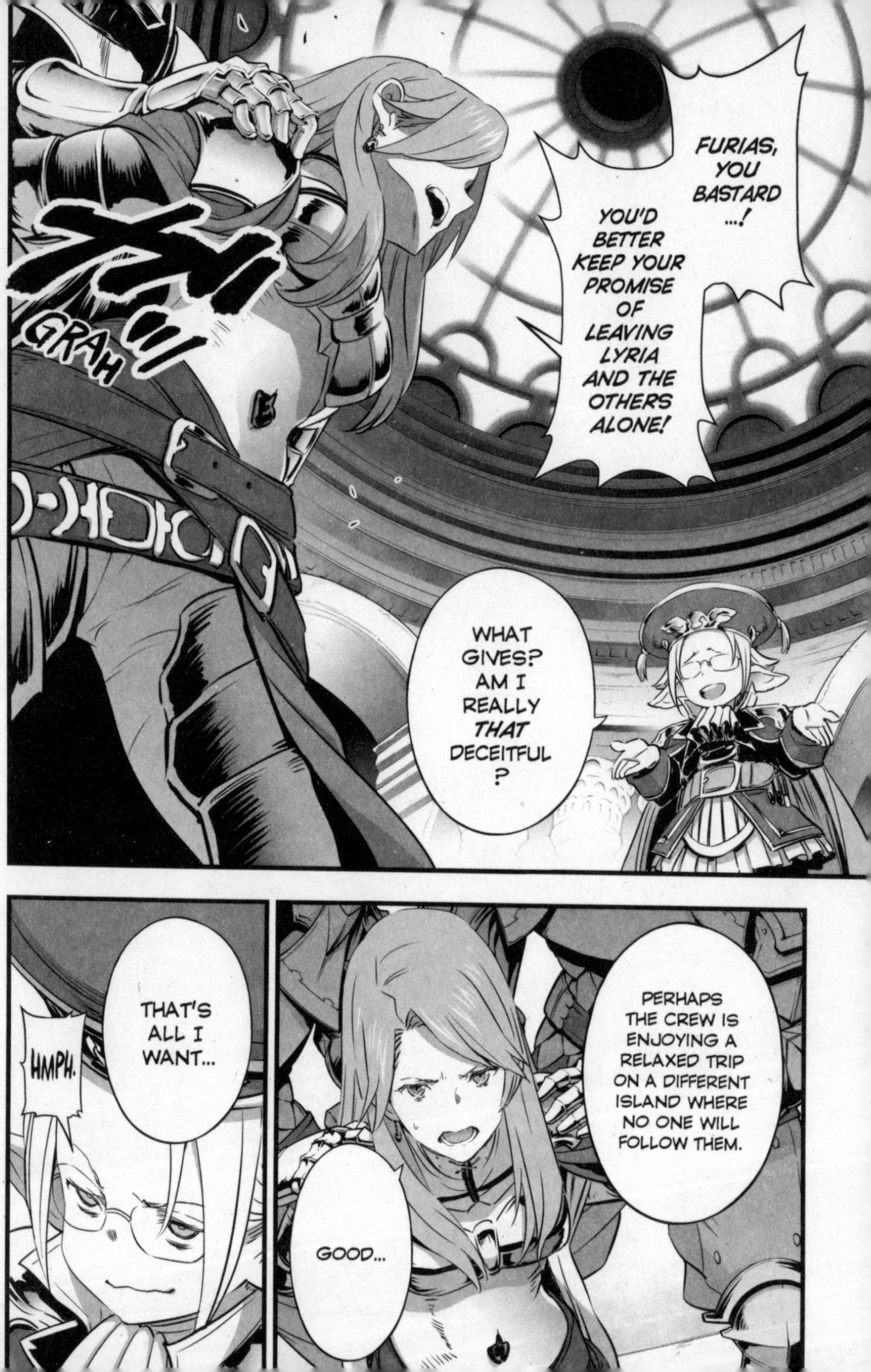
FURIAS, YOU BASTARD ...!
YOU'D BETTER KEEP YOUR PROMISE OF LEAVING LYRIA AND THE OTHERS ALONE!
GRAH
WHAT GIVES? AM I REALLY *THAT* DECEITFUL?
PERHAPS THE CREW IS ENJOYING A RELAXED TRIP ON A DIFFERENT ISLAND WHERE NO ONE WILL FOLLOW THEM.
GOOD...
THAT'S ALL I WANT...
HMPH.

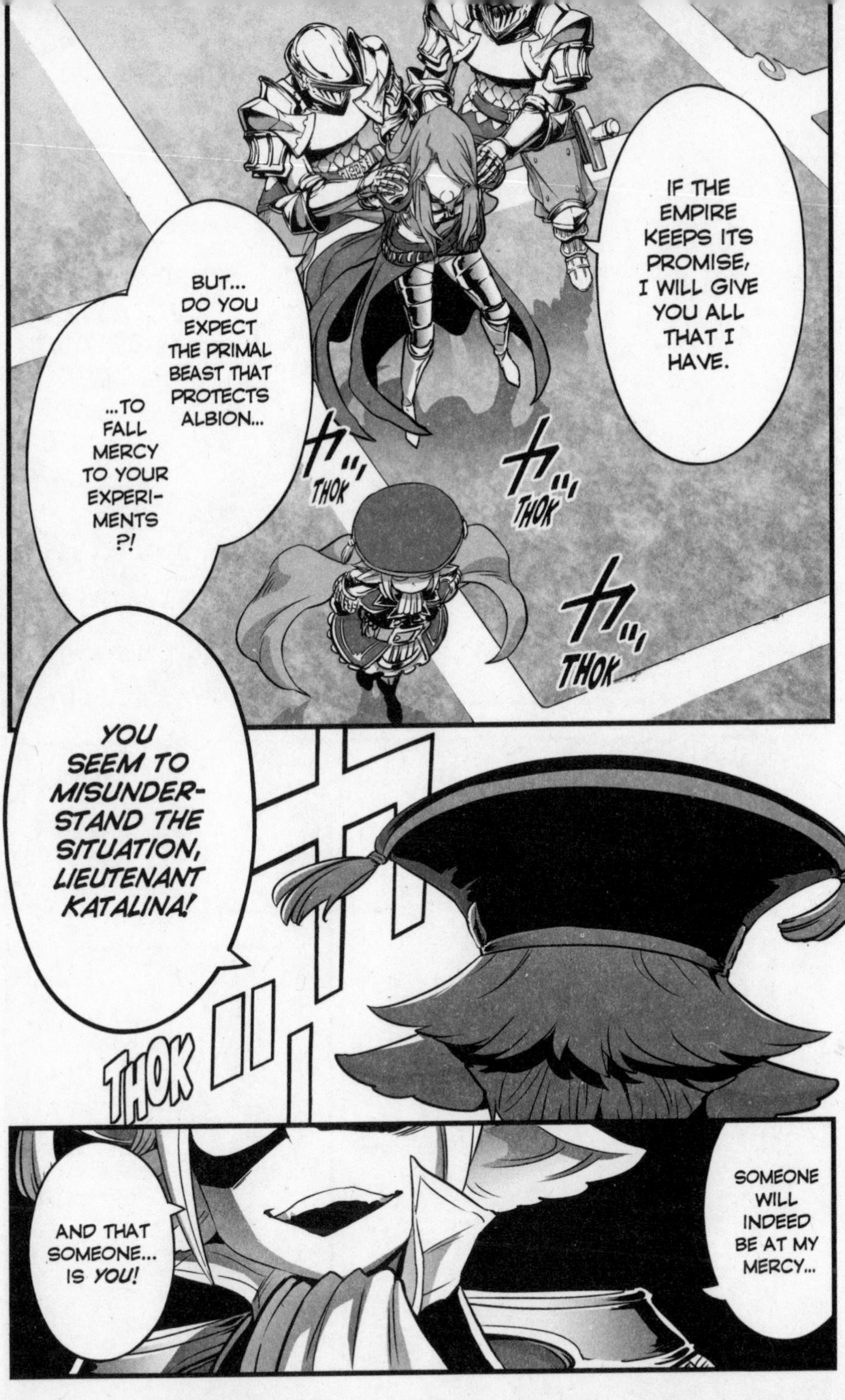
IF THE EMPIRE KEEPS ITS PROMISE, I WILL GIVE YOU ALL THAT I HAVE.
BUT... DO YOU EXPECT THE PRIMAL BEAST THAT PROTECTS ALBION...
...TO FALL MERCY TO YOUR EXPERIMENTS?!
THOK
THOK
THOK
THOK
YOU SEEM TO MISUNDERSTAND THE SITUATION, LIEUTENANT KATALINA!
SOMEONE WILL INDEED BE AT MY MERCY...
AND THAT SOMEONE... IS YOU!

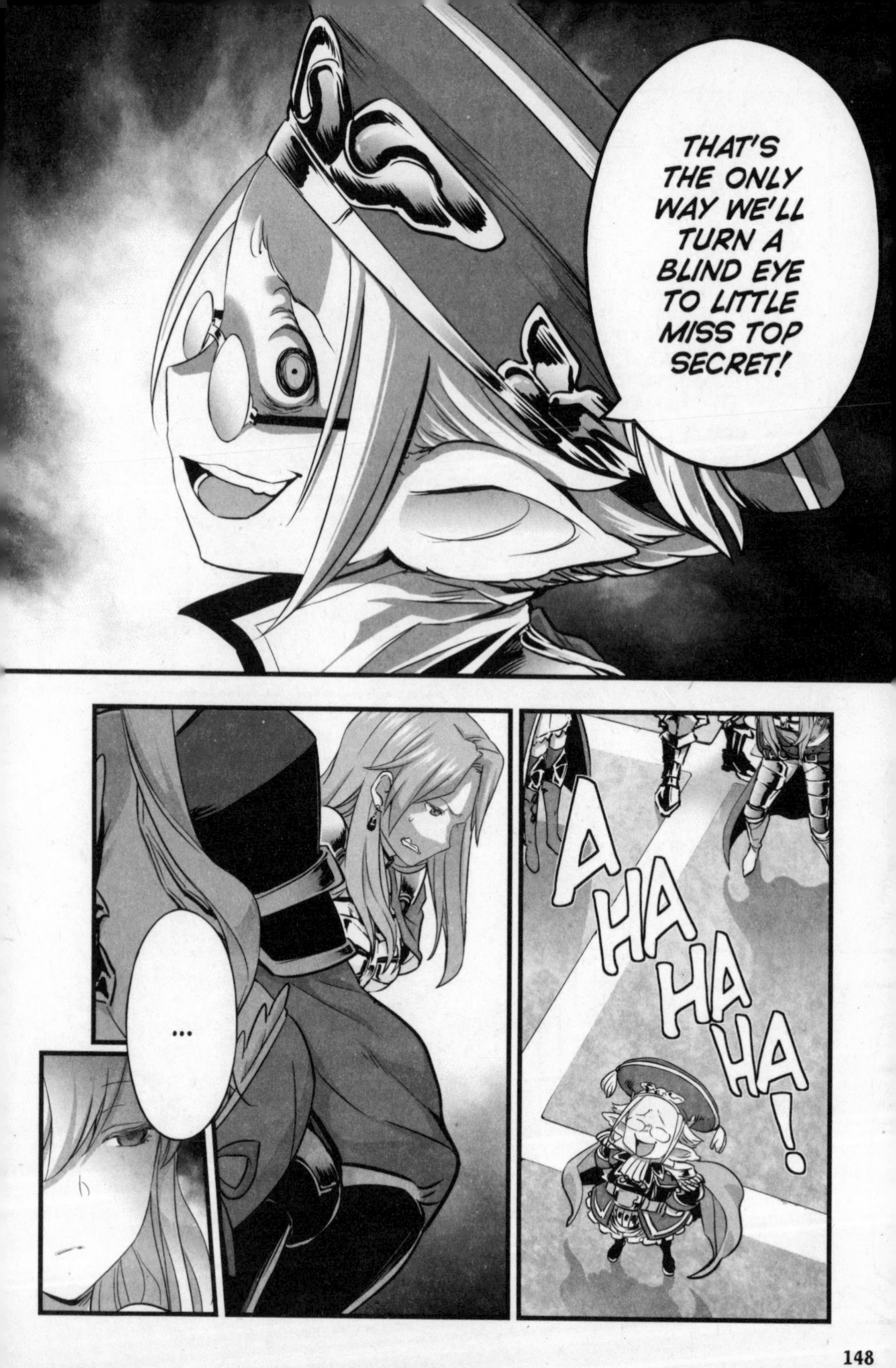
THAT'S THE ONLY WAY WE'LL TURN A BLIND EYE TO LITTLE MISS TOP SECRET!
AHAHAHAHA!
...

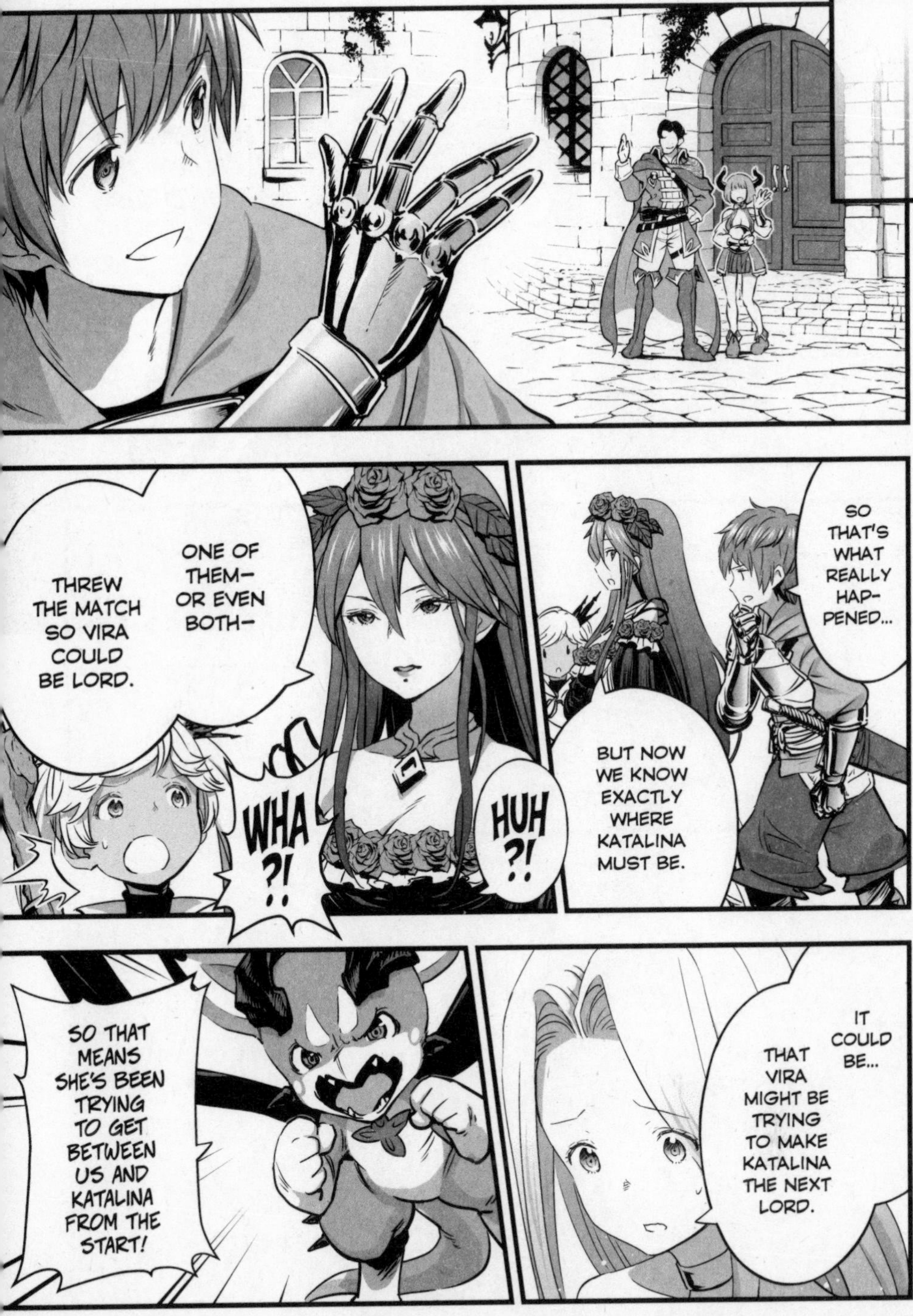
SO THAT'S WHAT REALLY HAPPENED...
BUT NOW WE KNOW EXACTLY WHERE KATALINA MUST BE.
ONE OF THEM— OR EVEN BOTH—
THREW THE MATCH SO VIRA COULD BE LORD.
HUH ?!
WHA ?!
IT COULD BE...
THAT VIRA MIGHT BE TRYING TO MAKE KATALINA THE NEXT LORD.
SO THAT MEANS SHE'S BEEN TRYING TO GET BETWEEN US AND KATALINA FROM THE START!

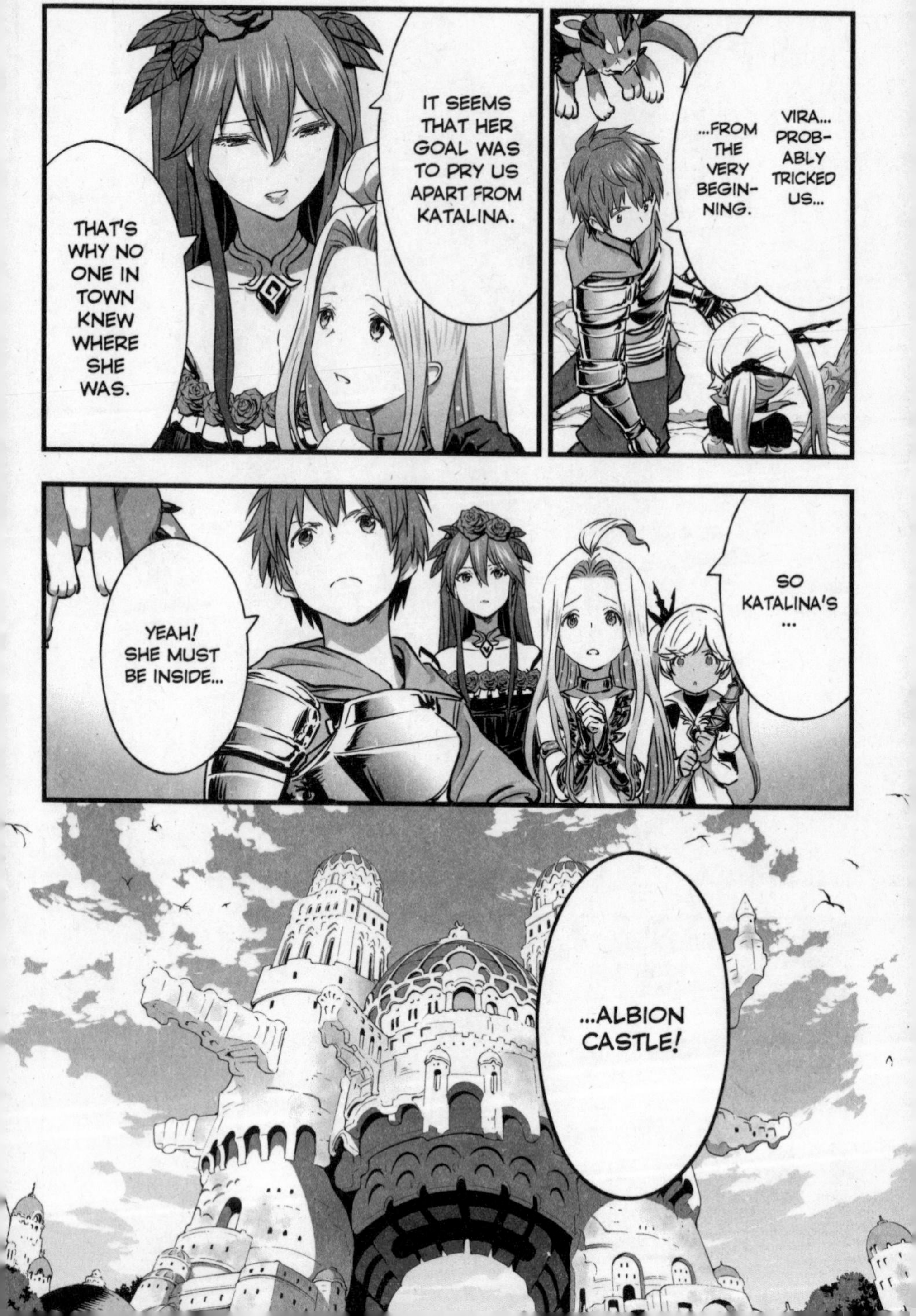
VIRA... PROBABLY TRICKED US...
...FROM THE VERY BEGINNING.
IT SEEMS THAT HER GOAL WAS TO PRY US APART FROM KATALINA.
THAT'S WHY NO ONE IN TOWN KNEW WHERE SHE WAS.
SO KATALINA'S...
YEAH! SHE MUST BE INSIDE...
...ALBION CASTLE!

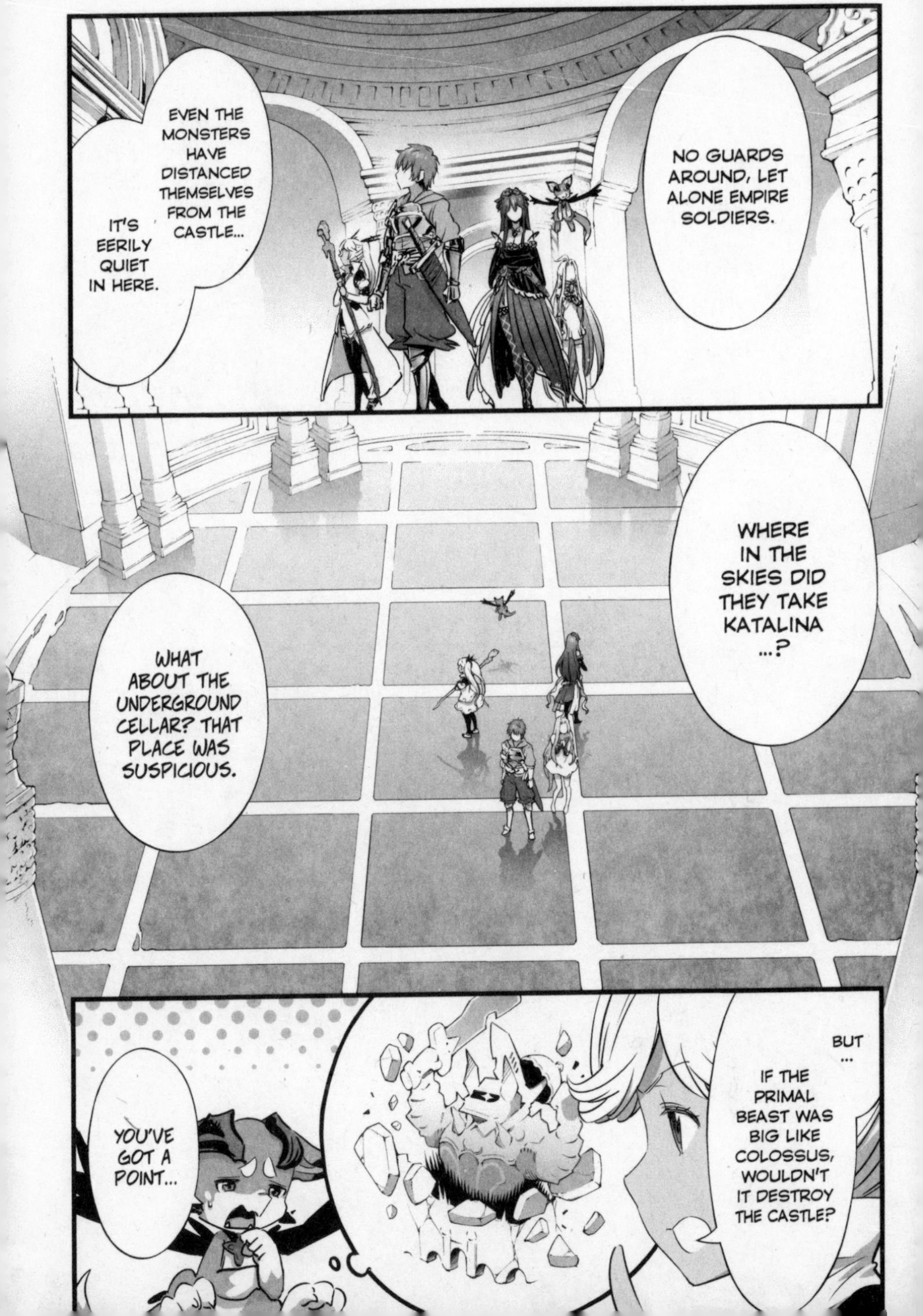
NO GUARDS AROUND, LET ALONE EMPIRE SOLDIERS.
EVEN THE MONSTERS HAVE DISTANCED THEMSELVES FROM THE CASTLE...
IT'S EERILY QUIET IN HERE.
WHERE IN THE SKIES DID THEY TAKE KATALINA ...?
WHAT ABOUT THE UNDERGROUND CELLAR? THAT PLACE WAS SUSPICIOUS.
BUT ...
IF THE PRIMAL BEAST WAS BIG LIKE COLOSSUS, WOULDN'T IT DESTROY THE CASTLE?
YOU'VE GOT A POINT...

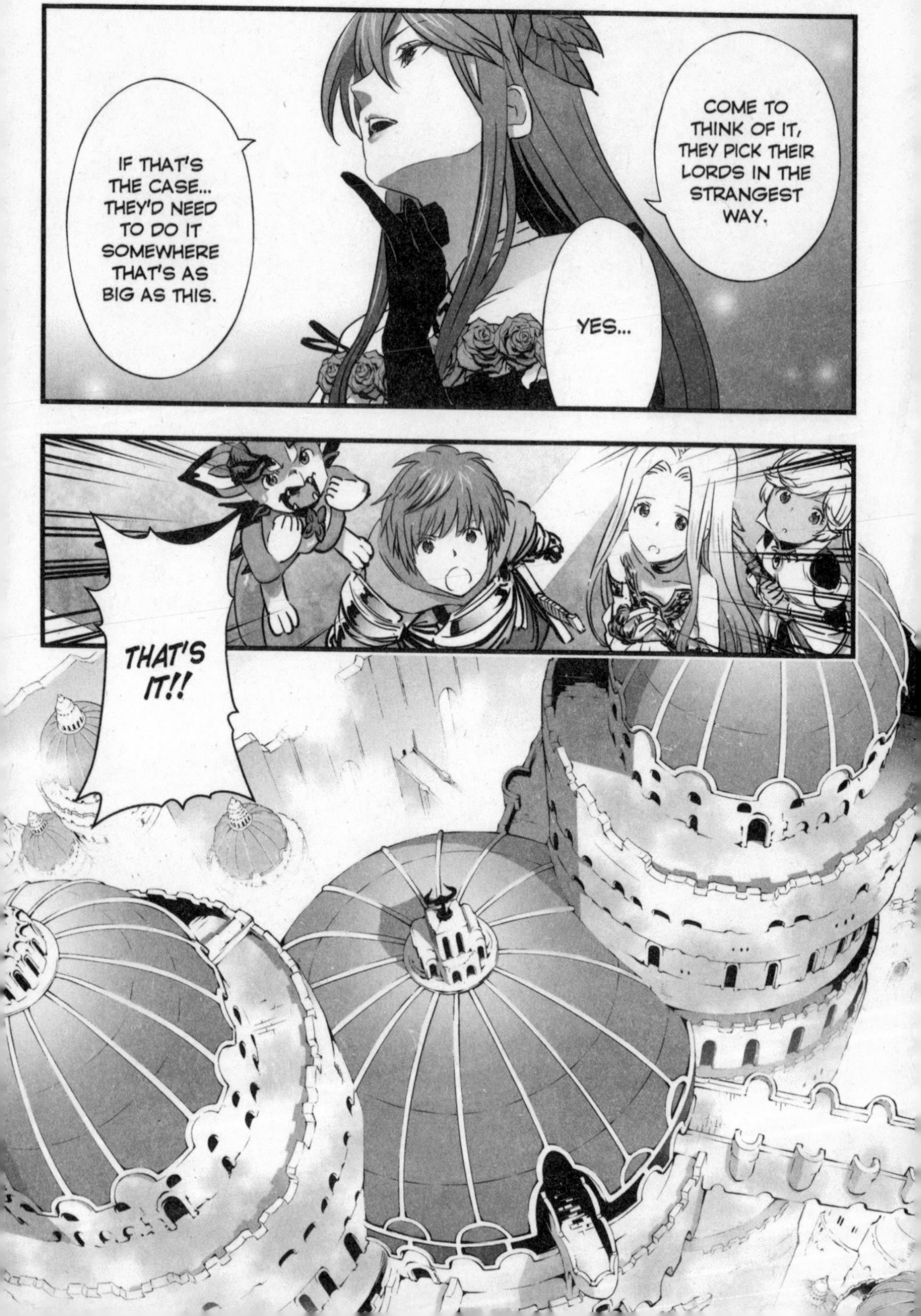
COME TO THINK OF IT, THEY PICK THEIR LORDS IN THE STRANGEST WAY.
YES...
IF THAT'S THE CASE... THEY'D NEED TO DO IT SOMEWHERE THAT'S AS BIG AS THIS.
THAT'S IT!!

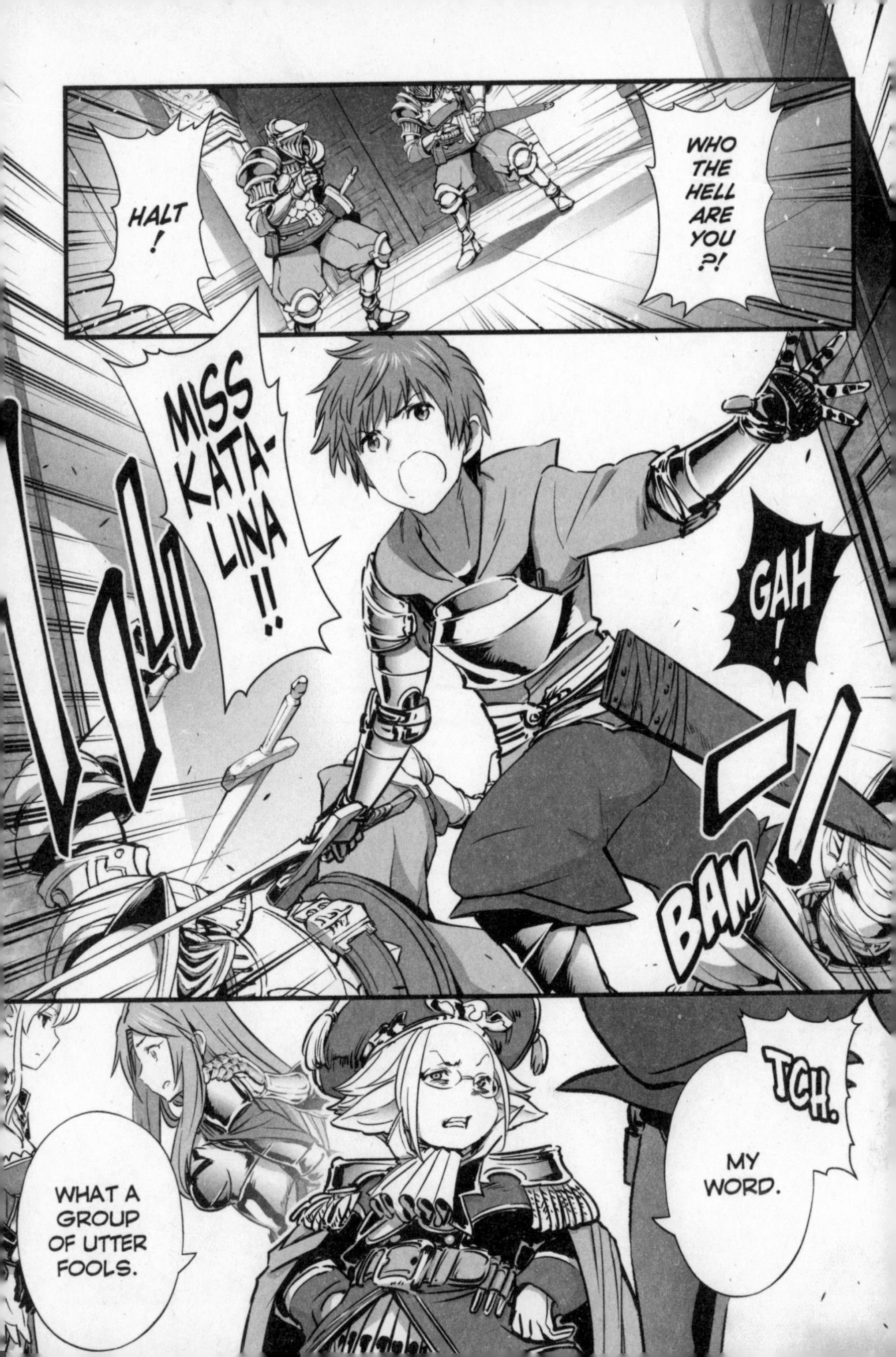
WHO THE HELL ARE YOU?!
HALT!
MISS KATA-LINA!!
GAH!
BAM
TCH.
MY WORD.
WHAT A GROUP OF UTTER FOOLS.

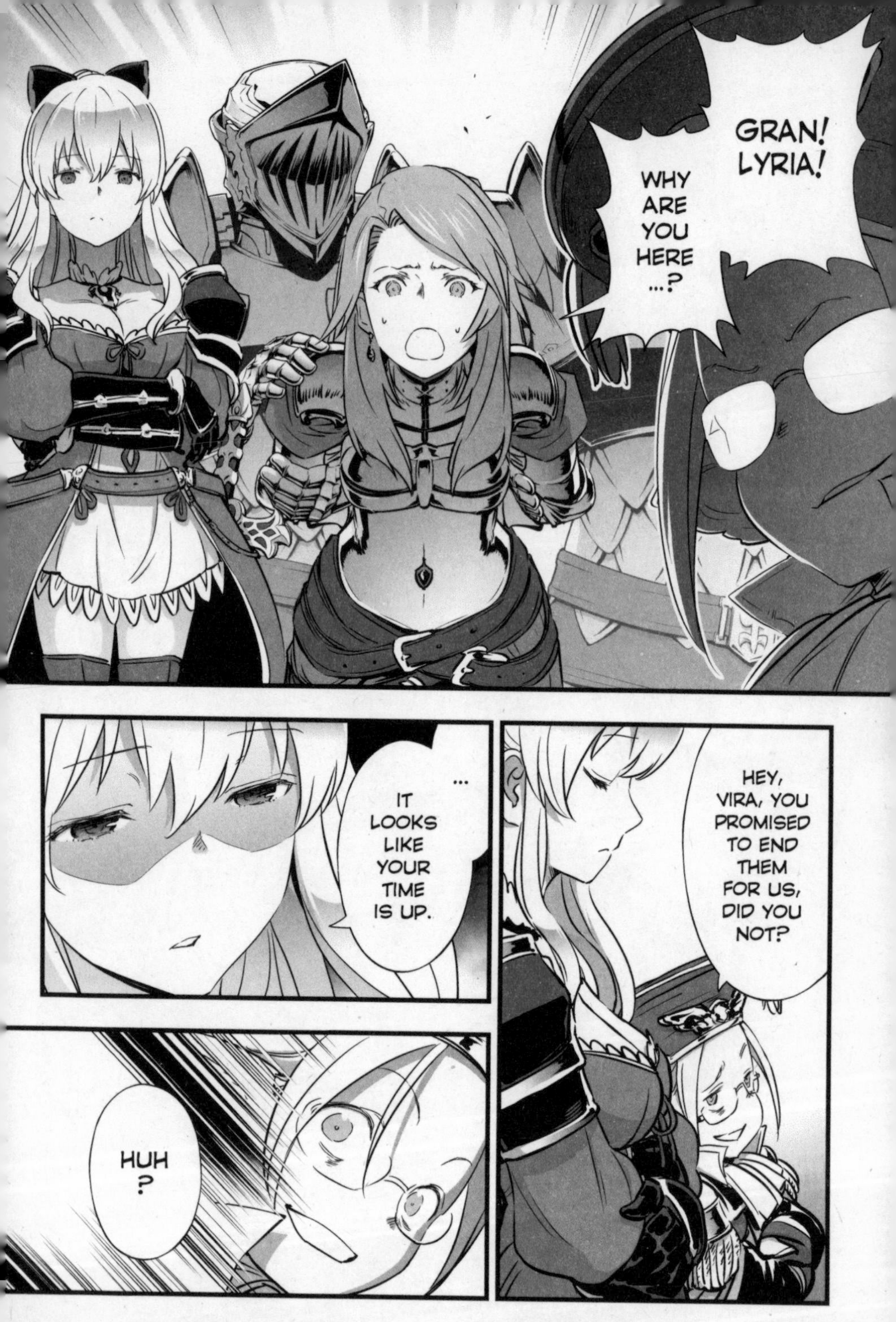
GRAN! LYRIA!
WHY ARE YOU HERE ...?
HEY, VIRA, YOU PROMISED TO END THEM FOR US, DID YOU NOT?
...
IT LOOKS LIKE YOUR TIME IS UP.
HUH?

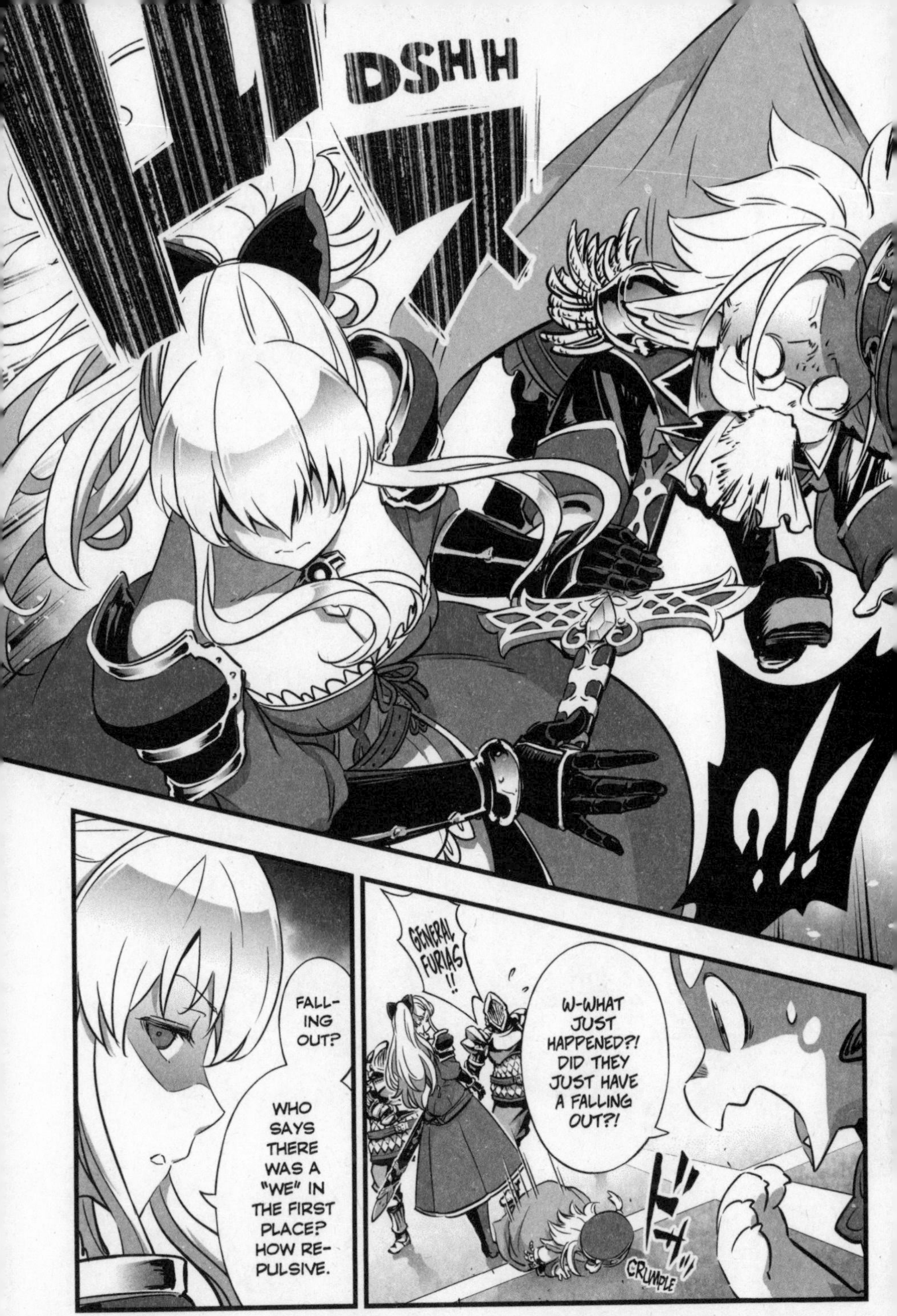
DSHH
?!!
GENERAL FURIAS!!
W-WHAT JUST HAPPENED?! DID THEY JUST HAVE A FALLING OUT?!
CRUMPLE
FALL-ING OUT?
WHO SAYS THERE WAS A "WE" IN THE FIRST PLACE? HOW RE-PULSIVE.

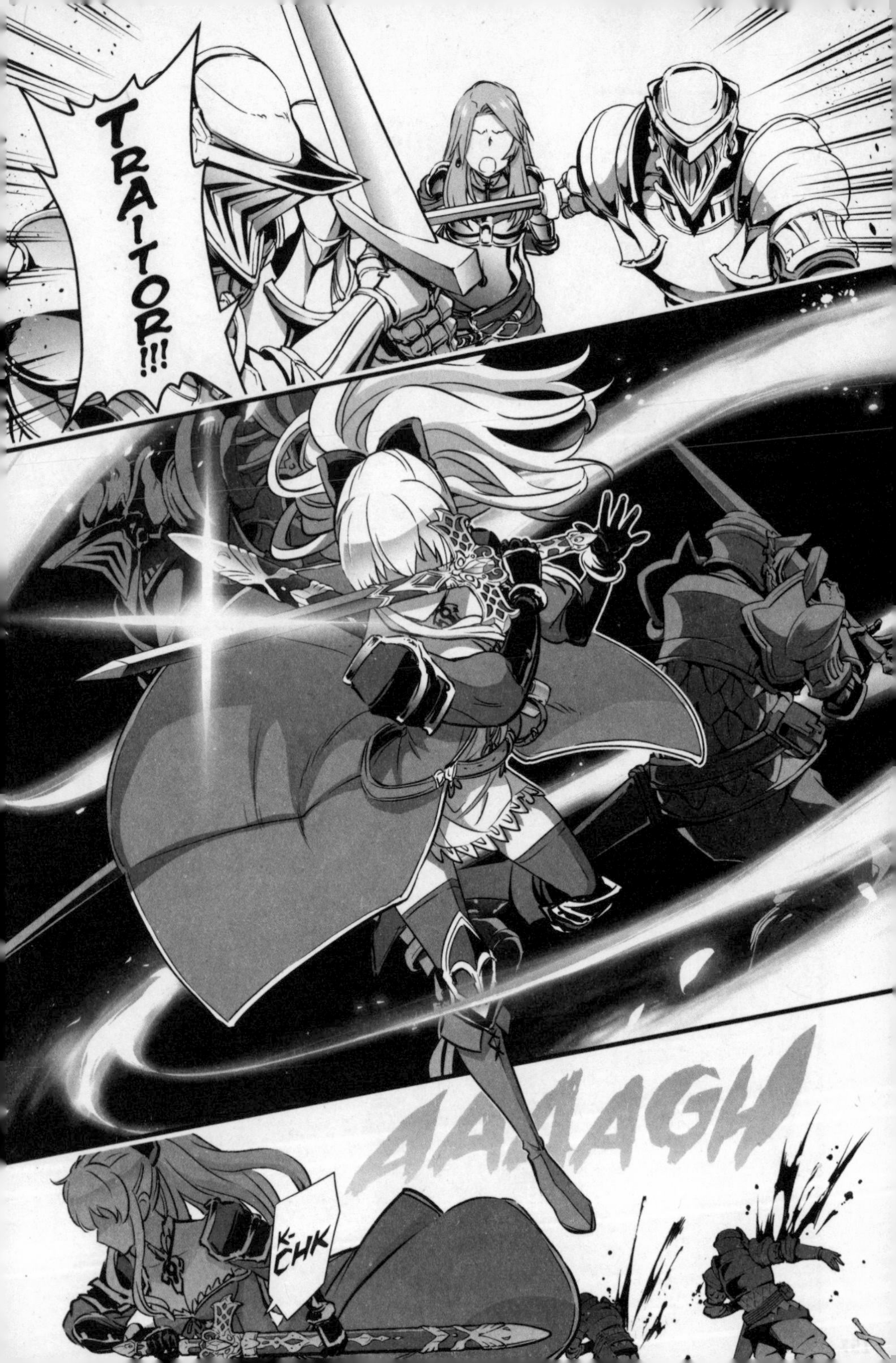
TRAITOR!!!
AAAAGH
K-CHK

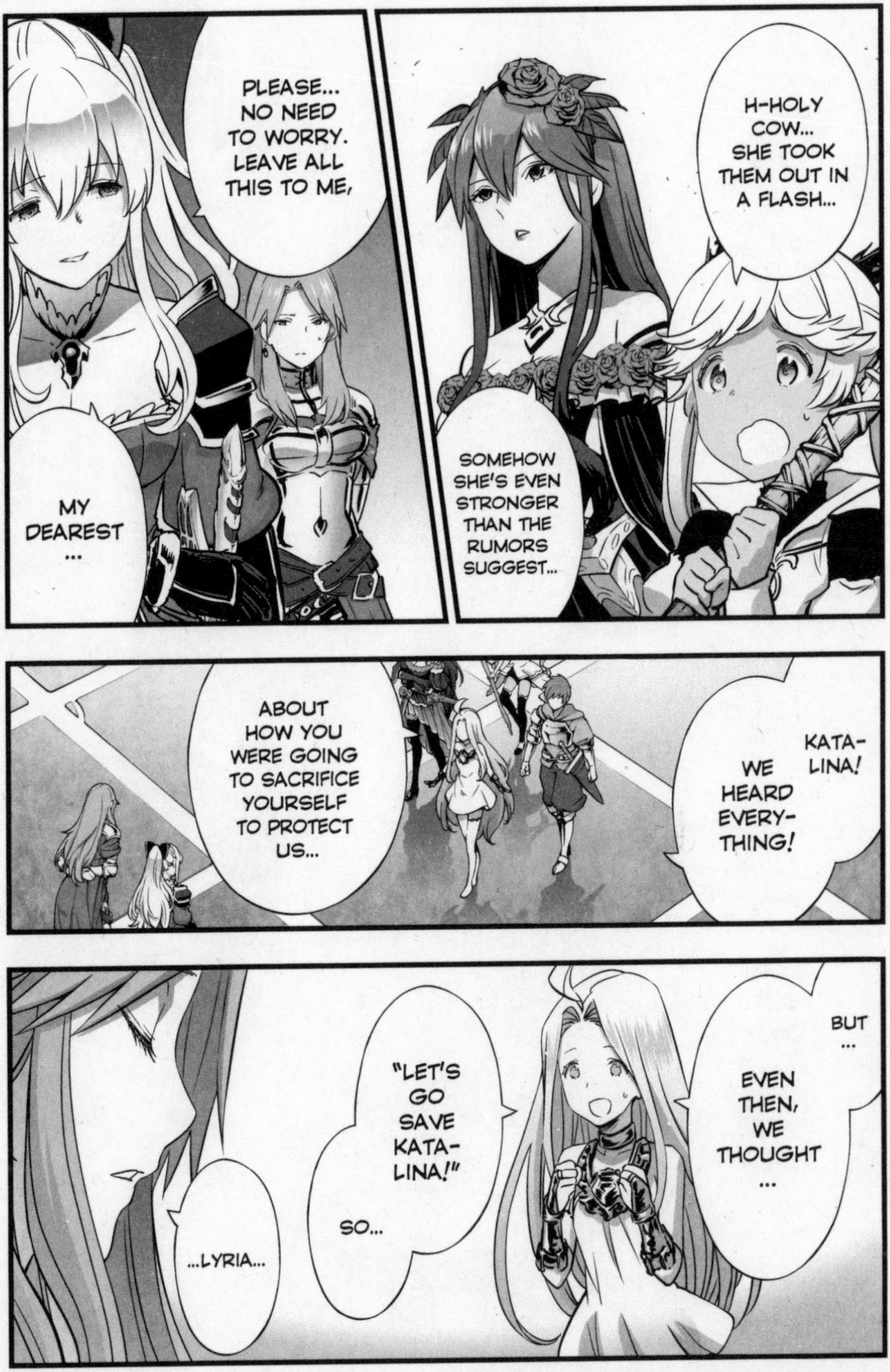
H-HOLY COW... SHE TOOK THEM OUT IN A FLASH...
SOMEHOW SHE'S EVEN STRONGER THAN THE RUMORS SUGGEST...
PLEASE... NO NEED TO WORRY. LEAVE ALL THIS TO ME,
MY DEAREST ...
KATA-LINA!
WE HEARD EVERY-THING!
ABOUT HOW YOU WERE GOING TO SACRIFICE YOURSELF TO PROTECT US...
BUT ...
EVEN THEN, WE THOUGHT ...
"LET'S GO SAVE KATA-LINA!"
SO...
...LYRIA...

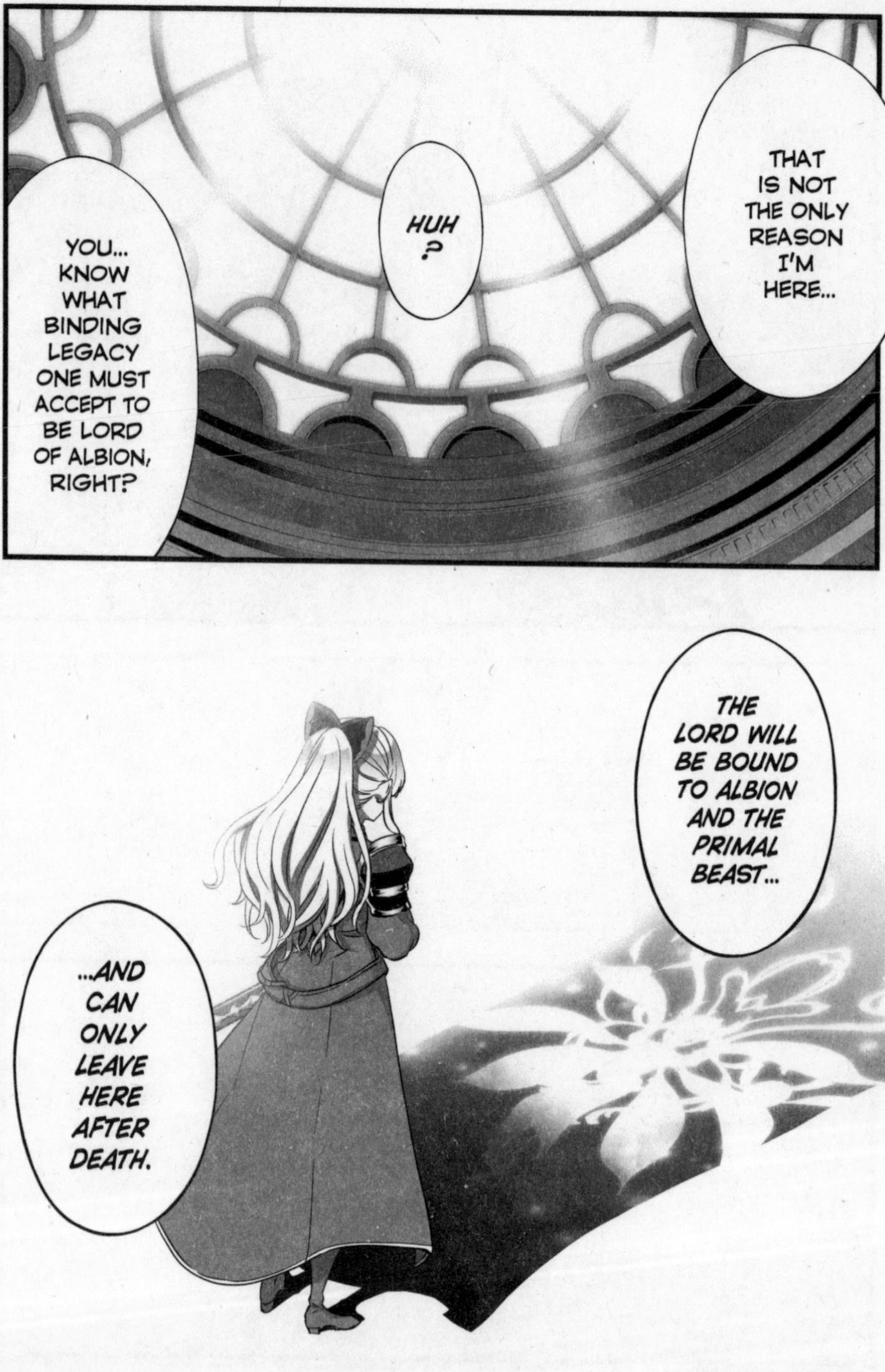
THAT IS NOT THE ONLY REASON I'M HERE...
HUH?
YOU... KNOW WHAT BINDING LEGACY ONE MUST ACCEPT TO BE LORD OF ALBION, RIGHT?
THE LORD WILL BE BOUND TO ALBION AND THE PRIMAL BEAST...
...AND CAN ONLY LEAVE HERE AFTER DEATH.

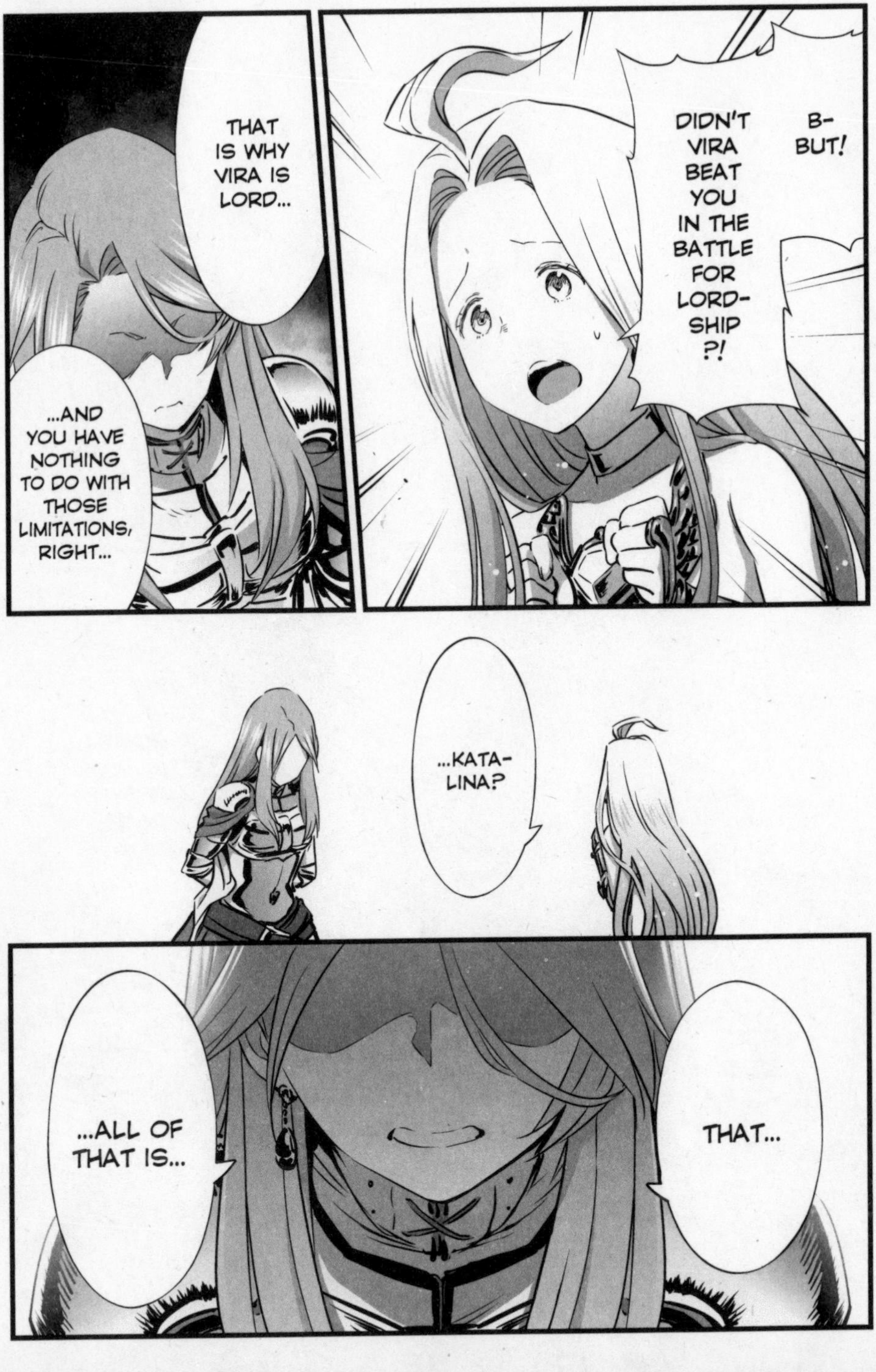
B-BUT!
DIDN'T VIRA BEAT YOU IN THE BATTLE FOR LORD-SHIP?!
THAT IS WHY VIRA IS LORD...
...AND YOU HAVE NOTHING TO DO WITH THOSE LIMITATIONS, RIGHT...
...KATA-LINA?
THAT...
...ALL OF THAT IS...

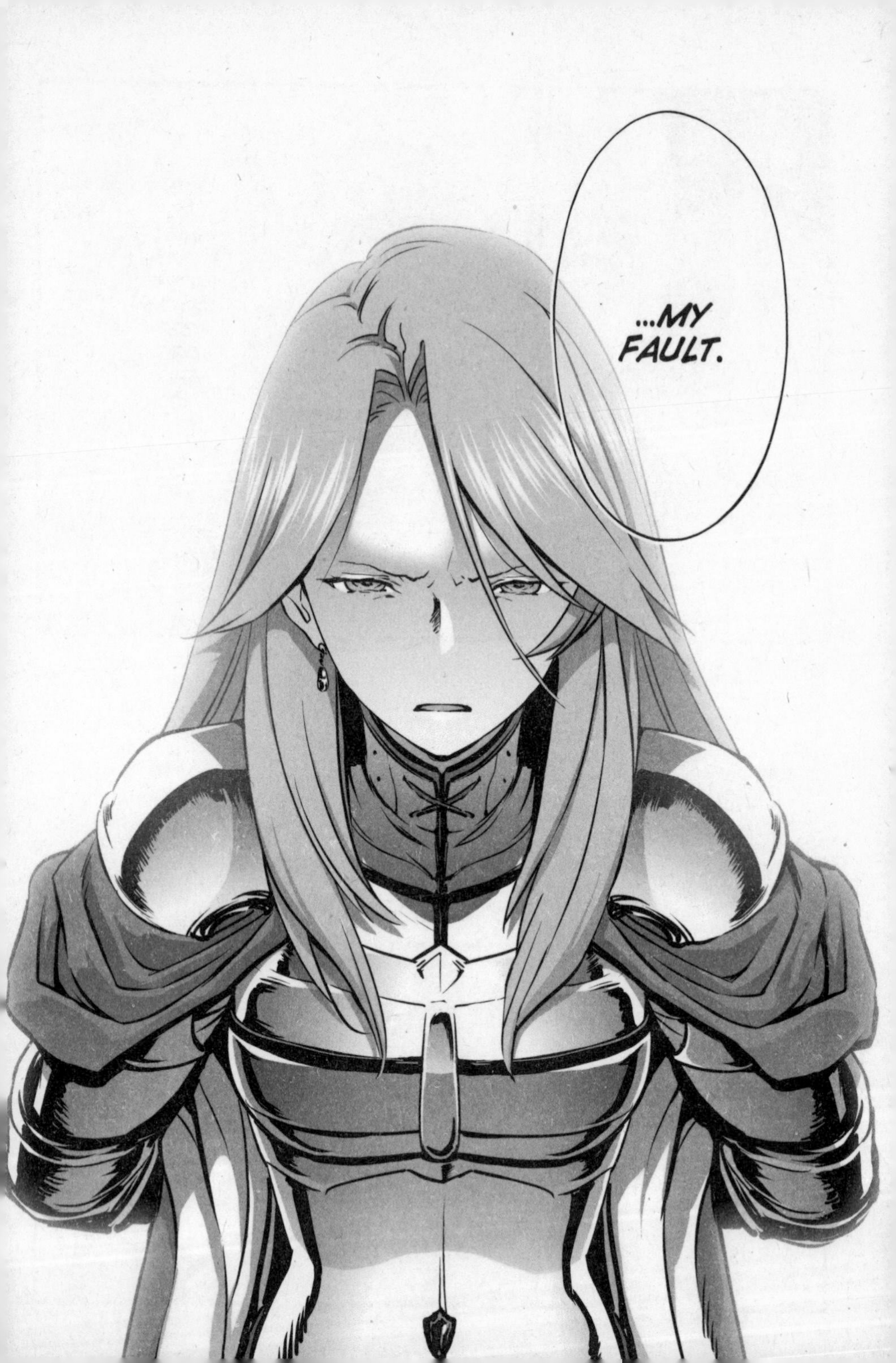
...MY FAULT.

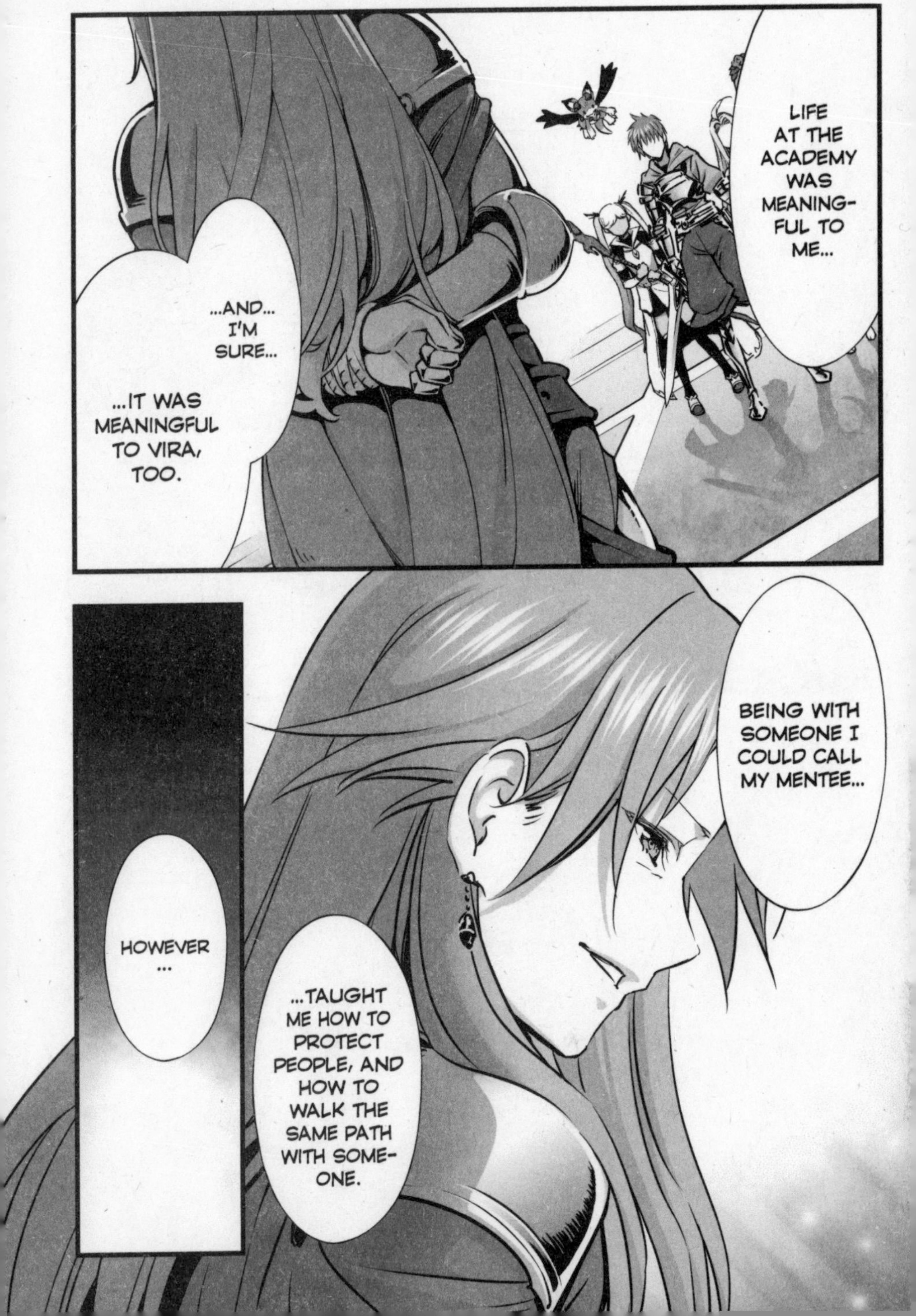
LIFE AT THE ACADEMY WAS MEANING-FUL TO ME...
...AND... I'M SURE...
...IT WAS MEANINGFUL TO VIRA, TOO.
BEING WITH SOMEONE I COULD CALL MY MENTEE...
...TAUGHT ME HOW TO PROTECT PEOPLE, AND HOW TO WALK THE SAME PATH WITH SOME-ONE.
HOWEVER ...

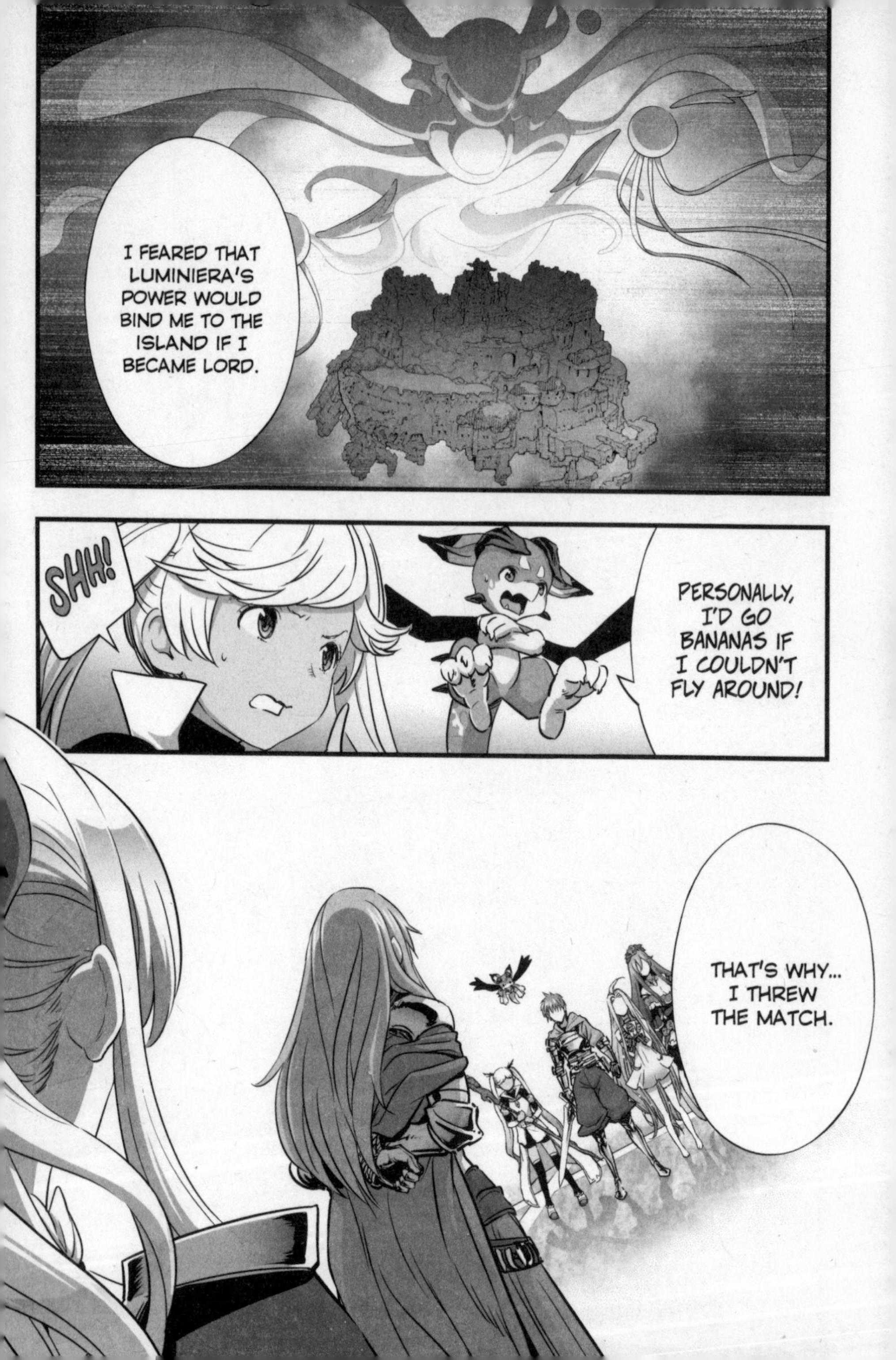
I FEARED THAT LUMINIERA'S POWER WOULD BIND ME TO THE ISLAND IF I BECAME LORD.
PERSONALLY, I'D GO BANANAS IF I COULDN'T FLY AROUND!
SHH!
THAT'S WHY... I THREW THE MATCH.

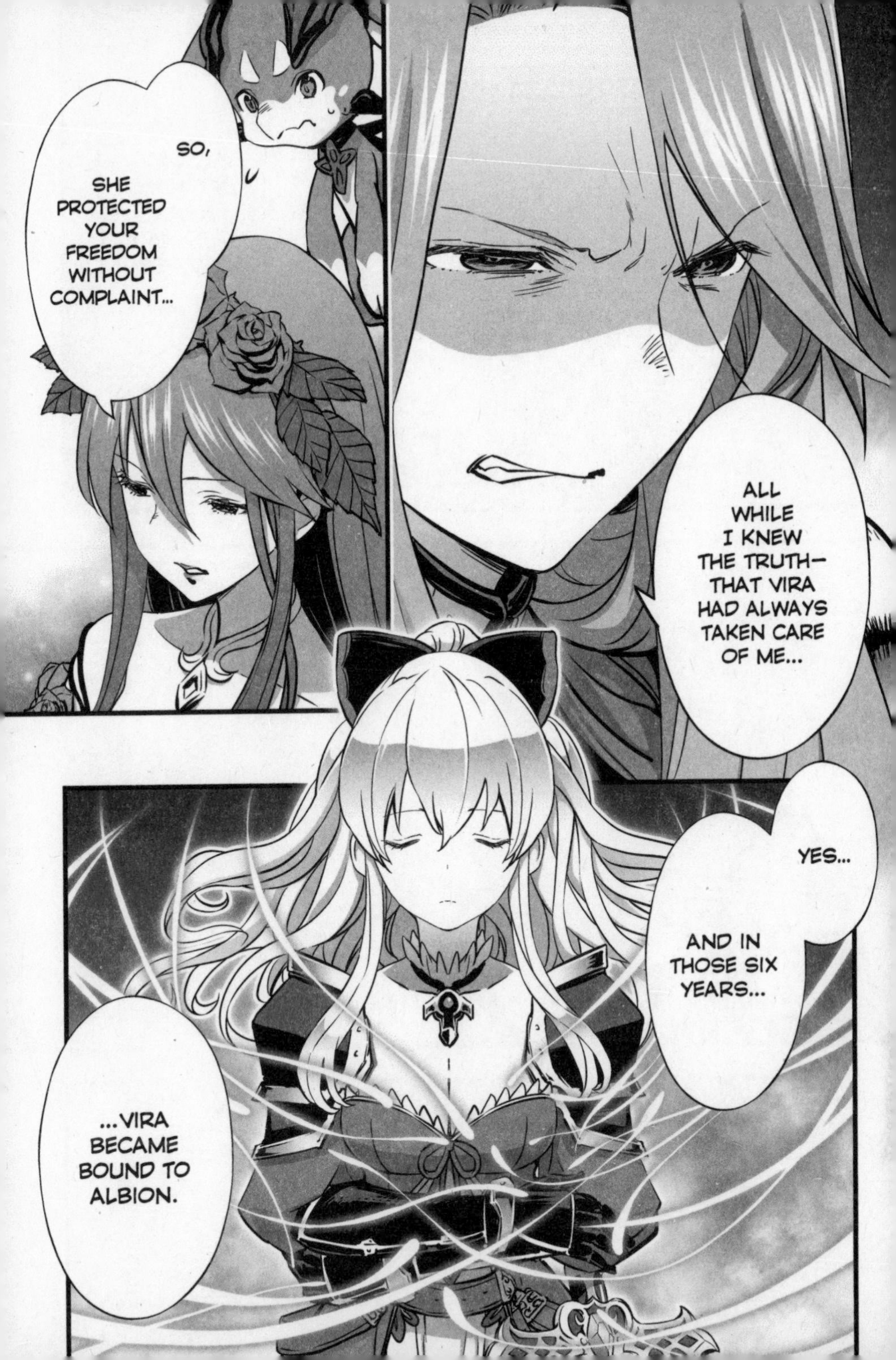
SO, SHE PROTECTED YOUR FREEDOM WITHOUT COMPLAINT...
ALL WHILE I KNEW THE TRUTH— THAT VIRA HAD ALWAYS TAKEN CARE OF ME...
YES...
AND IN THOSE SIX YEARS...
...VIRA BECAME BOUND TO ALBION.

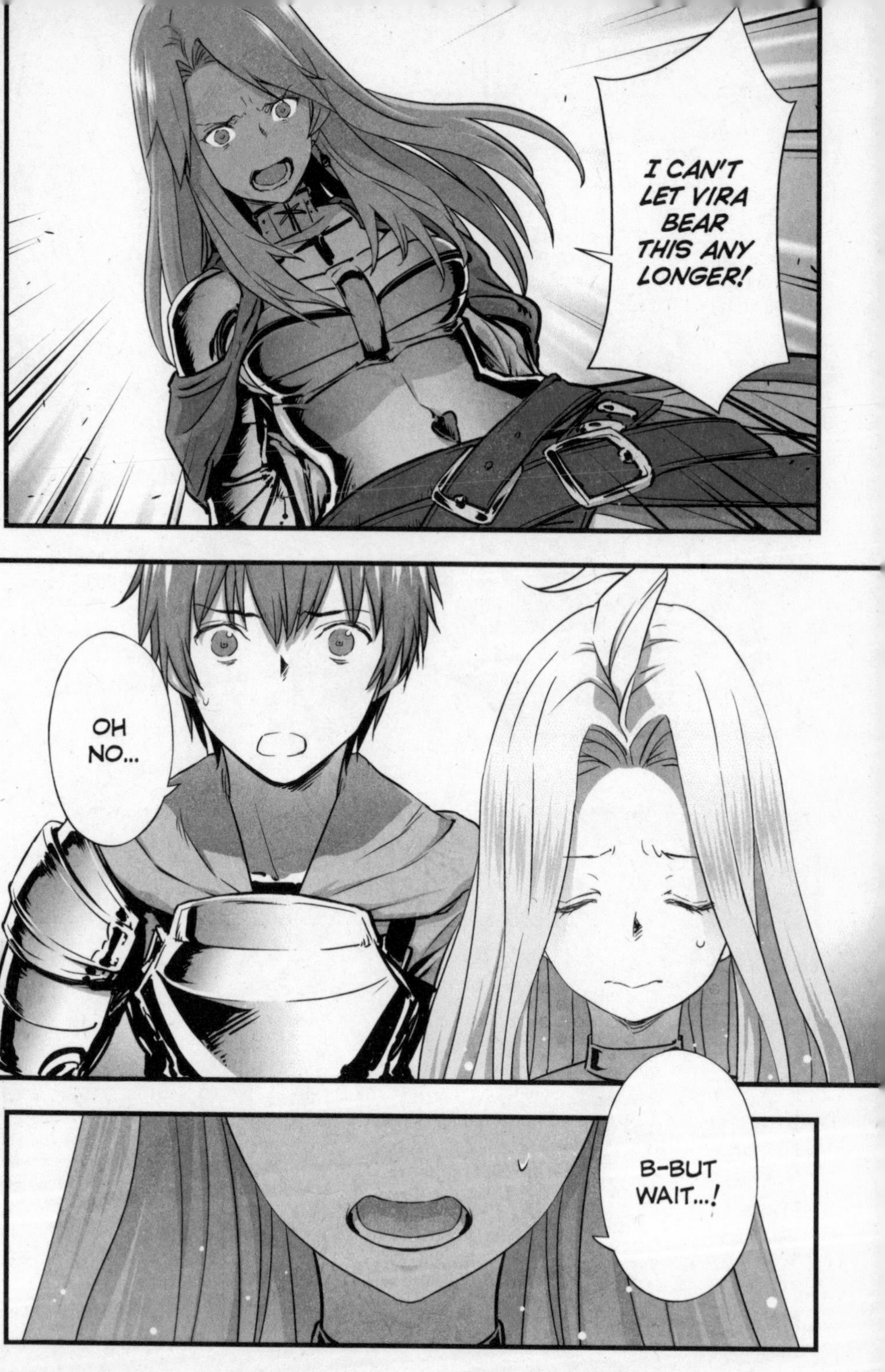
I CAN'T LET VIRA BEAR THIS ANY LONGER!
OH NO...
B-BUT WAIT...!

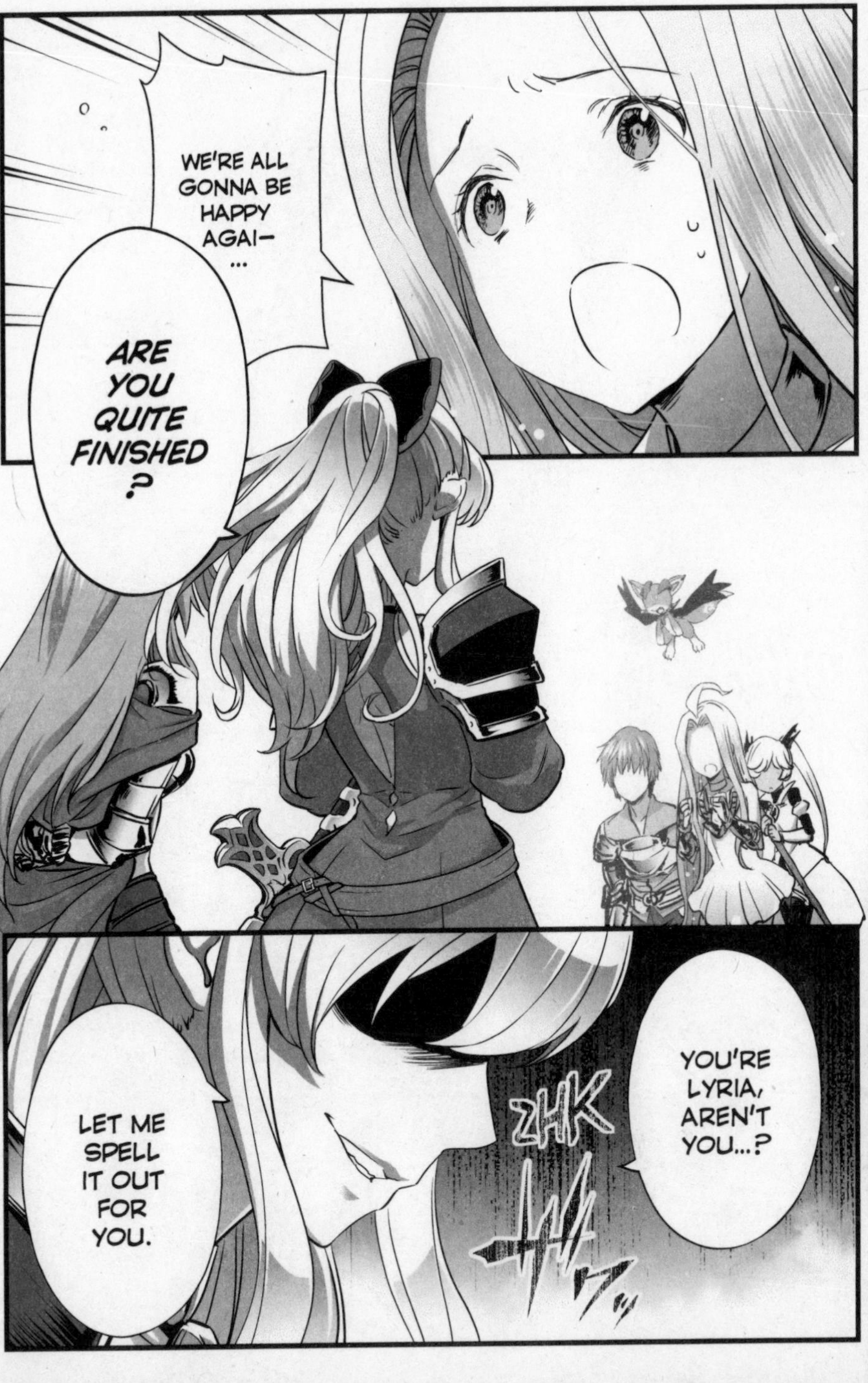

WE'RE ALL GONNA BE HAPPY AGAI—...
ARE YOU QUITE FINISHED?
YOU'RE LYRIA, AREN'T YOU...?
ZHK
LET ME SPELL IT OUT FOR YOU.

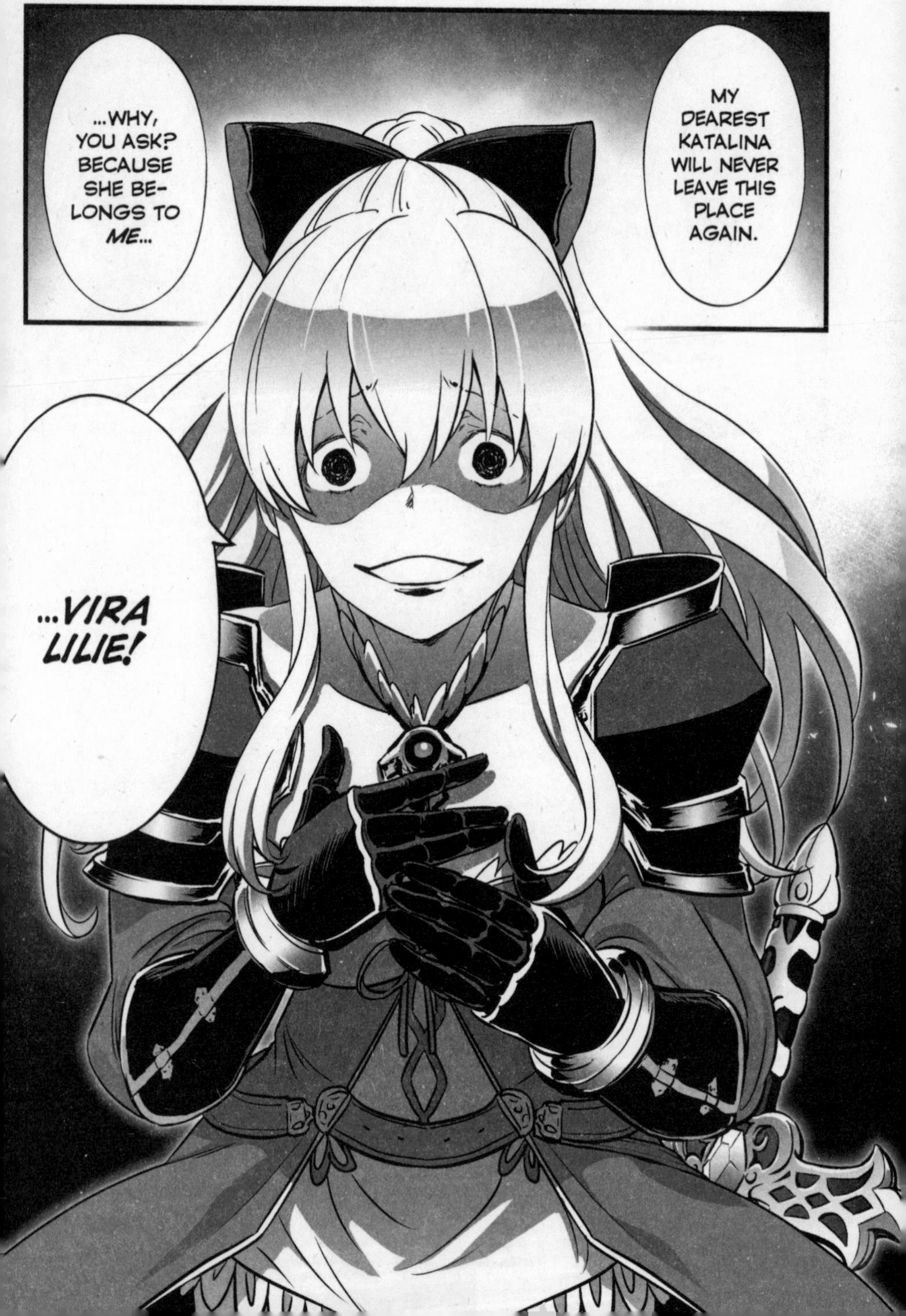
MY DEAREST KATALINA WILL NEVER LEAVE THIS PLACE AGAIN.
...WHY, YOU ASK? BECAUSE SHE BE-LONGS TO *ME*...
...*VIRA LILIE!*

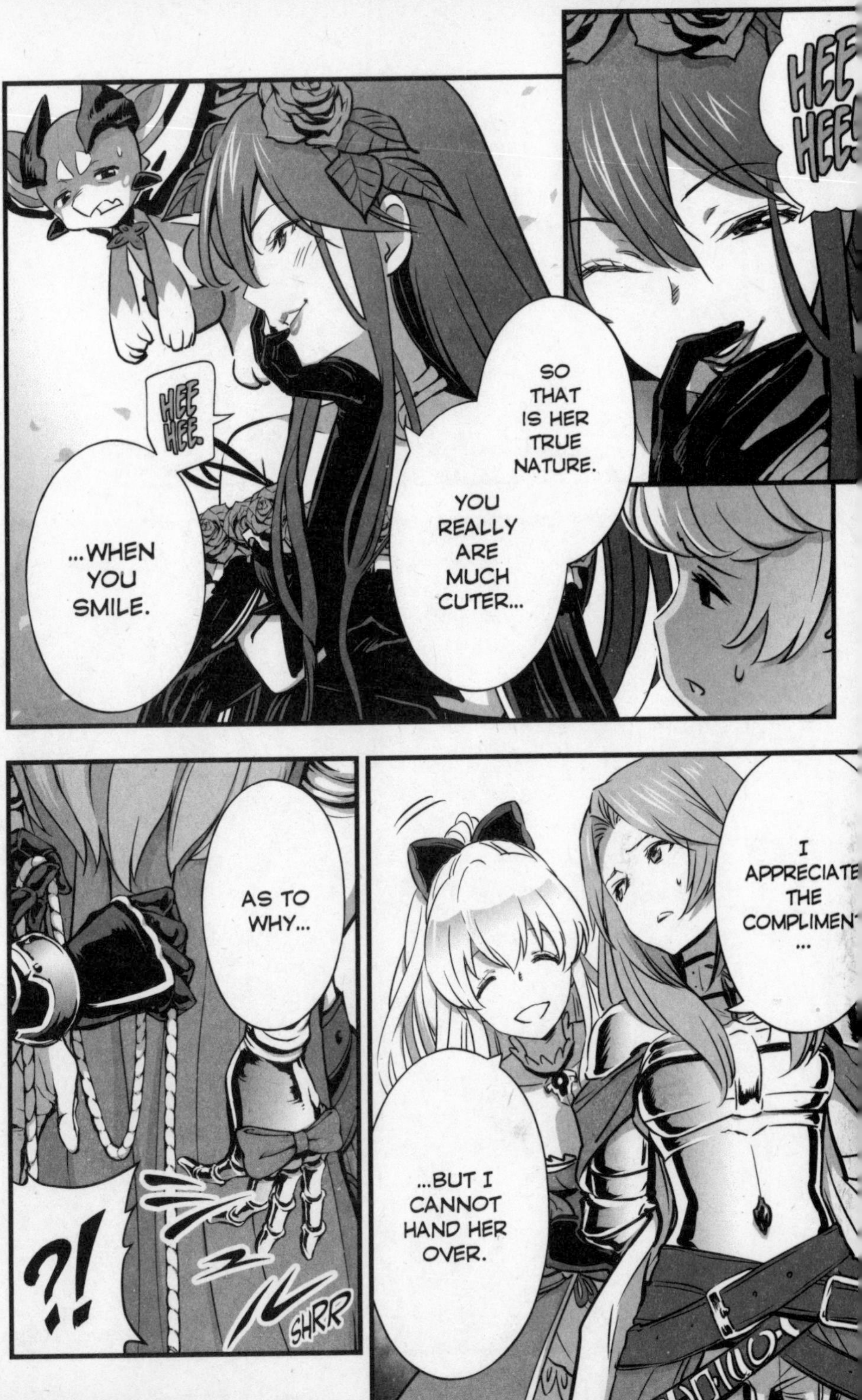
HEE HEE
SO THAT IS HER TRUE NATURE.
YOU REALLY ARE MUCH CUTER...
HEE HEE.
...WHEN YOU SMILE.
I APPRECIATE THE COMPLIMENT ...
...BUT I CANNOT HAND HER OVER.
AS TO WHY...
SHRR
?!

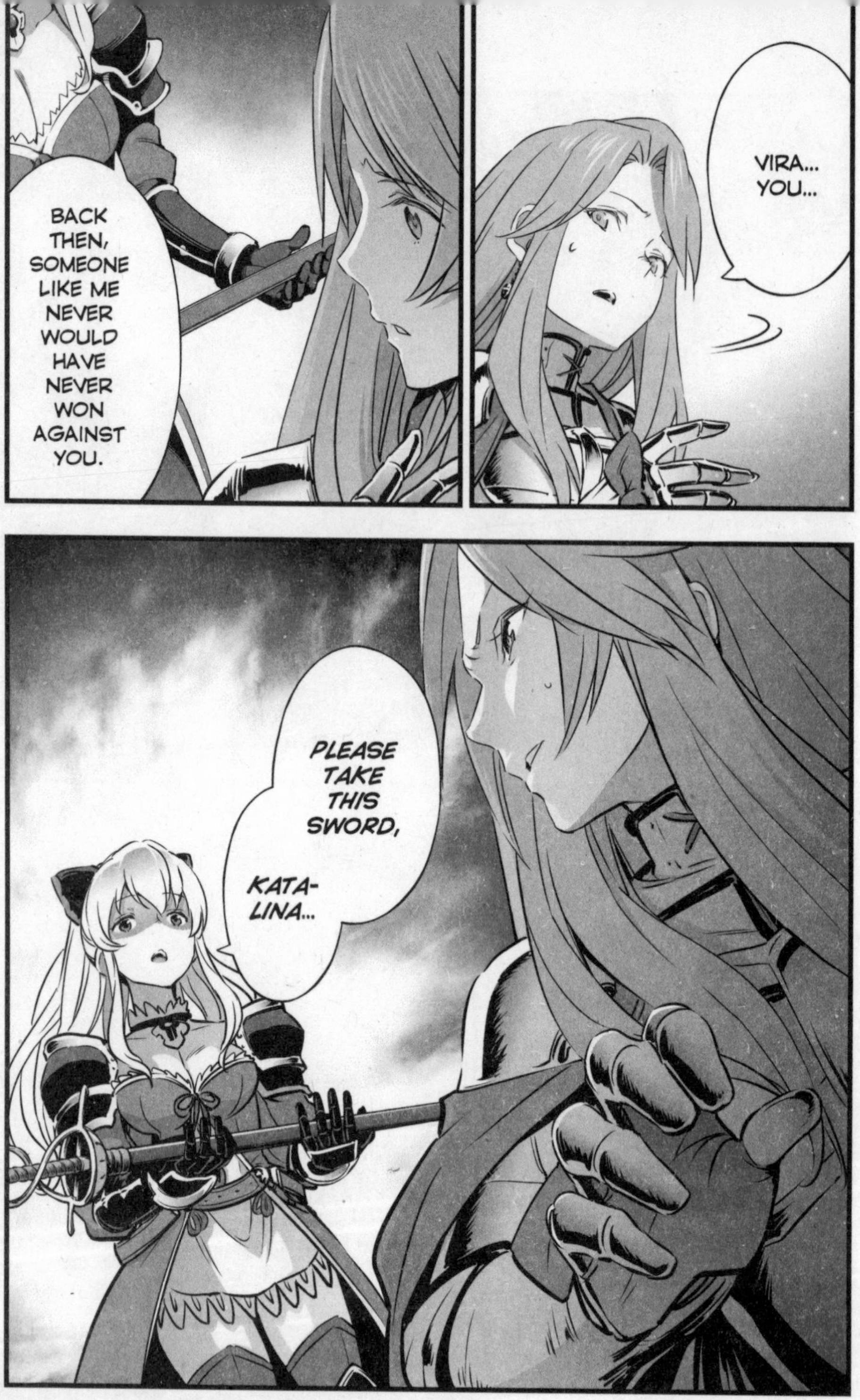
VIRA... YOU...
BACK THEN, SOMEONE LIKE ME NEVER WOULD HAVE NEVER WON AGAINST YOU.
PLEASE TAKE THIS SWORD,
KATA-LINA...

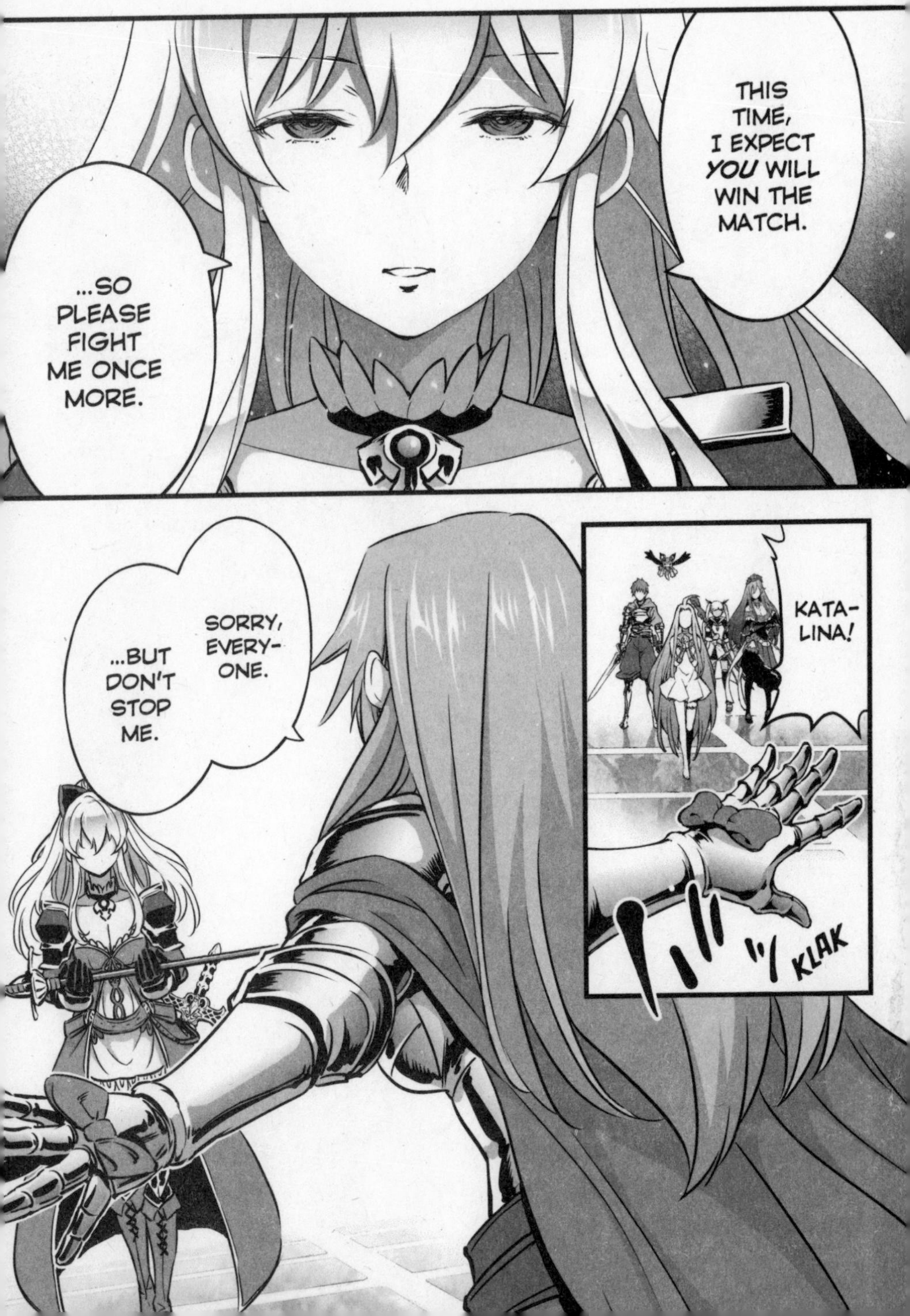
THIS TIME, I EXPECT YOU WILL WIN THE MATCH.
...SO PLEASE FIGHT ME ONCE MORE.
KATA-LINA!
KLAK
SORRY, EVERY-ONE.
...BUT DON'T STOP ME.

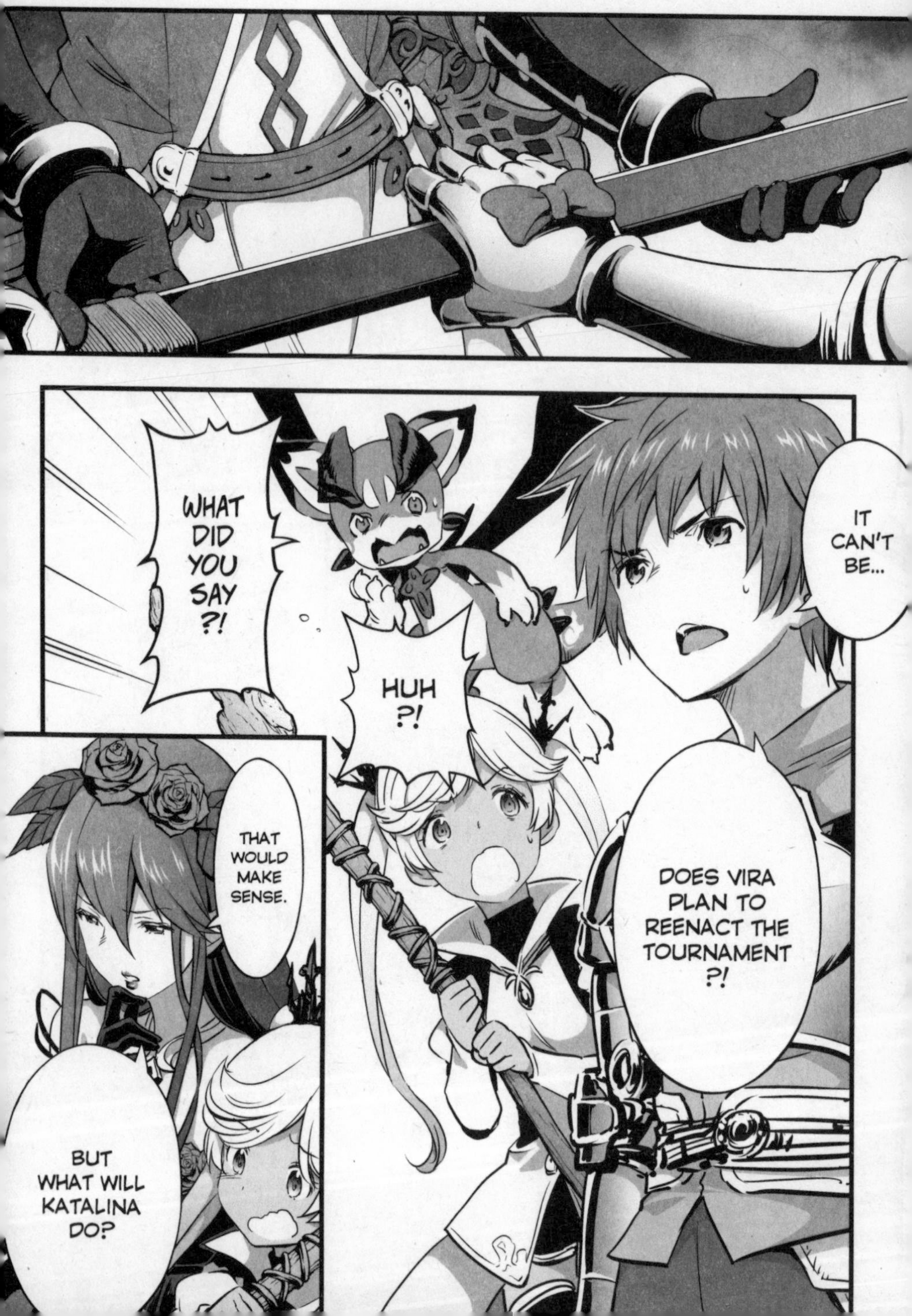
IT CAN'T BE...
WHAT DID YOU SAY?!
HUH?!
DOES VIRA PLAN TO REENACT THE TOURNAMENT?!
THAT WOULD MAKE SENSE.
BUT WHAT WILL KATALINA DO?

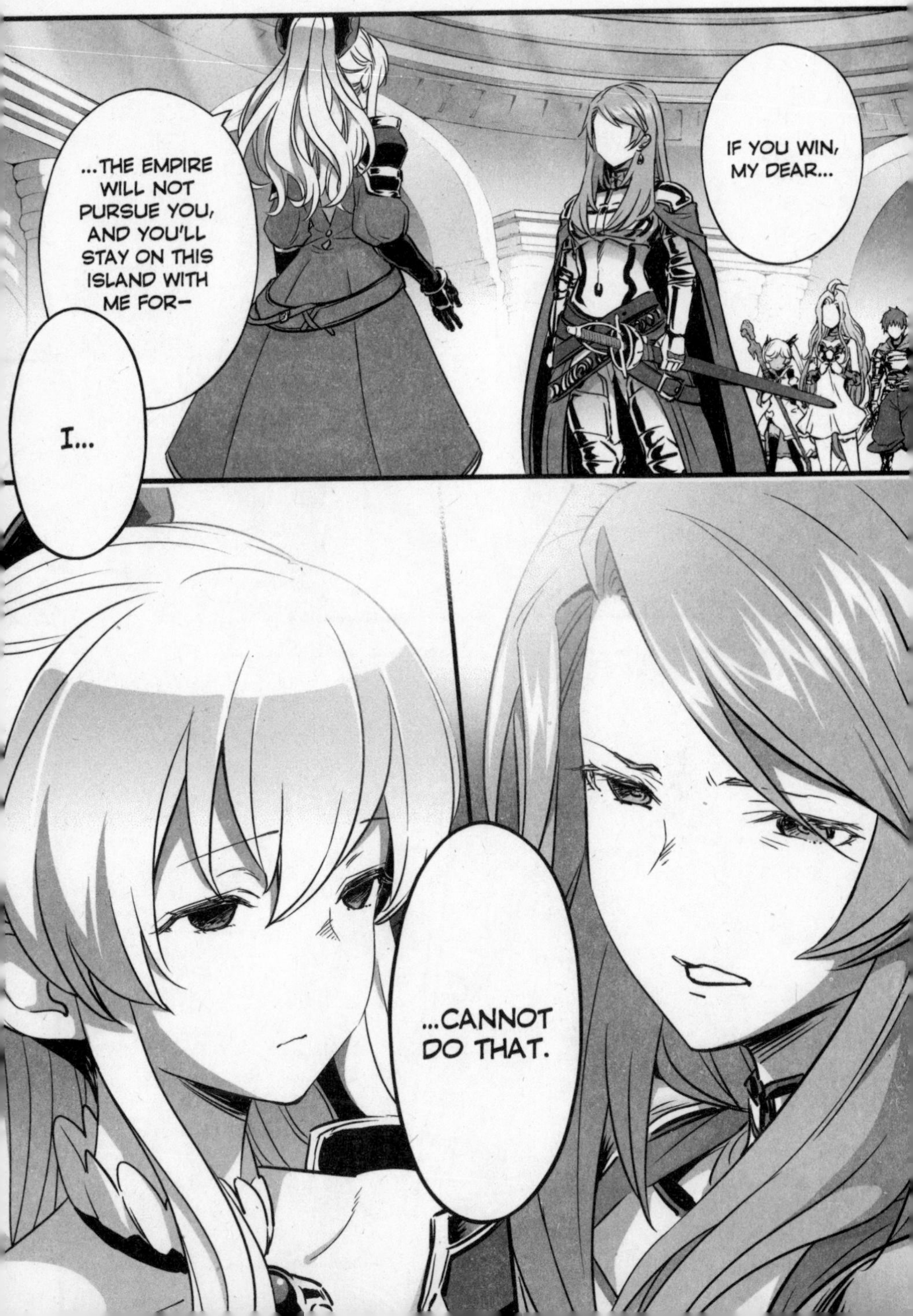
IF YOU WIN, MY DEAR...
...THE EMPIRE WILL NOT PURSUE YOU, AND YOU'LL STAY ON THIS ISLAND WITH ME FOR—
I...
...CANNOT DO THAT.

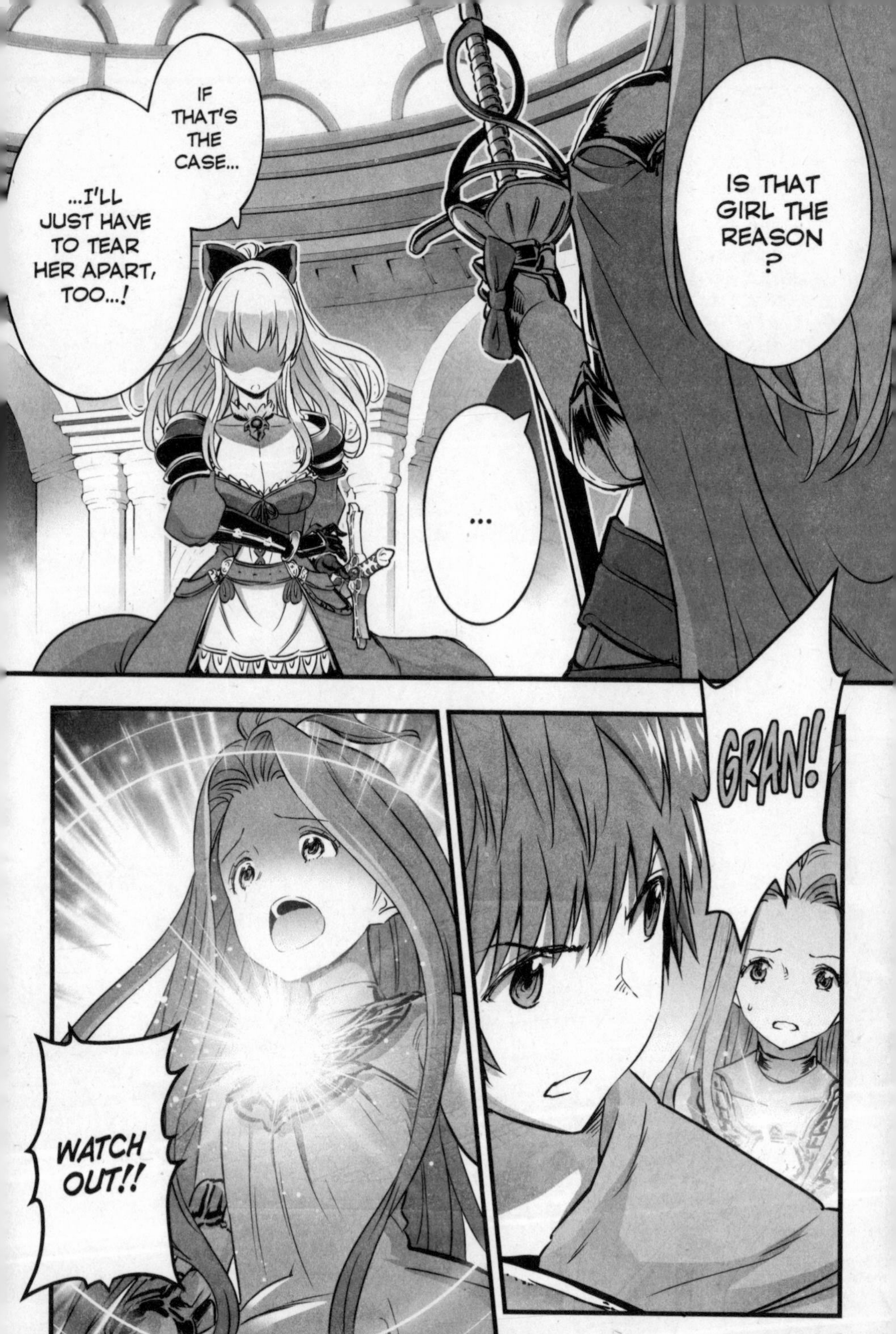
IS THAT GIRL THE REASON ?
...
IF THAT'S THE CASE...
...I'LL JUST HAVE TO TEAR HER APART, TOO...!
GRAN!
WATCH OUT!!

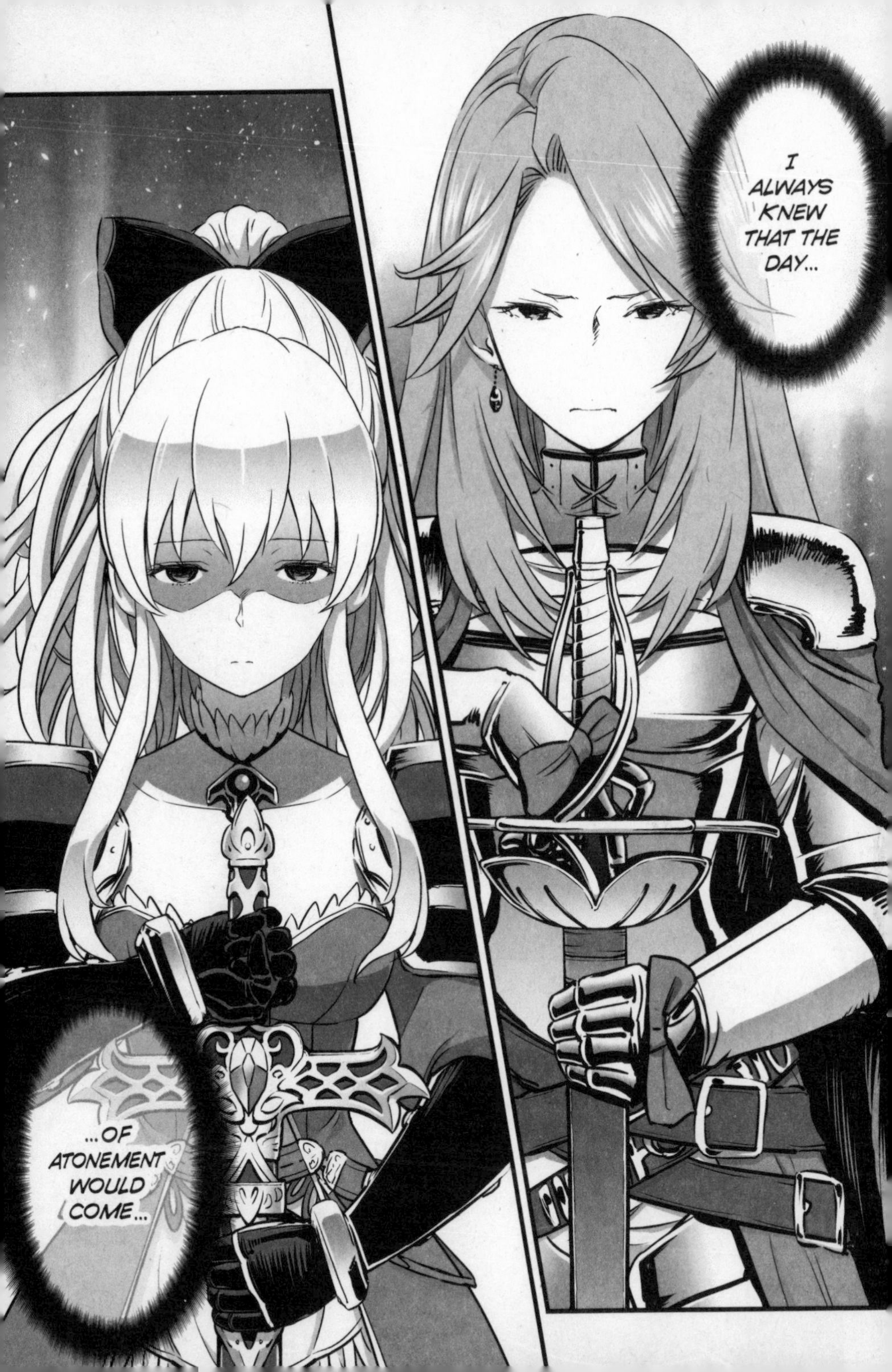
I ALWAYS KNEW THAT THE DAY...
...OF ATONEMENT WOULD COME...

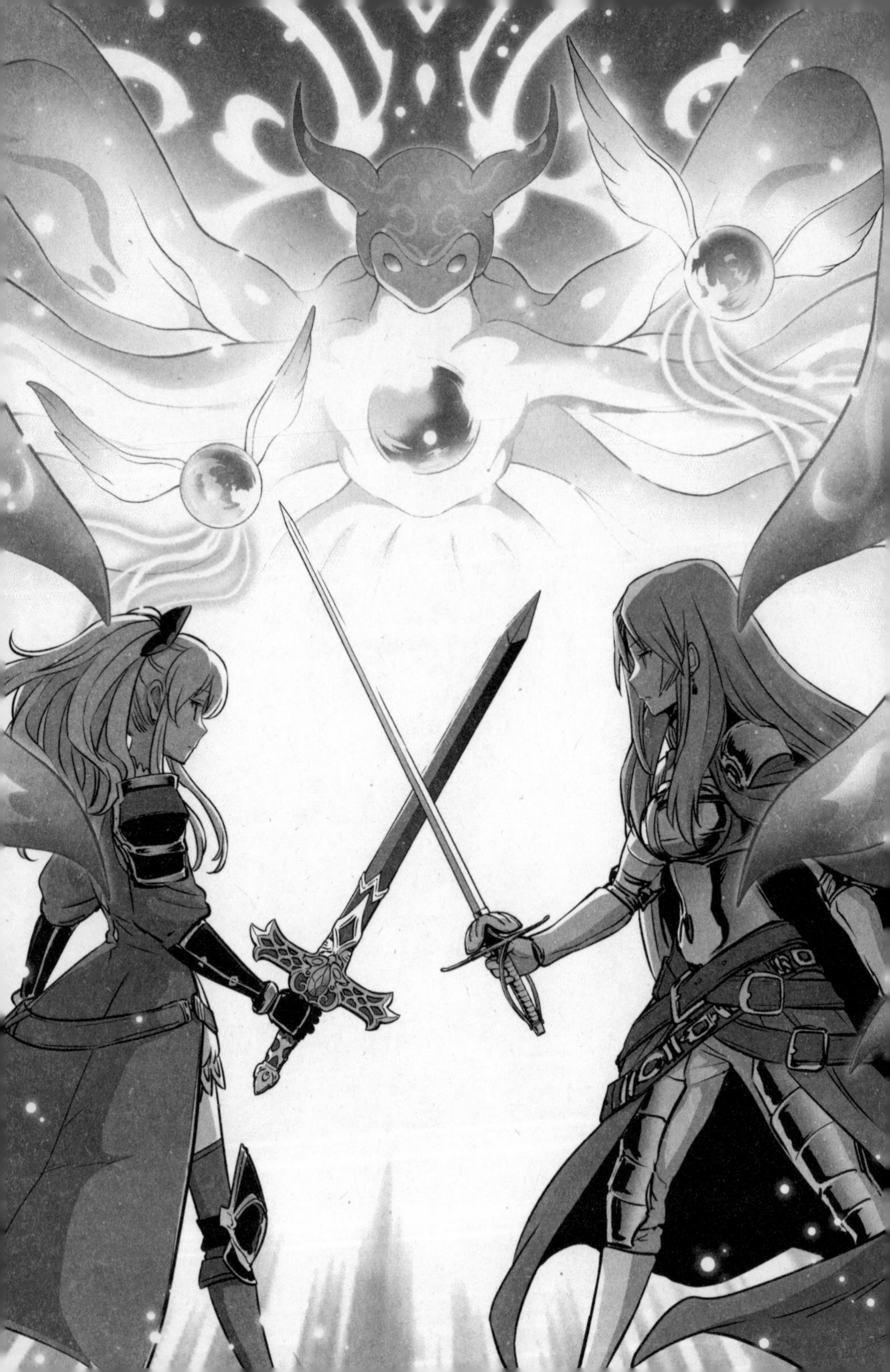

GRANBLUE FANTASY
グランブルーファンタジー

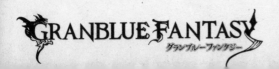

NEXT

NEXT VOLUME PREVIEW

Vira and Katalina lock swords once more!

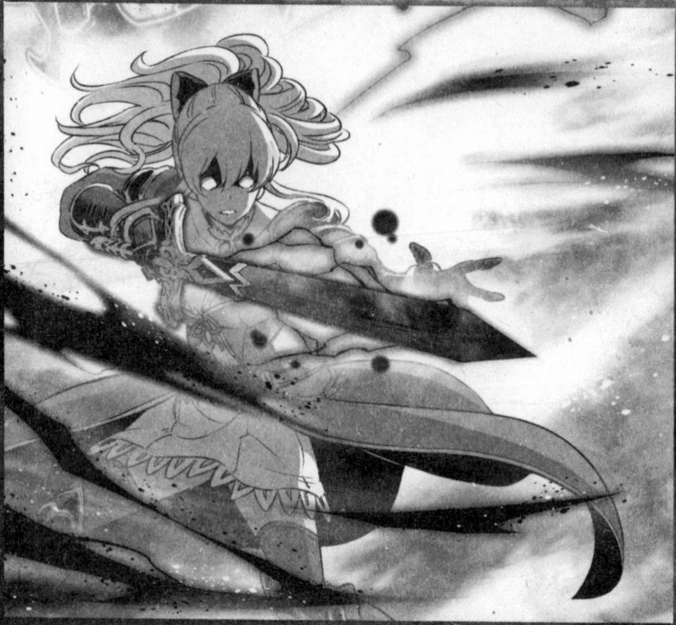

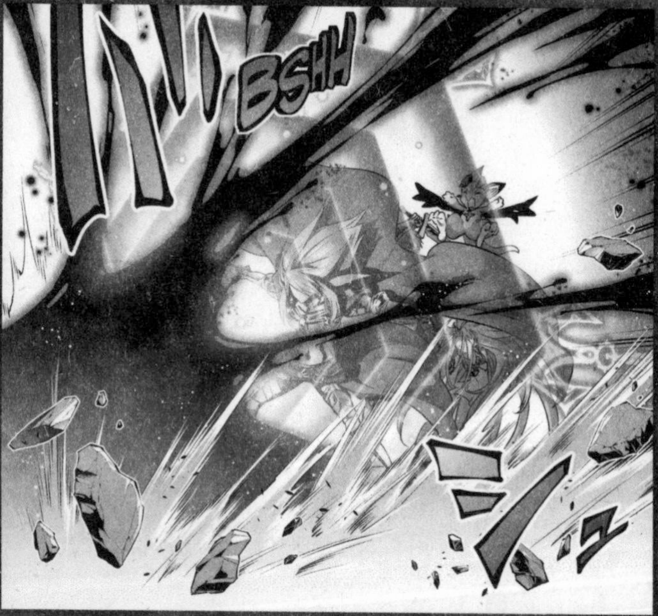
BSHH

Can Katalina respond as she battles her guilt ...?!

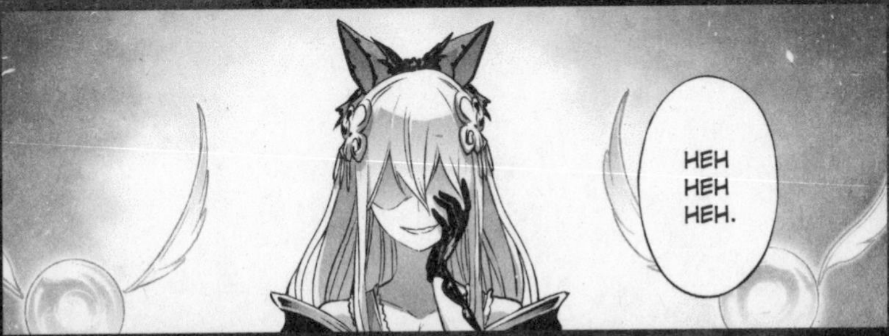
HEH HEH HEH.

And then...

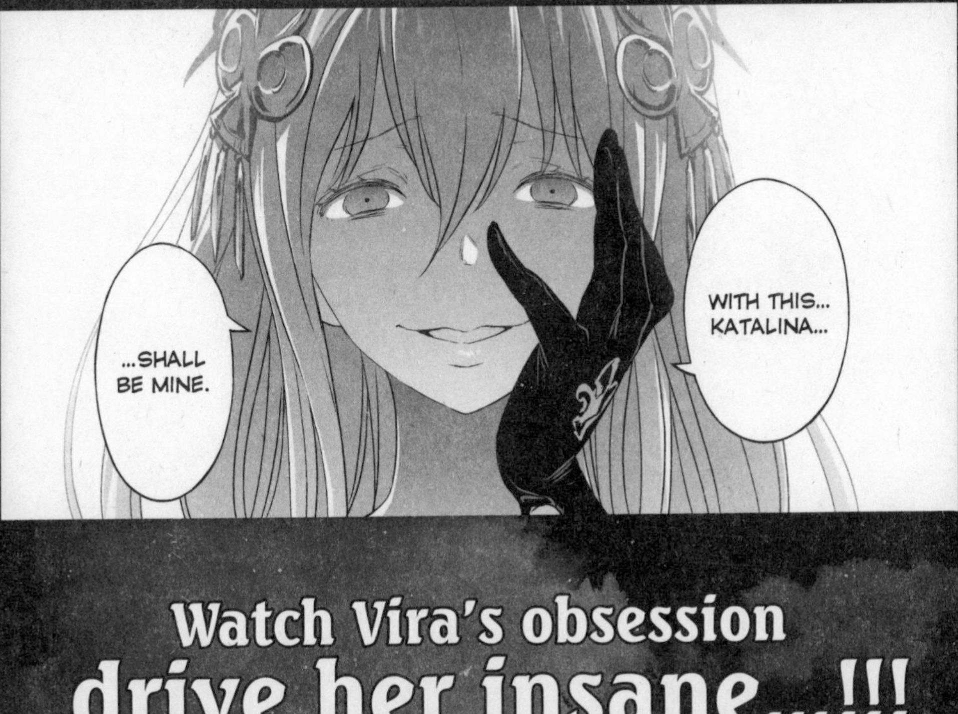
WITH THIS... KATALINA...
...SHALL BE MINE.

Watch Vira's obsession
drive her insane...!!!

GRANBLUE FANTASY
volume. 07 COMING SOON!!!!!

Knight of the Ice ©Yayoi Ogawa/Kodansha Ltd.

SKATING THRILLS AND ICY CHILLS WITH THIS NEW TINGLY ROMANCE SERIES!

A rom-com on ice, perfect for fans of *Princess Jellyfish* and *Wotakoi*. Kokoro is the talk of the figure-skating world, winning trophies and hearts. But little do they know... he's actually a huge nerd! From the beloved creator of *You're My Pet* (*Tramps Like Us*).

Chitose is a serious young woman, working for the health magazine *SASSO*. Or at least, she would be, if she wasn't constantly getting distracted by her childhood friend, international figure skating star Kokoro Kijinami! In the public eye and on the ice, Kokoro is a gallant, flawless knight, but behind his glittery costumes and breathtaking spins lies a secret: He's actually a hopelessly romantic otaku, who can only land his quad jumps when Chitose is on hand to recite a spell from his favorite magical girl anime!

KC
Kodansha
Comics

PERFECT WORLD

Rie Aruga

A TOUCHING NEW SERIES ABOUT LOVE AND COPING WITH DISABILITY

An office party reunites Tsugumi with her high school crush Itsuki. He's realized his dream of becoming an architect, but along the way, he experienced a spinal injury that put him in a wheelchair. Now Tsugumi's rekindled feelings will butt up against prejudices she never considered — and Itsuki will have to decide if he's ready to let someone into his heart...

"Depicts with great delicacy and courage the difficulties some with disabilities experience getting involved in romantic relationships... Rie Aruga refuses to romanticize, pushing her heroine to face the reality of disability. She invites her readers to the same tasks of empathy, knowledge and recognition."
—Slate.fr

"An important entry [in manga romance]... The emotional core of both plot and characters indicates thoughtfulness... [Aruga's] research is readily apparent in the text and artwork, making this feel like a real story."
—Anime News Network

KC
KODANSHA COMICS

◄ KAMOME ►
SHIRAHAMA

Witch Hat Atelier

A magical manga
adventure for
fans of Disney
and Studio
Ghibli!

Witch Hat Atelier © Kamome Shirahama/Kodansha Ltd.

The magical adventure that took Japan by storm is finally here, from acclaimed DC and Marvel cover artist Kamome Shirahama!

In a world where everyone takes wonders like magic spells
and dragons for granted, Coco is a girl with a simple dream:
She wants to be a witch. But everybody knows magicians
are born, not made, and Coco was not born with a gift for
magic. Resigned to her un-magical life, Coco is about to
give up on her dream to become a witch...until the day
she meets Qifrey, a mysterious, traveling magician. After
secretly seeing Qifrey perform magic in a way she's never
seen before, Coco soon learns what everybody "knows"
might not be the truth, and discovers that her magical
dream may not be as far away as it may seem...

KC
KODANSHA
COMICS

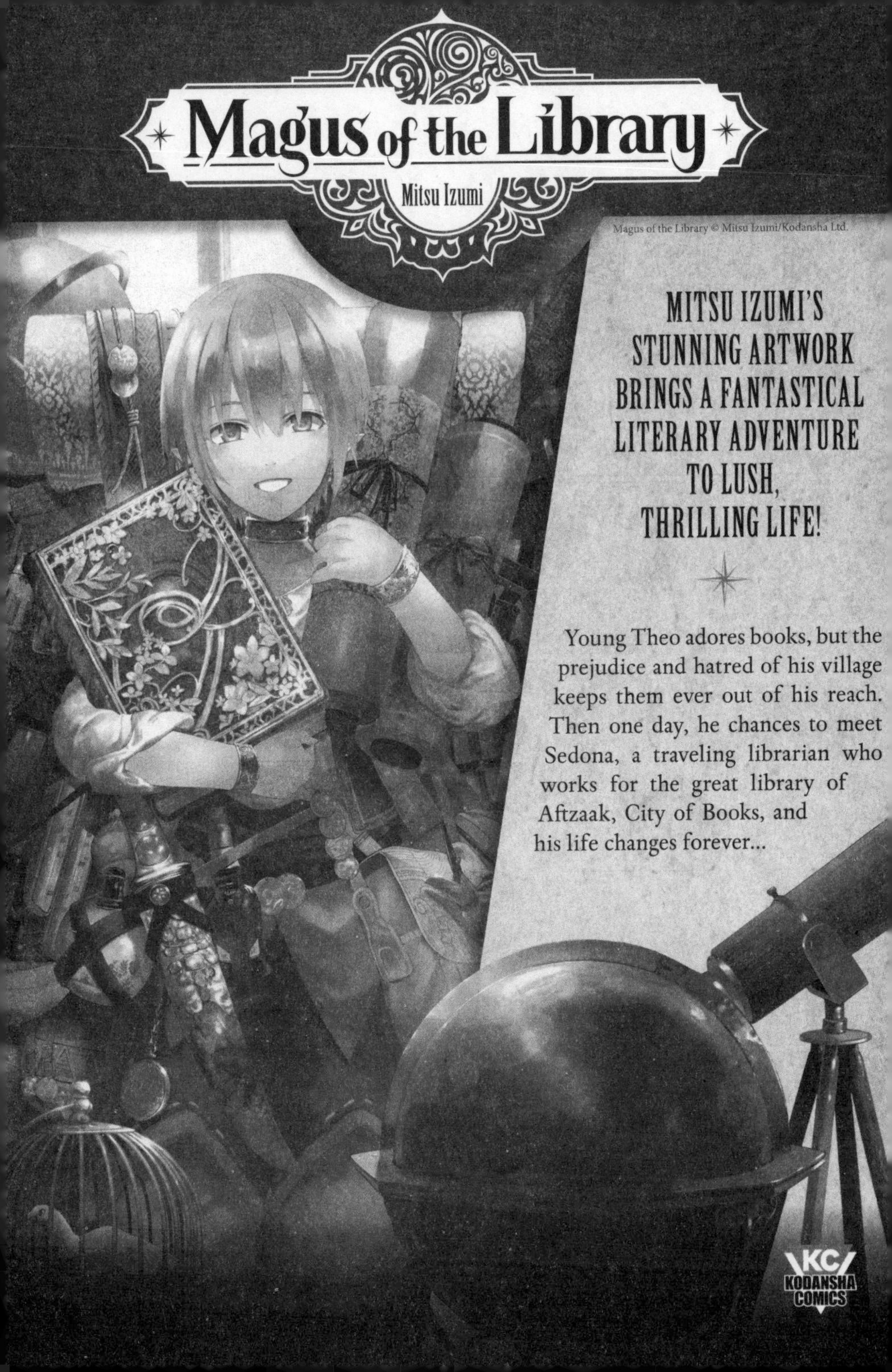
Magus of the Library
Mitsu Izumi
Magus of the Library © Mitsu Izumi/Kodansha Ltd.
MITSU IZUMI'S STUNNING ARTWORK BRINGS A FANTASTICAL LITERARY ADVENTURE TO LUSH, THRILLING LIFE!
Young Theo adores books, but the prejudice and hatred of his village keeps them ever out of his reach. Then one day, he chances to meet Sedona, a traveling librarian who works for the great library of Aftzaak, City of Books, and his life changes forever...
KC
KODANSHA COMICS

THE SWEET SCENT OF LOVE IS IN THE AIR! FOR FANS OF OFFBEAT ROMANCES LIKE *WOTAKOI*

Sweat and Soap © Kintetsu Yamada / Kodansha Ltd.

In an office romance, there's a fine line between sexy and awkward... and that line is where Asako — a woman who sweats copiously — meets Koutarou — a perfume developer who can't get enough of Asako's, er, scent. Don't miss a romcom manga like no other!

A SMART, NEW ROMANTIC COMEDY FOR FANS OF *SHORTCAKE CAKE* AND *TERRACE HOUSE*!

A romance manga starring high school girl Meeko, who learns to live on her own in a boarding house whose living room is home to the odd (but handsome) Matsunaga-san. She begins to adjust to her new life away from her parents, but Meeko soon learns that no matter how far away from home she is, she's still a young girl at heart — especially when she finds herself falling for Matsunaga-san.

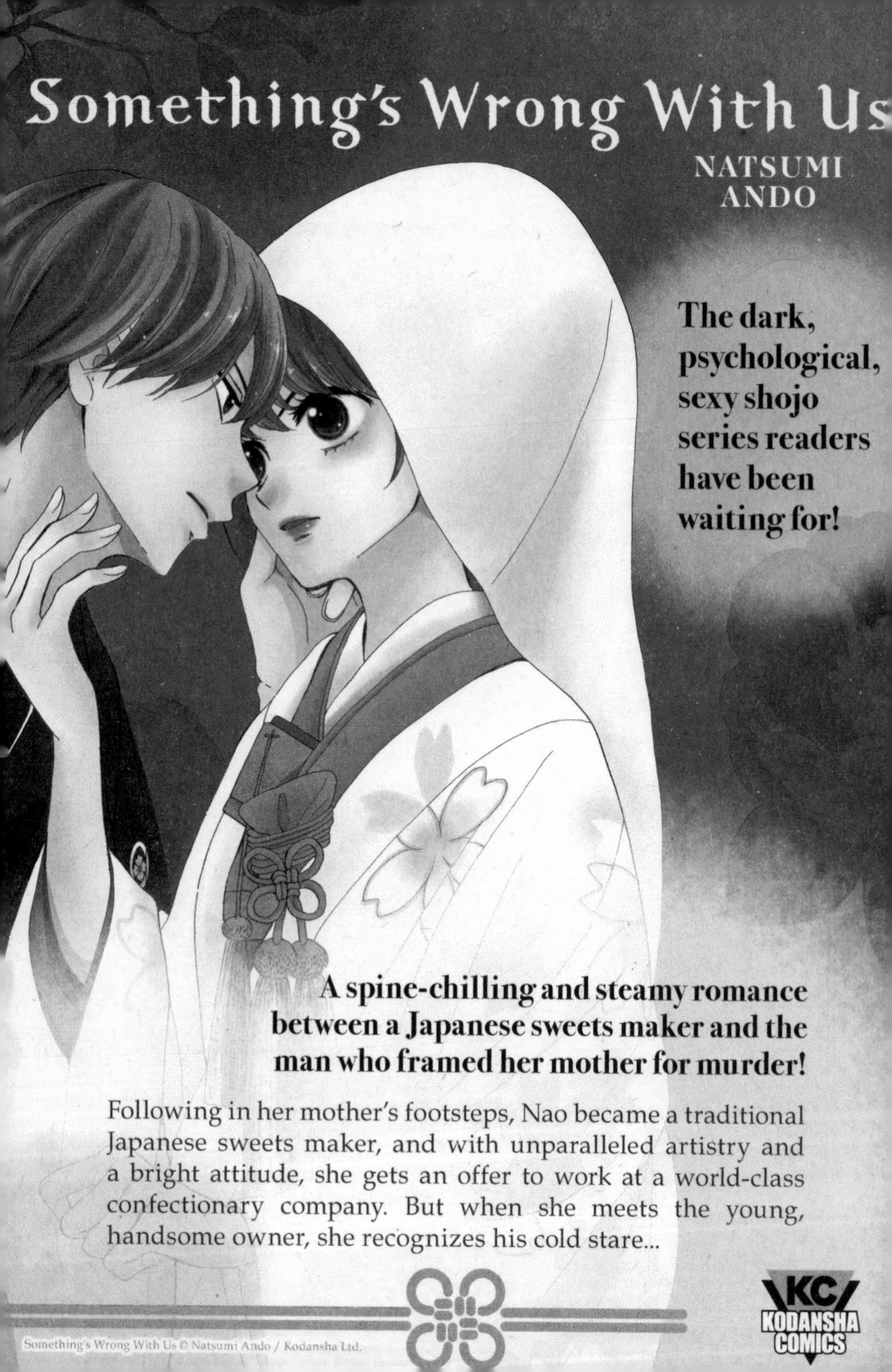
Something's Wrong With Us
NATSUMI ANDO
The dark, psychological, sexy shojo series readers have been waiting for!
A spine-chilling and steamy romance between a Japanese sweets maker and the man who framed her mother for murder!
Following in her mother's footsteps, Nao became a traditional Japanese sweets maker, and with unparalleled artistry and a bright attitude, she gets an offer to work at a world-class confectionary company. But when she meets the young, handsome owner, she recognizes his cold stare...
KC KODANSHA COMICS
Something's Wrong With Us © Natsumi Ando / Kodansha Ltd.

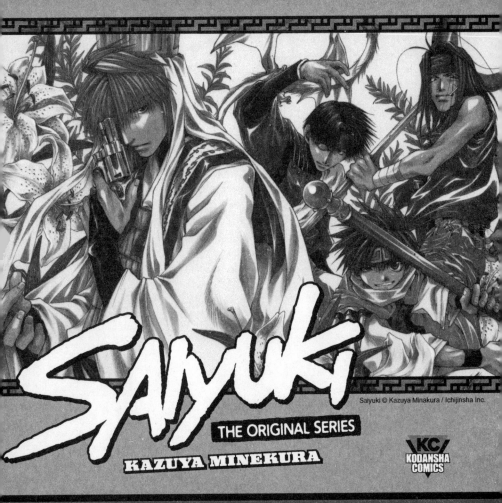

EDENS ZERO
エデンズゼロ

HIRO MASHIMA IS BACK! JOIN THE CREATOR OF ***FAIRY TAIL***
AS HE TAKES TO THE STARS FOR ANOTHER THRILLING SAGA!

EDENS ZERO © Hiro Mashima/Kodansha, Ltd.

A high-flying space adventure! All the steadfast friendship and wild fighting you've been waiting for...IN SPACE!

At Granbell Kingdom, an abandoned amusement park, Shiki has lived his entire life among machines. But one day, Rebecca and her cat companion Happy appear at the park's front gates. Little do these newcomers know that this is the first human contact Granbell has had in a hundred years! As Shiki stumbles his way into making new friends, his former neighbors stir at an opportunity for a robo-rebellion... And when his old homeland becomes too dangerous, Shiki must join Rebecca and Happy on their spaceship and escape into the boundless cosmos.

KC KODANSHA COMICS

Young characters and steampunk setting, like *Howl's Moving Castle* and *Battle Angel Alita*

Beyond the Clouds © 2018 Nicke / Ki-oon

A boy with a talent for machines and a mysterious girl whose wings he's fixed will take you beyond the clouds! In the tradition of the high-flying, resonant adventure stories of Studio Ghibli comes a gorgeous tale about the longing of young hearts for adventure and friendship!

Futaro Uesugi is a second-year in high school, scraping to get by and pay off his family's debt. The only thing he can do is study, so when Futaro receives a part-time job offer to tutor the five daughters of a wealthy businessman, he can't pass it up. Little does he know, these five beautiful sisters are quintuplets, but the only thing they have in common...is that they're all terrible at studying!

THE QUINTESSENTIAL QUINTUPLETS

negi haruba

KC/ KODANSHA COMICS

A dark and sexy body-horror action manga perfect for fans of _Prison School_ and _High School of the Dead_!

Shuichi Kagaya is a smart kid, and most smart kids his age would be thinking about college. Shuichi is also a monster, and he's smart enough to know that monsters don't go to college. But after he uses his monstrous form to save his classmate Claire Aoki, it doesn't matter what his plans for the future were, because he's not the one making the decisions anymore. Now that the seductive, sadistic Claire knows Shuichi's secret, she's got her own ideas about what a monster is good for—because he's not the first monster she's met...

GLEIPNIR

"You and me together...we would be unstoppable."

A Kodansha Comics Trade Paperback Original
Granblue Fantasy 6 copyright
© Cygames
© 2018 cocho

English translation copyright
© Cygames
© 2020 cocho

Published in the United States by Kodansha Comics, an imprint of Kodansha USA Publishing, LLC, New York.

Publication rights for this English edition arranged through Kodansha Ltd., Tokyo.

First published in Japan in 2018 by Kodansha Ltd., Tokyo as *Granblue Fantasy*, volume 6.

ISBN 978-1-63236-956-7

Original cover design by Yusuke Kurachi (Astrorb)

Printed in the United States of America.

www.kodanshacomics.com

9 8 7 6 5 4 3 2 1
Translation: Kristi Fernandez
Lettering: Evan Hayden
Editing: Vanessa Tenazas
Kodansha Comics edition cover design by Phil Balsman

Publisher: Kiichiro Sugawara

Director of publishing services: Ben Applegate
Associate director of operations: Stephen Pakula
Publishing services managing editor: Noelle Webster
Assistant production manager: Emi Lotto, Angela Zurlo

04/21